Eva Dick

Residential Segregation – Stumbling Block or Stepping Stone?

Politik, Gemeinschaft und Gesellschaft in einer globalisierten Welt

herausgegeben von

Rainer Dombois (Universität Bremen)
und Thomas Faist (Universität Bielefeld)

Band 7

LIT

Eva Dick

Residential Segregation – Stumbling Block or Stepping Stone?

A case study on the Mexican population of the West Side of St. Paul, Minnesota, USA

LIT

Bibliographic information published by the Deutsche Nationalbibliothek
The Deutsche Nationalbibliothek lists this publication in the Deutsche Nationalbibliografie; detailed bibliographic data are available in the Internet at http://dnb.d-nb.de.

ISBN 978-3-03735-936-5 (Schweiz)
ISBN 978-3-8258-0950-8 (Deutschland)
Zugl.: Dortmund, Univ., Diss., 2007

A catalogue record for this book is available from the British Library

Zweigniederlassung Zürich 2008
Dufourstr. 31
CH-8008 Zürich
Tel. +41 (0) 44-251 75 05
Fax +41 (0) 44-251 75 06
e-Mail: zuerich@lit-verlag.ch
http://www.lit-verlag.ch

LIT VERLAG Dr. W. Hopf
Berlin 2008
Auslieferung/Verlagskontakt:
Fresnostr. 2
D-48159 Münster
Tel. +49 (0)251–62 03 20
Fax +49 (0)251–23 19 72
e-Mail: lit@lit-verlag.de
http://www.lit-verlag.de

Auslieferung:
Schweiz/Österreich: Medienlogistik Pichler-ÖBZ GmbH & Co KG
IZ-NÖ, Süd, Straße 1, Objekt 34, A-2355 Wiener Neudorf
Tel. +43 (0) 2236/63 535 - 290, Fax +43 (0) 2236/63 535 - 243, e-Mail: mlo@medien-logistik.at
Deutschland: LIT Verlag Fresnostr. 2, D-48159 Münster
Tel. +49 (0) 2 51/620 32 - 22, Fax +49 (0) 2 51/922 60 99, e-Mail: vertrieb@lit-verlag.de

Distributed in the UK by: Global Book Marketing, 99B Wallis Rd, London, E9 5LN
Phone: +44 (0) 20 8533 5800 – Fax: +44 (0) 1600 775 663
http://www.centralbooks.co.uk/acatalog/search.html

Acknowledgements

Reaching the end of an approximately four-year work process implies uncertain feelings. I have thought about this moment many times, either wishing it had already arrived or fearing it would never do so. Now I am genuinely glad to hold a first version of this document in my hands, not without wondering about what to do next. But there will be new endeavors and challenges ahead, personal and professional.

I can with certainty say that this research would not have been possible without the support of many persons. I want to thank my supervisors, Professors Volker Kreibich from the University of Dortmund, Helga Leitner from the University of Minnesota and Einhard Schmidt-Kallert from the University of Dortmund, for their support. The regular contact with Prof. Kreibich from the beginning to the end of this work ensured getting and keeping me conceptually 'on track'. Prof. Leitner provided much backing for the framing of the research focus and methodology, as well as compiling interview questionnaires and organizing, at times, tedious work processes. She put me into contact with peer doctoral candidates at the "U of M", which was conceptually helpful and socially meaningful. I am very grateful to Prof. Schmidt-Kallert for reading and providing door-to-door advice to all of this document.

I spent the larger part of the work on the dissertation in Minneapolis/St. Paul, USA, in the context of a four-year stay in that country until July 2005. I am indebted to a number of persons and institutions who assisted me with the preparation and realization of the field work in the last nine months before leaving the United States. My colleagues from the Center for Urban and Regional Affairs (CURA) and Hispanic Advocacy and Community Development through Research (HACER) at the University of Minnesota helped me with first contacts in the West Side neighborhood, with understanding and managing impressive, but intricate US-Census systems, with research data and brown-bag flavored feed-back on my work-in-progress. I am particularly thankful to my resident and expert interview partners for conveying the principal information to this dissertation. I did not only *study* their social networks, but benefited from many of them due to kind referrals – reputed as *snowballs* in cool technical terms. I want to specifically mention the generosity of the "Hispanic Women in Action" group for having me participate, during seven months, in their wonderful events and dedicate two of these to my work – and eventual farewell.

On both a professional note and one of friendship I wish to thank Eric Myott from the Institute on Race and Poverty (IRP) of the University of Minnesota's Law School for his persistent and multiple support of this document. He has provided advice and propelled inputs for data analysis and illustration, repeatedly commented on chapters and offered cheerful opportunities of discussion during our weekly lunch-breaks back in Minneapolis.

I want to thank Margit Fauser for her meticulous comments on the conceptual part of this document and motivation to follow-through in the empirical chapters. I further thank Dr. Katrin Gliemann and Darja Reuschke for their critical observations and suggestions in crucial moments of the compilation of this document.

Thank you Eric and Ria for accompanying, sometimes enduring and always sustaining, as everything, the work on this dissertation.

Eva Dick, May 2007

Abbreviations

CBD	Central Business District
CDC	Community Development Corporation
CFR	Code of Federal Regulations
DI	Dissimilarity Index
ELL	English Language Learners
ESL	English as a Second Language
FHA	Federal Housing Administration
FMR	Fair Market Rent
GAP	Guadalupe Alternative Programs
HACER	Hispanic Advocacy and Community Empowerment through Research
HOPE	Housing Opportunities for People Everywhere Program
HUD	Federal Department for Housing and Urban Development
IPUMS	Integrated Public Use Microdata Series
LIHTC	Low Income Housing Tax Credit Program
LMC	Lewis Mumford Center
MHA	Mujeres Hispanas en Acción ("Hispanic Women in Action" group)
MTO	Moving to Opportunity Program
NeDA	Neighborhood Development Alliance
NGO	Non Governmental Organization
NH	Neighborhood House
PBA	Project-Based Assisted Housing Units
PHA	Public Housing Authority

REDA	Riverview Economic Development Association
STD	Sexually Transmitted Disease
WSCO	West Side Citizens Organization

List of Annexes, Boxes, Graphs, Tables and Maps

Annexes

Boxes

Graphs

Tables

Maps

1 Introduction

"[Residential] segregation is not a neutral fact; it systematically undermines the social and economic well-being of blacks in the United States. Because of residential segregation, a significant share of black America is condemned to experience a social environment where poverty and joblessness are the norm, where a majority of children are born out of wedlock, where most families are on welfare, where educational failure prevails, and where social and physical deterioration abound. Through prolonged exposure to such an environment, black chances for economic and social success are drastically reduced" (Massey/Denton 1993: 2)

These words, written by Douglas S. Massey and Nancy A. Denton, in their highly acclaimed and frequently quoted book "American Apartheid" from 1993, display three typical features of the academic discussion about residential segregation in the United States in the 1990s:

- Its perception as a barrier to social mobility and well-being,
- Its singling-out as a pivotal cause of urban poverty, and related social and behavioral dysfunctions, and
- The focus on the spatial and social segregation of black from white American citizens (the 'black-white paradigm') paying less or no attention to the segregation of other, immigrant, minorities.

Residential segregation and policy responses

Residential segregation, the concentration or uneven spread of residential locations across a city's region of residents with a different socio-economic and/or ethnical background, has been a prominent feature in both academic discussions and political discourse in the United States since the beginning of the 20th century. The civil rights struggles of the 1960s brought about the enactment of the Fair Housing Act in 1968, banning discriminatory practices in the public and private housing markets. With the enactment of the Act the main obstacles towards the vision of equal housing opportunities were believed to have been overcome.

The discussion about residential segregation has however regained momentum since the beginning of the 1990s, since, in spite of its legal ban in 1968, racially and economically based residential segregation has continued to be a hallmark of the American urban landscape. Policy makers and scholars alike started focusing on concentrated poverty, i.e. economic, even more than racial segregation, and its assumed detrimental effects on long-term urban sustainability and peace. Public housing programs of the Federal Agency for Housing and Urban Development (HUD) were identified as important contributors to concentrated poverty and racial segregation as intersecting phenomena.

The notoriety of large public housing projects as sites of urban 'blight', the shrinking governmental budgets for affordable housing, as well as several lawsuits filed against HUD on the grounds of racial discrimination in housing, lead to substantial modifications of the agency's housing programs from the late 1980s onwards: For instance, HUD started to impose significant restrictions on municipal public housing authorities (PHAs), implementing agencies for HUD-financed housing, for further construction and the geographic placement of subsidized housing. This was to prevent both racial and income concentration on project sites and in neighborhoods. On the basis of lawsuit settlements, e.g. in Chicago and Minneapolis, former public housing estates were transformed into mixed-income units and programs set up to relocate their residents to low-poverty or non-minority communities, partly against their will.

The notion of the limited success of these 'desegregation' initiatives constituted one of the starting points for the present research: Many of the dispersal programs showed unproductive success in terms of actually achieved desegregation, limited benefits for the desegregated households and were accompanied by frequent resistance from this latter target group. Resistance was particularly strong among racial or immigrant minorities.

A second starting point lay in the need to reconsider residential segregation from an immigration context. The US-American scholarly discussion on segregation has traditionally focused on black/white segregation. This was the case in spite of an increasing racial and/or ethnic diversification of US urban areas during the last decades of the 20th century. The diversification of the US city population was predominantly prompted by an accelerated immigration from Latin American and other countries of the Global South. Immigrant minorities also cluster in 'ethnic enclaves' inside cities, albeit to lesser degrees than the African American population. Questions thus evolved around the transferability of the African American segregation experience on social and spatial clustering of immigrant minorities.

The role of ethnic social networks and capital

Empirical studies conducted in Europe in the 1990s suggested that residential clustering, or segregation, may convey social and economic benefits to immigrants. This is as spatial proximity may favor the development of co-ethnic networks that assist immigrant newcomers to establish and accommodate themselves within the new society. In the context of the ethnic enclave economy debate, scholars in the United States have pointed to employment and skills transfers between co-ethnics inside 'Chinatowns' and 'Little Italies' of large American metropolis.

In the United States, however, research on immigrant groups and communities has historically been shaped by an integrationist or 'assimilationist' normative framework. Against the latter, the building and evolution of these communities was regarded with skepticism. Ethnic 'enclaves', even more so if spatially manifested, were not only considered a potential risk for national social cohesion, but also for the social, economic and cultural advancement of the immigrants themselves. However, in the late 1990s, scholars influenced by culturally pluralist theories, started to consider co-ethnic spatial clustering as a legitimate expression of cultural difference and identity.

In spite of the abundant body of literature about both residential segregation and immigrant networks in the United States, few research attempts have been made to link the two. The literature on residential segregation has extensively reflected the causes and 'neighborhood effects' of black/white residential segregation. However, few studies in the US have examined how exactly it influences the development of immigrant social networks and social or other resources – or *capital* – linked to these. Also outside the US, the conditions that influence positive vs. negative outcomes of social networks in ethnic communities, e.g. for social mobility or other measures of judgment, have rarely been studied in-depth. Hence the third starting point of this research.

Research gaps and main objectives

Against the background of the literature on residential segregation and ethnic social networks or communities in the United States, I have thus identified the following research gaps:

- Little research on the link between residential segregation and social networks and capital: Hitherto studies have relied on rather generalized assumptions about the impact of residential segregation on the development of social capital or mobility, be it in a positive or negative way. However, few studies have analyzed the neighborhood effect on the development of social networks and resources attached to these in a systematic way. Furthermore, inquiries into the concrete conditions for this impact being positive or negative are rare.

- Few studies on subjective perceptions and experiences of immigrants with segregation: As up until now most studies in the United States rely on quantitative, as opposed to qualitative data collection and analysis methods, the personal motivations of immigrants to live in ethnic clusters, and their perceptions and experiences with it are hardly ever explored.
- Relative neglect of increasingly multi-cultural urban reality: Demographic trends notwithstanding, even recent studies on residential segregation in the US focus on black/white residential segregation disregarding thereby the reality of an increasing cultural and ethnic diversity in US cities.
- Unsatisfactory policy responses: Desegregation as the hitherto dominant policy response to residential segregation in the USA has for several reasons proved to be of limited success. Yet, a comprehensive set of alternative policy responses is lacking.

Thus, against the background of these research gaps, the primary objective of this research is to

Assess the impact of residential segregation on the development of social capital and social mobility of immigrants.

A secondary, normative goal is to

Provide policy and planning indications that address both advantages and disadvantages of residentially segregated neighborhoods or ethnic clusters.

The intended contribution of the research is thus twofold: First, in analytical terms, it is to shed light on the link between spatial and social clustering of immigrants in the United States. Specifically it intends to provide a framework for distinguishing positive versus negative residential segregation, notably by exploring typical features of ethnic residential segregation and the conditions under which it is to be judged or plays out positively or negatively.

Second, in normative terms, the research intends to provide guidelines for appropriate policies to promote positive, while discouraging negative aspects of ethnic or immigrants' residential segregation. These should contribute to increasing housing options for residents potentially disadvantaged in the housing market while at the same time enlarging opportunities for satisfying their social, cultural and economic needs. The creation of a more socially just urban society, conducive to individual well-being, constitutes the primordial normative gauge for these guidelines. I assume that promoting (social and spatial) expressions of cultural specificity forms an integral part of it in today's increasingly multicultural urban realities.

Case study context

The above research gaps are explored by using evidence drawn from a case study research with the Mexican population in the "West Side" neighborhood of St. Paul, Minnesota, USA.

The Minneapolis/St. Paul, in short "Twin Cities", metropolitan area epitomizes a recent feature of urban demographics in the United States. This is that metro areas of the northern and (mid-) western US, with hitherto little migration experience, have become centers of a new 'wave' of immigration, this time not from European, but predominantly Latin American and other Third World countries. While in 1980, 89 percent of the population of the City of St. Paul was non-Hispanic white, in the year 2000 this proportion had decreased to 64 percent. These 'new' urban migration centers can be considered as relatively inexperienced with multi-cultural city and community politics, also compared to their US-counterparts in the Southwest and Northeast.

The choice of the West Side as the case study location came about for two reasons. The first is the adequacy with respect to the conceptual and literature framework: Regarding metro area and city figures, it shows a high presence of ethnic and/or racial minorities and inferior household incomes, housing values and higher poverty rates. The latter all constitute characteristics of ('problem') neighborhoods with which the literature of residential segregation is typically concerned. The second is that in the metro area and city context the West Side represents the neighborhood with the most longstanding and highest presence of Mexican and Latino population. Particularly since the 1990s immigration from Mexico and other Latin American countries has strongly increased.

The Mexican or Latin American immigrants do not constitute the only important 'new' immigrant group in the City of St. Paul. Hmong-immigrants from south eastern Asia have settled in the area in large numbers as well. The focus on the Mexican population in this research can however be justified due to its longstanding presence in the area – with ensuing methodological advantages - and its particularly large increase in the 1990s.

Structure of the document

As mentioned before, the academic discussion and political responses to residential segregation in the United States constituted one of the starting points of this document. Therefore, in Chapter Two I undertake a detailed examination and critique of the discussion on residential segregation in the United States, as well as its policy responses. Current trends of residential segregation of minority groups in the United States, and its identified effects and causes are discussed. Housing strategies of the past 30 years sought out to address the problems associated with residential segregation and their outcomes and impacts are assessed, against their self-set and broader social objectives. Alternative considerations of residential segregation are presented, against the background of increasingly multi-cultural city realities, changing normative frameworks and more recent empirical studies on segregation. Based on these considerations, the foregoing focus of this study on (immigrant) community networks and *capital* is justified.

This study focuses on immigrant or 'ethnic' social networks and capital as these networks appear as a missing link to explain and assess ethnically based residential segregation. Therefore, in Chapter Three of this document the concept of social capital adopted in this research is explained. Additionally a conceptualization of the mutual influence of the social and physical space is conducted. Both are based on the work of the French philosopher Pierre Bourdieu († 2002). In the chapter, I discuss several aspects of social networks and capital relevant for the operationalization of the empirical study. These are for instance the links between the different capital forms (social, economic and cultural), i.e. the link between social capital and mobility, objective vs. subjective measures for assessing capital benefits or disadvantages, spatial effects on the development of social capital and mobility and the meaning of social groups.

In Chapter Four, the discussion on residential segregation and social capital are put together. Assumptions resulting from the literature review and the concrete research questions guiding the empirical study are presented. The understanding between theoretical and empirical knowledge is explained. Finally the conceptual framework of the thesis and its operationalization in the empirical study is presented.

While the previous chapter (Four) illustrates the 'big picture' of the conceptual and methodological framework, in Chapter Five I elaborate on the chosen data collection and analysis methods in a more detailed manner. As this empirical research implied the use of a mix of secondary and primary, qualitative and quantitative data, I initiate the chapter by explaining the understanding and function of triangulation. In the subsequent chapters I explain the methods used. The explanation of the interviewing and interview analysis process, as the core data-collection activity, takes up a particularly prominent space.

Neighborhood and city contexts are assessed in Chapter Six, as they are crucial to understand the empirical data, as well as the scope and/or limits of validity of this study. This assessment is based on statistics from the American decennial Census of 1990 and 2000. The chapter starts by describing general characteristics of the Twin Cities metro area and City of St. Paul. Then demographic changes of this urban environment are described, specifically pointing to the development of a more ethnically and racially diverse population. Subsequently the focus is lead on the West Side neighborhood context. After providing a brief historical account, socio-economic and population, the characteristics of the West Side are described, first with respect to the total and then the Mexican population. A classification of the West Side with respect to other types of US ethnic neighborhoods is provided at the end of the chapter.

In Chapter Seven the results of the qualitative study are presented. The main data sources here constitute semi-structured interviews conducted with Mexican residents of the West Side neighborhood and experts working in institutions at different levels of intervention. Complementary information sources were neighborhood walks, participant observation and the review of neighborhood-related documents. The structure of the chapter follows the broad topics provided in the conceptual framework: Kinds of (ethnic) social networks and relationships, the value of these social networks and the 'neighborhood effect' on social capital and mobility. The chapter constitutes the heart of this thesis in that dominant patterns found in the study are presented, complemented with information about (typical or a-typical) single cases.

Many myths prevail about ethnic communities and the presence or absence of resources created in them, not least in academic discussion. On the one end of what could be termed a positive-negative continuum of myths lies the idea of homogeneous, solidaric communities in ethnic neighborhoods; on the other end the image of the immigrant neighborhood 'traps' or ghettos as points of no return. In Chapter Eight of this chapter I intend to differentiate between these ideas by concretizing distinct *features* of ethnic social capital and ethnic neighborhoods identified in the context of this empirical study. Another axis of differentiation constitutes the naming of the specific *conditions* on the individual, neighborhood and macro-social levels that have a stake in whether ethnic social networks and living in ethnic neighborhoods result as beneficial or pernicious for the individual person.

Whereas the previous two chapters have centered on responding to the principal analytical questions of this thesis, Chapter Nine is concerned with the normative conclusions resulting from this analysis. Here too the main data sources constitute the results of the expert interviews, as well as the interviews with West Side residents. While enlarging housing *choices* and *capabilities* is proposed as a guiding principle for the orientation of policy and planning strategies – instead of desegregation - further principles building on the results of this study on ethnic social capital are pointed out. Policy and planning recommendations are detailed for the housing and other policy and planning sectors and indicators provided that help recognizing positive from negative segregation, on the neighborhood level.

In Chapter Ten, the conclusion of this document, the most important results of this empirical study are summarized in the form of answers to its research questions. Furthermore, the transferability of the results of the West Side case study on other neighborhood and city environments is discussed. The thesis closes with an overview of starting points for future studies of residential segregation and ethnic social capital and mobility.

2 Residential segregation and housing policies in the United States

Research on residential segregation has a long tradition in urban studies. In theoretical terms, it relates to and sets forth theories of the 'early sociologists' like Marx, Durkheim and Weber, about social segmentation in industrialized and urbanized societies (Dangschat 1998: 207). The investigation of residential segregation in the context of the 'early' Chicago School marks the beginning of urban sociology. The researchers of the Chicago School recognized the growing differentiation of residential locations as the spatial representation of social differences (along socio-economic, cultural and racial terms), and the increasing differentiation of land uses (residential, industrial, commercial) as symptomatic for social changes occurring in the context of industrialization and urbanization and large scale immigration (Park 1974: 90).

A variety of models for an ideal-typical development of the spatial structuring of urban areas was developed based on the early studies of residential segregation in Chicago, between 1925 and 1945. The model of 'concentric circles' of Ernest Burgess and Robert E. Park is based on the assumption that spatial development in urban areas starts from the city center and according to the ecologist principles of "invasion", "succession" and "dominance" (Lichtenberger 1986: 25). According to the concentric model, the invasion of a neighborhood by a relatively homogeneous social group (of typically lower social status) successively leads to the displacement of the social group (of typically a higher status) who inhabited the neighborhood before (McKenzie 1974: 110).

The regularities stated by the ecological view laid the foundations for a spatial assimilation model according to which the residence in majority-white, suburban neighborhoods is identified with upwards social mobility (Zubrinsky/Charles 2003: 176f., Alba/Nee 1997: 836f.). This is as neighborhoods adjacent to the Central Business District – the so-called 'transitional zone' (in terms of land-use, but also of socio-economic characteristics) – were believed to typically evolve into a residential area of low-income groups and racial minorities. In contrast, middle- and higher-income groups 'fleeing' the invasion of lower social classes into their neighborhoods would typically move to the outer, suburban fringes of a city (see Park 1974: 92, Dangschat/Friedrichs 1988: 10).

While in classical human ecology segregation was considered a neutral fact and a quasi-natural expression of social distance between individuals (Fortuijn et al. 1998: 367, Lichtenberger 1986: 55), in the decades to follow it was looked at with increasing concern. Particularly from the Civil Rights Era onwards, the social fragmentation of urban areas represented one of the key preoccupations of academics, policy makers and planners and was attributed to illegitimate practices of socially powerful actors (Marcuse 1993: 360), and to undesirable effects of the segregated (Massey/Denton 1993: 97). Against this background, housing and other sector policies were formulated to address the persistent social and spatial segregation between the black and the white population.

As the assessment of the adequacy of the (still) dominant view and policy responses to minority segregation constitutes a key concern of this research, the present chapter will provide a review on the discussion on residential segregation by academics and in the policy field in the United States from the second half of the 20th century onwards. Such review is important in order to understand the analytical and normative context in which hitherto policy responses to residential segregation developed. It also serves as a foundation of the quest of this research for enhanced explanatory perspectives on, and policy and planning alternatives to residential segregation.

I first present the current trends and the hitherto assessment of segregation in the social science literature. Subsequently, I describe the most important policy and planning responses dealing with residential segregation, all this with respect to the US-American context. Afterwards, the role of residential segregation in the immigration context is discussed and possible implications for policy and planning outlined.

2.1 The persistence of residential segregation in the United States

Racial and/or ethnic residential segregation forms a key structural characteristic of cities in the United States. Segregation rates for African Americans continue to figure at high levels and the ones of Hispanics and Asians, albeit in the 'moderate' ranges, are increasing with the numbers of these ethnic groups growing in the past decades (Lewis Mumford Center 2001: 1, Fong/Shibuya 2005: 287, Zubrinsky Charles 2003: 167, Iceland 2004: 269). Although black-white segregation follows a downward trend, it is decreasing at a pace so slow that "it may take forty more years for black-white segregation to come down even to the current level of Hispanic-white segregation"

(LMC 2001: 1). Profiles of the typical neighborhoods of persons belonging to the dominant racial/ethnic groups of the United States (whites, blacks, Hispanics and Asians) starkly reflect segregation patterns: In the year 2000, the neighborhood of a typical black person in metropolitan America was 51 percent black, 33 percent white, 11 percent Hispanic and 3 percent Asian. A neighborhood where the typical white person lived was 80 percent white, 8 percent Hispanic, 7 percent black and 4 percent Asian (LMC 2001: 1)[1].

Box 1: Segregation indices

Several segregation indices were developed in order to measure, compare and follow-up on segregation tendencies among cities in the United States and, to a lesser degree, in other countries (Friedrichs 1981: 218ff.): the Dissimilarity Index (DI), Exposure Index and Isolation Index. The Dissimilarity Index (DI) expresses which percentage of members of a specific (income, ethnic, racial etc.) group would have to move to achieve a situation in which every census tract replicates the (income, ethnic, racial etc.) composition of the entire metropolis (view Blauw 1991: 394). It ranges from 0 to 100. Values of 60 or above are considered very high, values of 40 to 50 are considered moderate and values of less than 30 are considered low. The Index of group Isolation reflects the percentage of same-(income, ethnic, racial etc.) group members in the census tract where the average group member lives. It provides an idea about the exposure of a group to itself and ranges from 0 to 100. An interpretation of this index must however take into account the overall proportion of the respective group in a given metropolitan area, i. e. the isolation index 'automatically' tends to be smaller for members of a relatively under-represented ethnic group in a city. The Index of Exposure indicates the percentage of non-group whites a given racial minority group is exposed to in the average census tract it lives. It also ranges from 0 to 100.

Residential segregation has traditionally been and still is associated with racial inequality and barriers for social mobility and personal well-being (Zubrinsky Charles 2003: 167, Iceland 2004: 249, Kraus 2004: 484). The theoretical and empirical perspectives on characteristics, effects and causes of segregation that corroborate this view, are outlined in the present subchapter. The awareness about these perspectives is important in order to understand past and current strategies to deal with residential segregation, sought out by policy makers, planners and academics.

---

[1] In 2000, the typical Hispanic lived in a neighborhood that is 45 percent Hispanic, 36 percent white, 11 percent black and 6 percent Asian. The typical Asian in a neighborhood that was 18 percent Asian, 54 percent white, 9% black and 17% Hispanic.

2.1.1 Characteristics and effects of residential segregation

Although residential segregation has figured high in the academic and public interest in the United States since the early 1960s, a renewed research and policy focus on the topic developed from the late 1980s onwards (Massey/Denton 1993: 2, Zubrinsky Charles 2003: 168)[2]. This new focus was connected to the notion of increasing neighborhood poverty and to concerns about the development of an urban underclass in US metropolitan areas (Wilson 1990, Massey/Denton 1993, Jargowsky 1997)[3]. According to various scholars, the spatial concentration of the poor and, mostly, minority households, was a (if not *the*) major factor preventing social mobility and blocking opportunities among disadvantaged members of the US American society (Massey/Denton 1993: 1, Jargowsky 1997: 185).

According to Jargowsky (1990), the trends in neighborhood poverty and concentration of poverty became particularly alarming between 1970 and 1990. In these two decades, neighborhood poverty:

> "grew along virtually every dimension. Ghettos [high-poverty census tracts predominantly inhabited by blacks], barrios [high-poverty census tracts predominantly inhabited by Hispanics] and other slum neighborhoods **expanded in physical size**, **number of residents**, **number of poor residents**, and the **proportion of the metropolitan population living within them**. The proportion of African Americans living in ghetto neighborhoods increased, despite a slight decrease in that group's poverty rate. **Poor persons**, whether white, black, or Hispanic, **became increasingly concentrated** in high-poverty areas and **more isolated** from the rest of society. The fastest growing measure of neighborhood poverty, however, was the number of census tracts classified as high-poverty areas. In other words, the **physical space occupied by blighted urban neighborhoods expanded** faster than the number of residents of such neighborhoods" (ibid: 29, highlighted ED).

---

[2] According to Massey/Denton (1993), the neglect of residential segregation as a research topic in these decades may be explained with the enactment of the Fair Housing Act in 1968: Academics, politicians and civil rights leaders believed the problem of unequal access to housing to be solved and turned to specific sectors, e. g. education and employment (ibid: 4).

[3] According to Jargowsky (1997), the Los Angeles riots in 1992, sparked by the acquittance of four police officers accused of beating the black motorist Rodney King, powerfully recalled the image of inner city deterioration and violence in the collective memory of US citizens (ibid: 59). Goetz (2003) assumes the attention on inner city poverty to be connected to an overall concern on public law and order, inter alia related to the war on drugs (ibid: ix).

While the debate on residential segregation in the 1990s focused on poverty- as and not on racial or ethnic concentration, virtually no author negates the considerable overlap between poverty- and minority-concentration. On the basis of a study on neighborhood poverty and the concentration of poverty in all metropolitan areas in the USA from 1970 to 1990, Jargowsky (1997) points out that high-poverty neighborhoods (defined as census tracts with more than 40% of residents below the poverty line) are predominantly inhabited by members of minority groups[4]: "In 1990, nearly four out of five residents of high-poverty neighborhoods were members of minority groups" (ibid: 61). On the national average, non-Hispanic blacks accounted for half of the 8.4 million residents of such neighborhoods, Hispanics (primarily Mexicans and Puerto Ricans) for one fourth and non-Hispanic whites also for one fourth (ibid: 61). However, comparing the proportion of racial groups in the overall metropolitan population to their proportion in poor neighborhoods, blacks and - to a lesser degree - Hispanics are overly represented in the latter, whereas whites in the former (ibid: 61f.).

The exposure to and experience of poverty concentration vary substantially among different minority groups. While two-thirds of the white poor live in low-poverty areas (defined as areas with up to 20% of poor residents), this situation was only true for one-fourth of the black, and one-third of the Hispanic poor: "Thus, in addition to suffering much higher poverty rates than whites, minorities who are poor are much less able to draw on the resources of a financially healthy community" (Jargowsky 1997: 73). Notwithstanding this latter aspect, several authors notice a growing tendency among white poor residents to concentrate in high-poverty census tracts[5]. Even though the increase of poor households that live in high-poverty census tracts can be observed across racial groups, among Hispanics this is primarily a result of population growth, rather than of residential mobility (Jargowsky 1990: 43).

---

[4] The fact that the majority of residents of high-poverty neighborhoods are members of minority groups can be underlined with the following figures: The 8.4 million residents living in such neighborhoods make up less than 4% of the US population. Only 1% of all non-Hispanic whites lived in a high-poverty area in 1990. In contrast, 14% of all US non-Hispanic blacks lived in high-poverty neighbourhood. More than 9% of Hispanic households live in high-poverty census tracts, although figures vary strongly according to the respective country of origin. However still, most minority individuals do *not* live in high-poverty census tracts (Jargowsky 1997: 68f.).

[5] Doubting the assumption of other scholars on a possibly growing "white underclass", see Jargowsky 1997: 65f..

In spite of the increasing number of residents of high-poverty neighborhoods among all races, Massey/Denton (1993) state that residential segregation of blacks is unique, as compared to the segregation of other minority groups: Contrary to the more transient segregation of other groups it has sustained itself on high levels for decades, and many African American households continue to live in relatively segregated neighborhoods as they experience social mobility (ibid: 2, 9, Freeman 2000: 32, Zubrinsky Charles 2003: 171, Johnston et al. 2003: 578). However, neighborhood poverty concentration may diverge considerably among members of the same ethnic group with different national origins, socio-economic backgrounds, traditions and cultures: Among Hispanics, only 3% of Cubans lived in high poverty census tracts in 1990, whereas 9% of Mexicans and 19% of Puerto Ricans lived in this situation (Jargowsky 1997: 67f., also view Logan 2002: 6f.).

There are important regional variances in the incidence of neighborhood poverty and the concentration of poverty in the United States. The Midwest shows high rates of neighborhood poverty and concentration of poverty of every racial/ethnic group but Hispanics. Black-white segregation is particularly high in Eastern and Midwestern areas of the United States while lower in metropolitan areas in the West and the Southwest (Zubrinsky Charles 2003: 172, Kato 2006: 2285). A large proportion of poor blacks in the Midwest, namely 43%, live in high-poverty census tracts, i. e. under the situation of poverty concentration. The highest proportion of Hispanics living in poor neighborhoods can be found in metropolitan areas in the Northeast and the Southern US, i. e. in metropolitan areas with a (traditionally) large presence of Hispanic households (Jargowsky 1997: 69ff., Lewis Mumford Center 2001).

Many authors agree that the spatial concentration of economically disadvantaged households is most likely to impact negatively on their prospects for social and economic mobility (Goetz 2003: 7f., 26ff., Burgess et al. 2005: 1028, Cutler et al. 2005: 204). The spatial isolation of individuals and families in segregated urban neighborhoods is believed to lead to or at least aggravate social problems usually associated with the urban 'underclass': e.g. joblessness, dependence on welfare, out-of-wedlock births, single parenthood, school drop-out, drug use and proneness to violent crime (Wilson 1990: 46ff., Massey/Denton 1993: 2, Jargowsky 1997: 22ff., Goetz 2003: 22,

Galster 1992: 273, Zhou/Kim 2006: 4)[6]. Again, empirical studies indicate that poor African American and Hispanic households tend to be much more isolated in high-poverty areas than poor whites and particularly afflicted by the above mentioned symptoms of social disintegration (Wilson 1990: 58, Jargowsky 1997: 43).

Residential segregation is assumed to impact particularly strongly on *children* and *youth*: Firstly, recent studies suggest that it increases the likelihood of residence in a segregated neighborhood during adulthood (Dawkins 2005: 547). Secondly, if a neighborhood environment displays unemployment, welfare dependency and drug-use as the norm rather than the exception, this is believed to hamper the acquisition of hard and soft skills required for young persons' future success or social mobility in mainstream society (Wilson 1990: 57).

Goetz (2003: 26) points out six different ways neighborhoods may impact on residents, namely through:

1. The different <u>quality of services</u>, such as public schools, medical care, after-school care, child care and day-care centers, as well as a functioning social and physical housing environment in general (Wilson 1990: 57, Burgess 2005: 1029, Frazier et al. 2003: 132).
2. The <u>socialization of young people by adults</u>, impacting on young people's acquisition of both hard and soft skills and their general estimation of education (Wilson 1990: 57, Frazier et al. 2003: 132).
3. <u>Peer influence</u>, particularly with respect to drug use, sexual and criminal behavior of adolescents.
4. The composition and density of <u>social networks</u>, which affect the likelihood of a person hearing about job and other mobility-relevant opportunities.

[6] Since the 1970s, several arguments have been put forward to explain the development of 'the urban underclass' and the increase of behaviors associated with the underclass, particularly among urban blacks. Among these are the culture of poverty argument, welfare disincentives, institutional racism, demographics, structural economic change, and, ultimately, residential segregation. Arguing in favor of (albeit different) structural arguments such as economic restructuring, racial discrimination and residential segregation, as opposed to a 'culture of poverty' are Wilson (1990: 30ff.) and Massey/Denton (1993: 7ff.).

5. Exposure to crime and violence, with inherent risks of victimization or greater acceptance of norms of violence and criminality, and
6. The physical distance from employment and educational opportunities where job-suburbanization and disinvestments in inner-city neighborhoods lead to a job-housing mismatch situation (Orfield 1997: 66).

It is however important to note that in 1990 in the whole USA not more than 12% of all poor households lived in high-poverty areas. Among black and Hispanic poor households 26% and 19% were in this situation respectively. Thus, the majority of poor households live in metropolitan neighborhoods with low (37%) or intermediate (23%) poverty levels and thus *not* in *ghettos*, *barrios* or *slums* (Jargowsky 1997: 71).

2.1.2 Explanations for residential segregation

The question about the causes of residential segregation reflects in many ways the explanations for the persistence of 'black poverty' and the development of the urban 'underclass', particularly in terms of their underlying normative and ideological assumptions. However, the approaches for the explanation of residential segregation specifically focus on the phenomenon of spatial concentration and thus need to be considered separately.

Three explanatory approaches are commonly used to explain racially or ethnically based residential segregation (Iceland 2004: 250f., Kato 2006: 2285f.): 1. Economic status, placing the emphasis on income or status differentials that determine the ability of households to compete in the housing market and the volume of their actual housing choices. 2. Preferences, considering that the spatial segregation of racial or ethnic groups is a function of ethnocentrism and/or prejudice towards members of other racial or cultural groups. 3. Institutional causes, sustaining that the segregation of minority households is predominantly shaped by discriminatory practices of public and private housing stakeholders.

Authors who pinpoint the primacy of economic causes for residential segregation state that social status (income, occupation and education) is a stronger predictor than race for the explanation of differential housing access in city regions. The empirical fact of the residential concentration of black or minority households is explained by the overlap of income and race, in the sense that the majority of poor households also 'happen' to be black or minorities. Sustaining income or occupational status as being key factors for determining housing access, Clark/Blue (2004) show that in immigration gateway cities segregation indices decrease among households of growing education and income levels, especially so in the suburbs with higher proportions of middle- and upper-class residents (ibid: 685). The importance of income in shaping segregation patterns is also sustained using the example of an increasing proportion of middle-class African American households who successfully moved to the suburbs, i.e. leaving central city segregation behind them (Wilson 1990: 49f.). Other authors however maintain that suburbanization has not yet lead to a significant decrease in residential segregation for African Americans, but rather to re-segregation in particular suburbs, usually not the most attractive ones (Huttmann/Jonnes 1991: 348, Zubrinsky Charles 2003: 176f., Hanlon et al. 2006: 2138).

Wilson (1990) argues that poor black and minority households were particularly affected by the detrimental effects of economic restructuring, such as industrial decline, the shift from production- to service oriented economy, suburbanization of jobs and growing polarization between high- and low level jobs (ibid: 55, Zubrinsky Charles 2003: 168). As predominantly occupied in the industrial sector they were the ones hardest hit by ′blue-collar′ job losses from the 1960s onwards. Relatively low education levels prevented their entry into higher skill service jobs in the inner-city. Access to entry-level employment in the outer city areas became hampered due to problems of accessibility, i.e. job-housing mismatch. Finally, the better educated, middle-income black families followed the paths of suburbanization of white middle-class families once they were no longer legally prevented from doing so. As a result, only the ′truly disadvantaged′ and most vulnerable minority households stayed behind in the decaying inner-city neighborhoods (Wilson 1990: 55ff., Clay 1992: 95, Marcuse 1997: 228ff.).

Many authors reject that income differences alone, without accounting for race, provide a consistent explanation for the persisting residential segregation of minority households in the US (Johnston 1991: 255f., Massey/Denton 1993, Squires et al. 2002, Freeman 2000: 32, Huttmann/Jonnes 1991: 342, Dawkins 2005: 546). Massey/Denton (1993) have computed Dissimilarity Indexes for African American households of three income groups (ranging from under $2.500 a year to more than $50.000 a year) in the thirty largest black communities of the United States. The results of their study show that independent of income levels segregation indices of African American to white households remain relatively constant (Massey/Denton 1993: 85f., also view Fong/Shibuya 2005: 293, Kato 2006: 2286). Northern and Midwestern metropolitan areas fare particularly notoriously in this regard: “In no northern metropolitan area did blacks earning more than $50,000 a year display a segregation index lower than 72” (ibid: 87). By comparing DIs of Hispanic Caribbeans of different racial backgrounds in ten metropolitan areas of the United States, Massey/Denton (1993) came to the conclusion that Caribbeans who identify themselves as “black” in the Census[7] show significantly higher segregation rates than those who identify themselves as “mixed race” and “white” – even if adjustments are made for socioeconomic differences between the racial groups (ibid: 113f., Fong/Shibuya 2005: 287).

The relevance of preference as a determining factor for black-white segregation has been discussed in numerous studies (e. g. Freeman 2000: 15, Massey/Denton 1993: 89f., Quillian 2002: 197ff., Kryson/Farley 2002: 968ff., Bobo/Zubrinsky Charles 1996: 883ff., Wilson/Hammer 2001: 273). The hypothesis of blacks preferring to live apart from whites was in part triggered by the notion that contrary to former European immigrants to the US, for which residential segregation represents a transitional experience, African Americans have remained segregated for decades, also after experiencing upward social mobility (Freeman 2002: 15). Against the background of a history of century-long racial separation, the assumption that both black and white households may feel more comfortable staying amongst their ‘own kind’ seems not too far fetched. Finally, it is largely recognized that in the context of chain migration patterns, the most recent immigrant groups contribute to residential clustering by seeking out neighborhoods already inhabited by co-ethnics (Zubrinsky Charles 2003: 172, Zubrinsky Charles 2001: 242, Waldinger/Der Martirosian 2001: 231).

Studies that examine preferences for racial neighborhood compositions among black and white households show complex, albeit quite unanimous results: 1. Most African Americans prefer racially mixed neighborhoods to racially separate settings (Massey/Denton 1993: 89f., Kryson/Farley 2002: 937, Johnston 1991: 257). 2. Most African American households tend to express a strong reluctance towards moving into all-white neighborhoods. This reluctance however is primarily due to the expectation of white hostility

[7] The American Census determines the racial background of people on the basis of their self-identification.

and rejection in all-white areas, rather than a rejection of whites or white neighborhoods per se (Massey/Denton 1993: 90, Krysan/Farley 2002: 970, Fong/Shibuya 2005: 291, Vigdor 2003: 591). 3. However, to most white households a racially mixed neighborhood is not desirable or something they would value to put into practice (Massey/Denton 1993: 92f., Kryson/Farley 2002: 937, Galster 1992: 278f., Ihlanfeldt/Sacifidi 2002: 621). Rather, white Americans tend to move out of a neighborhood after a few black families have moved in. This causes a situation in which a transitional neighborhood mix of black and white families would almost invariably result in a racial turn-over and re-segregation from a formerly all-white into an all-black neighborhood (Quillian 2002: 222, Massey/Denton 1993: 96, Dawkins 2005: 547)[8]. Thus, white households' avoidance of predominantly black or mixed neighborhoods, or more generally *white* rather than black preference and prejudice have been confirmed as major factors upholding residential segregation (Quillian 2002: 197, Zubrinsky Charles 2001: 230, 237, Wilson/Hammer 2001: 273ff., Bobo/Zubrinsky Charles1996: 903, Huttmann 1991a: 347, Clay 1992: 99, Massey/Denton 1993: 94ff., Dawkins 2004: 396, Kaplan/Woodhouse 2004: 582).

Finally, some scholars stress the importance of <u>institutional practices</u> for the persistence of residential segregation. According to Massey/Denton (1993) white prejudice or even violent action cannot sufficiently explain the persistence of black/white residential segregation in US cities: "Whites can only avoid co-residence with blacks if mechanisms exist to keep blacks out of most white neighborhoods. […] Although white prejudice is a necessary precondition for the perpetuation of segregation, it is insufficient to maintain the residential color line; active discrimination against blacks must occur also" (Massey/Denton 1993: 97)[9]. Although discrimination in the public and private housing sectors has been officially banned since the enactment of the Fair Housing Act in 1968 and become almost none existent in its *explicit*

---

[8] White flight from neighborhoods where African American households move in is associated with pejorative stereotypes among whites, e.g. that property rates fall and crime rates rise after the entry of blacks into a hitherto all-white neighborhood (Massey/Denton 1993: 94).

[9] The argument of Quillian (2002) goes inversely: "Given the evidence of discrimination in housing markets, there is clearly a need for measures to combat racially discriminatory practices by housing brokers and lenders. […] Yct the strong evidence for White (sic) population decline in neighborhoods with more than a few Blacks (sic) indicates that efforts to counter housing discrimination may not be enough to curtail segregation without efforts to stem White (sic) avoidance" (ibid: 222).

forms since then, many authors still consider it as a principal cause for racially segregated housing in the US (Johnston 1991: 251, Wilson/Hammer 2001: 295, Clay 1992: 99, Squires et al. 2002: 156f., Massey/Denton 1993: 99ff.).

From an institutionalist perspective, both private *and* public actors in the US are blamed for discriminatory acts leading to housing segregation of ethnic or racial minorities. Although *direct* discriminatory practices have virtually disappeared after the enactment of the Fair Housing Act in 1968, according to Massey/Denton (1993) institutional racism exercised by private housing agents and government officials, continued to be effective, albeit in a more subtle way (ibid: 84, Kato 2006: 2286). It has to be taken into consideration however that the influence of the public sector on the housing situation of minorities is limited, with the US government represented by State, regional and local authorities owning only 2% of the housing stock in the country (view Johnston 1991: 252, Blauw 1991: 398, Massey/Denton 1993: 229).

This being said, governmental practices that are blamed for *directly* contributing to housing segregation in the first half of the 20th century are the Federal Housing Administration's lending activities, the enforcement of restrictive covenants[10], and the local authorities' deliberate concentration of public housing projects (and thereby minority households) in the central cities, often in the context of slum clearance and urban renewal programs (Squires et al. 2002: 157, Goering/Coulibably 1991: 307, Kaplan/Woodhouse 2004: 581, Kraus 2004: 483)[11]. In contrast, governmental policies in the second

---

[10] Prior to the Civil Rights Era, restrictive covenants were used as contractual agreements among at least 75% of property owners of a given area stating that they would not permit a black to own, occupy or lease their property. In case of the violation of one of the signatory parties, any one party of the agreement could call upon the *courts* for enforcement and sue the transgressor for damages. The US Supreme Court declared restrictive covenants to be unlawful in 1948 (Massey/Denton 1993: 36).

[11] In the context of the Housing Act of 1949 it was determined that for every unit built by public housing renewal one dilapidated unit had to be demolished. This aspect led to public housing being built in areas that were already characterized by high levels of poverty and predominantly inhabited by minorities. As these were areas on relatively expensive land adjacent to the Central Business Districts, the construction tended to occur at relatively high densities (Goetz 2003: 32). The second element leading to the spatial concentration of public housing units was that in 1935 local authorities came to own and operate the public housing program, and not the federal government (ibid: 31f.). Some cities, particularly in the suburban areas, simply did not create public housing authorities - a pre-condition for receiving federal

half of the 20th century have rather *indirectly* facilitated and nurtured racial segregation. Among these were exclusionary zoning ordinances[12], the construction of federal highways and the federal home mortgage interest deduction program that fostered suburban, at the expense of central city development (Squires et al. 2002: 157, Jargowsky 1997: 207). Finally, the Federal Housing and Urban Development Agency (HUD) has been repeatedly blamed for the lack of enforcement of anti-discrimination laws, such as sanctions for anti-discrimination violations by private housing agents (Massey/Denton 1993: 186).

An important number of empirical studies, as well as housing audits conducted by the US Housing and Urban Development Agency (HUD), have disclosed racially motivated housing discrimination of realtors, private lending agencies and insurance companies (Massey/Denton 1993: 102f., Squires et al. 2002: 162, Saltman 1991: 379, Galster 1992: 278, Chandler 1992: 290f.). One common practice is 'racial steering', implying that realtors do not inform minority households about vacant units in majority-white areas, but only show them housing units in majority-black or minority neighborhoods (Massey/Denton 1993: 102, Dawkins 2004: 393f.). Another recurrent practice is 'redlining' or 'blockbusting', in the context of which private lending agencies or insurance companies refuse to provide conventional mortgage loans in certain neighborhoods not considered credit-worthy – more often than not, these areas are located in the central cities and are predominantly inhabited by minority households (Massey/Denton 1993: 105f.)[13].

---

funds for public housing -just to keep public housing out of their jurisdictional area (ibid: 33). As principles of anti-discrimination did not exist at the time of the construction of the first public housing units, local politicians followed decade-long patterns of social and spatial segregation when deciding about their location (Goetz 2003: 33f.).

[12] For instance, municipal governments have recurrently foreclosed the entry of low-income and minority households into their jurisdictions by prescribing minimum lot sizes and floor areas, maximum residential densities and development fees for multifamily housing development (Orfield 1997: 59).

[13] Since the US Congress passed the Home Mortgage Disclosure Act in 1975, depository institutions in the US are required to identify the number and size of loans they make to specific neighborhoods. Since then, studies which intend to assess a possible racial bias in home lending come to the consistent conclusion that "black and racially mixed neighborhoods receive less private credit, fewer federally insured loans, fewer home improvement loans, and less total mortgage money than socio-economically comparable white neighborhoods" (Massey/Denton 1993: 106). Some studies have identified a U-shaped lending pattern of city loans, in which loan activities were high in all-white neighborhoods, very low in mixed, 55%

Redlining hampers the ability for asset creation by minority households and greatly contributes to a situation of generalized disinvestment and decay in the 'redlined' areas (ibid: 105, Frazier 2003: 131)[14].

2.1.3 Policy implications

Not surprisingly, each of the mentioned explanatory approaches for residential segregation (class-related, preference-related and institutional) comes to different conclusions as to what kind of policies and programs are required to respond to it. In spite of ideological differences on whether the supply- or the demand-sides of the housing market have bigger explanatory powers for residential segregation, most scholars agree that the answer lies in a combination of these (Blauw 1991: 396, Fossett/Warren 2005: 1894, Burgess et al. 2005: 1029, Clark/Blue 2004: 667, Dawkins 2004: 395f., Kaplan/Woodhouse 2004: 583). Zubrinsky Charles(2003) points out that the appropriateness of the causal perspectives is contingent on group membership: While the class-related explanations better characterize the situation of white Hispanics and Asians, the institutional model applies more to the black African and Hispanic Americans (ibid: 170, Dawkins 2005: 546). However, due to the assumed linkages of residential segregation with social and economic deprivation, scholars usually agree about the need to actively limit or decrease residential segregation, whether economically or racially based.

Thus, all of the scholars assume, implicitly or explicitly, desegregation to be a desirable outcome to improve the living situation of the poor and low-income minorities. Scholars who believe that the persistence or increase of residential segregation in US cities is a function of people's economic status coupled with neighborhood differences in housing prices, believe that (generalized *and* geographically targeted) economic and employment growth strategies, as well as improvements in education, are key elements to increase opportunities for social, as well as spatial mobility for the poor (Jargowsky 1997: 197f., Wilson 1990: 151ff., Clark/Blue 2004: 685f.). Spatial mobility is considered a 'natural' consequence of social mobility. Accordingly, desegregation would occur by itself once people have achieved a

---

black, and again higher in predominantly black neighborhoods. This suggests that lending institutions associate racially mixed neighborhoods with 'instability' and are thus apprehensive of providing credit to their residents (ibid: 107).

higher economic and educational position (Jargowsky 1997: 204, Wilson 1990: 158).

Scholars who assume white prejudice and racism to be major factors for residential segregation consider that more tolerant racial attitudes by whites are necessary to achicve higher levels of spatial integration of blacks and whites (Krysan/Farley 2002: 970f., Bobo/Zubrinsky Charles1996: 904, Fossett/Warren 2005: 1895). As the lack of inter-racial contact is considered a root cause of white prejudice, increased inter-racial exposure is seen as one means of increasing whites' readiness to live in racially mixed neighborhoods. Referring to the contact hypothesis, it is assumed that "peoples' racial stereotypes wither when they have the opportunity to live with neighbors of other races" (Galster 1992: 276). The contact hypothesis has been confirmed provided that white and black households living in the same neighborhood have a similar social status (Ihlanfeldt/Scafidi 2002: 619)[15]. Most authors however agree that increased inter-racial exposure does not take place 'naturally'. Rather aggressive pro-integrative housing policies and strategies are deemed necessary which seek to prohibit housing providers from discriminatory action and to lure prospective owners into racially mixed areas (Galster 1992: 280f., Saltman 1991: 388, Ihlanfeldt/Scafidi 2002: 633).

As preferences of minorities, e.g. African Americans, to live in a same-ethnic neighborhood have been largely attributed to their intention to escape discrimination in majority-white neighborhoods, policy recommendations have centered on ways of how to decrease this discrimination. Consequently, policy measures to accommodate possible 'genuine' preferences of native or immigrant minorities to live close to each other were discredited from the upstart.

Those who believe that institutional racism constitutes the decisive factor to maintain residential segregation, call for a wide array of governmental strategies to actively counteract racially segregated housing patterns and promote desegregation. These are, for instance, the stricter and more effi-

---

15 Ihlanfeld/Scafidi (2002) have ascertained that interracial neighborhood contact affects "preferences [for ethnically mixed settings] of Whites only if this contact is with Blacks of about the same or higher social status" (ibid: 633). Also for blacks, neighborhood contact has a stronger impact on their residential preferences if it is with whites of the same or higher social status. However, their preferences for racially mixed settings also increase with lower-income white neighbors (ibid: 633).

cient monitoring and enforcement of fair housing laws by the US Federal Department for Housing and Urban Development (HUD), the promotion of tenant-based, as opposed to project-based subsidies, HUD's increasing institutional and financial support for fair housing organizations operating at local levels, community reinvestment in inner-city areas, mobility programs and the promotion of fair share housing plans for municipalities of a given metropolitan region (Massey/Denton 1993: 231ff., Squires et al. 2002: 171ff., Kraus 2004: 489). Most of these strategies have been applied in the last decades and will be described in more detail in the following chapter.

2.2 Policy and planning responses to residential segregation in the USA

American scholars and practitioners have generally attributed more weight to the institutional, supply-side, as opposed to individual, demand-side explanations for residential segregation. Academic and public perception alike has focused on the coercive and non-voluntary character of residential segregation and implicitly neglected its possible voluntary sides. Thus, policy and planning efforts have concentrated on recommendations of how to halt segregation or discrimination (Blauw 1991: 401), generally considering desegregation as an obstacle to achieving a more egalitarian urban society.

Thus the purpose of this present chapter is to place desegregation policies in their historical and normative context, to describe the most important of them, and to assess their hitherto success. From the perspective of the present research, this is important for two reasons: Firstly, these planning responses are directly related to the causes of segregation described in the previous chapter. Secondly, their assessment and critique set the basis for the need to explore alternative views on segregation, as well as for new policy and planning approaches.

2.2.1 Two generations of desegregation policies

According to Goetz, the United States have witnessed two generations of housing dispersal policies (Goetz 2003: 43f.). The first generation policies manifested themselves in the context of the "open housing" and Civil Rights movement in the 1960s, and the second generation ones in connection with the concentration-of-poverty argument in the early 1990s (ibid: 43f., 53)[16]. These two generations of dispersal policies can be distinguished in terms of

- their underlying motivations,
- the main steps proposed for desegregation, and
- the changing housing policy landscape.

The main motivation of the first generation dispersal programs was to revert past wrongs, i. e. racial discrimination in housing, and thus to address one of the important *causes* of residential segregation (Goetz 2003: 44). As mentioned in Chapter 2.1.2, the US Federal Housing Administration (FHA) and the Federal Department for Housing and Urban Development (HUD) had actively contributed to concentrating racial minorities, e.g. by the geographically differentiated provision of housing loans and subsidies, the placing of public housing projects and the advocacy of restrictive covenants (ibid: 44). Due to the overlap in American society between race and income, the mentioned discriminatory strategies indirectly contributed to the concentration of poverty (ibid: 44). However, the first generation dispersal programs focused generally on *racial*, as opposed to *income* desegregation.

In contrast, the main motivation of the second generation desegregation programs was to counteract the social problems or assumed *effects* of residential segregation and poverty concentration: prolonged joblessness, dependence on welfare, educational failure, out-of-wedlock births, proneness to drug consumption and criminal behavior (Goetz 2003: 53, Massey/Denton 1993: 2). Concentrated poverty came to be perceived as the driving problem in American urban areas (Goetz 2003: 53). Thus, unlike "the first generation of dispersion efforts, which was tied to racial segregation, this generation was firmly tied to concentrated poverty" (ibid: 54) or *income* segregation.

[16] Also other authors mention policy shifts concerning residential segregation, from the 1960s to the 1990s. According to Popkin (2002), during the 1990s the US government "dramatically changed its policy for housing the poor" (ibid: 1), also involving important changes in its efforts for housing desegregation (ibid: 1). According to Massey/Denton (1993), the enactment of the Fair Housing Act in 1968 had the effect that the problem of residential segregation was dropped as a priority issue from the agendas of academics, politicians and the civil rights' community (ibid: 4). Jargowsky (1997) states an increasing attention among the general public and politicians towards the social problems associated with ghetto life in the 1990s, not least triggered by mass media accounts (ibid: 59, 89).

In the context of the first generation anti-segregation policies, the US government undertook some fundamental steps to reverse residential segregation (Goetz 2003: 44). It acknowledged racial discrimination to be the principal cause for segregated housing patterns in American cities and banished housing discrimination in the context of Fair Housing Legislation[17]: In 1962, President John F. Kennedy signed the Executive Order 11063 for federally assisted housing to "take all necessary and appropriate action to prevent discrimination (Massey/Denton 1993: 189). The Civil Rights Act of 1964 prohibited discrimination in employment and all organizations that received federal funds (Massey/Denton 1993: 191, Goering/Coulibably 1991: 307). In 1968, the government of President Johnson enacted the Fair Housing Act outlawing discriminatory practices in virtually all the housing stock in the country (Massey/Denton 1993: 44, Goetz 2003: 44, Helper 1991: 303). In 1974, the Nixon administration created the Section 8 program under the Housing and Community Development Act, instituting voucher-based affordable housing as an alternative to the hitherto project-based public housing (see below). The Act was amended by the requirement that communities prepare housing assistance plans taking notice of the needs of low-income families and complying with the Fair Housing Act, *before* receiving federal block grants (Massey/Denton 1993: 206). In 1975, the Home Mortgage Disclosure Act was passed, requesting lending institutions to disclose the geographic targeting of mortgage and home-improvement loans, to facilitate the prosecution of redlining practices (Frazier 2003: 126, Massey/Denton 1993: 206). The Community Reinvestment Act of 1977 required banks to show that loans were provided to low-income areas (Massey/Denton 1993: 206). Also in the late 1960s, the US government started supporting regional housing initiatives and fair share housing initiatives, with the intention of breaking opposition to public housing by suburban municipalities (Goetz 2003: 47, see chapter 2.2.2).

This impressive legislative record notwithstanding, most scholars agree that the impact of the Fair Housing legislation and first-generation desegregation strategies on the segregated housing patterns, was limited at best (Goetz

---

[17] Laws enacted in the 1960s were not the first to remove residential segregation. For instance, in 1917, in the context of the "Buchanan vs. Warley" litigation, city administrations were bared of the ability to enforce residential segregation by determining black vs. white areas in a city. In 1948, the Supreme Court declared restrictive covenants to be illegal. However, these laws were rather punctual and easily ignored (Massey/Denton 1993: 188f.).

2003: 44, Massey/Denton 2003: 14, 200). Scholars point out several reasons for this limited impact: 1. Little commitment on the part of policy makers and local housing officials to the cause of desegregation; 2. Limited means of enforcement of anti-discrimination in housing; 3. Small proportion of scattered-site units with respect to large high rise projects in the pool of assisted housing; 4. Sustained resistance of local governments to regionalized housing policies and programs (Goetz 2003: 44, 48f.). According to Massey/Denton (1993), only the Fair Housing Amendments of 1988 strengthened and remedied the main flaws of the Fair Housing Act of 1968, notably in the area of law enforcement (ibid: 209f.).

In the context of the second-generation dispersal policies, the US government continued and accentuated some first-generation strategies (scattered sites, Section 8 program) but also created new ones. In any case, according to Goetz (2003) the government's focus on desegregation changed: The intention was no longer to 'merely' correct past wrongs, i.e. the outcome of racial discrimination, but to address "what it [HUD] regarded as the most significant problem facing American cities at the end of the century" (Goetz 2003: 54): the socio-economic and spatial division of US cities and the growth of an urban underclass in dilapidated inner-city neighborhoods – in short, the "ghetto" (Wilson 1990: 38). HUD created a two-sided approach to fight segregation. This approach consisted on the one hand of mobility programs, as cities were helping low-income families to use their housing subsidies to move to no- or low-poverty areas. On the other hand, the government charged public housing authorities with instilling a higher income mix in public housing project sites and with improving the physical and functional conditions of public housing, not merely by demolishing some of the housing. The Clinton administration in the 1990s tried to settle most housing discrimination lawsuits using a combination of the approaches mentioned (Goetz 2003: 62).

The shift in the 1990s towards more demand-side oriented housing policy and the privatization of the public housing stock, needs to be placed into a broader and more long-term context of budget considerations and standpoints on housing and welfare provision. Tenant-based or 'Section 8' subsidies require low-income families to rent a unit in the private market at or below the Fair Market Rent of a given region[18]. Whereas the family pays up to 30% of its income for the rent, HUD subsidizes the difference between the so-defined affordability limit and a unit's market rent. The shift from unit-to project-based had developed since the passing of the Housing and Community Reinvestment Act in 1974, when the Section 8 program was started. Thus:

"Between the 1970s and early 1990s, the ratio of tenant-based to project-based subsidies increased from 0.6 vouchers and certificates to 4.75 vouchers and certificates for every unit of project-based public or subsidized unit (…). By 1997, 72 percent of new federal rental assistance funds went to tenant-based assistance and only 28 percent to project-based programs (…). By the end of the 1990s, roughly one-third of all households assisted by the federal government received allowances." (Goetz 2003: 51)

The embracing and accentuation of tenant-based subsidies in the 1990s occurred in the context of an increasing pressure on HUD to cut down on expenditure for subsidized housing development and to acquiesce to demand-side and privatized housing policy options favored by conservative policy makers (Goetz 2003: 54, Goering/Coulibably 1991: 307)[19]. The focus on tenant- as opposed to project-based subsidies in the 1990s continued trends which had already existed in the Reagan and Bush administrations in the 1980s: the budgetary retrenchment in the construction of public housing and the relaxation of race-related restrictions on local governments in the provision of subsidies, e.g. vouchers and/or block grants (Goering/Coulibably 1991: 307, Goetz 2003: 54, Galster 1992: 275). Thus, local authorities were left with greater decision scope on how to deal with federal housing subsidies (Goetz 2003: 54, Goering/Coulibably 1991: 310). This was at least implicitly rendering service to suburban communities, which had traditionally rejected federal impositions on the provision of a 'fair share' of affordable housing, through regional governing bodies (Goetz 2003: 47).

---

[18] Fair Market Rent units are those with a rent below of which 40 percent of standard quality rental units of an area are rented out. In areas with a particularly tight rental market (e.g. due to economic and job growth) the 50th percentile is used instead of the 40th (www.universallivingwage.org).

[19] According to Goetz (2003), in the 1990s under the Clinton administration HUD had to fight for its institutional survival. Both the Senate and the House of Representatives were controlled by members of the Republican party, some of them calling for the elimination of the agency (Goetz 2003: 54).

2.2.2 *First generation policies and their impact*

Since the enactment of the Fair Housing Bill in 1968 a large variety of desegregation policies and strategies have been implemented in the US. The most important ones are summarized in this section, arranged in chronological order and following the account of desegregation strategies described by Goetz (2003).

<u>Scattered site programs</u>

In the context of moving away from the public housing construction in high-rise buildings in the 1960s, the US government enacted scattered-site housing in its Section 23 program in 1965. Scattered-site units are mostly single-family units owned by local Public Housing Authorities, rented to the tenants. They were the first initiative to deconcentrate assisted housing in American cities, which was however occurring on a very gradual basis (Goetz 2003. 45): Less than one fourth of the housing authorities had started scattered-site housing by the end of the 1960, and by the early 1990s only 10 percent of all assisted housing in urban areas were scattered-site units (Goetz 2003: 45). Also, with the government moving away from public housing projects from the mid-1970s onwards, the construction or purchase of scattered-site housing was slowly abandoned.

The contribution of scattered-site housing to the intended impact of housing desegregation was limited. It is clear that the placement of public housing in single-family units implies a higher level of spatial or physical distribution than in high-rise buildings. Thus effectively, since 1970, public housing projects became less concentrated in central city areas (Goering/Coulibably 1991: 314)[20]. However, apart from the small number of scattered-site housing units[21] several reasons can be illustrated for the rather moderate desegregation effects of the scattered site program: 1. Public housing officials were not necessarily committed to the implementation of residential desegregation as quickly as called for by the fair housing legislation. 2. High costs of land and property outside areas adjacent to the central city, as well as the resis-

[20] In the period from 1980 to 1983, 44 percent of all units were built in the central city, as compared to the period from 1937 to 1949, in which 85 percent of subsidized homes were built there (Goering/Coulibably 1991: 314).

[21] According to Massey/Denton (1993) scattered-site units constitute only one third of all the public housing in the United States, which by itself represents only 2 percent of the country's total housing stock (ibid: 229).

tance of residents in the receiving wealthier communities, prevented a higher spatial distribution. 3. In the placement of scattered-site units, PHAs were limited to the borders of their own jurisdiction, usually preventing the dispersal of scattered site units across municipal borders (Goetz 2003: 45f.).

Fair-Share housing

Fair-share housing programs have occurred in the context of urban governance reforms seeking to strengthen the regional, with respect to the local government level. Regional fair-share housing initiatives started in the late 1960s and constituted a reaction to the "exclusionary practices of predominantly white suburban areas and the lack of subsidized, affordable housing outside the central cities" (Goetz 2003: 46). Such practices include the so-called exclusionary zoning in which municipalities determine, for instance, minimum lot-sizes, density limits of units per acre or impose additional development fees on developers for the construction of multi-family units (view Orfield 1997: 59). In the years after the Fair Housing Act of 1968, the federal government supported regional fair share housing in multiple ways. Examples are the funding of development of area-wide councils of government, provision of infrastructure funds based on local governments' compliance with fair share housing regulations under HUD's Open Communities Program, and the authorization of metropolitan area councils to review local governments' applications for federal aid for consistency with regional development plans (Goetz 2003: 47).

Although fair-share housing was started with considerable political impetus and experienced transitional success stories in some metropolitan areas in the country, these success stories were not permanent. HUD not only stopped funding regional initiatives in the second half of the 1970s, but also tended to accommodate suburban resistance to complying with regional affordable housing obligations and anti-discrimination in housing (Goetz 2003: 49).

Tenant-based programs

Tenant-based or 'voucher' housing was introduced under the Nixon administration in 1974, in Section 8 of the Housing and Community Development Act. Although it had been discussed as an alternative to unit-based housing since the creation of assisted housing in the 1930s and 1940s, it was not implemented until 1974 (Goetz 2003: 49f.). The Presidential Committee on

Urban Housing in 1968 recommended the introduction of tenant-based housing based on the following three arguments: 1. Costs: Tenant-based housing is less expensive than are unit-based programs; 2. Market: It leaves assisted families more choices for units and neighborhoods and implies less interference with the private market; and 3. Desegregation: It will reduce the degrees of segregation by race and income (Goetz 2003: 49). As mentioned in the previous chapter, tenant-based subsidies allow families to rent a unit at or below a HUD-established fair market rent (FMR) of a given region. The PHA then pays for the difference between 30% of the person's income and the unit's rent. In the 1980s the voucher program was introduced allowing families to rent units above the FMR provided they pay the extra cost and to use the certificate throughout the United States (ibid: 51). The principle of 'portability' of vouchers, sanctioned by Congress in 1998, institutionalizes the right of families to use their subsidy also outside of their municipality of residence, in any city in the United States (ibid: 52, Section 8 Portability Fact Sheet, PHA St. Paul). As mentioned in the previous chapter, tenant-based subsidies were greatly expanded between 1970 and 1990 and by the end of the 1990s provided to one third of all households that received subsidies from the federal government (Goetz 2003: 51). Due however to continuous budget cuts for affordable housing in the 2000s, HUD stopped providing additional vouchers in most jurisdictions.

Scholars assess the impact of tenant-based subsidies on desegregation in mixed ways, but agree that it is confronted by serious limitations. Some authors point out that tenant-based programs are the most promising type of governmental intervention to achieve higher levels of racial and income diversity in neighborhoods (Schuck 2003: 258) or they stress their potential in geographically expanding housing choices for poor and minority households (Goetz 2003: 51). However, experiences in many cities of the US have shown that Section 8 households face considerable obstacles when looking for housing in predominantly white, low- or non-poverty areas, for several reasons: property managers' unwillingness to accept these households; limited availability of affordable housing in non-poor areas, especially in situations of tight housing markets; and the reluctance of low-income or minority families to leave the neighborhoods familiar to them, i.e. out of fear from discrimination in the housing search and every day life (Goetz 2003: 239). Therefore, in many cases, "vouchers have proven to stimulate little geographic expansion of housing choice" (Galster 1992: 275). Furthermore, in most cities the impact of the voucher program is small in terms of sheer numbers (Massey/Denton 1993: 191).

Mobility Programs

Mobility programs are usually implemented in combination with tenant-based subsidies. They can be considered a consequence of HUD´s recognition that the scattering of public housing projects or even voucher-based housing programs *alone* are not sufficient to achieve racial and/or income desegregation. According to Goetz (2003), mobility programs may involve either of the following strategies: 1. Residents of a public housing project are required to move to non-racially concentrated areas, often by the so-called *vouchering-out* process. The latter implies the provision of Section 8 certificates to public housing families, not always on a voluntary basis (ibid: 55). 2. Counseling to assisted families in order to facilitate information about housing opportunities in areas outside the original or outside minority-concentrated areas. 3. Recruitment of landlords in e.g. suburb neighborhoods in order to increase their acceptance of Section 8 rental households (ibid: 55). One example for the large scale implementation of mobility programs is the *Gautreaux* lawsuit in Chicago[22]: It was initiated in 1966 and represents the largest of several lawsuits in the country fought against racially based housing discrimination since the enactment of the Fair Housing legislation. Its consent decree in 1981 involved the provision of housing vouchers to former public housing tenants, mobility assistance to the families as well as landlord recruitment (view Schuck 2003: 228, Goetz 2003: 52, Massey/Denton 1993: 190).

Assisting public housing families who wish to move to majority-white or non-poverty areas with counseling can hardly be disputed on moral grounds[23]. The situation is different in cases where families do not want to leave their projects and neighborhoods, but are still required to do so: Such procedure violates the right of families to decide about their housing situation and has shown little success in terms of the achieved housing desegrega-

---

[22] According to Goetz (2003) "the most notable lawsuit dealing with desegregation and deconcentration" (ibid: 52).

[23] One critique on voluntary mobility programs is their assumed 'creaming' effect: The families who decide to move or turn out selected in a screening process tend to be the most motivated, functional and capable ones (Goetz 2003: 242).

tion (Goetz 2003: 73)[24]. Apart from the problems of involuntary displacement, both the quantitative and qualitative impacts of mobility programs have been limited. Even *Gautreaux*, the hitherto largest desegregation program in the country, has been criticized due to its limited scale and slow pace (Schuck 2003: 230)[25]. Usually considered as successful, studies on the impact of *Gautreaux* on the participating families show mixed results. For instance, families who moved to predominantly white suburbs showed "significantly greater satisfaction with police and schools, but significantly less satisfaction with medical and transportation services" (Goetz 2003: 78)[26].

Integration Maintenance

Integration maintenance programs usually include the employment of a combination of preventive and repressive race-conscious strategies. Their objective is to facilitate the formation of racially balanced housing developments, neighborhoods or communities (Huttmann et al. 1991: 335, Massey/Denton 1993: 225)[27]. Similar to the authors of mobility programs, the advocates of integration-maintenance assume that racial integration in housing will not occur without governmental manipulation of housing demand and supply. Thus they intend to address what they consider as the root

---

[24] Several studies have shown that involuntarily movers of mobility programs have moved to neighborhoods with similar characteristics in terms of minority and/or poverty concentration (Goetz 2003: 73).

[25] At the end of HUD´s funding for the program, 7,100 black families out of 1.2 million former public housing residents had moved out of the segregated public housing and neighborhoods to 115 predominantly white areas of Chicago (Schuck 2003: 228, Goetz 2003: 52f., Massey/Denton 1993: 191). The limited scale of the mobility program however is not only due to obstacles in its implementation. In order to remain politically feasible and acceptable to the majority-white suburban families, mobility programs are almost required to work on a limited scale (Goetz 2003: 244).

[26] Several authors however pinpoint the positive, selection-related bias or creaming effect inherent in *Gautreaux* impact studies. The families interviewed about their experiences with the program were voluntary participants and probably above-average in terms of their social mobility-relevant skills and/or initiative. Hence the difficulty to determine what part of the found improvements in the living situation of participants can be actually attributed to their residential dispersal (Goetz 2003: 75f.).

[27] What is defined as 'racially balanced' depends on the overall racial composition of a given community. Usually, housing authorities determine a certain percentage above the area's or county's average minority proportion as the maximum proportion of minority in-movers (Chandler 1992: 292ff.).

causes of segregation: racist attitudes and behaviors, notably white "prejudice spawned by lack of inter-racial exposure" (Galster 1992: 277).

Examples of integration-maintenance strategies are affirmative marketing of mixed neighborhoods to prospective home owners, pro-integrative residential location counseling, bans on "for sale" signs in front yards of houses in neighborhoods in transition, financial incentives (e.g. low-interest mortgages) for households who move to a mixed neighborhood, promotion of non-discriminating real estate brokers, fair housing education, monitoring and testing with private lenders and in-place community development strategies (Galster 1992: 280f., Saltmann 1991: 388, Huttmann 1991: 355f., Massey/Denton 1993: 226, Kraus 2004: 489, Kato 2006: 2291). Some housing agencies have pre-determined racial quota in order to prevent the proportion of minority households, in a given neighborhood, exceeding a certain 'tipping point' (Chandler 1992: 292ff.)[28].

In the eyes of many, the use of racial quotas and entry restrictions for minorities into racially mixed settings[29] has strongly discredited the integration-maintenance approach. Agencies using the approach were criticized for practicing a reverse form of racial steering when "bowing to white wishes to what is an acceptable composition of an integrated neighborhood" (Huttmann/Jonnes 1991: 358, also see Schuck 2003: 210). Thus ironically, in some cases the well-meant goal of racial housing integration underlying integration maintenance strategies ended up *constraining* housing choices to minority residents and thereby violating the Fair Housing legislation (Chandler 1992: 297)[30].

---

[28] The 'tipping point' (determined on the basis of studies on racial preferences of white and minority households) refers to the maximum proportion of minority residents that is acceptable to the white residents of a given housing estate or neighborhood. Exceeding this 'tipping point' is expected to lead to white residents leaving the neighborhood ('white flight') or refusing to move in, i. e. to racial turnover and resegregation (Chandler 1992: 288f.).

[29] According to Massey/Denton (1993), typical target communities of integration maintenance strategies are those adjacent to black neighborhoods with a likelihood of being attractive for black home-seekers: they "all essentially work to maintain blacks as a minority" (ibid: 226).

[30] On the often quoted Starrett City court decision the Brooklyn housing authority was charged for housing discrimination due to imposing racial quota in this housing estate (Huttmann/Jonnes 1991: 336, Massey/Denton 1993: 227).

Further first-generation strategies

Beyond the mentioned first-generation housing desegregation programs, public and private agents engaged in numerous initiatives to strengthen the enforcement of the Fair Housing Act. These initiatives are, for instance, the prosecution of violators of the fair housing laws (e. g. developers and real estate agents), the realization of housing audits using paired testing methods[31] with the objective of detecting differential treatment of black vs. white home-seekers, and the filing of complaints against public housing authorities e.g. practicing racially biased assignments of rental units in their public housing projects. However, the effects of fair housing enforcement initiatives in the decades following the Fair Housing Act are generally believed to be weak due to their sporadic and punctual character (Massey/Denton 1993: 224).

2.2.3 *Second generation policies and their impact*

As mentioned in chapter 2.2.1, one of the differences between first- and second-generation dispersal programs lies in the focus on income of the latter, as opposed to the focus on race of the former. The first-generation desegregation programs engaged in race-affirmative housing policies (opening up housing options for blacks in majority-white neighborhoods), with the intention of providing remedies to past racial discriminations. In contrast, second generation dispersal policies from the 1990s onwards were essentially race-neutral and concerned on addressing concentrated poverty "regarded as the most significant problem facing American cities at the end of the 20th century (Goetz 2003: 54). However, as will be shown in the following paragraphs, most second generation dispersal strategies constitute complements or accentuations of already existing first generation strategies, rather than totally new approaches.

Moving to opportunity

The Moving to Opportunity (MTO) Program was enacted by Congress in the year 1992, in the context of the 1992 Housing and Community Development Act (Goetz 2003: 56). It can be considered a mobility program but differs

---

[31] Paired tests involve two individuals – one black and one white – presenting themselves to real estate or rental agents.
Apart from the racial differences the two applicants possess identical social and economic characteristics (see www.huduser.org/publications/hsgfin/phase1.html).

from first generation mobility programs such as *Gautreaux* in that both the original and the receiving neighborhoods are defined by their income levels, instead of their racial characteristics. Families who live in public housing in high-poverty neighborhoods (those with more than 40 percent of residents earning an income below the federal poverty line) are eligible to participate in the program. The program was started as a demonstration that assigned families on a random basis to an MTO experimental group, a (traditional) Section 8 comparison group and a public housing control group[32]. The MTO experimental group was different from the other two groups in that it received Section 8 certificates, received mobility counseling and was also required to move to low-poverty areas of their respective cities. The program operates in five cities: New York, Los Angeles, Chicago, Boston and Baltimore (Goetz 2003: 56f.). However, elements of the MTO program have been used in other cities, too.

In principle, the MTO program is subject to similar difficulties such as mobility programs that focus on race and not income as the decisive variable. The difficulties are similar in at least two aspects: suburban residents' and landlords' resistance to accept poor (and, due to the overlap between income and race, often minority) families in their midst and the limited scale of actual housing desegregation caused by the program (Goetz 2003: 56f.).

Mixed-Income developments

The objective of the approach of mixed income developments constitutes in achieving higher income diversity within a single subsidized housing project. The approach was legally sanctioned by the 1990 Cranston-Gonzalez National Affordable Housing Act and after a four-year demonstration program in four cities, institutionalized in the Public Housing Reform Act of 1998 (Goetz 2003: 58). It follows the inverse logic of scattered-site housing: Whereas the latter seek to disperse low-income and (according to their original logic) minority families across a city or even metropolitan area, mixed-income developments seek to achieve a bigger income mix *inside* of public housing projects by attracting higher income residents to these developments (ibid: 58). In the context of the 1998 Act, public housing authorities were required to "reserve as little as 40 percent of public housing units for the

[32] The decision to assign families randomly to their respective groups was made in order to prevent the methodological biases of the *Gautreaux* program.

very poor, opening the rest to families with higher incomes" (Goetz 2003: 58), for instance to households with 'low' instead of 'very low' incomes. They were also required to reserve 75 percent of all new vouchers to very low-income families, thus additionally facilitating their deconcentration (ibid: 58). The underling rationale is the same as in all dispersal strategies: Housing estates and neighborhoods with a high concentration lack long-term social and economic sustainability (see Chapter 2.1.1) - an assumption confirmed by evidence in many of the housing projects in the country, "literally crumbling and plagued by drug trafficking and violent crime" (Popkin 2002: 2).

Two sets of strategies are usually employed to convert public housing into mixed-income developments. The first consists of attracting higher-income residents to formerly concentrated project areas or communities. This in turn requires these areas to be attractive in terms of the building quality and design, amenities and conditions of neighborhood safety for market-rate residents – thus, community development or upgrading investments (Goetz 2003: 58). In order to improve housing structures, the demolition of often decrepit public housing projects may be necessary[33]. Furthermore, HUD monitors the performance of PHAs in preventing the concentration of lowest-income residents in their public housing units, also requiring the PHAs to submit yearly deconcentration analysis (view St. Paul PHA deconcentration analysis, January 2004). The second strategy involves assigning Section 8 vouchers to former low-income residents of housing projects, for use in alternative and, if possible, non-poverty neighborhoods (Goetz 2003: 58f.). Thus, mixed-income developments involve the use of both project- and tenant-based housing subsidies with a focus on household-based subsidized housing.

HOPE VI

Introduced in 1992, the since then official federal public housing revitalization program HOPE VI displays all the above-mentioned features. Its objective is to improve conditions in the worst public housing projects and increase economic opportunities and self-sufficiency among low-income hous-

---

[33] Until 1995, the one-for-one replacement regulation prevented PHAs from demolishing public housing sites. However, in 1995, under the Democratic Housing and Urban Development Departments's Secretary Henry Cisneros, Congress waived the rule and "permanently repealed [it] in the 1998 housing bill" (Goetz 2003: 60).

ing inhabitants (Popkin 2002: 1, Goetz 2003: 15, 60)[34]. It usually involves the demolition of part or all of these units, the rehabilitation and/or new development of housing units, i.e. through the combination of rental- and owner-occupied housing on the former project site, screening of prospective project-based housing residents, and the provision of Section 8 vouchers to low-income project residents, together with supportive services such as mobility assistance (Goetz 2003: 6f., Popkin 2002: 2).

Studies tracing the impact of the HOPE VI program arrive at mixed conclusions. According to Goetz (2003), contrary to earlier dispersal programs with relatively little desegregation effects, HOPE VI has "resulted in the immediate deconcentration of poverty" (ibid: 68) on former project sites. At least in the first years of its implementation, the biggest impact of HOPE VI lay precisely in *demolishing*, as opposed to providing public housing (ibid: 61). As many former public housing sites are located in areas adjacent to the Central Business District, public housing redevelopment under HOPE VI "must walk a fine line between triggering large-scale gentrification and being forced to heavily subsidize redevelopment in communities where the market is not so anxious to reinvest" (Goetz 2003: 69). Although replacement housing constitutes a goal of HOPE VI, the program often struggles with identifying and putting together alternative funding sources for public housing replacement (Goetz: 60f.).

Based on findings from a multi-city study about the impact of HOPE VI on former project residents conducted by Washington's Urban Institute, Popkin (2002) states that results were generally positive, as "many residents now live in better housing in less poor neighborhoods" (ibid: 1). However, similar to difficulties of tenant-based programs mentioned in the previous sections, challenges lie in Section 8 families struggling to find housing in non-poor

---

[34] HOPE VI was first targeted at only the worst-condition housing projects, however later was applied to all the public housing stock in the country, for which demolition and redevelopment are deemed economically feasible (Goetz 2003: 6). Between 1993 and 2001, HUD funded 165 revitalization grants, with a budget of $4.5 billion for redevelopment and supportive services: "HUD estimates that thanks to these grants some 71,900 units of distressed public housing will be demolished (of which about 50,000) were occupied and about 42,000 units will be replaced. These funds will also support construction of 15,000 homeownership units, 'affordable units' for the working poor and market rate units" (Popkin 2002: 2). The non-replaced units were to be compensated by the provision of housing vouchers (Goetz 2003: 60).

neighborhoods, particularly under conditions of tight housing markets, and in obstacles "to making the transition out of dilapidated public housing and to self-sufficiency" (ibid: 1). Particularly the more vulnerable public housing residents are exposed to significant risks if required to leave the housing projects and compete in the private market (ibid: 3, 5), hence a repetition of the 'creaming' effect inherent in many mobility programs (Goetz 2003: 68, 242f.). Furthermore, as the program involves the involuntary displacement of former public housing residents, chances of dissatisfaction among residents are high (ibid: 61)[35].

More recent housing policy developments

The policy trends for the provision and dispersal of affordable and/or minority housing instituted in the 1990s have greatly been continued in the present decade. *Budget cuts* for deeply affordable housing continue to materialize in the dismantling of old, dilapidated public housing units without adding new, as well as in the absence of incremental housing vouchers since the late 1990's (Testimony of St. Paul PHA-director to House of Representatives, May 2005). *Privately-run and shallowly affordable programs* are on the increase. For instance, the Low-Income Housing Tax Credit (LIHTC) program managed by the US Income Revenue Service has produced significant affordable rental units in the past years: up to 50% of all multifamily housing starts per year (www.novoco.com/low_income_housing/facts_figures/research_center.pdf). The program provides dollar-for-dollar credits against tax-payable for developers who agree to build affordable housing units for a minimum period of thirty years (Smit/Purchase 2006: 24). However, only moderately- (60% of area median income), as opposed to very poor households (30% of area median income) benefit from the program – otherwise it results as economically unfeasible for the developers (interviews K.NEDA, 4 May 2005; J.PHA, 1 June 2005, see Annex 3). At the same time, HUD-funded agencies and programs continue to *concentrate on income-*, as opposed to race (de-)segregation (interview A.PHA, June 14 2005).

35 The Hollmann v. Cisneros Consent Decree in Minneapolis included the elements of poverty deconcentration of HOPE VI, involved most of the dispersal strategies and presented virtually ALL the described problems (view Goetz 2003: 137ff., 173f.). As pertaining to my case study context, it is described in more detail in Box 10 in chapter 9.2.2.

2.2.4 *Summary assessment of desegregation programs*

Desegregation strategies can be classified according to their target groups: Some strategies have sought to influence the opportunities and decisions of individual households, i. e. the *demand* side of the housing market; others have sought to tackle the individuals and agencies that control housing *supply*. The classification can be extended by taking into account their levels of intervention: Some have focused on the *micro* level of the housing market, where individuals or households compete for or provide housing opportunities. Others have focused on the *meso* level, where organizations and institutions try to influence housing patterns and residential attitudes. Eventually, a third set of interventions has focused on the *macro* level in which the government defines the housing policy framework in which individuals and housing institutions operate. The following table places programs and particular strategies forming part of them into this classification:

Table 1: Housing desegregation strategies in the US

	Demand side		Supply side	
MICRO-LEVEL	**Target group**	**Approach**	**Target group**	**Approach**
	Public housing residents	Scattered site housing	Landlords	Counseling and recruitment to increase acceptance of Section 8 families
	Public housing residents	Provision of Section 8 certificates or vouchers	Landlords	Community development and rehabilitation activities
	Public housing residents	Mobility counseling	Landlords	Prosecution of fair housing violators
	Public housing residents	City- or metro-wide housing information systems (clearing houses)	Landlords	City- or metro-wide housing information systems (clearing houses
	Public housing residents	Demolition, vouchering-out		

	Demand side		Supply side	
	White middle-class residents	Affirmative marketing, incentives to pro-integrative movers		
	White middle-class residents	Bans on "for sale" signs in front yards		
	Whole community	Community development and rehabilitation strategies		
	Fair housing organizations	Financial and technical support		
MESO-LEVEL	**Target group**	**Approach**	**Target group**	**Approach**
	Housing agents and providers (public, private and NGOs)	Fair housing education		
			Housing agents and providers (public, private and NGOs)	City- or metro-wide housing information systems (clearing houses)
			Real estate agents	Promotion of fair housing agents
			Real estate and lending agents	Housing audits
			PHAs	Income restrictions for assignment of public housing units
			PHAs	Monitoring performance on racial/low-income deconcentration

	Demand side		Supply side	
			PHAs, real estate and lending agents	Lawsuits against and prosecution of fair housing violators
MACRO-LEVEL	**Target group**		**Approach**	
	Local governments, individual households		Fair share housing programs: development of regional development plans, including affordable housing objectives (since 1968)	
	Public housing authorities, local governments, individual households		Housing and Community Development Act: Creation of Section 8 tenant-based housing (1974)	
	Lending and home mortgage agencies, individual households		Home Mortgage Disclosure Act: Identification of redlining activities (1975)	
	Public housing authorities, local governments, individual households		Housing and Community Development Act: Creation/confirmation (?) of one-by-one replacement rule (1987)	
	Public housing authorities, local governments, private housing agents, individual households		Fair Housing Amendment bill: Stronger enforcement of fair housing violations (1988)	
	Public housing governments, local authorities, individual households		Housing and Community Development Act: Creation of HOPE VI, MTO (1992)	
	Public housing authorities, local authorities, individual households		Public housing Reform Act: Institutionalization of mixed-income approach, waiver of one-by-one replacement, merging of Section 8 / voucher program, portability of Section 8 voucher(1998)	

The classification of desegregation strategies shall now be linked with a summary assessment on their achievements and limits. I want to base this assessment on the following two criteria:

1. The success of the strategies in terms of their self-said objective of racial (or income) deconcentration in housing, and
2. The success of the strategies in terms of the underlying goal of improving individual's and families' living situation and opportunities.

Occurrence of residential deconcentration

In the light of continued segregated housing patterns of US cities in the 1990s and 2000s, especially between the black and the white population (view chapter 2.1.1), the effect of desegregation strategies to achieve racial and income dispersal have proved to be limited. This fact can be explained by several reasons:

1. Many strategies (e. g. shift from project- to tenant-based subsidies, scattered-site housing, mobility counseling) have focused on public sector housing – obviously the sector of the housing market that government has most influence on. Notwithstanding the importance of increasing housing choices for families assisted through public housing, HUD financed housing forms only a very small part, i.e. approx. two percent, of the total housing stock in the United States (Massey/Denton 1993: 229, Johnston 1991: 252). Accordingly, aggregate housing patterns are relatively few influenced by policy changes in public housing.

2. Even within the pool of public housing units, desegregation initiatives have encountered strong obstacles, such as the resistance to affordable housing on the part of suburban municipalities and residents of white and/or middle class neighborhoods. The fears of suburbanites associated with racial turn-over (e. g. property devaluation and increase in crime rates) tend to lead to re-segregation once only a few black households move into a neighborhood[36]. Although portability ensures that Section 8 vouchers can be used across jurisdictions, central city Public Housing Authorities still transfer little affordable housing to suburban communities (interviews with A.PHA, 14 June 2005 and S.HUD, 7 June 2005, see Annex 3). Thus, desegregation has little effect if only carried out on the

[36] However, it is clear that the resistance to public housing is greater in the case of big housing projects than with single-housing units, not least due to the former's higher visibility.

level of a single (usually central city) municipality, and not in whole metropolitan areas (Chandler 1991: 298). In times of tight housing markets the private market leaves little locational options for low-income families and (suburban) landlords can afford to refuse Section 8 households. Desegregation programs only apply to the housing stock built after 1972, i.e. leave large public housing high-rises untouched (Massey/Denton 1993: 201) – unless they are demolished under the new public housing revitalization program HOPE VI.

3. Initiatives to curtail segregation in the private housing market have, firstly, been less than in the case of public housing (see table 1), and secondly, have not proved very effective, at least not until the 1990s. The outlawing of discrimination in the entire housing stock of the United States in the Fair Housing Act of 1968 was enacted in conjunction with feeble means of law enforcement, e. g. a limited time to file a lawsuit against a potential discriminator, relatively small fines imposed on violators of fair housing laws, the need to identify and prove discrimination before filing the lawsuit – almost impossible for the individual complainant - and high cost implications for complainants (Massey/Denton 1993: 198). Until the end of 1980, very few cases of housing discrimination were actually prosecuted (ibid: 200), although serious biases among real estate and lending agents had been detected, e. g. in national housing audits. In the context of the 1988 Fair Housing Amendment Act the above constraints were partly rectified, e. g. extending the time to file a lawsuit, increasing potential fines for fair housing violators[37] and extending HUD's competences to initiate and file complaints. However, anti-discrimination enforcement measures have remained relatively ineffective.

In view of relatively little impacts of desegregation programs in changing housing patterns in American cities, Schuck (2003) considers that

"[The] tasks of defining and implementing diversity, however, have proved far more difficult than the courts imagined. Their Herculean efforts have borne little fruit. Indeed, Promethean might be a more apt adjective, as their efforts have entailed compulsive persistence, mythic hubris, and tragic failure." (Schuck 2003: 219)

[37] Whereas the hitherto limit of fines on punitive damages until 1988 was US$ 1,000, the 1988 Fair Housing Amendments Act empowered the Federal Housing Agency to impose up to US$ 100,000 to fair housing violators (Massey/Denton 1993: 209, Helper 1991: 303).

Impact on individuals and families

One of the key underlying assumptions of desegregation programs is that racial and/or income dispersal is beneficial for the affected families. This is believed to be the case for both the families moving to non-poverty and/or majority white communities *and* for the families left behind in the original neighborhoods – provided the latter are then characterized by a higher racial and income-mix. Desegregation is legitimated with the argument that it improves families' and individuals' situation in terms of access to and quality of services (schools, child care, medical centers), socialization for young people, social networks and access to employment (Goetz 2003: 27). Partly this is supposed to happen through diversified social networks and the increased contact with middle-class, white families (ibid: 81). However, hitherto experiences of desegregation suggest the following:

1. Impacts of desegregation on the affected families, e. g. of the *Gautreaux* program, are far from fulfilling all the expectations in terms of social and economic benefits. Although they are difficult to generalize across different dispersal programs (e. g. *Gautreaux* in Chicago and *Hollmann* in Minneapolis), some common features have been observed: Households dispersed in the context of desegregation programs report positive experiences in terms of neighborhood security, a higher quality of schools, as well as better hosing structures. On the contrary, households' experiences in terms of access to employment are sometimes positive, sometimes negative. Frequently reported detrimental effects of neighborhood dispersal are less access to transport and social services, such as health providers or childcare. Whereas moving to suburban neighborhoods tends to lead to more social interaction among white and minority children and adolescents, the situation tends to turn out very differently for adult movers: Many adults who have moved to suburban neighborhoods report higher degrees of social isolation, loneliness or even hostility in their new environments and few interactions with their higher income, usually white neighbors (Goetz 2003: 81f., 218ff.).
2. Voluntary vs. involuntary participation in dispersal programs seem to strongly affect households' appreciation of experiences. In the context of the *Hollmann* case in Minneapolis, voluntary movers reported higher levels of satisfaction in their new neighborhoods and

were also more able to actually 'improve' their neighborhood situation, in terms of indicators such as neighborhood poverty levels, proportion of residents on welfare, percentage of female-headed households and minority households (Goetz 2003: 204ff.). On the one hand, the latter is due to the fact that involuntarily displaced families are usually given full choice to find replacement housing, whereas voluntary movers have to comply with certain requisites in their choice of neighborhood (ibid: 71). On the other hand it points to the 'creaming' aspect repeatedly identified in mobility programs: As a consequence of self-and external selection[38] processes, the voluntary participants of mobility programs tend to be the households with the highest skills and initiatives (Goetz 2003: 242). On the contrary, poor households with little resources and/or weak credit histories often are not able to find replacement housing through the private market on which tenant-based subsidies rely. In order to prevent the possible destabilizing effects of mobility programs on such 'hard-to-house' families, comprehensive and enlarged supportive services are necessary (Popkin 2002: 4f.).

3. Many desegregation programs have faced considerable resistance from the affected, usually minority communities. This was especially the case with recent immigrant communities, e. g. in the context of the Hollmann consent decree the Southeast Asian families who displayed a strong reluctance to move away from their support networks (Goetz 2003: 202). Historically, leaders of African American communities or black fair housing advocates reject the objective of racial integration as paternalistic. Many minority leaders consider desegregation as yet another intention of the white majority to disrupt their communities, erode their power base and after all constraining, rather than enlarging their housing choices (Chandler 1992: 291, interviews with Expert 10, 14 June 2005; Expert 6, 10 May 2005; Expert 5, 4 May 2005, see Annex 3).

The ambivalence in the success of desegregation programs on the participating households points to an important policy dilemma: The promotion of more integrated housing patterns cannot necessarily be equalized with

[38] External selection processes involve tenants' screening in order to satisfy landlords or residents in receiving neighborhoods (Goetz 2003: 242f.).

enlarging peoples′ (housing) *choices*, although the latter constitutes a rather unquestioned social objective. Yet, many minority families would precisely *not* choose to live in racially integrated or majority-white neighborhoods. Among other reasons, this is due to the fact that many of these neighborhoods lack service infrastructure and support systems that are essential *assets* in the life of low-income and/or minority households[39]. The dependence on formal and informal support systems or *social networks* appears as a particularly sensitive aspect for immigrant households. Finally, desegregation programs have not only been compromised by the racially biased behavior of housing market door keepers and/or anti-discrimination law enforcers. Beyond the latter, they have experienced substantial opposition by the communities affected and assumed to benefit from them (Schuck 2003: 258ff.).

2.3 Residential segregation in the context of immigration

Although the academic perception about residential segregation in the United States continues to be predominantly negative, some scholars have criticized such outright negative assessment. On the one hand, the limited success of dispersal programs described above has prompted criticism on the ideal of housing integration and its underlying assumptions (Goetz 2003: 237ff., Young 2002: 217). On the other hand, scholars have criticized the focus of most hitherto studies on the black-white as opposed to multi-ethnic segregation experiences, and pointed to the possibly distinct function of residential segregation in the immigration process (Young 2000: 216f., Tomlins 2000: 163, Boal 2000, Häußermann/Siebel 2001). Whereas in the United States this criticism has remained theoretical, in Europe and, e.g. in Australia some empirical work has been carried out looking into positive and negative 'neighborhood effects' in the context of ethnic segregation.

Shifts in the perception of residential segregation in the US context can be explained against the following background factors:

1. Increasingly multi-ethnic urban areas,
2. The (discovery of the) relevance of cultural pluralism for housing,

---

[39] In other words, the type and quality of the housing top structure constitutes only one of several factors determining an individual's or a family's housing choices (Galster 1992: 277, Goetz 2003: 8, Vigdor 2003: 590). Offering affordable and decent public housing in a suburb does not necessarily make the latter a suitable housing option for a household formerly living in a central city neighbourhood.

3. The notion of the benefits of spatial clustering.

While for the first factor I will focus on the case of the United States, I will discuss the second and third aspects with respect to theoretical reflections and empirical studies both in- and outside the US[40].

2.3.1 Increasing diversity in US cities

In the last three decades of the 20th century, the foreign-born population[41] in the United States has grown dramatically and particularly its cities have become increasingly diverse in racial and/or ethnic terms (Fix/Capps 2002: 1, Camarota/McArdle 2003: 1, Logan 2002b: 1, Sandercock 1998: 2, Sandercock 2003: 3, Fong/Shibuya 2005: 285). In the year 2000, 11 percent of the total American population was foreign-born, a figure that had doubled since the 1970s (Fix/Capps 2000: 1, Schuck 2003: 88, Camarota/McArdle 2003: 1)[42]. As almost half of the immigrants who live in the US today arrived after 1980, their 'second-generation' is "an overwhelmingly youthful population" (Zhou 2001: 273). The increase of the immigrant population in the US can be attributed to global forces such as international political and labor migration (Sandercock 1998: 2f.), as well as to changes in its national legal and policy framework[43].

---

[40] I have included the non-US American literature in this section due to the more advanced discussion on 'positive' versus 'negative' segregation in e.g. European and other country contexts.

[41] For pragmatic reasons, in the present document the terms "immigrants" and "foreign-born" population will be used synonymously. This slightly differs from the definitions of the US Census Bureau, according to which "foreign-born" residents are persons living in the US who were not US citizens at birth, including naturalized citizens, legal permanent residents (e. g. green card holders), illegal immigrants and those possessing long-term temporary visas such as students or guest workers. In contrast, "immigrants" are only those possessing *legal* permanent residence (www.factfinder.census.gov, Camarota/McArdle 2003: 2).

[42] The growth of the immigrant or foreign-born population in the last decades of the 20th century is not the first one in industrial America's history. The "record level of 15 percent" (Fix/Capps: 1) of immigrants with respect to the total population was attained in the year 1900 (ibid: 1). On the discussion about differences and communalities between what are considered the two waves of massive migration to the US, the 'old' one of predominantly European between 1880 and 1920 and the 'new' one of predominantly non-European provenance since 1965, see Alba/Nee 1997: 841ff., Gans 1997: 876, Wind/Kasinitz 1997: 1097, Zhou 2001: 281.

[43] The relaxation of country-specific immigration ceilings or quota in the context of the 1965 immigration law can be considered a starting point for attracting large scale migration from Third World countries and particularly Latin America (Schuck 2003: 85, 88, Iceland 2005:

In the 1990s Latin America has become the most important sending region of immigrants to the US, accounting for 60 percent in the growth of the country's foreign-born population[44]. According to the Census 2000, 52 percent of the foreign-born population of the United Sates comes from Latin America, 32 percent from Asia, 16 percent from Europe and 0.2 percent from Canada[45]. By the year 2000, Mexico constituted the top sending country, accounting for 30 percent of the total foreign-born population[46] and for 43 percent of the latter's growth between 1990 and 2000 (Camarota/McArdle 2003: 1). The majority of undocumented or illegal immigrants coming to the United States are from Mexico (Zubrinsky Charles 2003: 171). Notwithstanding the Mexican predominance among the immigrants to the US[47], the number of 'new' Latinos from the Dominican Republic, as well as Central and South American countries has also increased in the 1990s (Logan 2002: 3)[48].

---

250). Other reasons include geopolitical events such as the end of the Vietnam war in the late 1970s – triggering a large scale immigration of the Hmong people -, as well as economic changes in the sending countries coupled by an important demand for inexpensive labor in the US (Kaplan/Woodhouse 2004: 580).

[44] Still, immigrants to the US "now arrive from every corner of the world" (Camarota/McArdle 2003: 1), as opposed to, for instance, from Europe or a single Asian country in the late 19th century (Schuck 2003: 81ff.).

[45] This significantly differs from the share of the immigrant population in 1960, before the enactment of the 1965 immigration law: In this time, 30% of the foreign-born population came from Europe, 40% from Mexico and Latin America, 12% from Asia and the rest from Canada (Schuck 2001: 89). Both the Hispanic and the Asian population grew significantly between 1990 and 2000, with 57 percent and 69 percent respectively. Whereas the population growth among Asians mainly stems from natural population growth, the increase in the Latino population can be attributed to immigration (Logan 2001: 1f., Logan et al. 2001: 3).

[46] In 1990, Mexico represented 22 percent, and in 1980 16 percent of the foreign-born population representing the main sending country for more than 20 years (Camarota/McArdle 2003: 1, 3). In 1970, Italy constituted the largest sending country, the Italian foreign-born representing 10 percent of the US' national immigrant population (ibid: 3). Historically, "for at least 120 years, no country has accounted for such a large share of the foreign-born as Mexico does today" (ibid: 6).

[47] Corresponding to representing the top overall immigrant nationality, Mexicans also represent the largest Hispanic group, i. e. two-thirds of all Hispanics. They are followed by Puerto Ricans and Cubans who according to the Census 2000 counts represent 10 percent and 3.5 percent, respectively (Logan 2002: 5).

[48] Whereas the 1990 Census counted 3 million 'new' Latinos, in the Census 2000 this figure rose up to 6.1 million (Logan 2001: 1, Logan 2002: 5).

In terms of the residential patterns of the immigrant population, the Census 2000 shows that the foreign-born population lives considerably more dispersed inside the United States than in the previous decades. The share of the foreign-born population residing in the traditional destination states of California, New York, Texas, Florida, New Jersey and Illinois fell from 75 percent in 1990 to 68 percent in 2000[49]. In the meantime, "new growth states" (Fix/Capps 2000: 3) located in the central areas of the country have emerged: Carolina, Georgia, Nevada and Arkansas show the highest increases in their foreign-born populations (Fix/Capps 2000: 3)[50]. Among the Hispanic foreign-born population, the Census 2000 shows different prime locations for different national groups: For instance, whereas the largest numbers of Mexicans live in the Southwestern states of California and Texas, most Puerto Ricans reside in New York and most Cubans in Florida (Logan 2002: 7f.). In spite of their concentration in the Southwest, in 2000 Mexicans showed the biggest foreign-born population shares in 30 states, among them Minnesota (Camarota/McArdle 2003: 9).

Cities, and particularly the largest ones, constitute the major destinations for migrants to the US (Logan 2003: 3, 8, Fong/Shibuya 2005: 285), which in the case of Latin American immigrants is usually labor-driven[51]. In 2000, eight out of fifty largest metro areas of the United States were majority-minority in 2000, with whites forming less than half of their populations (Zubrinsky Charles 2003: 171). In the same census year, 69 US metropolitan areas had a share of more than 10 percent of foreign-born residents (Logan 2003: 15f.). Although immigrants can now be found in many cities of the country, partly as a consequence of secondary migration, they are still unevenly distributed (Logan 2003: 14): Half of the nation's immigrants are concentrated in 13 metropolitan areas[52], whereas some areas continue to

---

[49] The growth rate of the foreign-born population in the 'top' destination state California even declined from 80 percent in the 1980s to 37 percent in the 1990s (Fix/Capps 2000: 2).

[50] In the 1990s, the foreign-born population more than doubled in 19 states. In the new-growth states together, the foreign-born population increased by 145 percent (e. g. 274 percent in North Carolina and 233% in Georgia), as opposed to 57 percent countrywide (Fix/Capps 2000: 3). The foreign-born population in Minnesota grew by 127 percent from 115,097 in 1990 to 261,030 in 2000 (Camarota/McArdle 2003: 9).

[51] Other immigrant types commonly depicted are: entrepreneurial, professional and refugee (Waldinger/Der Martirosian 2001: 239).

[52] The following are these 13 metropolitan areas, in order of the proportion of immigrants in 2000: Los Angeles-Long Beach, New York, Chicago, Miami, Houston, Orange County,

possess very small proportions of foreign-born residents, particularly in the Midwest of the US (Logan 2003: 4f.). While historically, immigrants have moved to central city neighborhoods the Census 2000 indicates a stronger growth of the foreign-born population in the suburbs (ibid: 8, Hanlon et al. 2006: 2138f.).

According to the Census 2000, "immigrants typically live in neighborhoods where about 30% of residents are immigrants and an even higher share of neighbors speaks a language other than English at home" (Logan 2003: 1). Although Hispanic-white and Asian-white segregation indices are generally lower than the black-white ones (view Jargowsky 1990, Massey/Denton 1993, Alba/Nee 1997: 859), they do oscillate between moderate and high levels, depending on factors such as the Hispanic immigrants' population size in a city, skin color and socio-economic status (Logan 2002: 6f., Lewis Mumford Center 2001, Alba/Nee 1997: 859)[53]: For instance, the predominantly non-white immigrants from the Dominican Republic, Puerto Rico and Central America show the highest segregation (DI) indices, i. e. 81, 57 and 64 respectively (Logan 2002: 6f.).

Segregation and isolation of Hispanics and Asians have increased parallel to their population growth in the USA (Zubrinsky Charles 2003: 172, Johnston et al. 2003: 577, Iceland 2004: 264). Thus, between 1990 and 2000 Mexican-white segregation has slightly increased, as indicated by the respective dissimilarity indexes of 51.4 and 53.1 (Logan 2002: 6). In 2000, the average Hispanic's neighbors are 45.5 percent Hispanic, as compared to 42.4 in 1990 (Logan 2002: 6f.). The neighborhood 'isolation' of Hispanics and Asians with respect to the white population increased between 1980 and 2000 (LMC 2001: 1, Zubrinsky Charles 2003: 174). This trend was observed to be almost the same for first and second generation immigrants and the case in

Washington DC, Riverside-San Bernardino, San Diego, Dallas, Oakland, San José and San Francisco. Most of them are situated in the Southwestern USA, notably California, with the exception of New York, Chicago and Washington (Logan 2003: 6). However, in some of the metropolitan areas with a very small foreign-born population, the latter have increased significantly. For instance the foreign-born population of Nashville, Tennessee tripled between 1990 and 2000 (Logan 2003: 5).

[53] Hispanics of different countries or regions of origin considerably differ in terms of their socioeconomic status. Whereas Latinos from South America and Cuba tend to be better educated and earn higher incomes in the US, Hispanic immigrants from Mexico, Puerto Rico, the Dominican Republic and Central America tend to have lower education levels and earn lower incomes (Logan 2002: 1f., Bohon 2005: 264).

both cities and suburbs (Lewis Mumford Center: 1, Logan 2003: 11f., Fong/Shibuya 2005: 292). Thus, suburbanization has continued patterns of residential clustering formerly confined to the inner city (Zubrinsky Charles 2003: 175)[54].

What is the consequence of all this? If cities in the US are becoming increasingly "multi-cultural, multi-racial, multiple" (Sandercock 1998: 3) and if this diversity is reflected in residential experiences and patterns, a focus of studies on black/white segregation has to be considered severely inadequate (Cornwell/Murray 1992: 359, Clark/Blue 2004: 669, White et al. 2005: 174). Whereas until recently immigrants from Third World countries concentrated in a few urban centers in the South West and East Coast of the US, in 2000 they have dispersed to urban areas that have historically attracted few immigrants.

Thus, multi-ethnic or –racial conditions apply to the reality of an ever increasing number of cities and experience of citizens in the US. Studies on residential segregation and its policy implications need to take into account these more complex demographic realities, for at least two reasons: 1. Statistical accounts, based on the Census, prove that spatial segregation is also experienced by Hispanics and Asians, the two most important immigrant 'groups', albeit at a more moderate level than with African Americans. 2. The motivation for, and experiences of these immigrant groups with residential segregation may considerably differ from those of the native African American population in the USA. They therefore deserve a particular study focus as well as separate attention from policy makers.

---

[54] The quoted authors evaluate the increasing segregation of immigrants in US cities in a mixed way. On the one hand, they assume that immigrant neighborhoods fulfill important cultural and socioeconomic bridging functions for new arrivals and living in an 'ethnic neighborhood' may be a result of choices rather than exclusively constraints (Logan 2002b: 9). On the other hand, they are extremely critical of the inequalities in public schools, safety, environmental quality and public health a segregated neighborhood environment imposes on blacks, Hispanics and Asians (Lewis Mumford Center 2001: 1, Logan 2002a: 4). Minority neighborhoods in the city *and* in suburbs tend to be characterized by lower income levels, poorer quality public services and schools, more crime and other social problems than majority-white areas (Zubrinsky Charles 2003: 176).

2.3.2 *The emergence of the pluralism paradigm*

Apart from the reality of an increasingly multi-cultural city context in the United States, the re-evaluation of residential segregation can be partly understood by what I term the (re-)emergence of the paradigm of cultural pluralism and multiculturalism in urban and housing studies. In the USA, the claim for pluralist policies and planning appeared as a reaction to what some social scientists consider an ethnocentric and paternalist bias in the visions of the 'melting pot' and 'assimilation' in American society (Wortham 2002: 9, Alba/Nee 1997: 827)[55]. The spatial assimilation model assumes that native or immigrant minorities will convert social mobility gains into an "improved spatial position, which implies assimilation with members of the majority group and suburbanization" (Clark/Blue 2004: 670, also Zubrinsky Charles 2003: 176, Waldinger 2001: 229, Hanlon et al. 2006: 2130).

From a theoretical standpoint the melting pot concept may imply a reciprocal assimilation of majority and minority groups in a given society. However, most authors agree that the American understanding of assimilation has historically relied on the assumption that immigrant groups successively abandon their culture of origin and adapt to the dominant, i. e. Anglo-Saxon culture and value system (Wortham 2003: 6, Alba/Nee 1997: 827, Schuck 2003: 41f., also view Borrie 1959: 292ff., Glazer 1975: 24)[56]. Whereas the melting-pot and assimilation concepts correspond to the political project of a homogeneous national culture and political identity (Schuck 2003: 45,

---

[55] The US scholarly debate on the meaning and desirability of assimilation is not new. It was prompted by the arrival of large immigrant populations from (mostly) Europe in the context of the first massive migration between the 1880s and 1920s and has re-gained momentum in the last three decades of the 20th century, when large immigrant groups from predominantly Third World countries arrived in the US. Cultural pluralism as an alternative analytical and normative concept of inter-ethnic co-existence in the US has emerged in the 1920s, too (Gordon 1964: 141ff.). However, the 'early' sociological debates on immigrant communities (view Thomas/Znaniencki 1996, Breton 1964, Price 1959, Petersen 1958) have rather focused on the social, and not so much the spatial dynamics of these communities. Therefore, in this document I focus on the scholarly debate on cultural pluralism and housing that has emerged only recently.

[56] Assimilation theories in immigration research have not only been criticized on ideological grounds. Also, the empirical validity of some their assumptions has been questioned, e. g. the one of an almost inevitable and straight-line acculturation process from first- to further-generation immigrants, independent of immigrants' providence and other influencing factors (Zhou 2001: 276).

Wind/Kasinitz 1997: 1097, Goldberg 1992: 203), pluralist visions highlight the importance of building on the notion of "'the presence of more than one 'we' community within the same political constitution'" (Benhabib, quoted in Sandercock 1998: 13)[57].

The emphasis some scholars place on 'difference' and 'multiplicity of identities' grows out of what they consider the historically repressive character of policies oriented by the assimilation ideal (Dunn 1998: 509). However, advocates of pluralist and 'identity policies' also pinpoint that social justice and a shared commitment to a democratic political community constitute core binding values, needed to prevent social polarization and fragmentation into self-centered micro-communities (Sandercock 2003: 103, Young 1990: 253, Young 2000: 231, Jacobs/Fincher 1998: 15, Amin 2002: 18). It is clear that the value placed on 'difference' as a salient feature particularly of *urban* life and the call for certain universal principles (e. g. social justice, equality of opportunity) guiding urban policics and planning may enter into conflict with each other (Jacobs/Fincher 1998: 16, Sandercock 1998: 122, Young 2000: 231).

Accordingly, from a cultural-pluralist point of view the evaluation of ethnically- or racially-based residential segregation in American cities faces certain dilemmas: Most authors recognize that there is a link between spatial and social mobility restrictions[58], and that residential segregation may impose significant constraints on people's systemic integration[59] and on their participation in civic and political life (Young 2000: 196ff., Wortham 2002: 11, Alba/Nee 1997: 837, Boal 2000: 277, Warr 2005: 288). Involuntary residential segregation, e. g. spurred by institutionalized discrimination (e. g. racial steering, redlining, blockbusting) or policies, is considered as extremely problematic (Young 2000: 200).

However, many pluralism advocates do not qualify residential segregation as outright negative: Young (2000) highlights the potentially voluntary charac-

---

[57] On the critique of the pluralist concept for being unable to accommodate the African-American experience, see Goldberg 1992: 207.

[58] For the mobility-relevant 'neighborhood effects' (job references, social role models, access to and quality of services and infrastructure, particularly schools) view Chapter 2.1.

[59] Usually, systemic integration refers to people's access to a country's or region's status-relevant functional systems, such as the labor and housing markets, educational opportunities and social services (Tomlins 2000: 166, Harnhörster/Mölder 2000: 390, Göschel 2001: 5).

ter of spatial clustering in ethnic neighborhoods (also view Marcuse 1997: 228). According to her, ethnic clustering may "arise from legitimate desires to form and maintain affinity grouping" (Young 2003: 197) and "serve as an important source of self-organization, self-esteem, relaxation and resistance" (ibid: 217). Tomlins (2000) states that "in terms of a pluralistic housing policy, a fundamental issue concerns the right of minority ethnic groups to express identity through residence" (ibid: 163, also Dunn 1998: 510) and highlights that ethnic residential segregation may offer important group resources to people (ibid: 163, also Schuck 2003: 209, Robinson 2005: 1421). He strongly argues against state interventions that "appear to be paternalistic majority ethnic 'solutions' on behalf of, and for 'the other'" (Tomlins 2000: 163). For Sandercock (1998) ethnic neighborhoods are among the "strategic sites for the formation of transnational identities and communities" (ibid: 92) in which the postmodern, multicultural city and resulting inter-ethnic relations and conflicts crystallize (ibid: 92, Amin 2002: 2, Amin 2006: 1012). Instead of deciding "who can do what and be where, and even, when" (ibid: 16), planners should assist people in negotiating these spaces, claiming them, shaping their hybrid identities and making them safe (ibid: 16). Amin (2002) considers the ideal of ethnic mixture through housing as a popular, but quite problematic policy fix: Many desegregation programs aim at moving presumably self-segregating minorities into white areas, rather than addressing 'white flight' and the exclusion of minorities from housing opportunities (ibid: 5, 11, Simpson 2005: 1230, Robinson 2005: 1412, Young 2000: 216f.[60]). Instead of promoting housing desegregation[61], policy makers and planners should concentrate on fostering dialogue and mutual understanding *inside* immigrant neighborhoods (ibid: 12). This even more so, as most 'ethnic' neighborhoods are much more socially and culturally diverse than suggested by the simplifying majority-/ minority-, white or non-white dichotomy on which most desegregation programs are based (Burnley 1999: 1312, Häußermann/Siebel 2001: 76, Amin 2002: 21).

---

60 According to Young (2000), usually it is the poor and minorities who are blamed for the failure of residential integration projects or programs (Young 2000: 216f., also Dunn 1998: 510).

61 Amin (2002) considers the ideal of greater ethnic mixing in housing as a myth, as "housing estates and public places fall short of nurturing inter-ethnic understanding (…), 'because they are not spaces of interdependence and habitual engagement'" (Amin 2002: 12), such as e. g. the workplace, schools, colleges, youth centers, sports clubs, community centers and neighborhood houses may be (ibid: 12).

What does all this mean? The criticism of some authors concerning the underlying paternalism of desegregation programs in the US (view chapter 2.2)[62] resounds in the arguments put forward by the advocates of cultural pluralism and politics of difference[63]. Even though residential dispersal programs are designed in the name of social justice and equality of opportunities[64], the pluralists blame them for disregarding another basic issue, at least under conditions of multicultural urban realities: the respect for and valuing of difference (Sandercock 1998: 110, Dunn 1998: 503)[65]. The latter are considered centerpieces of enlightened urban citizenship, but also necessary starting points for coming to terms with the challenges increasingly diverse cities pose to urban governments and planners, such as conflicts over socio-economic resources and differential value systems (Amin 2006: 1016)[66]. On the contrary, spatial desegregation strategies are believed to be futile - and normatively problematic - attempts to neutralize or even suppress manifestations of ´otherness´ and urban diversity. Furthermore, advocates of pluralism

---

[62] Paternalism is reproached to desegregation programs in connection with their implicit pro-white bias. The latter manifests for instance in the definition of the adequate racial or ethnic mixture of a neighborhood in accordance with white residential preferences (integration maintenance programs), or the assumption of suburban majority-white neighborhoods as the most desirable housing outcome (Moving to Opportunity and other mobility programs).

[63] However, some of the above quoted advocates of cultural pluralism do not refer explicitly to the situation of the US, e. g. Tomlins (2000) and Boal (2002) to the UK or Europe.

[64] The advocates of pluralism do agree with these overriding social goals (see Sandercock 1998: 182, Sandercock 2003: 149, Young 2000: 197, 229, Young 1990: 3f.). About other policy concerns that have influenced the deconcentration of poverty discourse (war on drugs, urban safety issues), view Goetz 2003: 95.

[65] These are not only differences of race or ethnicity. Socio-political identities have emerged alongside other axes of difference, e. g. gender, sexuality, religion or caste (Schuck 2003: 8, Nagar/Leitner 1998: 227; for Latin American cities García Canclini 1995: 80ff.). These may furthermore cut across racial or ethnic lines and thus lead to separate identities inside the same ethnic ´group´ (Jacobs/Fincher 1998: 8, Amin 2002: 21, Glick-Schiller 1992: 7). However, many advocates of pluralism bestow particular attention on ethno-cultural differences arising in the 'age of migration', as the most continuous and potentially most destabilizing ones (Sandercock 2003: 4).

[66] These social and spatial implications are, for instance, violent urban upheavals or the existence of ´no-go-areas´ in cities. The latter are usually perceived as sites under the regime of violence, drug use and all sorts of social misbehavior, by a given city's inhabitants (Wilson 1990, Sandercock 1998, Sandercock 2003). Consequently, Sandercock (2003) assumes that the ´fear of the other´, of recognizing and respecting the stake of the culturally and otherwise different in the city is "as great a threat to the future stability of cities and regions as the much more talked about economic forces" (ibid: 4, also view 115).

argue that from the perspective of those to be desegregated, i.e. minority and/or low-income households, desegregation programs are rather counter-productive. This is especially so as living in spatial proximity to co-ethnics may be a question of choice rather than constraints and may confer important contact-related assets to households (Tomlins 2000: 163). Thus, by focusing on the ′wrong′ problem (ethnically or racially based spatial clustering), desegregation programs are believed to fall short of complying with their own – and uncontested - objectives of increasing people's opportunities and contributing to higher levels of social justice (Young 2000: 197). Urban and housing policies should confer primacy to 'empowerment', mutual engagement and the right to difference over paternalism and social engineering (Tomlins 2000: 163, Amin 2006: 1012).

Although most of the pluralist advocates pursue strong ideological stances, concrete proposals for alternative policies and planning practice are rather scarce. I will point out some of these in Chapter 2.3.4. However before doing so, I will discuss the potential role of group resources developed in the context of residential segregation.

2.3.3 Group resources through residential clustering

In addition to the theoretical and ideological critique as to what is viewed as a connection between desegregation policies and assimilationism, some authors have pointed to empirical evidence about positive aspects of ethnic concentration[67]. These authors assume that the spatial concentration of immigrants in certain neighborhoods may favor the formation of 'group resources' or social capital (Tomlins 2000: 163). These group resources are believed to be beneficial or sometimes even imperative for the longer term social, cultural and economic integration of immigrants in the new society (Logan 2003: 9, Häußermann/Siebel 2001: 70).

Usually, the assumption of positive aspects of residential segregation goes along with differentiating 'good' and 'bad' types of residential concentration. For instance, Marcuse (1997) defines three different types of socio-ethnic spatial concentrations in today's urban areas:

"[The] *classic ghetto* as the involuntary spatial segregation of a group that stands in a subordinate political and social relationship to its surrounding society, the *enclave* as a voluntarily developed spatial concentration of a group for purposes of promot-

[67] As mentioned above, most of this research has been carried out outside the United States.

ing the welfare of its members, and the *citadel* as created by a dominant group to protect or enhance its superior position." (Marcuse 1997: 228)

Thus, the following criteria are frequently mentioned to distinguish 'positive' residential segregation from a 'negative' one:

1. Causes: Positive segregation is assumed to occur *voluntarily*, i. e. as a result of preferences the members of certain, e. g. ethnic groups "have for living near those with whom they feel affinity" (Young 2000: 203). On the contrary, negative residential segregation happens as a result of discriminatory attitudes and practices from the side of the majority population.
2. Duration: Scholars assume that positive segregation represents a rather *transitional* housing situation for e. g. first-generation immigrants (Häuβermann/Siebel 2001: 77, Young 2000: 197). In contrast, they believe that long-term residential segregation, across generations, may evolve into a mobility trap and into lasting structural disadvantages in the host society (Häuβermann/Siebel 2001: 77, Burnley 1999: 1296).
3. Intersection with poverty: Ethnic residential segregation is considered the more problematic the more it intersects with socio-economic poverty[68]. Furthermore, detrimental neighborhood effects (view chapter 2.1) are assumed to increase with the actual number households living in poverty or under situations of social distress[69].

It is clear however that it is extremely difficult to draw the line between positive residential clustering and negative segregation in multicultural cit-

---

[68] Many authors point out that income poverty, rather than ethnicity constitutes the decisive variable for identifying residential segregation as a problem (Häuβermann/Siebel 2001: 76, Young 2000: 212, Interview with D.NH, 29 May 2005, see Annex 3). Obviously this distinction can be made easier in theory than in practice, due to the frequent overlap between income- and racial or ethnic concentration. However, even though many immigrant neighbourhoods are predominantly inhabited by low-income families, this does not imply a causal relationship between the condition of poverty and spatial clustering (Burnley 1999: 1312).

[69] It is clear that no 'official' quantitative criteria or benchmarks exist for distinguishing good or bad residential clusters. However, many scholars refuse to accept the 'ghetto' image of US American cities to situations of ethnic or income clustering in cities outside the United States. They precisely point to lower levels of social distress existing in e.g. European cities and the smaller sizes of their ethnic clusters (Burnley 1999: 1297, Wacquant 1999: 131, Burgess et al. 2005: 1028).

ies, or to tell where one ends and the other begins (Young 2000: 203[70], Marcuse 1997: 229)[71]. It seems important to keep in mind that residential segregation may include both positive and negative effects and that these may evolve not least according to specific local (social, economic etc.) conditions. To identify the conditions that determine segregation effects on individuals seems therefore more promising than assessing whether it is positive or negative in absolute terms.

The group resources facilitated by residential segregation have been found to benefit immigrant households on a variety of dimensions: socially, culturally, economically and with respect to their political representation. In a qualitative study with the Indo-Chinese-Australian community in an ethnic neighborhood in Sidney, Dunn (1998) has found that the spatial concentration of immigrants works favorably for the provision of culturally specific social services needed, as it renders them more cost-efficient (ibid: 518f., also view Priemus 2000: 228). Being close to their co-ethnics provides the Indo-Chinese people with the social environment, consumer goods and (e. g. religious) services they value (ibid: 520). Beyond serving as a social and cultural support to the ethnic resident population, the area has developed as an "activity-space concentration of Indo-Chinese" (ibid: 520) far beyond the neighborhood context. Ethnic enterprises in the Indo-Chinese neighborhood provide important entry points for self-employment, as well as employment opportunities for newcomers. However, the author also highlights the partly precarious and exploitative character of the ethnic economy (Dunn 1998: 519)[72]. Finally, spatial concentration has provided Indo-Chinese residents

---

[70] Young (2000) proposes a broader set of criteria to recognize 'negative' residential segregation: 1. Stigma of a migrant neighborhood, 2. White "flight" out of the neighborhood, 3. Disinvestments and quality decline, 4. Disadvantage in service provision and quality in neighborhood, 5. Segregation a consequence of discriminatory attitudes, 6. Inferior housing quality, with respect to the rest of the city (ibid: 203). Zubrinsky Charles (2003) proposes eight criteria for stable integrated communities (ibid: 201).

[71] For instance, an initial ethnic cluster may develop into a long-lasting 'ghetto', also as result of suffering stigma from the side of the dominant society. Or, members of a minority group may 'voluntarily' chose to live in an ethnic neighborhood, but mainly due to anticipating discrimination in majority white neighborhoods.

[72] This assessment is consistent with other research responding to the so-called ethnic enclave-economy hypothesis. The enclave-economy concept assumes that ethnic self-employed persons and their employees operate relatively autonomously from the mainstream economy and to the benefit of its members with respect to earnings and skills acquisition for future self-entrepreneurship, as compared to comparable jobs offered by non-ethnic employers

and business people with the possibility of joined 'ethnic place' marketing through business associations, and gaining political influence in the City Council (ibid: 522).

Other studies suggest the differential impact of residential segregation with respect to individual characteristics, e. g. gender or social status. Peleman (2002) has conducted a qualitative study on the impact of residential segregation on the participation of Moroccan women in associations in three neighborhood contexts in the city of Antwerp, Belgium. She comes to the conclusion that living in an inner-city neighborhood, with relatively high proportions of Moroccans, impacts positively on the women's participation in ethno-religious activities and Dutch language courses, and thereby on their empowerment and their development of an ethnic group identity (ibid: 16)[73]. The proximity to other women and the existence of culturally compatible neighborhood activities (religious courses, cooking, health and school education) in thc central city neighborhood promoted the women's social activism beyond the core family confines. On the contrary, living in suburban neighborhood, with very few co-ethnic rather accentuated their social isolation (ibid: 14f.). However, according to Peleman (2002) this assessment would most certainly differ with regard to higher-income and – skills women, who are less dependent on neighborhood structures for their

---

(Alba/Nee 1997: 852, Sanders/Nee 1987: 745, Portes/Jensen 1987: 768, Bohon 2005: 252). These assumptions have been criticized on several grounds: 1. The ethnic economic 'niche' has been found to be rather small as compared to the proportion of immigrants working in the open economy and far from self-supporting with respect to out-group contacts and clients (Alba/Nee 1997: 852, Waldinger/Der Martirosian 2001: 233). 2. Whereas ethnic employers tend to benefit from the often exploitative labour conditions, the situation of immigrant-workers is often precarious and can even be limiting for career mobility (Sanders et al. 1994: 868, Sanders/Nee 1987: 745). 3. Ethnic business niches have been found to be marked by strong hierarchies and socio-economic divisions, usually between groups of different national and/or ethnic origins, rather than presenting a picture of ethnic solidarity (Li 1998: 499, Fong/Shibuya 2005: 295). According to Waldinger/Der Martirosian (2001) the quality of jobs offered in the ethnic economy greatly varies among groups (ibid: 244). What is rarely put into doubt however is the role of the ethnic social networks as providing economic entry ports for immigrant newcomers, and that immigrants of a certain ethnic group cluster in certain sectoral and occupational niches (Sanders/Nee 1994: 869, Waldinger/Der Martirosian 2001: 236ff.).

[73] According to the Flemish policy definition, the concept of *integration* focuses on the idea of emancipation. The ability to manage for oneself (empowerment) and the development of an ethnic group identity constitute the two key components of integration (Peleman 2002: 7). This demonstrates the key role of the policy and ideological framework, when interpreting questions of social and/or spatial integration.

social contacts and emancipation (ibid: 16). A study of Bowes et al. (2000) who conducted qualitative, life history interviews with Pakistani families in Glasgow is commensurate with Peleman's results. It shows that the proximity to family contacts, of public transport, and to ethnic social and cultural infrastructure – usually provided in urban ethnic neighborhoods - work as strong criteria influencing the housing choice of women (ibid: 176).

In short, the quoted scholars emphasize the role of ethnic neighborhoods as a "spatial contribution to cultural diversity" (Dunn 1998: 523) and as promoters of the maintenance of in-group identities – considering both as desirable attributes of urban life. Furthermore, the results of their studies suggest that the spatial proximity inside ethnic neighborhoods impacts positively on the generation of mobility relevant group resources, and that these group resources can contribute to promoting immigrants' stance and integration in mainstream society (ibid: 523f., Pelemann 2002: 16).

The results of these qualitative studies challenge the more prominent perception among scholars, policy makers and the general public that ethnic social and spatial clustering lead to isolation rather than integration with the wider society. The portrayal of 19th-century Chinatowns in the US by Uslaner/Conley (2003) reflect this perception:

> "These insular political, economic and cultural enclaves of ethnic Chinese (…) bound immigrants together by limiting contact with outsiders and by promoting associationalism primarily within the confines of the Chinese community. Immigrants who settle in largely self-contained Chinatowns are more socially isolated and slower to become acculturalized to the larger society (…) Although the dominant culture may appear alien, identification with the larger society is essential to establishing the cooperative spirit that underlies generalized trust. Otherwise, people will think in terms of *we* and *they*, and each will be less productive. A strong identification with one's ethnic identity might lead to the development of an alternative culture that perpetuates feelings of exclusion." (Uslaner/Conley 2003: 337, marked UC)[74]

This section has been indicative of at least three aspects: First, the analysis of residential segregation has to focus on the analysis of ethnic *group resources*, and how these are affected by residential proximity. Researchers

---

[74] Uslaner/Conley's distinction between particularized and generalized trusters is partly derived from Putnam's differentiation between inward- and outward-oriented people and/or social groups, or between bounders and binders (Putnam/Goss 2002: 11f.).

who feel skeptic with respect to co-ethnic socializing tend to be even more reluctant with respect to the impacts of spatial (residential) clustering. Second, the analysis of residential segregation needs to be sensitive to other influencing factors, e. g. individual social or demographic characteristics and social or housing policy frameworks. Third, the outcomes of the analysis of residential segregation is remarkably contingent on the methods applied: The few qualitative studies that have included the perspectives and interpretations of ethnic individuals or groups shed a more favorable light on residential clustering, compared to preceding, predominantly quantitative studies.

2.3.4 Alternative policy and planning responses

Concrete policy and planning approaches that respond to pluralists', and some ethnic communities' calls for a more self-defined housing policy, as well as to the empirically grounded assertion of advantageous aspects of residential segregation are rather scarce. This scarcity can be partly explained by the difficulty to find a practical way out of the normative dilemma 'ethnic' or pluralist housing policies are confronted with: On the one hand, the political consequence of assertions of cultural difference seems to be local self-determination and autonomy (Young 2000: 230). On the other hand, the claim for self-centered local, ethnic or non-ethnic, communities which are only accountable to their own members and interests, may run against the ideals of social justice and inclusion (Young 2000: 230, Young 1990: 234ff., Jacobs/Fincher 1998: 15f., view chapter 2.3.1). The claim for group-related[75], territorialized political autonomy is also at odds with the notion of dynamic and hybrid city landscapes and socio-cultural identities (Young 2000: 197, Jacobs/Fincher 1998: 7).

Alternative housing policy and planning approaches to residential segregation are also scarce due the latter's lastingly negative perception among academics, -politicians and the general public, in the USA and elsewhere. Many of the following proposals are rather ideas and have not been tested yet. Others do not diametrically oppose existing policies, but rather emphasize the need for their further accentuation, as in the case of anti-discrimination policies. I will summarize the alternative proposals according to their targeted levels of intervention: the macro-level of policy or legal frameworks, the

[75] And: Who defines who is a group and according to which criteria? I will reflect more on this point in chapter 3.2.

meso-level of intermediate organizations, or the micro-levels of individuals on the neighborhood levels.

On the macro-level, from a standpoint of social justice Young (2000) highlights the need for continued anti-discrimination policies and their enforcement to effectively "limit the liberty of property owners and housing-related institutions for the sake of promoting the freedom of individuals to live in decent housing in decent neighborhoods where some choose group-specific clusters" (ibid: 227). She considers the regulating and monitoring of private housing agents as a much more appropriate answer to existing inequalities of housing opportunities than desegregation programs (ibid: 226). In order to strike the balance between housing policies sensitive to localized group-specific concerns *and* to issues of city-wide social justice, she proposes a model of 'relational autonomy' (Young 2000: 227). According to this model, local municipal jurisdictions or neighborhood councils should be granted "non-trivial" (ibid: 231) decision-making power on issues of e. g. environment and public life. However, institutions of regional government should have the right to interfere in local decisions where they adversely affect or create conflict with other locales, for instance concerning the allocation of affordable housing units or regulations for revenue sharing (ibid: 231ff.)[76]. As mentioned before, this proposal does not counteract, but rather reiterates and supports already existing regional policy initiatives. Tomlins (2000) also highlights the need for housing and social policies that prevent the marginalisation of minority ethnic groups inside the city-wide functional system (employment, social services, education), albeit without elaborating on the needed mechanisms (ibid: 166f.).

On the meso-level, Tomlins (2000) considers the technical and financial support of ethnic organizations as a basic component of a pluralist housing policy. He presumes these ethnic housing associations to be more responsive to specific housing needs of minorities than majority organizations, e. g. with respect to the dwelling design and –management (ibid: 169). Thus, ethnic communities who receive housing services should at least partly be able to control these, either through their own organizations or by ensuring

[76] In the case of US cities, Young (2000) considers the regional level as the most adequate one for the making of justice-relevant decisions, as it constitutes a critical level of density of which people's lives "are intertwined in social, economic and communicative relations that tie their fates" (ibid: 229).

minority representations within majority-led organizations (ibid: 166, also view Amin 2002: 18).

On the micro level, a relatively wide array of strategies is proposed, also beyond the realm of housing: Young (2000) favors an approach of movement of resources (for housing renovation and development, commercial spaces and businesses, community centers, parks, playgrounds and job-creating enterprises), as opposed to one of movement of people, aimed at by integration policies (ibid: 227). She criticizes policies that require people to move to predominantly white, better-equipped neighborhoods, not least due to their relatively small impact on the overall causes of housing inequalities. In the meantime, she considers that a "policy that aims to move resources to people directly addresses the inequalities of material privilege and disadvantage processes of segregation produce" (Young 2000: 227) while not forcing people out of the neighborhoods they have chosen to live in. These upgraded neighborhoods may ultimately attract other, higher-income and/or white residents to the areas that have been invested in (ibid: 228).

In a similar vein, Tomlins (2000) states that funding should be directed to housing improvement or new construction in minority areas, and that such initiatives should involve the employment of local labor (ibid: 166). Also, residents should be involved in improvement projects, for instance in the design of dwellings, housing estates and/or communal areas (ibid: 169, also view Amin 2002: 12). Boal (2000) stresses the need for an integrated view on housing processes that evaluate residential situations, i.a. in the individual neighborhood, with respect to the availability of other opportunity structures, e.g. employment and education (ibid: 277). According to Häußermann/Siebel (2001) infrastructure and services relevant for systemic integration (schools, employment, language courses) should be concentrated in ethnic neighborhoods, as well as adjusted to the particular needs of immigrants (Häußermann/Siebel 2001: 77)[77]. In order to respond to the multi-ethnic character of most 'ethnic' neighborhoods in which different immigrant nationalities co-exist, the development of informal conflict management mechanisms is necessary. Early-warning systems for the timely indica-

[77] Schools are of particular relevance here. The schools in inner-city neighborhoods with relatively high proportions of immigrants are rarely adjusted to this 'challenge' in terms of their teaching materials, curricula, qualification of teachers and building design (Häußermann/Siebel 2001: 77).

tion of the emergence of violent conflicts should be developed. Informal economic activities operating in legal 'grey zones' should be tolerated in their quality as economic mechanisms and entry-points, instead of being discouraged by the application of strict legal norms (Häußermann/Siebel 2001: 77). Amin (2002) stresses the need to promote inter-ethnic understanding and cooperation in sites where dialogue and negotiations 'naturally' occur[78], for instance in schools, work-places, sports clubs and leisure centers (ibid: 12, for schools view Burgess et al. 2005: 1031). He considers the *youth* as strong potential for promoting future inter-ethnic understanding and living in peaceful togetherness (ibid: 15).

The above-mentioned, alternative policy proposals can be differentiated from more traditional responses to residential segregation in the following ways[79]:

- Emphasis on moving resources as opposed to moving people: A center point of most of the dispersal approaches described in Chapter 2.2 constitutes the desegregation of minority and/or poor households into majority-, non-poor areas. On the contrary, the alternative policy proposals highlight the need for technical and financial assistance and investments *inside* the very immigrant or 'ethnic' neighborhoods. Such policies address the social and economic disadvantages of the urban population mirrored in many of the multi-ethnic neighborhoods, while at the same time valuing their integrative potential.
- Accentuation of opportunity-relevant sectors beyond housing: Most of the programs promoting housing desegregation directly tackle housing quality and location. In contrast, the alternative approaches stress the importance of viewing housing as an integrated concept.

---

[78] As opposed to just living in the same neighborhood, which does not entail effective and lasting interchange and social contact (Amin 2002: 20). This also implies a critique of the ideal of new urbanism according to socializing and the building of social capital occurs by virtue of co-existence in a specifically designed housing estate or communal space (Goetz 2003: 60).

[79] This does not mean that commonalities do not exist. For instance, both housing dispersal as well as the 'alternative' policies, pinpoint the importance of interventions on multiple levels, e. g. the level of individual households as well as the level of housing polices. Furthermore, both approaches stress the need for effective anti-discrimination policies and their enforcement.

Accordingly, improving the housing situation needs to focus on enhancing opportunities with regard to access to the most relevant overall means of well-being, i.e. employment, education and social facilities, and on overall social and political empowerment.

- Importance of inter-ethnic negotiation and conflict management: A central assumption underlying most desegregation programs is that ethnic housing mixture leads to increased social contact and that this contact is benign, for overall social integration and social mobility of the minorities and poor. On the contrary, the above described approaches believe that proximity or 'exposure' alone does not lead to meaningful social contact, and this even less so of people of different social and ethnic origins (Amin 2002: 20, Robinson 2005: 1424, see chapter 3). Rather they stress the heterogeneous, conflictive character of multi-ethnic settings, in multicultural cities in general and inside 'ethnic' neighborhoods in particular. Hence the need to actively work on deconstructing interest- or value-based barriers for mutual dialogue and understanding. The objective lies in bridging, instead of eliminating, differences to improve the chances for peaceful togetherness and individual empowerment in today's urban areas.

2.4 Summary

In this chapter, I have started by describing the present situation of residential segregation in the United States, approaches for explaining its causes and policy implications of the latter. I have shown that residential segregation, and its persistence in American cities, is considered as a problematic aspect by most authors. Some even consider it as the main source of poverty and urban social problems. While segregation indexes have slightly decreased for the African American population in metropolitan areas, this population group still lives highly segregated from the white, and other racial or ethnic groups in American cities. In the 1990s, a higher proportion of poor African Americans lived in high-poverty neighborhoods, i. e. in areas where 40% of the residents have household incomes below the federally defined poverty index. Residential segregation and isolation have increased for Hispanic and Asian populations as these groups have become more populous in American cities. However, the segregation of these groups figures at moderate levels as compared to segregation of African Americans.

There are different approaches for explaining residential segregation: Some scholars maintain that residential segregation is a consequence of market mechanisms, i. e. the result of income-related distribution of housing supply and opportunities. Other scholars believe preference for living close to those for whom one feels affinity or, inversely, far from "the others", to be a pertinent explanation. Finally, some scholars believe that deliberate discriminatory actions from both public and private housing agents are the most important factor for persisting segregated housing patterns. While scholars tend to place more emphasis on one or the other explanatory approach most of them agree that the causes of residential segregation are rather multi-faceted. As a consequence, they also agree that segregation requires policy responses in both the housing supply and demand areas.

Subsequently, I have outlined the legal framework and what I consider the most important housing policy reactions to residential segregation, since the enactment of the Fair Housing Act in 1969. As policy makers have consistently considered residential segregation as an urban problem, albeit for different reasons and related to different motivations, policy efforts centered on promoting housing dispersal or desegregation – of poor and minority households. Among the most prominent policies are the granting of housing vouchers or certificates to minority and poor families to find housing in majority-white, non-poor areas (often in the suburbs), combined with mobility counseling and lately attracting higher-income families to formerly 'segregated' inner-city neighborhoods. I have shown that notwithstanding the good intentions of these approaches – enlarging social and economic opportunities for structurally disadvantaged population groups – their success has to be considered as limited. The latter is true both in terms of the spatial desegregation of poor and minority groups actually achieved *and* regarding the living situation of desegregated families.

The limited success of desegregation strategies, together with more affirmative views on social and cultural difference in cities in the context of an increasingly multi-cultural reality of American life, has also prompted a different assessment of residential segregation. In the context of a 'mosaic' – as opposed to a melting pot – city ideal "the composite parts are still recognizable, but together form something cohesive and fine" (Priemus 2000: 228). According to this point of view, residential clustering of e.g. persons with cultural and social affinities, is a legitimate expression of cultural difference and worth being promoted politically. On the contrary, desegregation policies are considered as a *futile* and problematic symptom of overall assimilationist and culturally ethnocentric policies. Ultimately, empirical studies have provided indications about group-related resources or social capital generated in the context of residential clustering of immigrant groups. The link between residential segregation and social capital seems to be particularly relevant for the understanding of segregation in the migration context, and calling for future conceptual refinement.

Although incidental qualitative research on housing segregation of immigrants has been carried out, this is far from being complete. With quantitative studies largely dominating the research spectrum on residential segregation in the United States, qualitative analysis possesses important potentials for future research activities. This is particularly the case for the exploration of subjective *experiences, attitudes* and *perceptions* of immigrant populations with respect to residential clustering, as these form important determinants for residential outcomes (Zubrinsky Charles 2003: 200). As a matter of fact, these can be better captured by open-ended, qualitative research designs than by quantitative methods.

I also believe that satisfactory policy responses to residential segregation, beyond desegregation, require additional, particularly qualitative, research on the following issues:

1. The specificity of immigrants' residential clustering as opposed to the one of long-standing minorities of the United States, such as African Americans.
2. How residential segregation impacts on the development of group resources or social capital, and how these resources are linked to the creation of other mobility-relevant assets (education, employment etc.) apart from housing.
3. The specific conditions under which ethnically based residential segregation is positive or negative, and in which way this is related to the role of ethnic social capital in 'ethnic' or immigrant communities.

Thus, in the subsequent chapter I will turn my attention to the issue of social capital in ethnic neighborhoods.

3 Social capital in ethnic neighborhoods

In this chapter I discuss the concept of social capital and its relevance for the assessment of the impacts of ethnically based residential segregation. Although the majority of scholars consider minority and income segregation as negative for the long-term mobility and/or social integration of individuals, some concede that valuable group resources may be generated in the context of ethnic segregation. 'Group resources' refer to certain assets (jobs, cultural encounters etc.) engendered by ethnic or immigrant networks or in short, the building of social capital. What however is exactly meant by social capital? In which way is social capital related to social mobility, i. e. the generation of status-relevant assets? How does spatial proximity influence the social position and the living situation of individuals? Is this influence positive or negative, or, under which conditions can it be evaluated in one way or another way?

Thriving to provide answers to these questions, in this chapter I discuss the concept of social capital, drawing on the work of the French sociologist Pierre Bourdieu. In his concept of social capital he describes the link between social capital and social mobility of individuals, critically reflecting on conditions for and dynamics of group building. Furthermore, the analysis of the role of physical space in the social world and social relationships forms an integral part of Bourdieu's social theory. As both aspects (the link between social capital and mobility, influence of spatial on social position) constitute core concerns of this research, Bourdieu's concept of social capital provides an extremely useful framework of analysis.

After placing Bourdieu's concept in the context of broader academic discussions on social capital, I proceed with a definition of the term, as well as explaining the relationship between social and other capital forms (economic, cultural and symbolic) relevant to individual mobility. I also critically reflect on the instrumentalist or objectivist nature of Bourdieu's concept and propose an alternative perspective which highlights the legitimacy using subjective criteria for the assessment of the value of social capital. Subsequently I discuss the link between the social and physical position of an individual. I present Bourdieu's concept of social groups and discuss their relevance for the analysis of ethnic social networks and capital. After this, I reflect on the different spatial levels in which ethnic social networks and social capital develop, and then terminate this chapter with a summary of its main contents.

3.1 Conceptualization of social capital and 'site effects'

During recent years social capital as a concept has gained particular prominence in scholarly discussions and often been considered as a political goal or "something of a cure-all for the maladies affecting society at home and abroad" (Portes 1998: 2). Originally it was used to underline a third value-building component of *individual* action, additional to physical and human capital (Coleman 1991: 392, Portes 1998: 5). Robert Putnam, one of the most prominent representatives of a functionalist and integrationist view on social capital, emphasizes the potential of social ties for enhancing productivity and wealth accumulation of neighborhoods, regions or entire nations, as well as individual and collective well-being (Putnam 2000: 18f., Portes 1998: 3, Siisiainen 2000: 2, Schnur 2005: 492, Middleton et al. 2005: 1713). According to Putnam, social capital is both constituted by and reinforces mutual trust, common values, reciprocity, cooperation, as well as civic attitudes and engagement (Putnam 2000: 21, Siisiainen 2000: 5).

Putnam´s and other researchers' rather idealistic view on the role of social capital has been criticized with respect to several issues (view Middleton et al. 2005: 1712ff., Colclough/Sitaraman 2005: 474ff., Schnur 2005: 492, Carpiano 2006: 166, Portes 1998: 18ff.):

1. <u>Analytical vagueness of the constitutive elements of social capital</u>, i. e. trust, norms, reciprocity and social networks. Putnam´s conceptualization does not clarify how they related to each other, on which level of analysis they are situated or how they can be operationalised.
2. <u>Inadequate extension of the concept of social capital to collectives</u>. Whereas it has been shown that individuals may derive advantage from their social networks, the functionality of social capital for economic and cultural growth of population *aggregates*, e. g. entire communities or regions, lacks empirical grounding.
3. <u>Weak conceptualization of the relationship and respective weight of (local) social capital and external factors</u> that shape the prosperity and well-being of collectives, for instance wealth, demographics, changes of urban and economic regimes. As a consequence, the in-

fluence of social capital tends to be over-generalized or over-estimated.

4. Identification of the sources of social capital (social networks or relationships) with its usefulness, without defining the concrete conditions that determine the relevance of social networks for the development of individual or collective social capital.
5. Lack of consideration of the vertical power relations between different kinds of collectives (e. g. poor and rich neighborhoods or -neighborhood associations) and tendency to judge social networks and associations as per se benign, in spite of their possible pernicious or exclusionary character (Kao 2004: 173).

The concept of social capital of Bourdieu not only considerably differs from the functionalist ones, but also holds up to most of the above criticisms. Rejecting the notion of disinterested action, diffuse concepts such as trust and norms of reciprocity do not play a role (Siisiäinen 2000: 13)[80]. He assumes the instrumentality of social networks or groups for advancing individuals' e.g. economic or cultural interests in social struggles, and explains under which structural conditions the accumulation of *capital* is more or less likely to be successful, from the individual point of view (Bourdieu 1986: 249ff., Siisainen: 13, 22, Wolfreys 2000). The State and macro-social forces, e.g. globalization, are considered key influences in shaping options for individual capital accumulation and power asymmetries - influences that distinctively manifest in the organization of the urban social and physical space (Bourdieu 1999: 129).

While agreeing with the above critique on Putnam's functionalist concept on social capital, I will get back to elements of it where this seems helpful for explanatory purposes. And, while this research focuses on the connection between social capital and mobility-relevant assets highlighted by Bourdieu, it also goes beyond the mere instrumentalist view. Taking into account additional, e.g. social or emotional, values of social capital[81] seems a necessary

[80] According to Bourdieu, the individual does not engage in reciprocal acts without having a stake or an "interest" in what she or he is doing, be this interest of economic, cultural or symbolic nature (Bourdieu 1998: 75ff.). This does however not mean that people are always – consciously - act in pursuit of a strategic objective (ibid: 80f.).

[81] In the light of the empirical results generated in this research, these rather subjectively noted aspects of social capital turned out to be highly relevant.

complement for the understanding of group resources generated in the context of ethnic residential segregation.

3.1.1 Definition of social capital

According to Pierre Bourdieu, social capital is

> "the aggregate of the **actual or potential resources** which are **linked to** the possession of a **durable network** of **more or less institutionalized relationships** of mutual acquaintance and recognition – or, in other words, to **membership in a group**." (Bourdieu 1986: 248, marked ED)

These relationships may exist in the practical, i.e. material, sphere and/or symbolic exchanges. In the practical sphere social capital is generated in the context of more or less regular encounters, conversations or exchanges of goods, such as presents. In the symbolic sphere social capital may be instituted and symbolically fixed by, e. g. the name of a family, a tribe, a class, a party or even a neighborhood.

According to Bourdieu, the amount of social capital depends on the *size* of both the formal and informal network of connections a person can mobilize, and on the *volume* of the economic, cultural or symbolic capital possessed by those to whom the person is connected. Social capital, just like possessions in economic or cultural spheres, needs permanent maintenance and reinvestment, for instance in terms of spending time, money and energy by participating in different social spaces, such as the workplace, kinship- or neighborhood relations. The investment of a person in her/his contacts and networks (in the context of voluntary work, informal neighbor visits, preparing and attending group events etc.) is a pre-condition for obtaining the possible profits linked to the possession of social capital (ibid 1986: 249ff.). Inversely, the perspective of benefits or profits to be generated from social networks is a precondition of their functioning.

Bourdieu assesses the nature of social capital from the perspective of individual actors inside the social class structure. (Siisiäiinen 2000: 12). In contrast, he centers less on the effects of social capital on social groups or bigger social aggregates, e.g. a region. However he states that benefits from social capital do transcend the level of individual actors. For instance, communities or networks that manage to accumulate high levels of social capital such as exclusive clubs, gated communities, convey a collective benefit also to those members not immediately engaged in group activities[82]. On the contrary, access to certain communities and hence the benefits of membership are selectively granted (e. g. only to wealthy households): Hence the exclusive side of social capital, on which the effectiveness of 'solidarity' inside a given group is partly contingent (also view Putnam 2000: 21f.). Further on I will elaborate on Bourdieu's critical consideration of the conditions for the evolution of social groups.

The concept of social capital of Bourdieu needs to be considered in conjunction with the three other types of capital, which according to Bourdieu dispose the base material for the functioning of the social world: economic capital, cultural and symbolic capital:

- Economic capital is mostly constituted by material possessions and revenues of a person, e. g. from income and other sources. Sometimes it is institutionalized in the form of property rights. It is the only capital form that is directly convertible into money[83].
- Cultural capital consists of intellectual skills and knowledge acquired by a person, by virtue of his or her socialization and through the education system. The institutionalized form of cultural capital consists of educational qualifications and titles. Under certain conditions (e. g. possession of a prestigious university certificate) it is convertible into economic capital (Bourdieu 1986: 243).

Apart from the 'tangible' manifestations of the different capital forms (e. g. social networks and group memberships in the case of social capital), Bourdieu emphasizes the relevance of symbolic capital as a form assumed by all three types of capital (Bourdieu 1990: 126, Siisiainen 2000: 13). Symbolic capital describes agents' *perception* of certain differences (e. g. living in one or another neighborhood) as socially meaningful and status-relevant (Bourdieu 1990a: 135, Bourdieu 1991: 237, Bourdieu 1998: 9). In the case of social capital, this includes the mutual cognition and recognition of a

---

[82] This may, for instance, be the case for the children of inhabitants of an exclusive community benefiting from the best schools and health care.

[83] While from Bourdieu´s perspective, economic capital is the dominant capital form, he considers monetary exchange to be only a particular, albeit the most direct, type of exchange of the "economy of practices" (Bourdieu 1986: 242). Social and cultural capital also effectively determine an individual's social position, but imply more concealed and long-term exchange relations (ibid: 252).

given group by its members, on the basis of more or less explicit signs of membership (e. g. club card, certain form of greeting, certain clothing style). It also implies the recognition of a certain group and its attributes and life-styles by outsiders, be it in the form of approval or stigma. However, the definition power about the 'legitimate', i.e. to be imitated capital forms (e. g. the 'good' society, the 'right' kind of company) is usually reserved for the dominant classes (Bourdieu 1990: 25, Wolfreys 2000).

3.1.2 The relevance of social capital for social mobility

In Bourdieu's perspective, social 'capital' does not suffice in itself. Its basic function is the improvement of an individual's social position, working as "a resource in the social struggles that are carried out in different social arenas or fields" (Siisiäinen 2000: 2). Social relations in this sense become instrumental to advance an actor's interest in a specific social field or functional universe, such as arts, science, religion, politics, economics, cultural production and others (Bourdieu 1998: 83, Bourdieu 1990a: 58). In short, "the profits which accrue from membership in a group are the basis of the solidarity which makes them possible" (Bourdieu 1986: 249).

Thus, according to Bourdieu, ultimately social capital obtains its value from its *convertibility* into economic and cultural capital, respectively the possibility of (upward) *social mobility* (Bourdieu 1986:252, Ream 2005: 205, Portes 1998: 3)[84]. An example for the conversion of social into economic capital is a person's learning of a desirable employment opportunity, through somebody she or he knows. Inversely, economic capital can be converted into social capital, e.g. if a social relationship is strengthened through a more or less precious gift transfer (Bourdieu 1986: 253). However, the conversion from social into economic capital does not necessarily occur in a direct way: An example of an indirect kind of conversion would be somebody's saving time (rather than money) in daily trajectories through a friend's or family member's helping out with child-care.

---

84 Economic capital in Bourdieu's perspective is at the root of social and cultural capital, even though all three forms have distinct elements and conditions of functioning. Without being convertible into economic capital, the other two capital forms would not be effective. Vice versa, very often the possession of economic capital is a necessary (albeit not sufficient) condition for accumulating social and cultural capital, for instance the ability for prolonged studies at the University (for acquiring an additional academic title) requires a relatively solid financial background of students (Bourdieu 1986: 252ff.).

Although Bourdieu emphasizes that the generation of social capital is as interest-guided as the one of economic capital, the two capital forms function rather differently (view Kao 2004: 173, Portes 1998: 4). For instance, social capital appears in less tangible and transparent forms and does not follow a logic of immediate pay-off: "[Social] capital of relationships (or social obligations) cannot act instantaneously, at the appropriate moment, unless they have been established and maintained for a long time, as if for their own sake, and therefore outside their period of use" (Bourdieu 1986: 252).

The possibility or actual incidence of social mobility, linked to the social networks of a person, can thus serve as a measure for the value of his or her social capital. Possible indicators for social mobility are, for instance, an improved occupational status or position, increase of income, access to (housing) finance or loan or obtainment of additional skills or educational degrees. The assessment of the volume or value of social capital may be realized on a subjective basis (using a particular person's own assessment) or using a to be determined 'objective' measure, e. g. overall society's valuation of a given occupation[85].

3.1.3 *The value of social capital or the role of the 'habitus'*

Bourdieu considers the capital forms (economic, cultural, and symbolic) as the basic resources according to the possession of which people act, dispose of power and exercise judgments (Bourdieu 1991: 128). However, he does not believe that individuals are entirely conditioned by their social status. Rather he transcends radical structuralism by introducing the theoretical construct of the *habitus* as the binding element between structure and agency (Bourdieu 1993: 277ff., Bourdieu 1992: 120ff., Siisiäinen 2000: 16, Wolfreys 2000). The "habitus develops through the internalization of the objective structures of the environment in the form of practices" (Siisiäinen 2000: 16).

Therefore, on the one hand the *habitus* as a system of durable, transposable dispositions (Bourdieu 1990a: 53), guides individuals towards specific

[85] For instance, a formerly unemployed person who, through the help of a friend, has achieved employment as cashier in a supermarket will most likely experience this as a considerable increase of his/her social position. In contrast, an external person would probably consider this a less than moderate social ascent, on the basis of the rather low esteem of supermarket cashier-jobs in overall society.

tastes, attitude and practices, according to their position in the larger social structure. It provides agents with a 'sense of their place' and with a sense of the other's place' (Bourdieu 1990: 131, Bourdieu 1993: 278), hence with the basis to classify the social world (Bourdieu 1990). On the other hand the *habitus* "like every art of inventing, is what makes it possible to produce an infinite number of practices that are relatively unpredictable (like the corresponding situations) but also limited in their diversity" (Bourdieu 1990a: 55). Thus, the *habitus* does not prevent individuals from making judgments of their own, but impacts on the *likelihood* (dispositions) of persons perceiving and acting in one or another way[86].

Although Bourdieu considers economic and cultural capital to be the main factors that shape the *habitus* of individuals and their dispositions to value and act in the social world, he highlights the plurality of (structuring) factors that may influence the practice of individuals, such as ethnicity, religion or nationality. As a consequence, individuals in the same or a similar social position (defined by their disposition of economic and cultural capital) make use of infinite and unpredictable practice alternatives (ibid: 126). Using the analogy of a game, according to Bourdieu the *habitus* marks the framework of rules or constraints of the game. Yet individuals can exploit an infinity of options to 'manipulate' the game or even to change its rules and contribute to structural change (Bourdieu 1990a: 141, Wolfreys 2000).

What does this mean for the purposes of the research questions about the social capital and mobility perspectives of immigrant households? Oriented by Bourdieu's concept of social capital, I would build my answer predominantly on the assessment of whether and what economic, cultural and symbolic assets a person is able to derive from her (ethnic and/or neighborhood-based) social capital. From Bourdieu's perspective, the different capital forms are mutually reinforcing, and therefore the social acquaintances of lower-class agents likely to consist of persons with similarly low mobility perspectives. As immigrants' co-ethnics tend to dispose of relatively little economic, cultural or symbolic capital, the volume of ethnic social capital needs to be low almost by implication (Warr 2005: 286).

---

[86] It also impacts on the combination of social properties of individuals, e. g. people who like drinking champagne are more likely to have antique furniture and to appreciate dressing in a 'classical' way, etc., see Bourdieu 1990: 132f., Bourdieu 1993: 212f..

Thereby, the stigmatization of low-income or immigrant groups, as well as their stereotyping by the dominant society (e.g. as those being on welfare, lazy, having many children, etc.) is also likely to work as a barrier on their social contacts and capital (Warr 2005: 298f.). The middle- and upper-classes' low esteem of minorities or immigrants is likely to be reflected in a more or less explicit disapproval of their places of residence – and even be adopted by the inhabitants of the immigrant neighborhoods in the form of a low auto-esteem (Warr 2005: 303)[87].

3.1.4 Limitations of Bourdieu's instrumentalist standpoint

The above statements on the implications of Bourdieu's theory for the assessment of the "value" of social capital need to be critically reflected. In spite of his seemingly 'objectivist' stance on the elements constituting or indicating the value of an agent's social capital, Bourdieu highlights that, in order to understand the social reality and change, "social science must take as its object both this reality [e. g. social and economic power structures] and the perception of this reality, the perspectives, the points of view which (...) agents have on this reality" (Bourdieu 1990: 130, also see Denzin/Lincoln 1994b: 199). By only using 'objective' or 'tangible' criteria for the value assessment of social capital (e. g. employment benefits through personal contact), the researcher would implicitly disregard the subjective perspectives of the individuals involved who may value their social capital in terms of their own criteria of *well-being*[88].

Concerns about the appropriateness of the external or 'objectivist' standpoint need to be complemented by those related to the adequacy of the criteria of value judgment. By focusing on (the presence or absence of) *instrumental*

---

87 For instance, Mahler (1985) has found out that Salvadorian immigrants tend to attribute rather little value to their inter-ethnic relationships (ibid: 14).

88 Although Bourdieu concedes a considerable epistemological and methodological relevance to the subjective representations of agents, he highlights the constraints the *habitus* imposes on individual's subjectivity, by adjusting their taste to what is possible in the framework of their status-induced structural limits (Bourdieu 1990a: 64, id. 1987: 285ff., Wolfreys 2000). From Bourdieu's point of view, individuals are much more likely than one would expect to be satisfied with what they (can) have, as opposed to critically assess their status quo situation (Bourdieu 1990a: 61, 64, also view Bourdieu 1993: 285). For instance, immigrants may confer a high value to their existing social networks as well as to their present neighborhood, as a consequence of the simple lack of alternatives.

benefits of an individual's social capital (e.g. wealth accumulation, employment gains) Bourdieu does not take into consideration more *intrinsic*, e.g. social or emotional, benefits or costs of social capital. For instance, residents may perceive their social network as an end in itself, or as a necessary means for achieving personal ends of *well-being* such as living in a culturally close 'community' or a feeling of social stability, as opposed to a perception of social networks as a means for economic ends (view Warr 2005: 300).

Box 2: The concept of 'well-being' of Amartya Sen

Seeking to counteract utilitarian and monetary definitions of quality of life, the Bangladeshi economist Amartya Sen has defined alternative criteria of individual *well-being*. According to Sen, the well-being of the individual should be the at the center of social development, as opposed to materialistic, de-personalized measures such as increases in per capita income or national economic growth. Sen's conceptualization of well-being has proved highly influential for the definition of indicators for the monitoring and evaluation of national and global development (Neubert et al. 2001: 4).

According to Sen, enlarging a person's *capabilities* defined as the "freedom to achieve well-being" (Sen 2000: 49), should be the prime objective of any development strategy. Sen criticizes that often economic or personal income growth is taken as a prime indicator for the improvement of people's quality of life (or well-being) and the alleviation of poverty. However, he considers income to be a highly inadequate indicator for individual or collective well-being, for a variety of reasons: First, the well-being of human beings is influenced by far more factors than income, such as the freedom to live long, the opportunity to have worthwhile employment, or to live in peaceful and crime-free communities (Sen 2000a: 291). Furthermore, the convertibility of income in personal quality of life highly depends on individual and external circumstances. For instance, two persons with exactly the same income may possess very different qualities of life, if one of them suffers of an incurable disease (Sen 2000: 103). Thus, in order to more adequately assess people's opportunities to "lead the kind of life (…) [they] have reason to value" (Sen 2000a: 285), a variety of variables outside monetary ones need to be considered.

Second, income or wealth constitute 'means' rather than 'ends' of development. While these 'means' (e. g. being well-nourished, attending primary school, having shelter, etc.) from an individual point of view may form important contributors of well-being or freedom, they say little about the actual "*freedom* to pursue one's objectives – well being and other objectives" (Sen 2000: 27). For instance, a white and a black American family disposing of exactly the same income may have very different possibilities to convert their income into their desired housing situation, due to the discrimination of the African American families in the housing market.

The ability to *choose* and *decide* between serious options is hereby considered as a constitutive aspect of well-being in itself (ibid: 41, 291), hence '*enlarging people's choices*' as a key criteria of development (UNDP 1992, Neubert et al. 2001: 3).

What people consider as the most important elements of their well-being, and the respective weighting of these elements, is dependent on subjective experiences and the particular local context (Sen 2000a: 4, Sen 1999). For instance, the weight of income as an indicator may be greater in urbanized societies with a higher commoditization of social services (e.g. care for the elderly) as in rural ones where the extended families complies with most of these services. Hence the need to define people's objectives and their opportunities in the context of their "actual living" (Sen 2000a: 73).

The relevance of Sen's concept of well-being for this research lies in the fact that it provides an alternative rational for the valuation of individual assets, compared to instrumentally oriented ones. Thus, a mere valuation of the social capital of immigrants in terms of its mobility-relevance (convertibility into economic, cultural and/or symbolic capital) means to prioritize the instrumental value of social capital as opposed to values or costs perceived from the perspective of the concerned individuals. Thus, a more adequate understanding of immigrant social capital and the related social practices (e. g. living in an ethnic neighborhood), requires its valuation in terms of people's own criteria of well-being – which may transcend instrumental ones. Furthermore, the emphasis Sen places on *choice* calls for taking into consideration the actual freedom people possess to choose between their present or an alternative living situation – and possible internal and external limitations of this freedom.

3.1.5 'Site effects' as an additional capital form?

One of Bourdieu's central statements is that the physical space strongly interacts with the social space. Thereby he disputes the notion of the physical space as a sort of 'container' in which social relations simply happen according to their own rules. On the one hand he highlights that social patterns inscribe themselves in the physical space, for instance socioeconomic inequality in the form of residential segregation (Dangschat 1998: 207). On the other hand, he pinpoints the distinctive role of the physical space in cementing social differences:

"Part of the *inertia* of the structures of social space results from the fact that they are inscribed in physical space and cannot be modified except by a *work of transplantation*, a moving of things and uprooting or deporting of people, which itself presupposes extremely difficult and costly social transformations." (Bourdieu 1999: 124)

Bourdieu differentiates between two ways social power and hierarchies manifest themselves in the physical space:

1. First, by the localization a person or a site is situated in with relation to others, in economic, spatial and symbolic terms. Economic and spatial terms refer to the proximity to rare and desirable agents and goods or services, such as good schools and health services. The symbolic aspects point to the recognition of the place in the social space, e. g. in the form of prestige.
2. Second, by the bulkiness (and quality) of a space occupied by a person, in terms of a "greater or lesser ostentation in the consumption of space being one of the forms par excellence for displaying power" (Bourdieu 1999: 124).

Individuals compete for physical sites or the benefits they procure, just as they compete for other rare goods, e. g. desirable employment positions or the acquaintance with an ´important´ personality. The ability of individuals to appropriate physical space is contingent on the possession of all three forms of capital. For instance, the appropriation or access to a residential location depends first and foremost on the economic capital of a person, in terms of his/her ability to choose between higher or lower priced residential locations (ibid: 127). But it also depends on the agent's social capital, in that his or her social relations and networks in a desired neighborhood may facilitate access to housing in it. Finally, the cultural capital lies at the basis of individual tastes and lifestyles that help a person to 'appropriate' her- or himself of a certain type of neighborhood:

> "A habitat can be occupied physically without really being inhabited in the full sense of the term if the occupant does not dispose of the tacitly required means of habitation, starting with a certain *habitus*" (ibid: 128).

As mentioned above, according to Bourdieu (1999) the interaction between the physical and the social space occurs in both directions. Thus, he employs the term of 'localization profits' in order to describe how the physical space, notably through residential segregation, influences the social position and situation of agents. Spatial profits can be derived from:

1. The proximity to desirable agents and goods. For instance, from the perspective of households with children the proximity of good quality schools constitutes an invariably important criterion. The proximity of the workplace may form another important aspect that people value, depending on factors such as their financial budget, the possession of a car, but also their lifestyle.
2. Profits of position or of rank. A person may for instance acquire these symbolic profits by being able to mention a prestigious home address. In contrast, a person living in a neighborhood with a 'bad' reputation is deprived of this kind of symbolic profit or may be even punished with more or less obvious stigmatization[89]. These profits may also take the form of occupation profits. In this case, owning a big housing estate symbolically marks a person's economic and social importance (ibid: 127).

Bourdieu acknowledges the effectiveness of spatial proximity in enhancing opportunities for the development of social capital:

"Proximity in physical space allows the proximity in social space to deliver all its effects by facilitating or fostering the accumulation of social capital and, more precisely, by allowing uninterrupted benefits from the meetings at once fortuitous and foreseeable that come from frequenting well-frequented sites" (ibid: 127).

It is clear that Bourdieu inherently disapproves of the exclusionary practices and policies underlying spatial segregation. With respect to cities in the United States, he acknowledges that the government yields a key power in the social construction of the physical space, for instance through national housing policies (e. g. urban renewal, construction of large housing projects) and laws framing the actions of both public and private housing agents (Bourdieu 1999: 129). Local governments strongly shape residential patterns, notably the "*construction of homogeneous groups on a spatial basis*" (ibid: 129, marked PB) through decisions on the placement of public housing sites, taxation or zoning. Although he does not claim specific policy re-

---

[89] One may however argue that different actors or different social groups may convey different types of profits of position or rank, e. g. as a result of their dissimilar (practical and emotional) priorities or value schemes. However, from Bourdieu's point of view the definition power on what is 'rare' and 'desirable' is usually on the side of the dominant classes and more or less uncritically adopted or interiorised by the relatively disadvantaged (1990: 126).

sponses to residential segregation, Bourdieu (1999) expresses himself extremely doubtful with respect to strategies of (imposed) spatial integration:

> "If the habitat shapes the habitus, the habitus also shapes the habitat, through the more or less adequate social usages that it tends to make of it. This certainly throws doubt on the belief that bringing together in the same physical space agents who are far apart in social space might, in itself, bring them closer socially: in fact, socially distanced people find nothing more intolerable than physical proximity (…)." (Bourdieu 1999: 128)

3.1.6 Assessing social capital in ethnic neighborhoods

From Bourdieu´s point of view, those who are most likely to benefit from the accumulation of social capital by virtue of physical proximity are individuals with strong possessions of economic and cultural capital[90]. In contrast, in stigmatized neighborhoods or low-income housing sites, e. g. public housing projects, the fact of "bringing together on a single site a population in its dispossession strengthens that dispossession" (Bourdieu 1999: 129). In terms of Bourdieu´s localization profits, the "neighborhood effect" (view Goetz 2003: 26, chapter 2.1.1) is most likely to work counterproductively on residents´ social capital and mobility, as

- Those living in spatial proximity are likely to be struggling with similar social and economic problems and unlikely to be conveyers of economic and cultural capital. Adolescents may be particularly exposed to behavioral patterns and values at odds with those of mainstream society (e. g. alcohol and drug abuse, violence, low esteem towards education), through adult or peer role models (see

---

[90] However, again, which residential sites are considered 'desirable' by a person may vary according to her position in the social space and the respective proportions of social, cultural and economic capital owned by her. The wealthier suburbs of a city are usually identifiable as such by all city residents and – by means of a biased definition power among city residents in favour of the upper classes – considered as 'good areas'. However, not everybody wants to live in these suburbs. Some city residents, like young and childless professionals tend to prefer to live in a neighbourhood closer to the downtown area, close to work and to a specific cultural and social infrastructure e. g. theatres, cinemas, opera and restaurants. Students usually prefer to live close to the university and to certain evening entertainment locations. Hence the influence of cultural capital, additional to the economic one, in generating – by way of the *habitus* - tastes and lifestyles of a person, e. g. for patterns of space appropriation. Poor residents also have lifestyles, however frequently imposed by economic constraints, e.g. the presence to live close to the inner-city due to the dependency on public transport (Bourdieu 1993: 587).

2.1.1). Opportunities for socializing may be limited through high levels of neighborhood violence and low police presence. Local services, e. g. schools are likely to be adversely affected by neighborhood-related social and economic problems. Small proportions of homeowners or high resident turn-over may disincentive residents to build social relationships (Brisson 2005: 646) (1st localization profit).

- The stigma of many minority and/or poor neighborhood may symbolically pass on a negative reputation on their inhabitants. Although this negative labeling is created from the outside, neighborhood residents may adopt it, e. g. in the form of low levels of self-esteem. Additionally, the physical opportunities for socializing in both public and private spaces may be hampered, due to relatively few parks and squares in an overall dense building environment and small-size (and often over-crowded) private housing. In contrast, the usually high densities of inner-city or low-income neighborhoods may increase the opportunities to build relationships (Brisson 2005: 646) (2nd localization profit).

Thus, most researchers presume that poor neighborhoods – in the USA usually corresponding to neighborhoods with a significant presence of minority residents – show a detrimental effect on the development of individuals' social capital. De Souza Briggs (cited in Goetz 2003: 217) suggests that these neighborhoods offer only a limited volume of social capital: both in terms of the one that helps people to '*get by'* on a daily basis (e.g. by a cup of flour, a ride somewhere), but even more regarding the one that helps them to '*get ahead'* (e.g. job references, connections), the latter being particularly mobility-relevant (ibid: 217).

Generally, supportive 'bonding networks' between low-income persons inside a neighborhood are considered as less relevant for the generation of 'valuable' social capital than 'bridging networks', which extend outside the neighborhood (Warr 2005: 304, Brisson 2005: 645). Some authors stress the possibly redundant character of social networks in poor and/or ethnic neighborhoods[91], the weakness of strong ties between deprived neighbor-

---

91 Redundancy occurs not only in terms of the limited size of social contacts, but also in terms of available flows of information, exchange of ideas and exposure to (other) ways of living and thinking (Warr 2005: 304).

hood-kins or -friends concerning their mobility relevance (Colclough/Sitaraman 2005: 491, MacDonald et al. 2005: 884) and the detrimental effect of ethnic clusters for immigrants' overall social integration and engagement (Uslaner/Conley 2003: 333, see chapter 2.3.3).

I want to question the above assessments from a normative, conceptual and empirical standpoint. In normative terms, I believe that by focusing on terms such as self-segregation or auto-exclusion the above authors fall short of taking into account the exclusionary practices of the 'dominant society' that co-produce social and/or spatial segregation (Dangschat 2005: 350). Furthermore, I assume that the existence of culturally diverse sub-communities in a social or urban setting may convey benefits to their inhabitants and still allow a politically and functionally integrated society (see chapter 2.3.2) - at least if these diverse communities are not characterized by strong social and economic asymmetries.

From a conceptual standpoint the influence of e. g. ethnic neighborhoods on the volume or quality of social capital possessed by their residents, should not be assessed in abstraction from the perspective of the involved individuals. In chapter 3.1.4 I have elaborated on this point, with reference to Bourdieu's claim to overcome the epistemological between "structure" and "agency". Whereas the 'objective' conditions in an ethnically segregated neighborhood (e.g. deficient housing and infrastructure, few green areas, deficient social services) may suggest that individuals want to move away from such neighborhoods, the subjective views 'from the inside' may differ. This may be due to the socio-psychological compliance with a lack of alternatives, turning constraints into preferences (Bourdieu 1986: 285), but it may also be due to the perception that the ethnic neighborhood responds to needs or dimensions of well-being that non-ethnic neighborhoods do not.

From an empirical standpoint, the assumption that the spatial proximity of co-ethnics impacts negatively on their social capital and/or well-being, can be questioned from at least two angles. First, studies in European and other cities have found that the spatial clustering of immigrants can impact positively on their personal well-being and empowerment (Pelemann 2002: 16, Chapter 2.3.3), as well as on neighborhood development (Schnur 2005: 502). Some authors have highlighted that strategies aiming at *ethnic* instead of income-related mixing may be focusing on the wrong criteria (Caesperlein/Gliemann 2003: 216, Amin 2006: 1018)[92]. Third, the experience in several housing dispersal programs in the US did not confirm, but rather disputed the assumption that vicinity of households with differing social and/or economic backgrounds enhanced their social relationships (view Goetz 2003: 26, view chapter 2.2.4).

3.2 Conceptualization of social groups

If the membership in a group, formal or informal, constitutes the precondition for the generation of social capital it is necessary to clarify the meaning of social 'groups'. This implies the question on

- Objective vs. subjective group constituting factors: Are 'objective' social conditions (e. g. income and occupational status, educational level, ethnicity) sufficient to identify social groups, or do further, subjective, criteria need to be taken into account? What does this imply for the notion of ethnic groups or 'communities'?
- Impact of social differences on social capital: How does the reality of internal group differentiation or of multiple identities (Jacobs/Fincher 1998: 7) influence the formation of ethnic social capital and the extent individuals benefit from it? Which are the implications for the assessment of the development of 'ethnic' social capital?

3.2.1 Objective versus subjective criteria for group identification

In his construction of a theory of the social space and the genesis of social 'classes', Bourdieu (1991) criticizes the Marxist tradition in social sciences to identify what he terms 'classes on paper' with 'real' social classes. Structuralist or Marxist scientists tend to deduce the likelihood for the existence of 'social groups' from the notion of objective status-related differences among individuals, i.e. from their differential access to economic and cultural capital[93]. They assume that

---

92 These researchers qualify the readiness with which ethnically and class-based segregation are equated in the political and planning discourse as at the same time notorious and extremely problematic (Caesperlein / Gliemann 2003: 215ff.).

93 Although Marx distinguished between a 'class-in-itself' and a 'class-for-itself', according to Bourdieu (1991) he failed to clarify the conditions and mechanisms that lead to the transition from one to the other status, but rather takes this transition for granted – hence the reproach of determinism (ibid: 233).

"sets of agents who occupy similar positions [e. g. occupational, social status] and who, being placed in similar conditions and to similar types of conditioning [by way of the habitus] have every chance of having similar dispositions and interests, and thus of producing similar practices and adopting similar stances." (Bourdieu 1991: 231)

However, according to Bourdieu, the problem with this approach is that the 'classes on paper' form mere theoretical constructs and therefore fail to explain actual group-based identities or practices (ibid: 229, Bourdieu 1998: 11). In Bourdieu's perspective, status-related social differences are necessary, but not sufficient conditions for the formation of social groups. Thus, social groups should be identified taking into account both 'objective' social differences *and* the subjective perceptions of individuals. For, the latter are constitutive of a given group's identity, its common actions and/or social struggles.

Bourdieu considers the possession of or access to economic and cultural capital as the two most effective differentiating principles in advanced societies, such as the United States, Japan or France (Bourdieu 1998: 6). However, he does recognize that other categories of distinction (e. g. gender, race, ethnicity, sexuality, religion, caste) intersect with social class and that, depending on a particular local or historical context, may possess considerable structuring, organization or identity-building power (Bourdieu 1991: 233). Especially in the case of temporary social movements (e. g. a fight against construction of a highway), alliances and identities are often built across class-related social positions, which consequently fall short of explaining them (Bourdieu 1998: 233)[94]. The construction of personal identities, or boundaries, rests on a wide array of differences. This is although in the context of social or political struggles singular identity categories tend to be prioritized and isolated (e.g. sexual orientation in gay/lesbian movements), often on a temporary basis (Jacobs/Fincher 1998: 7f.).

---

[94] As from his point of view social practices and/or political struggles are by no-means self-evident and merely mirroring 'objective' structural inequalities, Bourdieu (1991) highlights the importance for a social group and its concerns being recognized on a symbolic level. This implies that both members and non-members of a group perceive the differences it is constituted upon as meaningful (ibid: 239, view Schuck 2003: 23). According to Bourdieu, conferring legitimacy and quasi-objectivity to a group's constitution is one of the main functions of a spokesperson or group leader (ibid: 236)

'Objective' and 'subjective' notions of social proximity or distance may diverge considerably from each other. According to Bourdieu (1990a), people tend to mark the biggest differences with respect to actors who, from an external point of view are in a similar situation, e. g. with respect to their socioeconomic status. On the one hand, this is "because what is 'closest' [to social actors] presents the greatest threat to [their] identity" (ibid: 137). On the other hand, Bourdieu assumes that people, guided by the *habitus*, tend to adjust their claims or complaints to real chances, and thereby "limit subjective pretensions to the immediate neighborhood" (ibid: 137, Bourdieu 1993: 589), instead as to the fundamental social cleavages.

The above considerations resound in a study on the social relations of Salvadorian immigrants in Long Island, carried out by Sarah Mahler (1995). Rather than emphasizing factual episodes of solidarity inside the ethnic community as reactions to common problems, the interviewed immigrants consistently placed emphasis on experiences of competition, jealousy and exploitation inside their 'community' or between immigrants of different national origins (Mahler 1995: 4). The isolation from the mainstream American society and their reliance on, at times, exploitative small business- and informal activities is seen by Mahler as one important reason for immigrants directing their resentments towards each other or native minorities (e. g. African Americans, Puerto Ricans), rather than towards the dominant US American society, i.e. the more fundamental social antagonisms (ibid: 227)[95].

From a research perspective, the above reflections on objective versus subjective definitions of social groups have important implications: Researchers of ethnic social networks need to be wary of adopting simplifying ideas about ethnic networks and 'solidarity' (Mahler 1995: 225, Glick-Schiller et

95 Hence the importance to analyze immigrant networks against the background of external perceptions and political and economic opportunity structures. Immigrants may socialize with kins or co-ethnics due to the (invisible) social wall established by the members of the receiving society, thus, not as a result of entirely free choice. They may work in the (partly informal) 'ethnic economy' due to constraints for (legal, better paid, more formalized) employment opportunities in the mainstream economy. Finally, in an overall context of high power asymmetries they may adopt the devaluation of the dominant group towards their own and its (assumed or real) practices.

al. 1992: 16f.)[96]. Such ideas, as they ignore social cleavages among co-ethnics, may radically differ from the views of the people and thereby miss out on what is constitutive of people's social practices and 'reality' (Bourdieu 1990: 130, Bourdieu 1990a: 141). People may not consider certain groups as their 'co-ethnics', e.g. due to different national or regional origins, and identify 'group'-based conflicts of interests on the basis of differentiating criteria not immediately obvious to the outside observer (e. g. white vs. non-white Hispanics, Central- vs. South Americans). Hence the imperative for researchers to include the auto-assessment of people in their analysis of social relations and to understand social networks in terms of common *practices*, rather than of ascribed structural similarities.

3.2.2 The impact of social differences on ethnic social capital

In the research on the residential segregation of immigrants, I implicitly assume that shared 'ethnicity' has a strong potential for group- and identity-construction, as well as for the formation of social capital. Yet, other categories of difference may also be relevant for the understanding of social networks or, for that matter, cleavages. The use and disposition over physical, e.g. neighborhood space, may differ among co-ethnic sub-groups. Therefore, the intersection of social class-, gender- and age-disparities within and with respect to ethnic communities will be discussed in the following paragraphs[97].

According to Bourdieu, the volume of social capital that can be used and mobilized by an individual depends foremost on his or her position in the social space, or his or her social class (Bourdieu 1986: 249, see chapter 3.1.2). Thus, individuals are most likely to entertain social relations with persons of a similar capital volume and relative weight of their economic and cultural capital (Bourdieu 1998: 5ff., 1991). The potential social benefits of the social 'capital' of individuals of lower social classes are intrinsically limited and likely to consolidate existing social and power asymmetries

---

[96] According to White et al. (2005), most studies on residential segregation are based on over-simplifying notions of group affiliations limiting themselves to the measurement of segregation among broad panethnic groups, e. g. 'whites', 'blacks', 'Hispanics' and 'Asians' (ibid: 175ff.). However, their study shows important inner-group residential distance or clustering, e. g. according to national origin (ibid: 193, also view Johnston et al. 2003: 568).

[97] I concentrate here on class, gender and age, as these were among the most important differentiating factors in the empirical part of this research.

(Bourdieu 1986, 1987, 1990, 1991, see chapter 3.1.2). Socioeconomic hardship may limit an individual's time- and financial means to engage in 'meaningful' social relationships and thereby accumulate social capital (Wuthnow 2000: 68ff., Brisson 2005: 651). It may also undermine their experiences of social solidarity, respect and honesty, something Mahler (1995) has found in her research about poor Salvadorean immigrants in Long Island, New York (ibid: 30).

In terms of gender, Pessar (1998) points to the limitations of social network theories that part from conceptions of ethnic households as 'unitary entities', failing to consider conflicts or the possibility of exploitation within the migrant households (ibid: 59). She highlights that male and female family members tend to use different kinds of social networks, and that women often have restricted access to network resources, as a consequence of their domestic responsibilities and the role imposed on them in the framework of patriarchical structures (ibid: 60f., Colclough/Sitaraman 2005: 486, Aguilera 2005: 574f.). In a similar vein, Mahler (1998) criticizes assumptions about the counter-hegemonic character of transnational ethnic networks and highlights that participation in, and benefits from many of these networks may reproduce gendered domination patterns (ibid: 82)[98]. Peleman (2002) finds gendered impacts of residential segregation on Moroccan immigrants in Antwerp. Her study results indicate that spatial proximity through life in an inner-city ethnic neighborhood specifically favors social networks among females as opposed to male migrants, and indirectly contributes to the enhancement of a cultural-religious identity and self-empowerment of these women (ibid: 1, 15ff., see chapter 2.3.3).

In terms of age, it seems evident that the experiences of adult and youth immigrants differ, with respect to social activities and peer groups and to the costs or benefits of ethnic versus non-ethnic social networks. Referring to studies on transnational social networks, Mahler highlights that the pursuance of such ties should be observed across generations and the little attention directed to this issue up to present (Mahler 1998: 84). Although the predominant assumption among scholars is that ethnic ties will gradually disappear with immigrants' advanced acculturation in the host society (Gans

[98] According to Mahler, these social networks may have counter-hegemonic functions from a class-based point of view, however she highlights that intersecting structures of domination (class, race, ethnic, gender etc.) should not be ignored (Mahler 1998: 82).

1997: 878), evidence has proved for e. g. Jewish, Polish and Irish Americans in the US that they persist and develop across generations (Guarnizo / Smith 1998: 17). In the case of the children of non-white immigrants in the US, ethnic social networks may be maintained as a response to discrimination from the dominant society (Portes 1997: 815).

The above elaborations have illustrated several important issues: First, in sub-chapter 3.2.1 I have shown that social groups need to be defined with respect to the subjective perceptions of agents, rather than with respect to the proximity of agents in the social space (Bourdieu 1991: 231). Second, in this present sub-chapter I have concretized how benefits or costs accrued from membership in a social group or from the residence in an ethnic neighborhood may play out according to categories of differentiation different from ethnicity. An essentialist consideration of only one axis of difference, e.g. ethnicity, would miss out key aspects and dynamics of ethnic social and spatial, conflictive rather than harmonious, togetherness.

3.3 The geography of social capital

In the 1990s, an increasing number of social scientists drew attention to the concept of transnationalism, notably transnational social networks. Transnationalism, as defined in 1990 considers itself as a new analytical framework for understanding migration and refers to “processes by which immigrants build social fields that link together their country of origin and their country of settlement” (Glick Schiller 1992a: 1). These social fields can be family, economic, social, organizational, religious and political relations that span borders, connecting its members simultaneously to two or more societies and territories (ibid: 74). They can be reinforced by migrants entertaining temporary, rather than establishing permanent residency in the receiving country (Jones 1992: 217, Rouse 1992: 43f.)[99].

Most scholars consider the emergence and growing relevance of transnational, as opposed to primarily ‘localized’ social spaces as a consequence of macro-structural influences. The first major influence constitutes the globalization of the economy and its destabilizing effects on less industrialized countries of the Global South, prompting labor-migration as a risk-reduction

---

[99] Temporary or circular migration has been found to be a pattern particularly prominent among the Mexican migrants, not least due to the proximity of this country to the US (see *Box 3* in chapter 6.1).

strategy on the part of individuals and households. A second one lies in the technological revolution in the means of transportation and communication that facilitates and lowers costs for transnational mobility, as well as the use of information and communication tools such as radio, television and the internet[100]. A third reason forms an increasingly multinational regulatory context since the middle of the 20th century (view i. a. Guarnizo/Smith 1998: 4).

As opposed to studies that stress the increasingly globalized linkages of political and businesses *elites*, the transnationalism scholars focus on the daily lives, activities and social relationships among *non-elites*[101]. Transnationalist scholars distance themselves from the notion of the local' as something static and backward′, but stress its dynamic character. They consider the social ties, cultural practices and identities of every-day people as coping strategies inside global economic forces, in part strongly encouraged by nation states (Glick Schiller 1992a: 8f.)[102]. Countering essentialist viewpoints on local communities and cultures, they stress their link to values, knowledge and practices from the outside (Pessary 1999: 56).

With respect to immigrant social networks, some authors underscore their transnational – as opposed to exclusively local - character (e.g. Goldring 1998, Smart/Smart 1998, Amin 2006: 1020). For instance, Mexican immigrants to the United States continue to be involved in home town organizations or community development projects, even a long time after having settled in the US (Goldring 1998: 165f., Rouse 1992: 44, Lauria-Perricelli 1992: 256). The need for a critical analysis of the functions of transnational social networks and 'loyalty-based' practices was also recognized in light of a tendency among scholars to idealize these networks as inherently counter-

---

100 Interestingly, the scholars recognize the supportive effect of communications technologies on the development and maintenance of transnational social networks (and capital), whereas other social capital theorists consider technological innovation as a key factor for declining social capital, spurring withdrawal of people from public social spaces (Putnam/Goss 2002: 18).

101 In this regard, transnationalism can be considered as a normative concept, as grassroots′ social relations and coalitions are considered as motors of - desirable - social change and resistance to the hegemonic structures of global capitalism (Mahler 1998: 67ff., Guarnizo/Smith 1998: 5, Glick-Schiller et al. 1992: 11).

102 The interests of national governments lie in building or maintaining political and economic relations with the US government, via immigrant organizations (Glick-Schiller et al. 1992: 2ff.).

hegemonic and resistant (Mahler 1998: 88, Guarnizo/Smith 1998: 5, Pessar 1999: 62)[103].

Transnational social networks or 'capital' refer to both organized and unorganized ways immigrants of a common national origin entertain relations across borders. According to Mahler (1998), studies that focus on a limited set of transnational activities such as the engagement in voluntary associations and/or ethnic organizations are problematic, as these practices are only performed by a relatively small proportion of the transmigrants and by no means 'typical' (ibid: 82). Rather, the whole array of formal *and* informal transnational social practices should be considered, including remittances, communications (letters, tapes, telephone calls, videos, e-mail), home town-oriented projects (planned in organizations), home travels, cultural activities and others (also Glick-Schiller et al. 1992: 2).

Several scholars highlight the relevance of *social status* to understand the instrumentality of transnational social networks (Glick-Schiller et al. 1992: 11, Goldring 1998: 167f., Rouse 1992: 38). Goldring (1998) has found that, by maintaining social relations and a stake in their home community, "immigrants can improve their social position and perhaps their power, make claims about their changing status and have it appropriately [symbolically] valorized, and also participate in changing their place of origin" (ibid: 168), i. e. improve their social and political capital in their home places. Social practices (formal, and informal; individual and collective)[104] are more likely to convey benefits in the context of the home community or region, than in the host country:

"[Transnational] social spaces and the locality of origin in particular, offer a special context for claiming and valorizing status. (...) [Community] involves a sense of shared history and identity, and mutually intelligible meanings (...) that allow status claims to be understood [on a symbolic level] through the interpretation of practices,

---

[103] Their counter-hegemonic character may be motivated by the conscious or unconscious intention of immigrants to resist forces of acculturation in the USA, the resistance to social and economic inequalities in the US or their participation in political anti-hegemonist projects.

[104] Examples of these social practices range from the organization of infrastructure projects in the home community, over communication in the English language, up to individual 'conspicuous' consumption patterns such as driving of an imported vehicle, paying a round of drinks, extending the house in the home community, dressing in US-American clothes etc. (Goldring 1998: 174).

rituals, goods and artifacts in the context of transnational communities and broader transnational fields" (Goldring 1998: 173).

The discussion about transnational social networks suggests that the analysis of social capital of immigrants (both in terms of the involved social practices *and* their benefits from the perspective of the individual actors) should not be limited to a consideration of the 'local' level. Many immigrants, and not only of the first generation, entertain social relations that range beyond. Importantly, the use of products and cultural references of the home country, region or community may convey tangible and symbolic benefits in the host and home countries (Smith 1998: 19f.). Social mobility gains in the home country may also contribute to compensating relatively low mobility prospects in the host country.[105] In the long-run they may even impact positively on the social position in the receiving society (Goldring 1998: 184ff.). However, as pointed out in the former chapter, transnational social obligations may impose financial and time limits on the social engagement of immigrants in the host country or the respective residential neighborhood (Mahler 1995: 219).

The effect of residential clustering (segregation) versus dispersal of immigrant households on the functioning of *transnational* social networks needs to be additionally considered. It has been shown that transnational social networks in the host country do not stop on the neighborhood or – level of an individual city, but may be maintained among immigrant kins and friends across several cities and states in the host country (for the US, view Goldring 1998: 179). However it can be assumed that the development and maintenance of infrastructure that facilitates local, as well as transnational connectivity (e. g. 'ethnic' supermarkets, money exchange shops, 'ethnic' organisations) require a critical mass that can more easily be achieved when the demand for this infrastructure is concentrated in a specific neighborhood (view also Peleman 2002: 13).

---

105 Referring to a study about Ticuani youth in New York City, Mahler points to the status-related function of transnational ethnic social networks from the specific perspective of these youth. Whereas they occupy among the lowest social strata in New York, by the "over-accentuation of their Ticuani identity (…) they create an alternative niche, on that bulwarks being associated with the negative stereotypes attributed to other poor minorities" (Mahler 1998: 85).

3.4 Summary

In this chapter, I have discussed the concept of social capital and its relevance for this research. I started with the definition of social capital based on the concept of the French sociologist Pierre Bourdieu. He defines social capital as the '*aggregate of the actual or potential resources linked to a possession of a durable network of acquaintances or membership in a group'*. His concept is particularly instructive for this research, as it explains the instrumentality of social networks, and the place of residence, for an individual's social status and mobility. Thus, according to Bourdieu, social capital has little or no value by itself. Rather, the latter is derived from its convertibility into economic, cultural and symbolic capital.

According to Bourdieu the volume of an individual's social capital depends on the volume of the capital possessed by those to whom she/he is connected. He argues therefore that the social networks of the middle or upper classes tend to consolidate and/or reiterate their dominant position. In contrast, the social networks of the lower social classes have the opposite effect, as socializing with agents of a similar low position tends to imply rather bleak mobility prospects. This is even more so if the disadvantaged position of an individual in the social space is reflected by him or her living in a 'poor' neighborhood.

In my point of view, this does not mean that the value of immigrants' social capital is 'low', as derived from social contacts with individuals of a mostly disadvantaged social position. Hence my critique of Bourdieu's instrumentalist view on social capital that favors tangible and mobility-relevant benefits or costs, at the cost of more intrinsic, e.g. emotional, social ones. For instance, people may value their (ethnic) social networks beyond their economic instrumentality, but according to their own criteria of well-being. In methodological terms this means that the assessment of the value of ethnic social capital – and living in ethnic neighborhoods - requires taking into account the subjective views and experiences of people.

The physical and social spaces interact and are mutually reinforcing. Not only do social relationships and hierarchies inscribe themselves in the physical space, but the latter has a distinct impact on social relationships. According to Bourdieu, 'site effects' occur through tangible and symbolic localization profits. Tangible or material effects form the proximity to certain agents and goods and the size of the space one occupies. Symbolic effects constitute the prestige or stigma attributed to a certain location. Against this background one would assume that living in low-income or 'ethnic' neighborhoods can hardly contribute to enhancing an individual's social capital. A number of authors presume that social capital that helps people to get 'along' and 'ahead' is lacking in minority neighborhoods. However, both empirical evidence and social theory indicate that spatial integration is by no means a panacea for gains in terms of social mobility and/or integration.

In the section on the conceptualization of social groups I argue that social groups or networks considered as such from an outside perspective are not necessarily experienced as such from the inside. This means that ascriptions by the external observer (researcher) on possible common interests and actions may remain entirely inadequate if not confirmed by people's subjective perceptions. Whereas the researcher presumes the existence of a certain 'group' with unitary interests and identities, e. g. due to a common ethnicity, the situation of individuals forming part of this group may be far from homogeneous, due to other differentiating factors, such as social class, gender and age. Finally, in the sub-chapter on the locality of social capital I argue that the analysis of the social capital of immigrants should not be limited to the local (i. e. neighborhood) level, due to the potentially trans-local character of these networks *and* their benefits.

4 Conceptual and methodological framework

The objective of this chapter is to synthesize the theoretical reflections of the preceding two chapters and to operationalize them for the purpose of the empirical study. Whereas in chapter two I have discussed different analytical and normative approaches towards residential segregation, in chapter three I have defined my perspective on social capital and an analytic approach to assess the impact of residential segregation on the development of social capital and social mobility. In the present chapter I outline:

- the research objectives, assumptions and questions of this research,
- the understanding of the relationship between theoretical and empirical knowledge and its methodological implications, and
- the conceptual proceeding and model.

4.1 Research objectives, assumptions and questions

The research gaps or shortcomings prompting this research were already pointed out in the introduction of this document. They were:

- little research on the link between residential segregation and social networks,
- neglect of the subjective perceptions and assessment of immigrants on residential segregation, primarily as a result of the reliance on statistical data,
- relative neglect of multi-cultural US-urban and housing conditions through focus on black/white-segregation, and
- unsatisfactory policy responses to residential segregation.

Against the background of these research gaps, ***assessing the impact of residential segregation on the development of social capital and social mobility of immigrants*** constitutes the primary objective of this research. ***Providing policy and planning indications that address both advantages and disadvantages of residentially segregated neighborhood or ethnic clusters*** constitutes a more normative goal. A case study with the Mexican immigrant population in the neighborhood "West Side of St. Paul" in St. Paul, USA was used to address the indicated research gaps.

The literature review on residential segregation and social capital has lead to narrowing the research interests, according to certain identified gaps (see above). It has also contributed to shaping certain assumptions that orientate the empirical proceeding. While I do not formulate hypothesis requiring the subsequent testing of empirical results against them[106], the assumptions comply with two important functions:

- Methodological: They form the basis for the formulation of research questions. They further inform the empirical proceeding in that they help to define data collection methods, the 'right' interview partners and questions, and approaches for the interpretation of data (Denzin/Lincoln 1994a: 11, ibid 1994b: 199).
- Epistemological: They help to articule the author's theoretical pre-knowledge and/or normative preconceptions (Glaser 1992: 25). These are based on the topic-related literature review, but may also relate back to prior scientific work and general world view (Meinefeld 2003: 273). Being aware of these preconceptions helps to employ alternative interpretation tools in data analysis. (Strauss/Corbin 1994: 280, Meinefeld 2003: 270f.). They may also allow the reader to recognize possible research biases.

The following are the central assumptions underlying this research:

1. Contrary to the more frequent assumption that ethnic social networks and ´capital´ represents a social mobility obstacle for immigrants, I assume that they may convey important benefits on individuals to be able to get 'along' and 'ahead' in their lives.
2. Many seemingly 'local' ethnic social networks are of a translocal nature, both in terms of activities and goods involved, and also in terms of their functions (e. g. intended status gains in their home country).
3. The relevance of ethnic social capital for individuals´ social mobility depends on individual characteristics, particularly their social class. Upwardly mobile immigrants are likely to engage less in co-ethnic relationships and attribute less importance to them.
4. Spatial proximity and clustering, happening in the context of an ethnic neighborhood, can be favorable for an individual's development

[106] The formulation, and falsification or verification of hypothesis in the context of an empirical experiment constitutes a common practice in particularly quantitative methodological proceeding.

of social capital and social mobility, for instance through the facilitation of social encounters or the provision of partly mobility-relevant social infrastructure. However, it may be negative in the case of neighborhoods that display high economic and educational poverty, e. g. limiting an individual's exposure to opportunity-related social contacts and infrastructure.

5. Housing policy strategies should be sought out that contribute to strengthen positive aspects of clustering, instead of focusing on residential dispersal, as residential segregation or clustering may have the potential to contribute to mid- or longer term social inclusion of immigrants.
6. A fundamental problem of desegregation as a political objective is that it attacks a symptom (spatial concentration) rather than the underlying causes of urban poverty: the limited access to housing and other opportunities of low-income or minority families. Furthermore, desegregation strategies implicitly neglect the relevance of a housing location as an expression of a person's cultural identity or difference. Housing strategies that include (i.a.) culturally-based needs and choices of immigrants would ultimately lead to higher levels of well-being without hindering perspectives of upward social mobility.

Thus, against the background of the mentioned assumptions, this research seeks to answer the following sub-questions:

1. What kind of social networks and connections can be found among immigrant households, in a segregated neighborhood? How can these networks be described, in terms of their degree of formality and/or institutionalization, as well as in terms of their socio-demographic characteristics?
2. What can be said about the geography of these social networks or 'connectivity'; are they of a local, city-wide, national or transnational scale?
3. Do the ethnic social networks generate or hinder resources that impact on social mobility and other assets of 'value' for the individual immigrant? How do the answers to these questions change with varying individual characteristics, e.g. gender, social class (income), first/second generation immigrants?

4. Does residential clustering in an ethnic neighborhood impact positively or negatively on the development of social networks and capital, and how? Are these networks bound to physical spaces and encounters in- or outside the neighborhood?
5. How can dominant housing policy and planning responses to residential segregation be assessed, or which are more adequate ones?
6. How can these be related to the challenges and (e.g. asset-creating) potentials of ethnic social networks?

4.2 Relationship between theoretical framework and empirical research

The empirical proceeding in this research is characterized by a predominantly inductive research approach, although combined with a few deductive elements. The following table illustrates the differences between an inductive and a deductive approach, with respect to the generation of knowledge, the role of existing concepts and theories, and the assumed characteristics of scientific knowledge:

Table 2: Inductive versus deductive research approach

	Inductive	**Deductive**
Generation of knowledge	Exploratory, generating concepts	Verificational, testing hypothesis
Use of existing concepts and theories	Consulted in the process of data analysis	Basis of formulation of hypothesis
Characteristics of scientific knowledge	Provisional, historically and locally contingent	Objectively and universally valid until falsified

An inductive approach implies the generation of concepts and theories on the basis of the empirical data applied to a specific case, in an *exploratory* process often achieved through qualitative research methods. Existing theories are rather consulted in the process of data analysis, and to the extent that they possess specific explanatory power, with respect to the data at hand (Strauss/Corbin 1990: 49, Caesperlein/Gliemann 2003: 37).[107] Inductive

[107] Researchers who call for inductive theory-building tend to reject the use of ex-ante hypothesis as it influences the researcher in the interpretation of the data from the upstart, i. e. reduces the likelihood of achieving results that diverge from the pre-conceived models. However, other researchers warn that by rejecting the use of hypothesis as a rule, 'inductionists' fail to confront the fundamental epistemological problem of the positionality of the researcher

approaches emphasize the provisional character of theories i.e. their contingency on certain historical and geographic conditions, as well as the importance that theories can be traced back to the subjective standpoints of individual actors, i.e. to the data (Strauss/Corbin 1994: 279f., Dey 1999: 4, Kuzel 1992: 33, Miller/Crabtree 1992: 6).

In contrast, a deductive approach denotes the formulation of hypothesis from theory (literature), and the testing of these hypotheses with empirically generated data, often, but not necessarily on the basis of quantitative data. It aims at generating 'objective' theories, which retain validity across historic moments and individual cases.

In the present research, the deductive elements consisted of the following: Instead of renouncing the use of existing literature and concepts prior the empirical research as a strictly inductive approach might suggest, these were used for the definition of broad themes, assumptions and research questions. The ex-ante formulation of assumptions and research questions was necessary to center the empirical research on the hitherto gaps in an otherwise extensively studied topic. For instance, Bourdieu's conceptualizations about the link between social and other (economic, cultural and symbolic) capital were drawn on for the definition of the research focus. The empirical research also lead to an assessment of the completeness of these conceptualizations, for instance with respect to 'instrumentalist' versus 'intrinsic' elements constitutive for the value of social capital (see chapter 3.1.4, 8.1.2)[108].

This proceeding is in line with the standpoint of defendants of inductive methodologies such as grounded theorists who state that existing theories may be used beforehand to guide the researcher towards possible relevant aspects or research gaps (Strauss/Corbin 1990: 50f., Ryan/Bernard 2003: 275, Meinefeld 2003: 270). However, to what degree existing theories or knowledge should guide the analysis process is one of the questions for discussion among grounded theorists themselves (Dey 1999: 14)[109].

---

and thus the impossibility of complete immersion in a research subject's world (Dey 1999: 16f., Fontana/Frey 1994: 363, Meinefeld 2003: 270f., Bourdieu 1991 et al.: 44f.).

[108] The critique of Bourdieu's concept from the point of view of a more subjectivist understanding of elements of *well-being* was informed by the development theory of A. Sen (see chapter 3.1.4).

[109] For instance, Glaser (1992) emphasizes that a research needs to be started without studying existing theoretical literature, even though the latter is very extensive (ibid: 32). Yet he

Thus, while my assumptions and research questions served as a conceptual framework (Ryan/Bernard 2003: 275), I chose a qualitative, exploratory approach to fill the identified research gaps: For instance, existing literature does not provide sufficient indications about the concrete interaction between social and other capital forms, the value attributed to them by the social agents, or the influence of physical space on the development of social and other capital. Thus these gaps were filled on the basis of generated empirical data through semi-structured open-ended interviews, observation and the analysis of secondary data. The analysis of the interviews was guided by the methodological principles of *grounded theory* (Strauss/Corbin 1994, Strauss/Corbin 1990, Glaser 1992)[110].

The perspectives of the inhabitants of the chosen segregated or 'ethnic' neighborhood and those of other stakeholders, e.g. community workers, planners and policy makers were used as the starting point for my contributions to the topic of residential segregation, not just by repeating, but by making 'sense' of them in the process of concept building (Strauss/Corbin 1994: 274)[111]. This proceeding is also based on Bourdieu's assumption according to which agents′ subjective *perception* of social reality, although limited by structural base conditions (social hierarchies, power asymmetries), needs to be accounted for in whatever empirical research process, as

> "(…) on the one hand, the objective structures which the sociologist constructs in the objectivist moment, by setting aside the subjective representations of the agents, are the basis of subjective representations and they constitute the structural constraints which influence interactions; but, on the other hand, these representations also have to be remembered if one wants to account above all for the daily individual and collective struggles which aim at transforming or preserving these structures. This means that the two moments, objectivist and subjectivist, stand in a dialectical relation." (Bourdieu 1990: 126)

---

nevertheless concedes disciplinary knowledge to be important for data-based concept-building (ibid: 28, also view Strauss/Corbin 1994: 280).

[110] These principles, as well as the applied methods in the research will be explained in more detail in chapter 5.

[111] Strauss/Corbin (1994) consider the development of 'substantative' theory as the prime objective of grounded theory methodology. Substantative theory-building refers to specific topics and is seen as a strategic step towards, however not identical with, higher-level formal theories (ibid: 281).

Graph 1 illustrates the way inductive and deductive approaches interplay in the present research.

4.3 Conceptual proceeding and model

I have derived the general concepts and themes guiding this research from literature on residential segregation and social capital. For the topic of residential segregation, the literature review has contributed to defining the key categories for its *causes*: Income and social status, housing preferences and experiences, and institutional factors such as housing laws and policies. Based on Bourdieu's reflections on 'site effects' and localization profits, I have defined two ways in which the *effects* of residential segregation manifest themselves in individuals' social capital: Proximity to co-ethnics and to infrastructure and services, and inside and outside perception of a neighborhood including size of spaces.

Bourdieu's theory has also provided the basis for defining the *types* of social networks (formal and informal interpersonal relationships), important *factors* influencing their nature (social differences, locality of social networks), and other capital forms constitutive for the determination of the volume of social capital, in terms of its relevance for social mobility (economic, cultural and symbolic capital). Following 'objectivist' definitions of social status based on the measures of occupation and income (Lamnek 1989: 698), I have determined the following two indicators for social mobility: job options and housing opportunities. I have included housing opportunities as an indicator due to the important role of ownership housing for wealth-based asset generation.

Graph 1: Relationship between literature and empirical proceeding in research

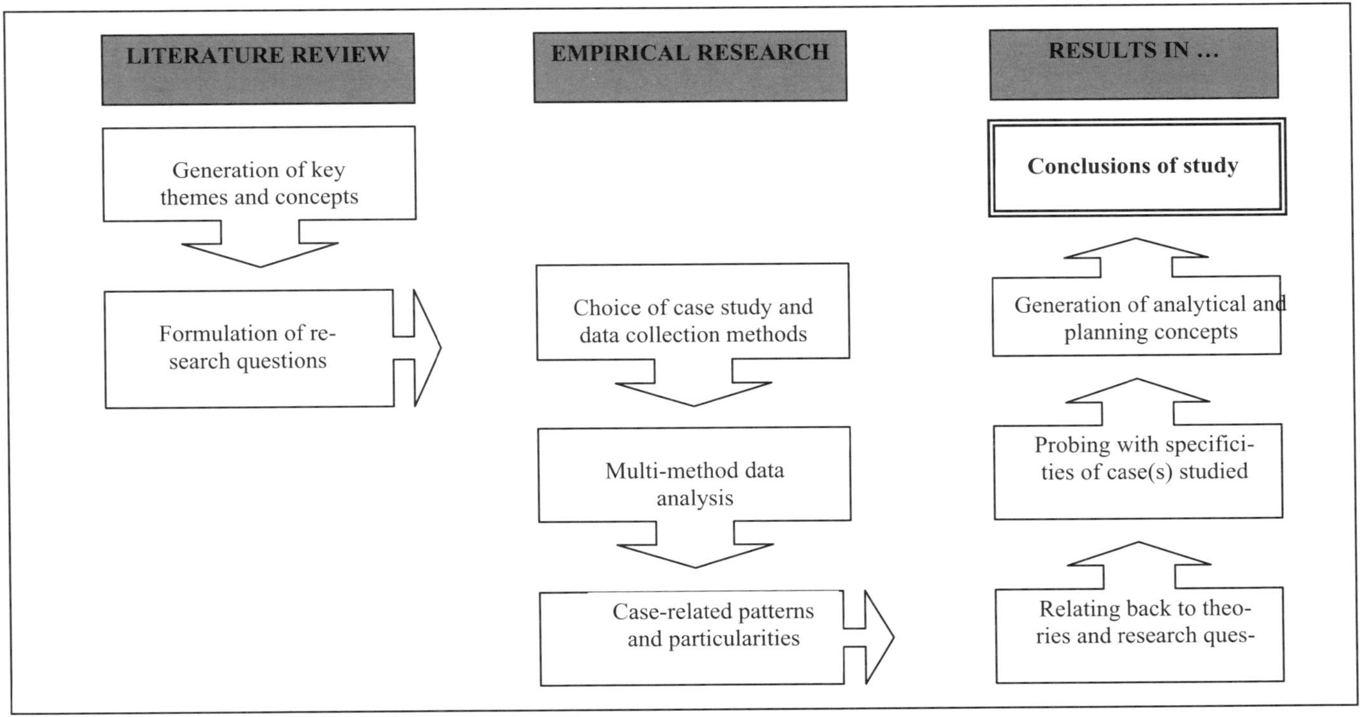

Source:Own compilation

The following elements were inductively developed in the context of the analysis of the empirical data, my primary source for conceptualization:

- Additional mobility-relevant categories and indicators[112],
- the concrete manifestations of social capital/mobility and 'site effects' in the life of the residents of the researched ethnic neighborhood, and
- patterns and relationships between the core categories.

My key sources of information formed the semi-structured interviews with residents living in the studied 'ethnic' neighborhood, and with housing and community development stakeholders working at community, city, State- or national levels. The structure of the resident interview guidelines was broadly informed by the categories mentioned above, i. e. including sections about ways "to get along and ahead", the residents' "social networks" and "pros and cons of the ethnic neighborhood". Whereas the resident interviews focused primarily on the experiences related to their social networks and life in the ethnic neighborhood, the expert interviews primarily focused on community development and housing policy and planning issues. The process of the interview design, implementation and analysis will be explained in more detail in the following chapter on the research methodology (5).

In the context of the interview analysis, the results were conceptualized and related back to existing concepts and the research questions and assumptions. Particularities of the treated case study (e.g. the city and neighborhood environment, as well as those of the studied immigrant group) are reflected on, also in terms of their implications for the possibility of generalizing the study results.

Graphs 2 and 3 illustrate the theoretical framework for the influence of residential segregation on social capital, and the relationship between social and other capital forms:

---

[112] For instance, in the phase of the conceptualisation of the research and the design of the interview guidelines I did not think about "skills development", "self- and outside-group image" and "social or emotional comfort" as relevant indicators of mobility. However, these proved to be of particular relevance in the context of the resident interviews. They can also be directly related to Bourdieu's concept on site effects. The indicator of social comfort goes beyond Bourdieu's conceptualisation (see chapter 3.1.4).

Graph 2: Conceptual framework for relationship between social and other capital forms

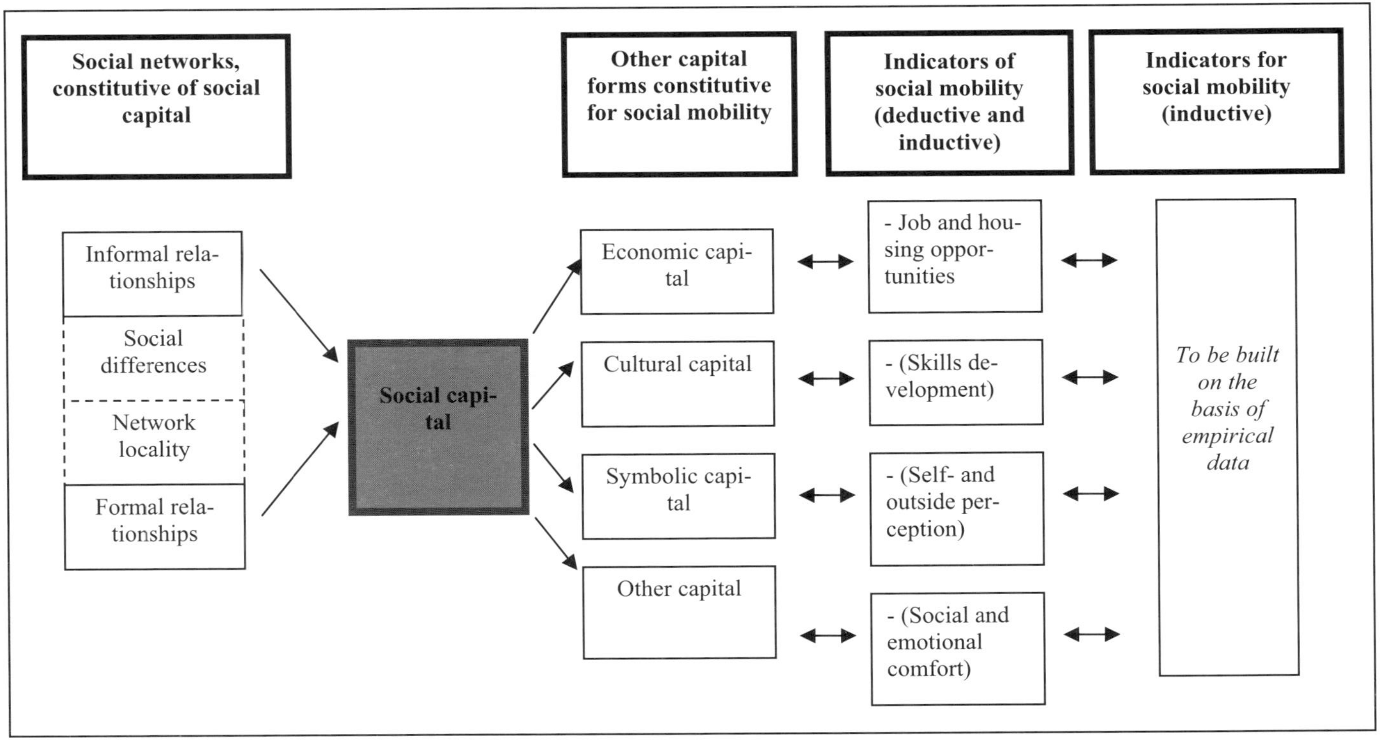

Source:Own compilation

Graph 3: Conceptual framework for influence of residential segregation on social capital

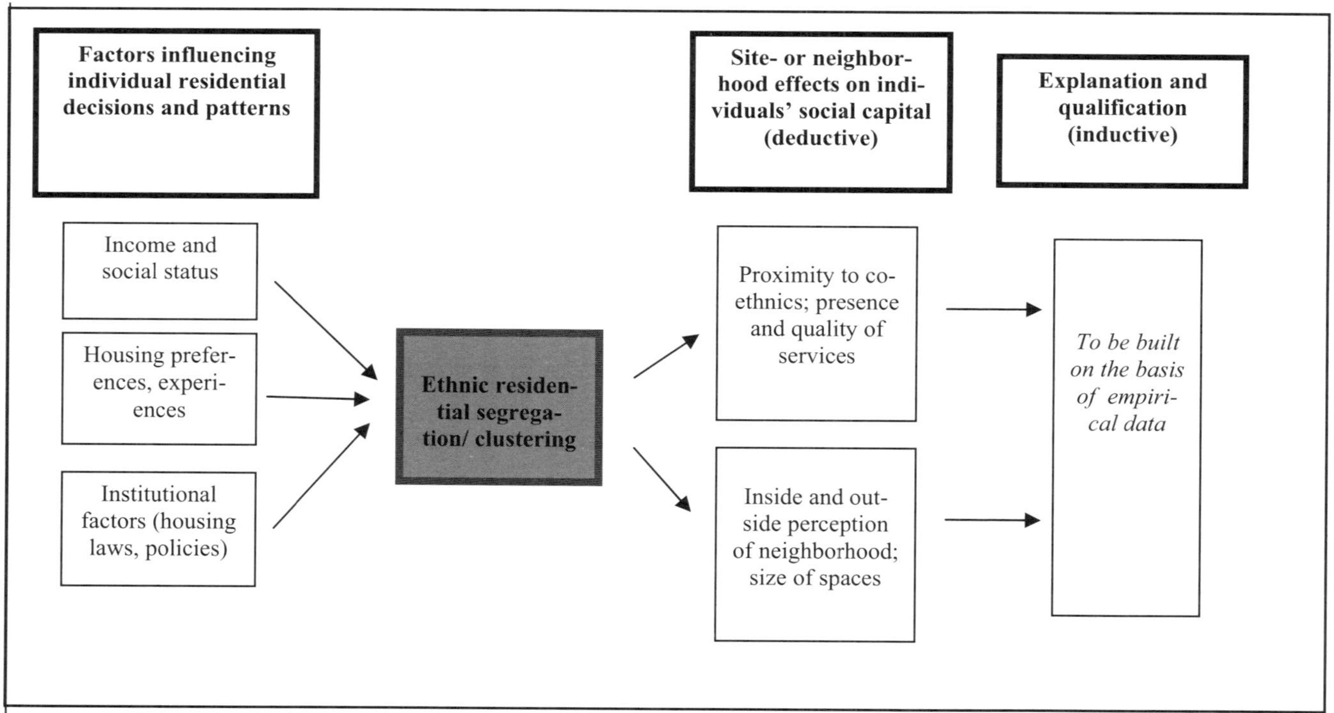

Source:Own compilation

5 Research methods

The present chapter complements the previous one, in that the methods and research tools applied in the research are discussed in more detail. As pointed out in chapter 4.3, the research was characterized by a predominantly inductive research approach. However, deductive elements were also used, for instance, the formulation of research questions and the development of a conceptual framework based on a previous literature review. The empirical methods implied the use of secondary and primary data, the first including the review of documents and statistical data, and the second the realization of interviews, observation and neighborhood walks.

Graph 4 illustrates the research methods applied, in terms of their function and with respect to the time frame of the study:

In the present chapter the focus lies on the methods I have used in the context of the *empirical* research. Since in the preceding chapter on the conceptual and methodological framework I have explained the function of the literature review in this research, this is not further elaborated on here. As the combination of different data gathering methods constituted a central aspect of the empirical proceeding in this research, the function of *triangulation* is explained before explaining each of the methods used. The description of the methods used starts with the secondary methods, followed by a more detailed elaboration of the primary methods. The process of conducting and analyzing the resident interviews, as the core data source of the study, is hereby explained in particular detail. I close this chapter with a summary assessment of the selected methodology.

5.1 Function of triangulation

Triangulation refers to the combination of multiple methods in an empirical research (Denzin/Lincoln 1994a: 2, Gilchrist 1992: 87, Miles/Hubermann 1994: 438, Flick 2003: 309). This may imply the use of different sources of information, the application of different instruments of inquiry (e. g. interviews, observation), the involvement of varying investigators or teams or the adoption of multiple theoretical perspectives (Denzin/Lincoln 1994a: 2, Gilchrist 1992: 87, Flick 2003: 310, Miller/Crabtree 1992b: 99). For the purposes of this research, the use of different instruments of inquiry constitutes the most relevant aspect.

Graph 4: Steps in research methodology, in chronological order and mutual relationship

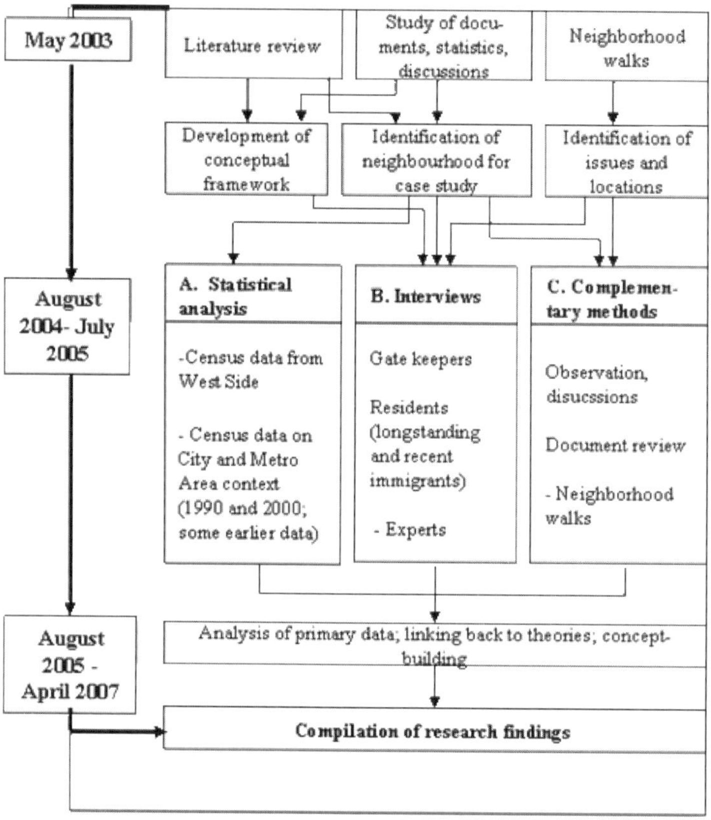

Source of graph structure: Godehart 2007

The understanding of the function of triangulation has changed in the last decades. Originally, the mixing of methods and research perspectives was considered as a means of increasing the research validity through the cross-checking of results gained with, e.g. one data collection method through evidence provided by another (Flick 2003: 310, Kelle/Erzberger 2003: 303f.). This view was cast into doubt in the context of a critique of a positivist research tradition, which inherently negates the possibility of multiple perspectives or realities (Flick 2003: 311, Caesperlein/Gliemann 2003: 100). Today, triangulation is considered "as a strategy that adds rigor, breadth and depth to any investigation" (Denzin/Lincoln 1994a: 2), and helps to achieve a more complete and better reasoned answer to a given research question (Neubert et al. 2000: 33f., Caesperlein/Gliemann 2003: 100, Kardoff 2003: 247, Flick 2003: 311, Kelle/Erzberger 2003: 304)[113].

This latter view of triangulation, as providing *complementary* views on a research topic, is crucial to this research. I have analyzed statistical data (see chapter 5.2) in order to provide additional background information on the case study neighborhood and population. My expert interviews with housing and community development stakeholders aimed at addressing the topic of ethnic clustering from a different, complementary perspective to the one of the interviewed residents. The review of the interview transcriptions of a previously conducted study on the West Side (HACER 2002) contributed to gaining additional information on the history and organizations of the West Side, and to corroborate interpretations realized through the resident interviews. I have used several of the other applied qualitative methods to re-address issues mentioned in the interviews.

[113] However, the understanding of different perspectives or approaches complementing each other is not without problems as different (e. g. quantitative and qualitative) methods are rarely able to consider the same aspects of a phenomenon with the same degree of depth. However, this does not mean that their combination leads to a 'complete' picture of this phenomenon. Rather, different research methods are attached to different and sometimes opposing research paradigms and world views (e. g. positivism, constructivism). These need to be taken into account, for instance when analyzing 'contradictory' research results (Denzin/Lincoln 1994af.: 4, Flick 2003: 310f., Caesperlein/Gliemann 2003: 100).

5.2 Use of secondary data

The most important secondary data sources constituted city and neighborhood statistics and different kinds of (non-technical) documents reviewed prior to and during the research.

5.2.1 Analysis of statistical data

I compiled and analyzed statistical data on the Minneapolis/St. Paul Metropolitan Area, the City of St. Paul and the neighborhood of the West Side. All the statistics were extracted from Census data from 1990 and 2000. The data can be freely accessed on the internet through the American Fact Finder (factfinder.census.gov)[114]. The variables accessed in the Fact Finder are indicated in the tables displayed in this document and listed in Annex 1. For the purpose of the research, data was gathered on the level of metro areas, cities and census tracts, the latter forming the third-smallest geographic entity the Census provided information about.

The census tract constitutes the most appropriate statistical unit in order to gather data for a particular neighborhood. This is since neighborhoods do not constitute separate statistical entities in the US Census. The residential area of the West Side of St. Paul, the selected neighborhood for this research, consists of four census tracts, which in their totality provide a relatively precise overview of the West Side neighborhood. A map with the West Side census tracts and their respective borders in the Census year 2000 can be viewed in chapter 6.2.3 (map 5). The demographic and socio-economic differences between these census tracts provide additional information on the demographic and socioeconomic differences inside a neighborhood.

---

[114] In the American Fact Finder, the Decennial Census data is gathered in four "Summary Files". The Files differ in terms of the sampling procedure, the variables included, and their degree of geographic (dis-) aggregation. Summary Files 1 and 2 are 100-percent samples, which means that every person and housing unit in the United States was asked some basic questions on their age, sex, race, their family situation and housing tenure. The smallest available geographic level is the census tract (approx. 4,000 residents). Summary File 2 additionally contains detailed data on people's nationalities. Summary Files 3 and 4 contain data from a sampled questionnaire collected from 1 in 6 households in the United States. Summary File 3 contains the highest number of variables, e.g. on people's socioeconomic status, housing situation etc. down to the geographic level of the block group (approx. 1000 residents). Summary File 4 contains additional data on people's nationalities with the smallest geographic area being the census tract level (factfinder.census.gov).

The following were the main purposes of the review of the statistical data in the present research:

1. Assessing the presence of the Hispanic or Mexican population in the Minneapolis-St. Paul Metropolitan Area and in its neighborhoods, and using this as an indication for the neighborhood in which the case study will be carried out[115].
2. Gathering demographic, socio-economic and housing background information on the West Side of St. Paul, as well as on the Hispanic or Mexican population in this neighborhood.
3. Compare results of the resident interviews, if adequate.

5.2.2 Review of documents

The documents I reviewed in the context of this research were, among others, the transcriptions of qualitative interviews conducted in the context of a previous study on the West Side of St. Paul (HACER 2002)[116], historic accounts of the West Side neighborhood (www.rchs.com, McClure 1992, Boyte 1984) and informational brochures from the institutions of the interviewed experts (view list in bibliography). I have reviewed the HACER-interview material prior to and after conducting my own case study. The original purpose of the review was to provide some qualitative background information on the history of the West Side and the institutions relevant to Hispanic population groups. However, in the course of this research the interview transcriptions also proved important for the appreciation of my own interview results: For instance, notwithstanding the different interview questions some issues were recurrently mentioned both in the HACER- *and* in my own interviews[117].

---

[115] Again, the West Side of St. Paul as a "neighborhood" of St. Paul and administrative entity does not form a statistic entity for which separate Census data can be gathered. Rather, census tracts located *inside* neighborhoods were compared.

[116] In the context of this study ("Latinos on the West Side of St. Paul"), interviews on the history and Hispanic community life on the West Side were conducted with 37 individuals and four focus groups (HACER 2002: 7). With kind assistance of HACER, I received the transcriptions of 12 interviews that were carried out with community leaders and employees of neighborhood organizations from the West Side.

[117] One of these issues was the perceived contrast between the former small and 'tight' Mexican community and today's one (view chapter 7.1.1). About the advantage of combining reactive, with non-reactive research methods, view Flick 2003: 313.

I reviewed documents (e.g. reports, leaflets, websites) of neighborhood and city institutions prior to, and following the expert interviews. The basic purpose of this review was to complete the picture of the institutional activities, objectives and standpoints acquired in the interviews, as well as to assess other institutional characteristics, such as the organizational structure and decision-making processes.

5.3 Use of primary data

The primary data gathering instruments applied in the study comprised resident and expert interviews and neighborhood walks, observation and group discussions. While the resident and expert interviews lay at the heart of the empirical study, the other methods provided valuable additional information on some of the aspects brought up in the interviews.

5.3.1 Sampling, conducting and analysing resident interviews

I carried out 27 open-ended interviews with Mexican residents of the West Side neighborhood in St. Paul. The resident interviews were carried out between November 2004 and May 2005, and most of them (21) between January and March 2005. In November 2004 two pre-test interviews were conducted.

As the research aimed at exploring the perceptions and experiences of immigrants or individuals with an immigrant family background with respect to the impact of residential clustering or segregation on their social capital and well-being (see chapters 2.5, 4.1), conducting interviews with the individuals involved seemed the most promising method to find information-rich answers to these questions (view Miller/Crabtree 1992: 17, Denzin/Lincoln 1994a: 5).

In the following I will outline the interview process including its different components.

<u>Sampling</u>

The aspect of sampling involves the decision on: the focus and boundaries of the investigation, the criteria for the selection of data sources, the most information-rich data sources, the data collection method and the appropriate number of data sources (Kuzel 1992: 32f.). In the following, all these issues are addressed in respect of the present research.

The question on the *focus and boundaries of the investigation* seems particularly relevant with respect to the selected immigrant group and neighborhood. It is relevant for all methods used in this research, although the use of some of the methods (literature and document review) preceded the decision on the immigrant group and neighborhood to be studied.

The Mexican population was selected for the following reasons:

- Importance out of immigrant population in city context: According to Census data, Mexico became by far the leading immigrant sending country to the State of Minnesota. Mexicans experienced a population growth of 42% between 1990 and 2000, followed by a 11%-growth of immigrants from Laos (Camarota/McArdle 2003: 9). In the Minneapolis-St. Paul Metropolitan Area, in the same period, the Hispanic population experienced the highest growth with respect to other racial groups (Asians and Blacks), more than doubling from 1.5% in 1990 to 3.3% in 2000[118]. Most of these Hispanics are Mexicans, 64% in 1990 and 66% in 2000 (www.lewis-mumford.com)[119].
- Relationship with segregation literature and conceptual framework: The characteristics of the Mexican immigrant population correspond with those of minorities the literature on residential segregation and social capital is most concerned with: adult migrants with relatively low-incomes and low education levels, at least upon their arrival[120]. With respect to other national minorities with an important presence in the Twin Cities (e.g. the Hmong from Laos and the Somalis) and similar socio-economic characteristics, the Mexicans show one important advantage: They have been coming to the area for almost 100 years, albeit with varying intensities (HACER 2002: 7). This

---

118 The Hispanic population proportions for the central city are higher than for the entire Twin Cities' Metropolitan Area: from 3% in 1990 to 7.7% in 2000.

119 For the central city the proportions of Mexicans out of the total Hispanic population, is slightly higher: 66% in 1990 and 70% in 2000. Other Hispanic national groups of much smaller numbers and proportions than the Mexicans, but with high increases of residence in the Twin Cities from 1990 to 2000, are: Ecuadorians (15 times), Salvadorians (six times) and Peruvians (3 times).

120 The notion of the typical, low-income and –skilled Third World migrant is however disputed by some scholars who highlight their increasingly socio-economic diversity and the growing importance of high-skilled labor migrants (Waldinger/der Martirosian 2001: 238).

provided an invaluable opportunity for this research to track experiences of residential clustering across different migration generations.

- Practicability of empirical research: Due to my fluency in the Spanish language, as well as relative familiarity with the Latin American cultural context, the selection of a Hispanic population group seemed more appropriate than the selection of an Asian national and/or ethnic group. In the latter case, neither of the two conditions (language skills and cultural understanding) would have been fulfilled.

The focus of the study on the 'case' of the West Side neighborhood occurred based on the following criteria and reasons:

- Important presence of immigrant, especially Hispanic or Mexican population in the neighborhood: The West Side of St. Paul is the neighborhood with the highest percentage of Hispanic or Latino residents in the Twin Cities and, by implication, in the City of St. Paul. According to the Census 2000, approximately 5,266 residents of the 16,133 residents of the West Side are Hispanic or Latino, corresponding to 33% of the neighborhood population (HACER 2002: 44). In two of the four census tracts of the West Side, more than 40% of the residents are Hispanics or Latino. Half of the Hispanic or Latino population of St. Paul lives on the West Side. While the immigration of Mexicans and Hispanics has become more geographically dispersed in the last 10 years, the West Side constituted the traditional migrant destination quarter in St. Paul.
- Relationship with literature and conceptual framework: The socio-economic and ethnic profile of the West Side corresponds to the type of neighborhood the literature of residential segregation is typically focusing on: With respect to the entire city of St. Paul, the West Side shows inferior household incomes, housing values and higher poverty rates (see table 8 in chapter 6.2.2). Having started up as a working class neighborhood with nearby inner-city industries it has attracted immigrants of diverse background since the early 20th century. This has lead to a
- Perception in the 'rest of the city' as an immigrant neighborhood: Although in the context of the increase in the Hispanic and Mexican population in the 1990s other ethnic clusters developed in the City of

> St. Paul and in the Twin Cities' Metropolitan Area, the West Side continues to be perceived as 'the' Hispanic or Mexican neighborhood of the Twin Cities. This is due to its long history of Mexican and Mexican-American immigrant and community life.

The 'case' of the West Side will be further discussed in chapter 6.4, in the context of a classification of different ethnic neighborhood types.

The *criteria for the selection of the data sources*, i. e. informants, were related to the conceptual framework. Due to the study focus, the interview partners had to be of Mexican origin and residents of the West Side. I used a purposive or theory-based, as opposed to random sampling design (Kuzel 1992: 40, Merkens 2003: 290ff.) choosing interview partners of varying social class backgrounds, gender, age and length of stay. I assumed these factors to be constitutive for differences in social capital-related outcomes of immigrants living in ethnic neighborhoods. However, following a principle in grounded theory, I intended to maintain a certain flexibility and responsiveness to interview results with respect to the data collection criteria (Strauss/Corbin 1990: 178). For instance, during the interview process, former residence on the West Side proved to be an additional concept-relevant variable[121].

The above paragraph already answers on the question of the *data source* I considered most appropriate: Residents of the West Side with varying socio-economic or demographic characteristics, or those who used to live on the West Side, were considered 'valuable' informants. The matrix of resident interviews in Annex 2 provides an overview of the interviewees and their characteristics. The names of the interview partners have been replaced by pseudonyms. Maximal difference with respect to the above-mentioned variables (socio-economic status, gender, age, immigration cohort/generation) constituted a guiding principle during the sampling, as well as during the

[121] I discovered this variable 'by accident'. In the very first interview that served as a pre-test, the person (Carmen, view Annex 2) had moved away from the West Side, in order to be better able to pursue her college studies. This seemed an interesting phenomenon to pursue. Therefore, I conducted four further interviews with informants who had moved away from the West Side. In the interviews, the motivations for moving away from the neighborhood were addressed.

interview analysis (Strauss/Corbin 1994: 280, Denzin/Lincoln 1994b: 202, Caesperlein/Gliemann 2003: 90, Merkens 2003: 291)[122].

I used a variety of interviewee recruitment or collection strategies to guarantee the intended heterogeneity of the sample. The first interview partners were contacted through referrals of four "gatekeepers" (Kuzel 1992: 36, Merkens 2003: 288): a colleague from the University and former resident of the West Side, a young community organizer from the community development corporation West Side Citizens Organization (WSCO), the leader of the Hispanic women self-help group "Hispanic Women in Action"[123], and the Director of the community development corporation Riverview Economic Development Association (REDA)[124]. The gatekeepers provided direct referrals to other interviewees, or helped with indirect referrals e.g. inviting me to events in the context of which I recruited additional interviewees[125]. Two of the informants were recruited at their work places: an ethnic, Mexican super-market and a Mexican restaurant. By way of the different recruitment approaches and 'snowballs' thrown out, a relatively diversified

---

122 Socio-economic status was the hardest variable to address by a direct sampling process. This variable was rather indirectly accounted for by talking to informants of different immigrant cohorts or generations: Those in the 2nd to 4th generations tended to dispose of more socio-economic stability than very recent immigrants. Choosing Mexican or Mexican-American residents of different sub-areas *inside* the West Side neighborhood could have served as a 'dummy' variable for socio-economic status. However, the geography of residence was not used as a criteria for data collection, partly due to the difficulty of controlling it in a process of snowball sampling.

123 Original: *Mujeres Hispanas en Acción.*

124 I also conducted expert interviews with three of the four 'gatekeepers' (Experts 8, 2 and 4, view Annex 3). Whereas the first of them was a personal acquaintance, I was referred to the three other gatekeepers by a University employee involved in community education on the West Side, whom I explicitly sought out to gain entry into the field. A further referral by the same University employee was a long-term community leader and employee of Neighborhood House. The interview with him (Expert 1) had to be cut short due to a death in his family the day before the interview, but forms part of the conducted expert interviews (see Annex 3).

125 This happened with all the interview partners contacted with the help of the leader of the women's group "Hispanic Women in Action" (Expert 4): Rather than providing me with names and/or telephone numbers of female group members, she invited me to the group meetings. I met two other interviewees (Theo, Raul) in the context of a West Side church celebration in the Lenten time. One interviewee (Arturo) was a young man whom I had met in the context of a previous interview with his mother (Dora).

sample could be achieved, in terms of the socio-economic and demographic characteristics of the interviewed residents[126].

Altogether, I carried out 27 resident interviews deeming a sample size of at least 20 interviews as necessary due to the required heterogeneity of the sample (Kuzel 1992: 41). However, the exact number of the interviews had not been determined at the beginning, but occurred considering the saturation point reached after a certain number of 'snowballs' were thrown in one direction and additional sampling efforts could not be justified with respect to the (relatively little) new information they helped to bring out (ibid: 40)[127].

The sampling process was confronted with several challenges: First, certain Mexican or Mexican-American sub-groups were particularly hard-to-reach: These were very recent immigrants (with a presence in the US of less than five years) and/or males[128]. In order to overcome this difficulty, towards the end of the interview period, I asked interviewees if they could recommend potential informants specifically belonging to these sub-groups. As this strategy did not prove successful[129], I directly asked (previously unknown) employees of an ethnic supermarket and a restaurant if they were ready for an interview. Second, some Mexican or Mexican-American residents of the West Side I had been referred to refused the interview, due to lack of inter-

---

[126] Whereas the informants recruited by the REDA-contact tended to be more longstanding Mexican-American residents of the West Side, those recruited by the "Neighborhood House" self-help group were relatively recent, first generation, female immigrants.

[127] This was, for instance, the case of the relatively well-organized, first generation, female immigrant population.

[128] The reason for the difficulty of reaching very recent immigrants may lie in the frequent undocumented status and legal and economic vulnerability of this sub-group. Very recent immigrants may be the least organized, not least due to their vulnerability. Hence the bias risk when sampling upon a certain type of, e. g. organized, 'gatekeepers' (Merkens 2003: 288). The reason for the difficulty of recruiting male informants – recent and longstanding – may lie in a lower level of family-extern social activities of this sub-group. However, this still does not mean that little effort was required to recruit informants of the other sub-groups. For instance, conducting interviews with members of the group "Hispanic Women in Action" occurred upon repeatedly participating in its meetings, rather than due to mere contact with its leader.

[129] For, the female self-help group members could not 'force' their husbands or male extended family members to agree to be interviewed. Or, longstanding Mexican-American residents of the West Side were hardly acquainted with recent Mexican immigrants.

est[130] or for self-protection. Third, not all previously sought-out recruitment methods were successful. For instance, a bilingual leaflet placed in November 2004 in several 'ethnic' locations in the neighborhood (Mexican restaurants, supermarkets, the Church, REDA) did not prompt any response. Fourth, the predominant method for the recruitment of interview partners (using members or leaders of neighborhood organizations as starting points of snowballs) may have lead to a certain bias in favor of the *organized* Mexican or Mexican-American population.

Interviewing

This section describes the resident interview situation and structuring. The following aspects are discussed:

- Interview pre-tests,
- contact with interviewees,
- context, e.g. interview location, language, use of technical facilities,
- structuring and focus of the interviews and its guideline,
- capturing of the interview information, and
- compensation for the interview.

As mentioned in the previous chapter, I initiated the resident interview process with two pre-test interviews (Carmen, Francisco). The main purpose of the pre-test interviews was to assess the appropriateness of the questions included in the interview guideline, as well as the timing of the interviews[131]. The interview guideline was considerably modified after the pre-tests, for instance in terms of the formulation and order of questions[132].

---

130 The reasons for a stated lack of interest are not entirely clear. In one case an older first generation Mexican women stated that she had already provided an interview for a previously conducted research about the West Side. In another case I was brusquely rejected, but without reasons. In a third case, the interview was politely refused, also without providing any reason.

131 Although the actual duration of the interviews differed depending on the personalities and narratives of the interviewees, the idea was that the interview could be finished in one hour, without rushing through it.

132 For instance, one question of the pre-test interview guideline ("What does it mean for you to have these Mexican contacts?") was not understood and therefore eliminated. A further important adjustment of the pre-test to the definite interview guideline lay in first asking about ways to access certain resources (getting started, finding a job, finding housing, being helped, celebrating, view questions 6 to 10 in Annex 4), before asking about the social and

I contacted the interviewees in a variety of ways. In most cases, the contact and agreement for an interview was established by phone, after I had received the telephone number from a 'gatekeeper' or a former interview partner. In other cases (Theo, Raul), I directly asked residents for the possibility of an interview, in the context of neighborhood events or celebrations. In two cases (Carmen, Juana), the contact and agreement for an interview was established per e-mail. In a further two cases (Ronald, Leon), a former interview partner (Dora) asked for the opportunity of an interview on my behalf. In the case the contact was established per telephone or e-mail, I asked the interviewees if they preferred to meet 'informally' prior to the interview. Only one interview partner (Monica) conceded to this proposition, whereas the others preferred the interviews to be conducted without a previous meeting.

In order to ensure a comfortable setting and atmosphere during the interview and to minimize inconvenience for the interviewees (Fontana/Frey 1994: 366f., Hermanns 2003: 367), I asked them for their preferences in terms of the interview locations, language and recording techniques. As a result, most of the interviews (16) were carried out at the interviewees' homes. Seven interviews took place at the interviewees' work places – in all of these cases the interviewees were male. Four interviews were conducted in other places, e. g. in cafés or a school. Usually, the interviews started five or ten minutes after meeting the informant, as a certain time span before starting the interview was used for informal conversations, looking at the apartment or at photos.

The informants were asked about their preferences in terms of the language used during the interview: 15 interviews were conducted in English, 11 in Spanish and one in both languages[133]. At the beginning of the interviews, the

---

particularly co-ethnic contacts of interviewees. This was in order to prevent interviewees feeling they needed to defend their co-ethnic contacts or describe them in the most favorable way. Also, following discussions with university colleagues the questions were grouped into categories derived from the conceptual framework, in order to make sure that important issues were addressed and that this was done in a systematic way. The general information on people's family, professional and personal situation was placed at the end of the interview guideline.

[133] Usually the question of the interview language was clear from the outset and a function of the immigrant group the respect interviewee belonged to. Most of the longstanding Mexican-American residents of the West Side wanted to conduct the interview in English – many of them did not speak Spanish. In contrast, the first generation immigrants felt more comfortable

interview partners were ensured confidentiality of the interview results, and asked for permission to record the interview. Only one interviewee (JEV) refused the use of the tape recorder, for privacy purposes. In this and one other case[134], the interview content was computerized on the basis of notes taken during the interview, immediately after conducting the interviews.

The interviews were semi-structured, based on an interview guideline including 22 open-ended questions and a few additional questions on the person. Questionnaire versions were compiled both in English and in Spanish (see Annex 4). The use of a semi-standardized interviewing technique, as opposed to narrative interviews (Fontana/Frey 1994: 366, Hopf 2003: 355ff.) seemed most appropriate due to the relatively narrowly defined focus of the research. The intention was thus to strike a balance between

- on the one hand, an open interview process in which every interviewed person was allowed sufficient space to elaborate on his/her views on the topic at interest, as well as bringing up aspects not anticipated (Hopf 2003: 354), and
- on the other, an interview situation focusing on previously identified research gaps, in the large research context on residential segregation and social capital (see chapter 4).

After providing a brief and general introduction about the objective and topic of the research[135] and the interview process (Wolff 2003: 344ff., Hermanns 2003: 367), I organized the interviews along broad, theory-informed topics, marked as headings in the interview guideline (Annex 4). These are: Life history on the West Side, Getting along and ahead, Social networks and spaces, Pros and cons of the West Side and Future plans. Although the questions in the guideline are pre-formulated and organized in a chronological

in Spanish. An exception was the young recent immigrants (Tamara, Marco) who stated they were fine with either of the two languages, and one adult recent immigrant (Elena) who switched from Spanish to English in the course of the interview.

[134] Due to a technical problem with recording the interview, a further interview (Monica) was equally not recorded and could thus not be fully transcribed.

[135] This introduction laid out the research topic in quite general terms: "(…) about the living situation of the Mexican population in the West Side of St. Paul". This was done with the intention of not influencing the informants' responses too much. On the other hand, as a matter of research ethics it was important to provide genuine, albeit general, information about the topic of the research and its purposes (view Caesperlein/Gliemann 2003: 82, Wolff 2003: 346).

order, with respect to the above-mentioned topics, I tried to maintain a maximum of flexibility during the interview (Strauss/Corbin 1990: 178, Hopf 2003: 358). This means that in the case the interview partners addressed certain topics prior to the moment anticipated by the interview guideline, I did not impose the latter order[136]. Or, depending on specific concerns of the respective interview partner, I interposed questions not asked of other informants[137]. At the end of the interview, the interviewees were asked some additional questions on their migration, housing, family and working situation (Annex 4). These questions served as a guarantee of the availability of socio-economic and demographic context variables deemed concept-relevant. The duration of the interviews was between one and two hours. In only one case I visited the informant (Dora) a second time, the whole interview taking roughly three hours.

I captured all but two interviews with a tape recorder, for their subsequent transcription. Simultaneous to the interviews, I took written notes about the responses of my informants[138]. In the two or three hours following each interview I compiled notes on the interview atmosphere, the characteristics of the interviewee and certain 'surprising' specifics, e.g. with respect to the informant's life history or the interviewer-interviewee relationship[139]. This was in order to account for non-verbal elements in the communication situa-

136 The choice and organization of topics by the informants may, for instance, provide an indication about their prioritization of issues. For instance, one interviewed resident (JAS) from the outset talked about the experiences of violence in his family and the neighborhood – obviously a central issue to understand his subsequent value judgments and perceptions.

137 An example for this are questions on the legal status of immigrants, an issue of concern to many recent immigrants, with important repercussions on employment and other mobility relevant opportunities. Whereas at the beginning I was adamant in asking about the legal status of the respective interviewee, in the last resident interviews I directly addressed this topic – and usually got straight answers.

138 This process proved important at least in one opportunity when the recording technique did not function.

139 The influence of the interview context on its outcome is particularly highlighted by deconstructivist and feminist researchers (Fontana/Frey 1994: 369, Denzin/Lincoln 1994a: 12). For instance, class-based hierarchical or gendered relationships between the interviewer and the interviewee may lead to a 'strategic narration' (view Caesperlein/Gliemann 2003: 47) or to certain experiences or feelings of the informant not being expressed at all. Likewise, the subjectivity of the interviewer and/or researcher influences his or her attitude during the interview and subsequent data interpretation (Fontana/Frey 1994: 372, Addison 1992: 111).

tion that may have influenced the responses of the questions (Fontana/Fey 1994: 371, Caesperlein/Gliemann 2003: 49).

At the end of each interview, I expressed my gratitude towards the interview partner by handing over a gift certificate from a local department store. Furthermore, on two occasions I presented some preliminary results of my field work in front of the women self-help group "Hispanic Women in Action" [140], also seeking their feed-back and complementary information to my hitherto interpretations (Strauss/Corbin 1990: 252, see chapter 5.5). This happened after having participated for several months in the meetings of this group and interviewing some of its members. Additionally, I was explicitly asked for a presentation. To other interview partners, information about the ongoing interview process was provided in the context of informal meetings in the case where this was requested[141].

Interview analysis

Out of the 27 resident interviews conducted, I fully transcribed 22. The remaining five interviews were the last ones carried out (Arturo, Esteban, Mercedes, Fermin, Marco) and selectively summarized, according to the most relevant research issues, as narrowed down through the analysis of the previous interviews.

The proceeding in the analysis of the interviews was oriented by the principles of grounded theory: Varying intensity in the analysis of interviews, focus of analysis on maximal differing cases with respect to the variables identified as relevant (gender, class, immigrant group, etc.), building links to existing theories or generation of new conceptual links by use of different coding-techniques and connectedness of conceptual and theoretical conclusions to empirical data at their origin (Strauss/Corbin 1994: 280, Strauss/Corbin 1990: 30f., Dey 1999: 7, Glaser 1992: 38ff.). The adherence

[140] Original: *Mujeres Hispanas en Acción*.

[141] Such meetings only occurred with very few interview partners (Dora, Ronald, Theo, Harry), in the context of West Side neighborhood events. On the (limited) use of research results for the informants, see Wolff 2003: 348.

to these principles helped to systematize the interpretation of the empirical data and thereby maximize its plausibility[142].

The use of a relatively large number of interviews, at least in qualitative terms, seemed appropriate due to the intended heterogeneity of the sample (Kuzel 1992: 41). The interviewees should show heterogeneity in terms of their socio-economic background, gender, immigrant group and age (see chapter 3.2). The idea behind adopting multiple perspectives was that in this way a maximum spectrum of outcomes became possible, e.g. in terms of the occurrence of social mobility or in terms of judgments on neighborhood effects. Based on a first reading, I initially identified some salient issues and patterns.

After conducting and reading all the interviews at least once, I selected five very different cases (Carmen, Roland, Elena, John and Linda) for a more in-depth analysis. Variation was established in terms of the interviewees' gender, socio-economic background, immigrant group and age, and also the interviewees' valuation of their co-ethnic contacts and the consequences of living on the West Side. Based on the intensive analysis of these interviews, typical as well as untypical or exceptional cases or situations were identified, for instance the "typical member of an ethnical support organization" or the "untypical case of life-long engagement in neighborhood organizations" (view chapter 7.1.2). The property of being a "typical" (or untypical) case was attributed on the basis of the comparison with structurally similar cases from the entire interview sample[143].

The broad concepts derived from the literature (social networks, social mobility, benefits and disadvantages) were used as starting points for the text

---

142 The focus on plausibility rather than representativity constitutes one of the key differences in data validation procedures of qualitative and quantitative research (Strauss/Corbin 1994: 278).

143 The consolidation of a "typical" case can be illustrated by way of an example. For instance, for Linda, a recent female Mexican immigrant, the contact with the "Hispanic Women in Action Group" (MHA) was instrumental in achieving some social mobility via access to training courses and a first, part-time job. The interviews with some other members of the same or similar support groups (Hermosa, Rita, Tonia) show that they gained similar benefits. The participation in the group's weekly events (see "observation" in chapter 5.3.3) however also showed that the comparison only holds good for married females, as, e.g. single-educating Mexican immigrant mothers do not have the time to participate in large social networks and are thus deprived of a number of benefits related thereto.

analysis, in the course of which I added more themes and sub-themes (Ryan/Bernard 2003: 275, Miller/Crabtree 1992b: 99f., chapter 4.4). However, afterwards I made use of open and axial or selective coding, each of these constituting a different tool in the progressive concept-building on the basis of a qualitative data set (Strauss/Corbin 1990: 59ff., Glaser 1992: 75ff.). Additionally, I used contextual notes taken a short time after completing each interview for data interpretation (Fontana/Frey 1994: 369).

In the present document, in order to empirically ground the conceptual interpretations realized in the process of the interview analysis, the presentation of cross-case or general patterns is complemented with the presentation of five individual, 'typical' or 'untypical' cases, with respect to conceptually relevant aspects (e. g., the 'typical' and the 'untypical' member of an ethnic neighborhood group, see chapter 7.1) (Addison 1992: 116, Hubermann/Miles 1994: 436ff.). These cases correspond to the interviews analyzed in in-depth (Carmen, Ronald, Elena, John, Linda). Further ways of enhancing the validity and reliability of the results is by comparing results achieved from multiple sources and methods of inquiry, i.e. triangulation (ibid: 438, Gilchrist 1992: 87).

5.3.2 Expert interviews

All together I conducted 15 expert interviews, between November 2004 and June 2005. The first three expert interviews (Experts 1,2 and 3) were carried out before or at the beginning of the interviews with residents. The purpose of these interviews was primarily explorative, i.e. to gather information about the organizations in which the experts worked and to gain a first impression on the institutional landscape of the West Side. Furthermore, the first interviewed experts were asked about referrals for resident interviewees.

The majority of the expert interviews (12) were carried out between April and July 2005. The purpose of this main round of expert interviews was to focus on housing policy and planning issues related to ethnic segregation or clustering, as well as to assess the benefits and costs of ethnic clustering from a different point of view than the one of the interviewed residents (see chapter 5.5 on triangulation, see Flick 2003: 310, Kelle/Erzberger 2003: 303).

The sampling of expert interview partners was purposeful (Kuzel 1992: 40), following a broad set of criteria: The experts should be individuals working in organizations fulfilling one of the following conditions:

- Location **on** the WS, with important connections to the Mexican or Hispanic population and/or a focus on community and housing development,
- Location **outside** of the West Side, with a specific present or past working relationships with the West Side and/or the Hispanic population,
- Location **outside** of the West Side, with an influence on housing and community development sectors in the West Side and Twin Cities' areas.

Inside the West Side neighborhood, I conducted interviews with representatives of the West Side Citizens' Organization (WSCO), Neighborhood Development Alliance (NeDA), Riverview Economic Development Association (REDA), Hispanic Women in Action, Neighborhood House, Guadalupe Church and Roosevelt Elementary School. Outside the West Side, representatives from Hispanic Advocacy and Community Empowerment through Research (HACER), City of St. Paul Planning and Economic Development Department, St. Paul Public Housing Agency (St. Paul PHA, two experts), the Federal Department for Housing and Urban Development (HUD), Housing Link and the Minnesota House of Representatives were interviewed. An overview of the characteristics of the organizations of the experts is provided in Annexes 3 and 7.

The interviews were semi-structured, based on interview guidelines with open-ended questions. Eight interviews (Experts 1, 2, 4, 5, 6, 7, 8 and 9) followed a standardized interview guideline about the respective organizations´ main activity fields and objectives, and/or issues of interest or concern regarding the Mexican or Latino population on the West Side (Annex 5). The remaining interviews (Experts 3, 10, 11, 12, 13, 14 and 15) were prepared individually before every interview and included some more specific questions on the expert's work fields[144]. All the expert interviews were con-

[144] Initially the intention was to use the same guideline for *all* the expert interviews. This however proved unsatisfactory particularly towards the second half of the expert interviews when it became necessary to probe deeper into e.g. housing or educational policy specifics.

ducted in English, except one (Expert 4) that was carried out in Spanish. The interviews took between 45 minutes and 2 hours and, in all but two cases (Expert 4, Expert 2a), these took place at the informants' work places[145].

Notwithstanding the different work fields and/or environments of the interviewed experts, the following topics were addressed in *each* of the interviews conducted between April and July:

1. Advantages and disadvantages of the spatial concentration of ethnic households, and/or
2. Costs and benefits of ethnic social capital.
3. Community and housing development in ethnic or segregated neighborhoods.

All the interviews were tape-recorded, for their subsequent transcription. Whereas I transcribed the first eleven interviews word by word, I transcribed the last four interviews selectively, focusing on the answers most relevant to the research. The transcriptions of the expert interviews can be viewed in a separate document from this thesis. The analysis followed the topics established in the context of the analysis of the resident interviews.

5.3.3 Complementary qualitative methods

Additional to the resident and expert interviews, the following research methods were used:

- Observation,
- Neighborhood walks, and
- Group discussions.

I sought out these methods to complement and/or cross-reference findings from the resident and expert interviews.

<u>Observation</u>

I used observation as a research method from the beginning until the end of the interview process (November 2004 to July 2005), mostly by participating in neighborhood events and/or meetings of neighborhood groups. I participated in the weekly meetings and in some training sessions of the Hispanic

---

[145] In both mentioned exceptions the interviews took place in the restaurant of a Latino supermarket on the West Side.

women self-help group "Hispanic Women in Action" (MHA), in several neighborhood events (e. g. *Cinco de Mayo* celebrations), attended a Spanish Church service and parish gatherings as well as two meetings of the West Side Citizens Organization (WSCO). The events I participated in are illustrated in the table in Annex 6.

The purposes of the observation were twofold: On the one hand, it served to complement already existing information on the community organizations on the West Side. For instance, in the two community gatherings of WSCO, important information could be gathered about the socio-economic and ethnic characteristics of residents typically attending WSCO-meetings[146]. In the meetings of MHA, important impressions on the interaction between the women could be gathered, as an additional source of information to what some of these women had referred to in the interviews[147]. On the other hand, the observation served to corroborate information gained in the interviews. For instance, the assistance at several Guadalupe Church services or gatherings – separate ones in the English and Spanish languages - illustrated the social and cultural divide between different Hispanic residents on the West Side in a particularly vivid way.

<u>Neighborhood walks</u>

After deciding to conduct my case study on the West Side and gathering some initial quantitative and qualitative information about the neighborhood, I walked through the neighborhood on several occasions[148]. The purpose of these neighborhood walks was to familiarize myself with the neighborhood and its different parts (commercial, residential, industrial; higher and lower income), as well as to achieve a visual impression of the Hispanic imprints in the neighborhood, e. g. murals representing elements of Mayan or Aztec culture.

---

[146] As a matter of fact, very few Hispanics attended these meetings. Both included debates between the community and real estate professionals about a big residential and commercial development project on the West Side.

[147] For instance, the statement about women's empowerment through participation in the group was vividly illustrated by seeing some of them conducting education sessions on Sexually Transmitted Diseases (STDs) and HIV/AIDS in front of the other women. Also the atmosphere of confidence and solidarity among the women was starkly confirmed in these meetings.

[148] I was accompanied on one of this walks by one of the gate-keepers, a Hispanic employee of the West Side Citizens' Organization (WSCO). The others I conducted alone.

Group discussions

Towards the end of the interview process, once in May and once in July 2005, I presented some tentative results of my research to the "Hispanic Women in Action" group. As I had participated in this group for six months, conducted interviews with several members of it and had been asked to make the presentation, this seemed an appropriate way to express my recognition of the support I had received from the women. I also used these opportunities to inquire about issues that had remained unclear during the interview process, or to corroborate my findings till then by the communicated feed-back (Strauss/Corbin 1990: 228, Flick 2003: 316). In the presentations and the questions I focused on the aspects of the research I assumed to be of most relevance to my audience (Strauss/Corbin 1990: 228)[149].

5.4 Summary

In this chapter the methodology chosen in this research was presented. I aimed at complying with two imperatives every research endeavor is confronted with: The one is to take into consideration the existing state of research on a given topic and its present research gaps. This was realized here with the combination of an inductive and a deductive research approach. The second one is to ensure the methodological adequacy with respect to the research questions. On the one hand, this was intended by focusing on qualitative, open-ended (resident and expert) interviews as the main source of information. On the other hand, additional methodologies (e.g. observation, neighborhood walks, review of statistics and documents) were used to complement and cross-check the results from the interviews. The chosen, predominantly qualitative methodology seemed adequate for providing answers to the research focus on the subjective perceptions and experiences of immigrants or individual with an immigrant background towards ethnic clustering. A discussion on future research needs on our topic and their methodological implications will be held at the end of this document.

[149] For instance, I asked about the relationships between the Hispanic groups on the West Side, as well as on the quality of schools on the West Side.

6 The city and neighborhood context

The objective of this chapter is to assess the local context in which the empirical study of this research took place: the neighborhood of the West Side of St. Paul, the City of St. Paul and the Twin Cities' Metropolitan Area[150]. On the one hand, this is important as it provides necessary complementary information to that collected in the case study: For instance, most of the longstanding Mexican-American immigrants of the West Side refer to the neighborhood's history when describing personal experiences of discrimination and neglect. Also, the perception and practice of Mexican or Mexican-American residents of the West Side occur under certain context-related conditions (e.g. demographic, socio-economic), some of which will be discussed here.

On the other hand, being aware of the urban and neighborhood context of the case study (with respect to history, culture and socio-economic opportunities) helps to reflect on the applicability of its results to other neighborhoods or city regions of the United States (Kaplan/Woodhouse 2004: 579). In other words, what might be a plausible research result for a relatively prosperous Midwestern metropolitan area such as Minneapolis-St. Paul with relatively low immigration and segregation levels, might not be applicable to economically struggling urban regions with a much higher minority population and/or internal socio-economic disparities. What might be true for an ethnically and economically diverse neighborhood such as St. Paul's West Side may not be valid for an economically depressed majority-minority neighborhood elsewhere in the United States.

The present chapter is structured as follows: In the first sub-section, the main demographic and socio-economic characteristics of the City of St. Paul and the Minneapolis-St. Paul Metropolitan Region are described. Particularities of the 'case' of St. Paul and the Twin Cities are clarified by comparing demographic and socio-economic characteristics of the latter metro area with others in the United States. The second and third sub-sections are dedicated to the neighborhood of the West Side. After providing a brief historical ac-

150 "Twin Cities" due to the existence of two major urban centers, Minneapolis and St. Paul, in close proximity of approximately 15 km from each other. Although the two cities grew independently from each other, they now form the city centers of a closely connected urban region or "Metro Area".

count, its socio-economic and demographic characteristics are described, as well as the situation of the Mexican and/or Latino population in the neighborhood. Based on a classification scheme in the literature (Johnson et al. 2003), the West Side is categorized with respect to other possible types of ethnically and culturally diverse neighborhoods. I close this chapter with a summary.

6.1 City of St. Paul and Twin Cities Metropolitan Area

The City of St. Paul is the capital of the State of Minnesota, bordering at its south-eastern edge with the State of Wisconsin, in the northern Midwest of the United States. It forms part of the Minneapolis-St. Paul Metropolitan Area, usually referred to as the "Twin Cities" metro region. While the City of St. Paul has a total population of approximately 290,000 inhabitants, and Minneapolis 350,000, the Twin Cities Metro Region hosts a population of almost 3 million people (http://mumford.albany.edu/census/data.html). The location of the city and metro area, as well of as the West Side neighborhood - the study area of this research - is illustrated in maps 1 and 2.

6.1.1 Administrative and governance structure

The City of St. Paul is internally organized into seven Council Wards and thirteen Planning Districts. Whereas the Wards form political entities under the direction of one of seven elected City Council members, the Planning Districts constitute administrative and technical divisions within the wards. On the scale of Planning Districts, District Councils represent the citizens' concerns with planning and land use questions. The West Side of St. Paul is identical with the Planning District number 3 of the same name and forms part of Council Ward number 2. The West Side Citizens Organization (WSCO, see Annex 7) acts as its District Council.

Map 1: St. Paul in United States of America

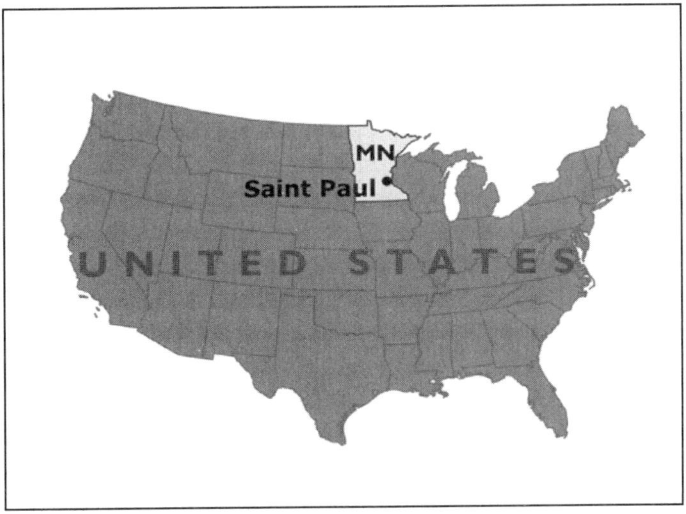

Map 2: Twin Cities Metro Area and West Side

Source: Eric Myott

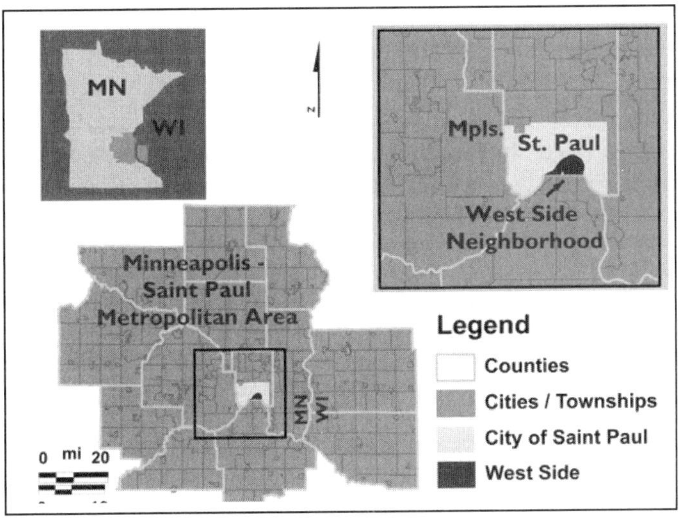

Source: Eric Myott

As mentioned before, the Twin Cities Metropolitan Region consists of two urban cores, Minneapolis and St. Paul City respectively. Including the latter big urban cores, the metro area hosts 188 cities and 7 counties[151], St. Paul forming part of Ramsey County (www.metrocouncil.org).

Since its creation in 1967, the Twin Cities' Metropolitan Council acts as a regional policy and planning agency, as a provider for certain public services (e.g. transport, water and wastewater management), and implementing agency for affordable housing in municipalities not served by their own Public Housing Authority (www.metrocouncil.org, Goetz 2003: 96)[152]. The St. Paul Public Housing Authority (PHA) manages the public housing programs in the jurisdiction of St. Paul, owning a total of 4,258 public housing units and administering 4,059 Section 8 voucher units (PHA Monthly Management Report).

6.1.2 Economic and demographic characteristics

The City of St. Paul emerged as a water and rail crossroads of fur and lumber trade in the mid 19th Century[153]. While at the beginning of the 20th Century constituting one of the main livestock and meatpacking centers in the Midwest of the United States, St. Paul today is predominantly service-sector oriented (http://mumford.albany.edu/census/data)[154]. However St. Paul, along with the City of Minneapolis, shows one of the largest concentrations of high-technology industry in the United States, including the manufacture of computers, electronics and medical instruments. The economic situation of the Twin Cities' Metro Area can be considered as healthy: compared to the 22 biggest US metro areas, it shows the second-highest adult labor force participation rates, the lowest unemployment rate and the fourth-highest

---

[151] In contrast, the U.S. Census Bureau defines the "Minneapolis-St. Paul Metropolitan Statistical Area", short "Metro Area" as a 13-county area surrounding the Twin Cities and going into Wisconsin (http://minneapolis.about.com).

[152] The effectiveness of the Metropolitan Council in promoting affordable housing throughout the Twin Cities' urban region, has however been viewed as negligible, particularly from the 1980s onwards (Goetz 2003: 97ff.).

[153] In 1847, St. Paul became the capital city of the State of Minnesota (www.st-paul.com). The river trade was substituted by railroad commerce in the last three decades of the 19th century.

[154] Whereas occupations in the service sector showed a 153%-rise between 1990 and 2000, occupations in the production sector rose only slightly (9%) and agricultural and forestry occupations fell by 42% (http://mumford.albany.edu/census/data).

share of residents working in educational, health and social services (www.brook.edu)[155].

As many other cities in the United States, the City of St. Paul has become more multi-ethnic and -cultural in the past decades. From a city with a predominantly Anglo-white population it has attracted an increasing number of immigrants from different parts of the World. This is reflected in a decreasing proportion of the non-Hispanic white population of St. Paul, from 88.6% in 1980 to 63.6% in the year 2000 (http://mumford.albany.edu/census/data). The foreign-born population of the Central Cities of the Twin Cities Metro Area more than doubled from 6.6% in 1990 to 14.4% in 2000 (http://mumford.albany.edu/census/data). Tables 3 and 4 display the presence of the major racial and/or ethnic groups for both the Twin Cities Metro Region and the City of St. Paul, between 1980 and 2000.

Table 3: Racial and ethnic composition of Twin City Metro Area, 1980 - 2000

	Total population	**Non-Hispanic White**	**Non-Hispanic Black**	**Hispanic**	**Asian**
1980	2,150,767	2,031,700	49,426	22,425	19,855
		94.5%	2.3%	1%	0.9%
1990	2,538,089	2,322,898	88,149	37,879	65,580
		91.5%	3.5%	1.5%	2.6%
2000	2,979,485	2,514,503	180,006	99,121	138,066
		84.7%	6.1%	3.3%	4.7%

Source: http://mumford.albany.edu/census/data.

Table 4: Racial and ethnic composition of St. Paul, 1980 - 2000

	Total population	**Non-Hispanic White**	**Non-Hispanic Black**	**Hispanic**	**Asian**
1980	270,230	239,341	13,099	7,864	2,695

155 However, other sources point to manifestations of poverty in the metro area, arguably due to its accentuated socio-economic polarization. For instance, according to the "Living Cities" report of the Brookings Institution one in six children in the metro area lives in a family with no parents in the labor force, ranking 16th with respect to the other 23 metro areas (www.brookings.edu/es/urban/livingcities/MinneapolisStPaul.htm).

		88.6%	4.8%	2.9%	1%
1990	272,235	218,750	19,569	11,476	19,197
		80.4%	7.2%	4.2%	7.1%
2000	287,151	183,898	37,062	22,715	38,374
		64.0%	12.9%	7.9%	13.4%

Source: http://mumford.albany.edu/census/data.

The graphs indicate an increase of black, Hispanic and Asian inhabitants between 1980 and 2000, in both absolute and relative terms. This is coupled with a clear decrease in proportions of the non-Hispanic white, with respect to the total population. Although these patterns can be stated in both the Twin Cities' Metro Area and the City of St. Paul, the decrease of the non-Hispanic white population is much more significant in St. Paul in which the latter group even experienced an absolute population loss[156]. Out of the mentioned racial and/or ethnic groups, Asians have seen the highest growth in the period from 1980 to 2000. While the Asian racial group is composed of nationals of different countries (Cambodian, Chinese, Filipino, Japanese, Korean, Vietnamese), the Hmong from Laos form the biggest ethno-national group[157]. When considering the period between 1990 and 2000, Hispanics grew most in the City of St. Paul.

Mexicans constitute the strongest country group among all immigrants to the Twin Cities. Among the Twin Cities' Hispanic population, 66% are of Mexican origin. However, some Latino country groups have grown much

[156] In this regard, the Twin City- and St. Paul-related figures reflect the common characteristic of the socio-spatial organization and evolution of the American metropolis: A decrease of the white population is paralleled by high growth rates of the non-white population in the central cities. The population growth in the Metro Area clearly exceeds the one in the Central City that tends to be abandoned of the economically stronger and predominantly white population. However, the fact that the City of St. Paul shows a positive absolute population growth indicates a relatively lower urban-suburban exodus as this is the case in other American metropolis (http://mumford.albany.edu/census/data).

[157] The root of the refugee status of the Hmong, an ethnic minority group mainly from Laos, lies in their alliance with the US in the Vietnam War. While the Hmong altogether represent no more than 0.5% of the US's foreign-born population, in the Minneapolis-St. Paul metro area they constitute the second-biggest immigrant group after the Mexicans, forming 19% of the area's foreign-born population in 2000 (www.migrationinformation.org, www.brookings.edu/es/urban/livingcities/MinneapolisStPaul.htm).

more than Mexicans in the ten years between 1990 and 2000[158]. For instance, the presence of 'new Latinos'[159] from Ecuador and El Salvador has highly increased in the Twin Cities between 1990 and 2000, similar to occurrences in other metropolitan areas in the US (Logan 2001, also view chapter 2.3.1). Table 5 illustrates the population numbers and changes of common Hispanic or Latino country groups in the year 2000, in the Twin Cities′ Metro Area:

Table 5: Hispanic or Latino country groups in Metro Area, 1990 - 2000

	Total Hispanic or Latino population	**Mexico**	**Puerto Rico**	**Ecua-dor**	**Cuba**	**El Salva-dor**	**Colom-bia**
1990	37,879	21,889	2,706	145	1,118	284	1,003
%		57.8	7.1	0.4	3.0	0.7	0.3
2000	99,121	65,469	5,333	2,163	1,841	1,721	1,671
%		66.0	5.4	2.2	1.9	1.7	1.7
%Growth	161.8	199.1	97.1	1391.7	64.7	506.0	66.6

Source: http://mumford.albany.edu/census/data.

In what kind of neighborhoods do the different racial and ethnic groups live in the City of St. Paul? This question is directly related to the concerns of researchers and policy makers that an 'unfavorable' neighborhood environment with respect to certain status-related and ethno-racial variables may negatively impact on people's long-term social and economic opportunities (view chapter 2.1.1). Table 6 compares characteristics of the census tract of the average non-Hispanic white, black, Hispanic and Asian resident in the City of St. Paul in 1990 and 2000. This will help to put into context the West Side's census tract- and neighborhood characteristics further on in this document (tables 10 and 11).

---

158 Although it needs to be taken into account that mathematically small population numbers show higher relative growth figures than large ones, with absolute growth figures remaining constant.

159 As opposed to Latino migrants who have been coming to the US for a longer period, notably Mexicans, Puerto Ricans and Cubans.

Table 6: Census tract characteristics of racial/ethnic groups in St. Paul, 1990 - 2000[160]

Indicator	White		Black		Hispanic		Asian	
	1990	2000	1990	2000	1990	2000	1990	2000
INDICATORS OF ECONOMIC AND HUMAN CAPITAL								
Median HH income	36.61	42.19	27.97	33.61	30.26	35.78	26.74	33.78
% Below Poverty	14.5	12.9	27.9	20.6	22.2	18.5	30.9	22.2
% Homeowners	55.4	56.9	43.2	46.3	50.1	50.5	40.9	48.4
% College educated*	27.6	35.8	19.8	23.1	17.4	21.5	18.2	20.0
% Professional	34.8	39.4	28.2	30.6	26.9	28.7	25.8	27.8
INDICATORS OF IMMIGRATION								
% Foreign-born	6.3	11.6	10.3	17.8	9.9	19.0	16.6	21.4
% Recent immigrants**	3.9	6.2	7.3	10.0	6.8	10.9	12.5	11.4
% Language other than English***	9.9	17.8	15.1	26.3	17.1	29.9	24.1	32.6
INDICATORS OF ETHNCO-RACIAL COMPOSITION[161]								
% Members of own racial/ethnic group	84.3	71.8	27.8	23.8	10.2	15.3	20.6	23.9
% Presence of whites	84.3	71.8	56.2	49.4	71.5	53.3	62.4	48.6

Source: http://mumford.albany.edu/census/data.

*Respondents with at least a Bachelor degree.

** Respondents who have come to the US in the 1990s.

---

160 In the tables on "Neighborhood Inequality", the Lewis Mumford Center presents some additional socio-economic and housing variables for each of the USA's cities (http://mumford.albany.edu/census/data). For the presentation in the present document, I have limited myself to the variables later used in the chapter on the West Side, in order to allow easier reading.

161 In the Lewis Mumford Center tables, these indicators were termed as "indicators of isolation and integration". Due to the inherent value statement in these terms, I modified them into a more neutral terminology.

*** Only those respondents that do not speak another language than English are excluded here.

The figures in the table show that, for all racial and ethnic groups, the neighborhood-indicators of economic and human capital have evolved favorably between 1990 and 2000 – an indicator of the overall positive economic climate in the City. However, both in 1990 and in 2000, the average white inhabitant of St. Paul lives in an environment where his or her neighbor fares much better in educational and economic terms than the neighbors of the average black, Hispanic and Asian[162]. The average Hispanic resident of St. Paul lives in a neighborhood environment in which co-residents fare better economically than in the neighborhood of the average Black and Asian resident. This is less true with respect to educational and professional achievements of neighbors, which are higher for the average black resident of St. Paul.

All the racial and ethnic groups of St. Paul included in table 6 today, i.e. by 2000 live in more diverse neighborhoods than in 1990, as shown by the indicators of immigration and ethno-racial composition. This is not surprising in view of the migration the City has experienced in the last decades. This predominantly Hispanic and Asian migration leads to whites and blacks living in neighborhoods with less members of their own race in 2000 than in 1990, whereas Hispanics and Asians now live in neighborhoods with higher proportions of same-race or –ethnicity residents. All racial groups live in neighborhoods with a higher proportion of own-group members than the overall proportion of each group in the City would suggest (view tables 3 and 4). This discrepancy is highest for the black population (11%), and roughly alike for the other three racial and/or ethnic groups (7-8%)[163].

Although the neighborhood environment variables in the above table seemingly present 'objective' facts and figures, one needs to beware of easy interpretations: It is certainly important to know that the average white resident of St. Paul lives close to neighbors in a more favorable income and educational position than residents belonging to any of the stated minority groups.

---

[162] While the economic discrepancy between white and non-white neighborhoods has slightly diminished between 1990 and 2000, the educational gap has rather widened.

[163] However surprisingly, unlike the national trends, Dissimilarity Indexcs are higher for the Hispanic and Asian, than for the black population in St. Paul: In order to achieve an even distribution of its group with respect to the white population, 43.1% of blacks, 44.2% of Hispanics and 50.7% of Asians would have to move (http://mumford.albany.edu/census).

This may represent a result of discriminatory practices such as 'racial steering' or 'blockbusting' in the private housing market (view chapter 2.1.2). However, the socio-economically unfavorable neighborhood situation of neighbors does not necessarily mean that the individual's social status is directly influenced by this. Furthermore, equating the presence of neighbors of one's own group with 'isolation', or the exposure to white neighbors with 'integration' (as suggested both in the academic and political discourse, as in http://mumford.albany.edu/census/data), implies problematic and unfounded value statements. Not only do the figures not indicate the actual choices and experiences that lead to a given demographic neighborhood setting. They also suggest that 'integration' is only possible by mixing with non-Hispanic *white* residents – by itself a reduced understanding of the idea(l) of increased neighborhood diversity (see chapter 2.3.2).

6.1.3 The Hispanic migration to St.Paul and the Twin Cities

In the following, I want to look at the historic presence of the Hispanic population in St. Paul and the Twin Cities urban region. Such an undertaking is confronted by some data-related challenges: The American decennial Census has only been accessible to the public in digitalized form since 1990[164], variable names related to ethnicity have been modified in the course of the decades[165] and data on the presence of ethnic groups in urban areas is not available for every Census of the 20th Century[166]. The federal censuses have not

---

164 For 1970 and 1980 Census data can be found in hard copy form. Some of this data has been digitalized by research institutions, and is not publicly accessible. Data of censuses from the decades prior to 1970 is gathered in the Integrated Public Use Microdata Series (IPUMS), which consist of sample data posteriorily drawn from all surviving American censuses from 1850 to 2000. Unlike Census data that is provided for population aggregates e. g. census tracts or cities, the IPUMS avails data on individual persons and households. As codes across the censuses are unified, the IPUMS constitute an important resource for historic population research (http://usa.ipums.org/usa/index.html). Pre-1990 data drawn from the IPUMS and from digitalized data of the 1970- and 1980 census was kindly made available to me by the Institute on Race and Poverty of the University of Minnesota's Law School.

165 In the Census years prior to 1980, the US Census enumerated the Hispanic population by using the Spanish surname of the respondent. The 1970 Census form additionally included a question on Hispanic origin. Only from 1980 onwards was ethnicity or nationality determined by self-attribution of the respondent.

166 For confidentiality reasons since 1940, the individual-level data of the IPUMS was not compiled for geographic areas with fewer than 100,000 inhabitants. In the years 1960 and 1970 this limit was 250,000 inhabitants. The strict confidentiality measures also applied to other small aggregates, e. g. population groups, hence the problem of a limited data availabil-

extracted data on single national ancestry before 1980; hence they do not provide digitalized information on the Mexican population either[167].

Table 7 shows the evolution of the population with Spanish surnames (until 1950) and the Hispanic population (from 1970 to 2000) in the Twin Cities Metro Region and the City of St. Paul:

Table 7: Population with Spanish surnames and Hispanic population in Twin Cities Metro Region and City of St. Paul, 1920 - 2000

TWIN CITIES METRO REGION				CITY OF ST. PAUL		
Year	**Total population**	**Population with a Spanish surname**	**% of total population**	**Total population**	**Population with a Spanish surname**	**% of total population**
1920	661,090	1,515	0.2%	227,565	909	0.4%
1930	593,498	3,538	0.6%	209,252	1,518	0.7%
1940	943,700	2,326	0.2%	N/a	N/a	N/a
1950	1,119,040	5,108	0.5%	N/a	N/a	N/a
Year	**Total population**	**Hispanic population**	**% of total population**	**Total population**	**Hispanic population**	**% of total population**
1970*	1,810,649	14,251	0.8%	309,835	6,155	2.0%
1980	2,196,169	22,752	1.0%	270,139	7,845	2.9%
1990	2,464,124	37,448	1.5%	272,235	11,476	4.2%
2000	2,968,806	99,121	3.3%	287,151	22,715	7.9%

Source: Institute on Race on Race and Poverty, based on Integrated Public Use Microdata Series (1920-1940), US Census (1970-2000)
*Also enumeration by using the Spanish surname.

Until today Hispanic migration is relatively small in the Twin Cities' Metro Area and the City of St.Paul as compared to other urban areas of the US (see chapter 6.1.4). However, the figures show that this immigration grew con-

ity about the Hispanic population in St. Paul in the years from 1940 to 1960. It is clear that for the same reasons no ethnicity-related historic data can be extracted from the IPUMS on the level of single neighborhoods, e.g. the West Side (http://usa.ipums.org/usa/index.html).

167 The fact that Mexicans constitute the largest majority among the Hispanic immigrants even today, and much more so in decades prior to the 1990s, needs to be remembered here.

tinuously in the 20th century[168] and marked a particular increase in the last decade from 1990 to 2000. In this period, the Hispanic presence almost tripled in the Twin Cities, a jump previously only experienced in the 30-year period from 1950 to 1970 and to a lesser degree, in the 1920s and 1950s[169]. Already at the end of the 19th century, the Minnesota Sugar Company had recruited the first Mexican and Mexican-American migrants from the southwestern United States for seasonal farm work. However, the history of permanent settlement of Hispanics or Mexicans in Minnesota started with them becoming city-dwellers and working in the St.Paul meat packing industries and railroad construction (McClure 1992: 6f.)[170].

Box 3: Mexican migration to the United States

The history of Hispanic – mostly Mexican – migration to the Twin Cities and the City of St. Paul needs to be considered against the background of transnational labor market dynamics, global politics and US migration law changes (Kaplan/Woodhouse 2004: 580). From the early 20th century onwards, Mexicans enjoyed the dubious privilege of being considered "an ideal back-door source of cheap labor for US-employers" (Calavita 1995: 236), predominantly for agriculture work and railroad construction in the Southern states of the US. Due to their relative geographic proximity and high economic vulnerability, the US could handle immigration policies and restrictions towards Mexico according to its own convenience, depending on the respective levels of labor shortage. For instance, during the 1920s, US employers deposited 20 percent of the pay of Mexican agricultural workers with immigration officials at the border, to ensure the departure of their Mexican workers at the end of the harvest season (ibid: 237). During the depression years in the 1930s, many Mexicans independent of their citizenship status were sent back to Mexico – St. Paul reputedly being one of the first cities in the United States where these kinds of forced expatriations took place (McClure 1992: 9).

---

[168] With an exception of the Depression years between 1930 and 1940, during which very few immigrants entered the United States (Schuck 2003: 84) – Mexicans may have even returned to their country during those years.

[169] Due to the methodology used in the Census until 1970 to determine Hispanic origin by surname, the comparability of the 1950 and 1970-figures is obviously compromised. The latter figures may under-represent the Hispanic population. One reason for this underestimation until 1970 may be that women of Hispanic descent married Anglo-American husbands, thus abandoning their Spanish maiden names.

[170] The transition from seasonal farm work to permanent industrial work-based settlement did not happen directly. Rather, most Mexican families worked on the Minnesota sugar and vegetable fields in the summer months and moved to the City during the winter months.

Table 8: Year of entry of foreign-born Mexican population to St. Paul

Total foreign-born Mexican	**6,016**	
1990 – March 2000	4036	67%
Naturalized citizen	234	6%
Not a citizen	3,802	94%
1980 – 1989	1,344	22%
Naturalized citizen	353	26%
Not a citizen	991	74%
Before 1980	636	11%
Naturalized citizen	403	63%
Not a citizen	233	37%

Source: Census 2000, SF 3 (PCT 20). Own compilation.

Due to the predominantly temporary and/or circular character of migration of Mexican's migration to the United States (Rouse 1992: 25), immigration restrictions were imposed later on Mexicans (by 1965), as on other groups, e.g. migrants from Eastern Europe. The latter had been faced with increasingly severe entry quotas since the 1920s (McClure 1992: 8, Calavita 1995: 236). The *Bracero* Program from the end of the Second World War until 1964 attracted five million Mexican farm workers to the US, plus an equal number of illegal immigrants (Calavita 1995: 237, Schuck 2003: 85): "By the time the *Bracero* Program ended in 1964, a relationship of symbiosis between Mexican immigrants and US employers had become well-entrenched, facilitated and nurtured by over fifty years of policy making" (Calavita 1995: 238). The 1965 Immigration Act contributed to the growing ethnic and cultural diversity of the country by a general relaxation of migration quotas (Goldberg 1992: 202). Whilst the 1965 law posed the first quota on immigrants from Mexico and Latin America, these were relatively favorable towards countries of the Western hemisphere and did not prevent further Mexican immigrants from entering the US (Schuck 2003: 88).

From the last three decades of the 20th century until today, US Immigration policies towards Mexico reflect the conflict between national economic interests seeking cheap labor supply and political restrictionism. The latter has partly been nurtured through an anti-immigrant nativism and the resistance of organized labor against a domestic 'race to the bottom' in labor conditions (Calavita 1995: 238). The Immigration Reform and Control Act of 1986, as well as subsequent immigration bills, combined measures of legalization of undocumented and farm workers with the establishment of a sanction system against employers hiring illegal workers (Calavita 1995: 239f., Schuck 2003: 86). Sanctions against employers have however remained relatively ineffective mostly due to their slack enforcement.

Today, more than 11 million illegal immigrants are estimated to live in the United States, most of them (78%) of Hispanic origin. Their occupational profile has diversified with Hispanics working predominantly in housekeeping, agriculture, food industries, restaurants and hotels (Le Monde, 21 April 2006). Oscillating between policies of repression and regularization, the present administration seeks to establish measures for enforced border control on the one hand, and ensuring the conservation of cheap labor for US employers, on the other (Le Monde, 21 April 2006).

6.1.4 St. Paul and Twin Cities in the national urban context

A further way to illustrate the urban context of my case study is to compare it with other urban areas of the United States, with respective to a set of relevant variables. The ones chosen here are: population size, percentage of foreign-born population, percentage of non-Hispanic white population, poverty rate, dissimilarity index and city-suburb disparities. The following metro areas[171] are compared in table 9: New York City, Detroit, Chicago, Los Angeles and Minneapolis-St. Paul. The choice of the metro areas occurred with the intention of providing a certain variation with respect to their geographic location and their demographic and socio-economic characteristics.

Table 9: Classification of Metro Areas with respect to their demographic, economic and socio-spatial structure in 2000

	New York City	**Detroit**	**Chicago**	**Los Angeles**	**Seattle**	**Mpls.-St. Paul**	**St. Paul City**
Population	9,314,235	4,441,551	8,272,768	9,519.338	2,414,616	2,968,806	287,151
% Foreign-born (*)	33.7 (1)	7.5 (21)	17.2 (3)	36.2 (2)	13.7 (18)	7.1 (25)	14.3
% Hispanics	25.1	2.9	17.1	44.6	5.2	3.3	7.9

[171] The comparison is provided on the level of metro areas, as opposed to city center municipalities, for two reasons. The first is content-related: The metro area rather than the city represents the economic opportunity context of a neighborhood or city dweller. The second is related to data availability: The Lewis Mumford Center compiled metro area profiles in the context of its American Community Survey, based on 2000 Census data. These profiles constitute an excellent source also for more complex measures, such as the Dissimilarity Index (DI) or the city-suburb disparity index.

	New York City	Detroit	Chicago	Los Angeles	Seattle	Mpls.-St. Paul	St. Paul City
% Non-Hispanic white	39.6	69.7	58.0	31.1	76.3	84.7	64.0
Median HH income (**)	41,053 (264)	49,175 (72)	51,680 (54)	42,189 (252)	52,804 (17)	53,450 (13)	38,774
% Below poverty	19.5	10.7	10.5	17.9	7.9	6.7	15.6
Hisp.-white Dissimilarity Index	66.7	45.7	62.1	63.2	31.1	46.6	44.2
City-suburb disparity (***)	289	306	286	149	73	251	(251)

Source: For Metro Area: http://mumford.albany.edu/census/data. For St. Paul: Own compilation from Census 2000, Summary File 1 (P1, P7, P8, P4, P21), SF3 3 (P53, P57).

* In parenthesis, a ranking of this metro area with respect to all metro areas in the US from 1 to 331, in terms of its attractiveness to immigrants – based on the percentage of foreign-born population.

** In parenthesis, a ranking of this metro area with respect to all metro areas in the US from 1 to 331, in terms of economic well-being indicators of income levels, unemployment and educational achievement.

*** The position of this metro area in a ranking system of all metro areas in the US from 1 to 326, in terms of disparity level in economic well-being indicators between cities and suburbs.

Based on the above comparison, some of the already discussed demographic and socio-economic patterns of the Twin Cities' Metro Area stand out: With respect to other big metropolitan areas of the United States the foreign-born population is relatively small in the Twin Cities. The same can be stated with respect to the number of Hispanics living there – especially if compared to the situation in traditional Mexican-Hispanic migration destinations, such as Los Angeles, New York and Chicago. However, out of 331 metropolitan areas in the United States, the Twin Cities' region constituted the 25th most attractive one to immigrants in 2000. In 1990, this ranking indicator figured at 32 (http://mumford.albany.edu/census/data), which indicates not only an increasingly diverse urban population, but also a rising popularity of the Twin Cities as a migration destination relative to other urban regions in the US.

The figures above suggest that this (new) attractiveness to immigrants is related to the relatively favorable economic situation of the Twin Cities. Compared to the other cities, the Twin Cities possess the highest median household income, and fewer households with an income below the federally determined poverty line. Even more important, in a national economic well-being ranking the Twin Cities in position 13, are much better positioned than all the other metro areas mentioned here, except Seattle. The Hispanic-white Dissimilarity Index figures in the middle ranges, may partly be explained by the relatively small Hispanic population in the Twin Cities[172]. In spite of its relatively positive economic indicators, the Twin Cities' shows relatively high city-suburb disparities. This corresponds to the relatively inferior economic indicators of the City of St. Paul with respect to those of the Metro Area.

The above comparison clearly suggests the need for caution in trading results or recommendations of findings across highly disparate city contexts. Thus, the results of this case study should be compared to neighborhoods located in urban areas and cities of similar demographic and socio-economic characteristics such as the Twin Cities and St. Paul: economically prospering, majority-white, but of growing ethnic diversity (also see Kraus 2004: 283). This is important, as perceptions on residential segregation may be more optimistic, or not an issue at all, in a relatively wealthy urban environment such as Minneapolis-St. Paul, both on the part of immigrants and on the part of the 'majority-white' population. Or, they may be more negative in such a context, as city inhabitants are less used to, and have not yet learnt to live with diversity compared to inhabitants of more longstanding migration destinies. Dealing with ethnically-based spatial clustering may be easier for policy makers and planners in a relatively small urban area, with relatively low segregation levels. Or, it may be harder for them, because of the non-availability of support infrastructure and a lack of policy and planning exper-

---

172 As pointed out in chapter 2.1.1 and 2.3.1, many researchers have found that the segregation levels of Hispanics tend to increase in relation to their population in urban areas (e.g. Zubrinsky Charles 2003: 172, Iceland 2004: 264). However, it is clear that size is not the only factor: In this example for instance Seattle has a lower segregation index than the Twin Cities, but a slightly higher Hispanic population. For the problems related to comparing Dissimilarity Indices across urban areas of different sizes or different spatial configurations see www.census.gov, Jargowsky 1997: 261f.).

tise in dealing with ethnic and racial diversity. These aspects will be addressed again in chapters 8 and 9.

6.2 The West Side of St. Paul

The neighborhood of the West Side of St. Paul, focus of the case study of this research, has a total of 16,133 inhabitants (Census 2000, SF1, P1)[173]. It is located south of downtown St. Paul[174] and marked by distinct physical boundaries: While it is surrounded by the Mississippi River in the north, west and east, the West Side's Southern border coincides with those of the City of St. Paul and Ramsey County (see map 3)[175]. Topographically, the West Side includes the lowlands or so-called "Flats" bordering the Mississippi river and occupying the north-east of the neighborhood, and the highlands or "Bluffs" located south-west of Wabasha and Concord Street in the neighborhood (HACER 2002: 7, see map 3). In its eastern part, the I-52 Freeway cuts across the neighborhood in a north-south direction. The St. Paul Downtown Airport is located between the Freeway and the eastern neighborhood border with the river.

The West Side includes a considerable variety of land uses. The "Flats" area is predominantly used for industrial purposes, with a general office-service district at its northern border with the river[176]. The "Bluffs" area is predominantly residential, with varying densities: While single-family structures predominate in the southern and western part of the "Bluffs", multi-family

---

[173] In the following, 1990 and 2000 Census data referred to will be indicated by the respective variable names and the location of the original tables in Summary Files (SFs) 1 to 4 in the American Fact Finder (http://factfinder.census.gov). A list of the consulted variables can be viewed in Annex 1. The sorting system of the digitalized Census data has been explained in chapter 5.2.1.

[174] The neighborhood's name "West Side" of St. Paul can be explained taking into account the general flow of the Mississippi River from north to south in the US, and historic settlement patterns on the 'west bank' of the River today referred to as the "Flats" (HACER 2002: 7, www.rchs.com).

[175] Municipalities bordering the West Side in the South are: West St. Paul, South St. Paul and Mendota Heights. All of these belong to Dakota County.

[176] This area has been the object of land use-related disputes between the City of St. Paul, private developers and West Side residents represented by the West Side Citizens' Organization (WSCO), about a planned high-end commercial, service and residential development at the Riverview. Issues of controversy run around building design and heights, but also touch on questions of economic and social viability, in the context of the City of St. Paul in general and the West Side neighborhood in particular (www.WSCO.org).

residential usage prevails in the north and east. The main commercial activities of the neighborhood are concentrated around the junctions of Concord Street, Robert Street and Wabasha Avenue, continuing southwards alongside Concord. Additional commercial clusters run alongside Smith and Stryker Avenues, although on a smaller scale[177]. The businesses (small- to mid-size grocery stores, hair dressers, bakeries etc.) located in the commercial areas of the neighborhood are predominantly community-oriented, although some of the Mexican restaurants and grocery stores serve a clientele beyond the West Side neighborhood.

Map 3: West Side neighborhood

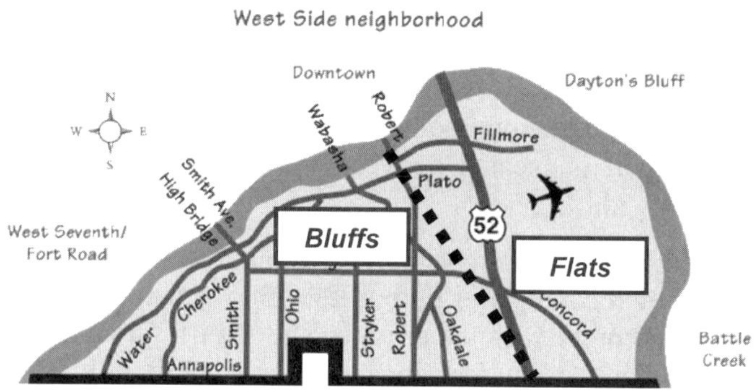

Source: www.stpaul.gov

The West Side's population is served by several social service institutions, including three elementary schools[178], two high schools[179], one clinic, a vari-

177 The commercial routes of today coincide with the original streetcar lines, e.g. in Robert, Concord and Stryker streets. Furthermore, commercial buildings were formerly concentrated along routes ascending the Bluffs (www.RCHS.com).

178 The elementary schools are: Roosevelt (from Kindergarten to grade three), Cherokee (from grade four to six) and St. Matthews (Kindergarten to grade eight). While the two former are public schools, the latter is a private school owned by the Catholic Church. The St. Matthews community also runs a child-care program (West Side Neighborhood Learning Community brochure).

179 The high schools are Humboldt Junior and Senior High and Guadalupe Alternative Programs (GAP). The latter is directed to youth who have experienced problems in the mainstream educational institutions (West Side Neighborhood Learning Community brochure).

ety of social and community development-oriented organizations and several catholic and other churches[180].

6.2.1 *History of the West Side*

The history of the West Side is closely entrenched with the history of migrants to the City, among them Mexicans (Boyte 1984: 43). First occupied by the Dakota Indians and later by French, Irish and German immigrants, the 'west bank' of the river was only linked to the little community of St. Paul by ferry boats and the Wabasha Bridge that opened up in 1859 (Boyte 1984: 40, http://www.rchs.com). In 1874 it was annexed by the City of St. Paul and became part of Ramsey County, after forming part of Dakota County in its first years. Due to its location on the Mississippi River frontage and to natural caves forming inside the river bluffs, the West Side gave way to its location for early industries such as breweries, foundries, quarries and manufacturing plants located on the "Flats" along the river (Boyte 1984: 42).

The jobs in the West Side industries attracted immigrants, starting with the Germans and Irish who arrived in the 1870s and followed by European and Russian Jews during the 1880s and 1890s, but also other population groups such as Syrians, French Canadians and Italians (Boyte 1984: 50, http://www.rchs.com)[181]. The migrants settled in the lower "Flats" of the West Side, which remained a predominantly Jewish neighborhood until after the First World War (Boyte 1984: 45)[182]. In the year 1895, Neighborhood House was founded by the Mount Zion Hebrew Ladies' Benevolent Society, and has since remained a service provider to all immigrant groups coming to the West Side (McClure 1992: 6). Other institutions also continue to testify to the diverse ethnic background of the early settlers of the West Side: the Church of St. Michael founded in the 1960s by the Irish[183], the Church of St.

---

[180] Some of these institutions are of great relevance to the Hispanic and/or Mexican population. I will come to this aspect in chapters 7 and 8 of this document.

[181] Several historians stress the polyglot character of the West Side at the beginning of the 20th century (Boyte 1984: 50, McClure 1992: 7f.). One of the chief reasons why the West Side attracted large numbers of poor immigrants was its cheap land, subject to periodic floods, leading to a low attractiveness to wealthier population groups (ibid: 43).

[182] In the 1920s, many Jewish residents of the West Side started moving to other neighborhoods of St. Paul.

[183] Today, only the tower remains of this Church. It has been remained the "Torre de San Miguel" and thus symbolically been appropriated by the Mexican-American community (www.rchs.com, HACER 2002: 2).

Matthew in 1901 by the Germans and the Church of Our Lady of Guadalupe in 1930s by the Mexicans (www.rchs.com)[184].

Mexican farm laborers had been working on the sugar and vegetable fields in Southern Minnesota since the end of the 19th century[185]. They started coming to the West Side in the 1910s and 1920s, as winter laborers in the packing industries and railroad construction adjacent to the West Side in South St. Paul (McClure 1992: 7). Many of the rural migrants became permanent settlers in the 1930s at a time when, in the context of the Great Depression, the original employers in the countryside stopped recruiting Mexican seasonal workers[186]. Due to the constrained access to employment opportunities, partly prompted by the racial prejudice of the native population, the poverty of the Mexican community manifested in crowded and unhealthy housing conditions on the West Side Flats (Boyte 1984: 50): "[A] survey made by the University of Minnesota showed this area to be the largest slum area in the Twin Cities" (NH quoted in McClure 1992: 10). In the context of the prosperous years after World War II, the living conditions on the West Side improved somewhat and more Mexican families settled in the neighborhood.

Serious floods – a problem negatively impinging on settlement in the area since its beginning - in the West Side Flats in 1952 and 1957, damaged the homes of many families. After the second of these floods, the City of St. Paul decided to build a massive flood wall on the Mississippi riverfront, and to remove the houses, schools, churches and other buildings of the, predominantly Mexican-American, community. The Riverview Industrial Park was built on the site of the old neighborhood, and families were relocated to other areas of the West Side or outside of it (McClure 1992: 12). The displacement of the West Side community is considered by many as an example of urban renewal policies of the time aimed at "eradicating neighborhoods that were occupied by low-income people and people of color" (McClure 1992: 12).

---

[184] Several authors testify to the prominent role of these early institutions in fighting racial prejudice and supporting the migrants to resist the pressure towards assimilation exercised by the native society (Boyte 1984: 60, McClure 1992: 12).

[185] According to McClure (1992), "it is doubtful that the region's fledgling sugar beet and vegetable industries could have survived without the help of these workers, who labored as families in the hot sun" (ibid: 6). In the fields, the housing and general living conditions of the Mexican workers were extremely poor (ibid: 7).

[186] However, also city employers, e. g. the railroad, did so (McClure 1002: 9).

Today, the West Side continues to be one of St. Paul's and the Twin Cities' most culturally and ethnically diverse communities. Representing one of many immigrant populations that have settled on the West Side over time, the Mexicans form the most longstanding and presently the biggest minority group in the neighborhood (see chapter 6.3). The presence of Mexicans and Hispanics has strongly increased in the last decades, not only on the West Side, but also in other neighborhoods, particularly on St. Paul's East Side[187] and in some neighborhoods in Minneapolis. Notwithstanding the development of other Latino clusters, the West Side is considered to be the hub of Latino culture of St. Paul and the Twin Cities, and the site of numerous 'ethnic' events[188] and institutions.

6.2.2 Demographic and socio-economic profile

The population of the West Side (16,133 inhabitants in 2000) has grown by 6% with respect to the population of 15,207 in the year 1990 (http://www.stpaul.gov). This represents a slightly higher population growth than the one of 5.5% of the entire City of St. Paul (HACER 2002: 44)[189]. Compared to the population of the whole City, the West Side population is relatively young: In the year 2000, school-age children (5-17 years) formed 22.8% of its population, as compared to 19.5% in the City of St. Paul[190]. The proportion of school-age children among the total West Side *Latino* population is considerably larger, namely 26.3% (Census 2000, SF1, PCT12, PCT12H).

Between 1990 and 2000, the West Side has become more racially and/or ethnically diverse, as shown by the following figures and graph: developed

---

187 The East Side is located in the north-eastern part of St. Paul and includes the planning districts Payne-Phalen, Dayton's Bluff, Greater East Side and Sunray-Battlecreek-Highwood. With a total population of 95,918 inhabitants in 2000 it is far more populous than the West Side. Almost 10% of the East Side's population in 2000 was of Latino origin (HACER 2002: 7).

188 For instance, since 1983 the *Cinco de Mayo* celebration is realized on the West Side. It memorizes the French defeat by the Mexicans on May 5th 1863 (HACER 2002: 3, McClure 1992: 12).

189 And a 17.4% increase of the entire Twin Cities' Metro Area (http://mumford.albany.edu/census/data).

190 The proportion of school-age children has also been augmented by 24% between 1990 and 2000. In the meantime, the proportion of pre-schoolers (age 0-4) decreased by 7% (HACER 2002: 44).

in the following way (Census 1990, SF1, P006, P009, P010; Census 2000, SF1, P8):

- The non-Hispanic white population decreased from 66% to 49%.
- The Hispanic population increased from 21% to 33%.
- The Asian population remained steady at 8%.
- The non-Hispanic black population grew from 3% to 6%, and the
- The American Indian population slightly fell from 3% to 2%.

Graph 5: Racial and ethnic composition of West Side, 1990 - 2000

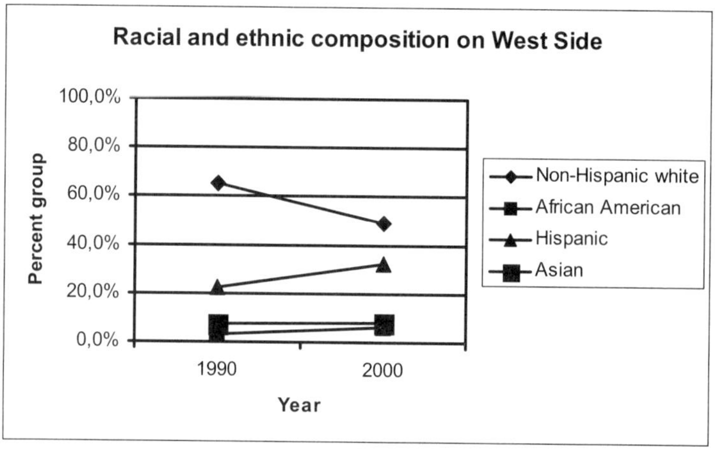

Source: http://mumford.albany.edu/census/data, own graph

In the Census 2000, 3% of the residents of the West Side considered themselves as multi-racial[191]. The cultural diversity of the neighborhood also reflects itself in the fact that for 50% of the public schoolchildren English is not the primary language spoken at home (Hacer 2002: 44). However, the racial profile of the neighborhood is sensitive to age: While only 21% of the

---

[191] In the Census 1990, the category of "two or more races" did not exist as yet. "Hispanic" is not considered a race as by the Census, but as an ethnic category (http://factfinder.census.gov).

elderly (residents above age 65) are people of color, 78% of public school students in the neighborhood are people of color (ibid: 45).

How does the West Side compare with the City of St. Paul, in demographic and socio-economic terms? Table 10 provides an overview over some selected variables, allowing evaluation of the demographic and socio-economic profile of the West Side inhabitants with respect to the one in the whole of St. Paul.

Table 10: Demographic and socio-economic characteristics West Side and City of St. Paul in 2000

	St. Paul City		**West Side**	
	1990	2000	1990	2000
Population	272,235	287,151	15,312	16,133
% Foreign-born	7.3	14.8	12.6	19.4
% Language other than English	11.2	21.8	21.2	34.5
% Recent immigrants*	4.8	7.7	6.6	12.4
Median HH income	26,498	38,774	22,675	36,392
% Below poverty	16.7	15.6	20.1	16.0
% Homeowners	53.9	54.8	56.8	58.6
Median hou-sing value	70,200	105,400	61,275	85,350
% College educated	26.5	32.0	12.8	19.4
% Hispanics	4.2	7.9	22.1	32.5
% Non-Hispanic white	80.4	64.0	65.4	48.8

Source: Census 1990, SF1 (P001, P009, P010, H003), SF3 (P042, P031, P036, P080A, P117, H061A, P057,)
Census 2000, SF1 (P1, P3, P4) and SF3 (P19, P22, P52, P87, H7, H76, P37). Own compilation.
* For 1990, refers to those who have arrived between 1980 and 1989.

The comparison with the City of St. Paul provides important indications about the demographic and socio-economic characteristics of the West Side neighborhood. It has a much higher proportion of foreign-born residents, and a higher attractiveness to the recent immigrant population than the City of St. Paul as a whole. The proportion of Hispanic residents far exceeds that of the

City. With respect to economic indicators, such as the median household income and the percentage of residents with an income below the poverty level, the differences between St. Paul and the West Side are surprisingly small, taking into account the neighborhood's relatively high proportion of recent immigrants. They even decreased between 1990 and 2000.

Map 4: Census tracts in the West Side neighborhood, in 2000

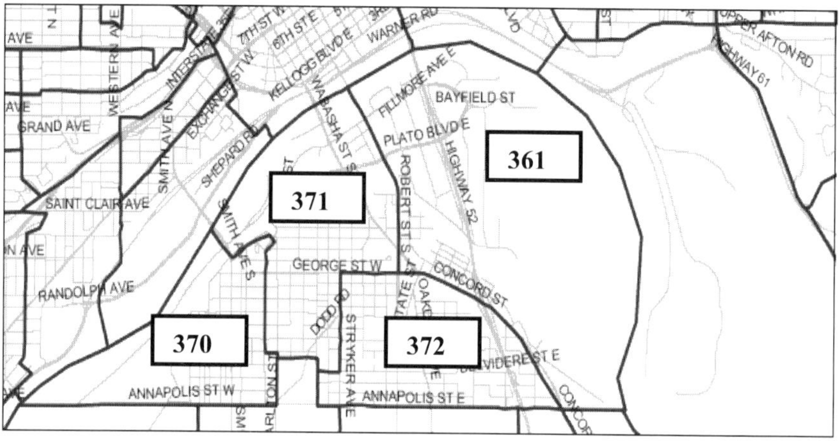

Source: www.wilder.org

Although the West Side shows considerably higher housing ownership rates than the entire City of St. Paul, both in 1990 and in 2000, the values of owner occupied homes are clearly lower and increased less between 1990 and 2000 than those of St. Paul's[192]. Finally, the West Side fares far worse than St. Paul in terms of the percentage of college-educated residents out of the population of 25 years and older. In spite of improvements of this educational achievement indicator between 1990 and 2000, the West Side continues to lag far behind the city average at the latter date.

[192] However, the development of different price segments inside the West Side shows big differences. While housing properties in the segments below US$60,000 have dramatically decreased between 1990 and 2000, in the segments above US$100,000 they have greatly increased (view Annex 9). This implies a growing difficulty for lower income households to acquire new housing property on the West Side. However, it also implies an improved asset-building potential who already own housing property in the neighborhood – both aspects confirmed in the resident and expert interviews.

6.2.3 *Sub-areas of the West Side*

It is also important to take into account the internal differences of the West Side, in terms of its residents' demographic and socioeconomic characteristics. The division of the West Side into four census tracts (see chapter 5) facilitates such differentiation. The census tract borders concur at least partly with topographic ones and reflect socio-economic variations inside the neighborhood. Map 4 illustrates the census tract borders and their respective enumeration in the 2000 Census. Whereas census tract 361 corresponds to the "Flats" area, the other three tracts (370, 371, 372) are situated uphill on the "Bluffs".

Table 11 shows the demographic and socio-economic characteristics of the sub-areas on the West Side. The variables shown in the previous table are complemented by the following housing-related variables: percentage of detached (single family) units, median housing value and percentage of houses built before 1940. The housing information is important as an indicator of socio-economic status[193], additional to income and poverty levels.

Table 11: Demographic, socio-economic and housing characteristics in sub-areas of the West Side in 2000

	West Side total	**Tract 361**	**Tract 370**	**Tract 371**	**Tract 372**	**Aver. Hispanic St. Paul**
DEMOGRAPHIC INDICATORS						
Population	16,133	1,807	2,995	5,155	6,176	
% Foreign-born	19.4	36.7	7.6	18.0	21.2	19.0
% Lan. other	34.5	62.2	18.2	35.3	34.1	29.9

193 Residence in single family units can be considered a status-indicator as it usually overlaps with housing ownership.

	West Side total	Tract 361	Tract 370	Tract 371	Tract 372	Aver. Hispanic St. Paul
than English						
% Recent immigrants	12.4	26.9	1.1	11.4	14.1	10.9
% Hispanics	32.5	41.5	16.4	29.0	41.0	15.3
% Non-Hispanic white	48.8	15.7	73.3	52.2	43.6	53.3
SOCIO-ECONOMIC INDICATORS						
Median HH income 1999	36,392	21,667	47,131	34,722	42,046	35,783
% Below poverty	16.0	27.8	6.8	18.8	14.8	18.5
% College educated	19.4	8.2	32.8	20.1	14.7	21.5
HOUSING INDICATORS						
% Owner occupancy	58.6	37.8	78.3	50.7	60.2	50.5
% Single family units	53.3	29.0	70.3	45.8	57.2	N/a
Median housing value	85,350	81,600	86,900	89,000	83,900	N/a

Source: Census 2000, SF1 (P1, P3, P4, H4) and SF3 (P19, P22, P52, P87, H7, H30, H76, P37). Own compilation.

It is obvious that the West Side neighborhood displays enormous internal differences, with respect to the demographic and socio-economic profile of the population living in the different sub-areas or census tracts[194]. Tracts 361 and 370 are farthest apart, with respect to all variables. The former (tract 361) has the highest minority-population, the lowest income and educational levels, and the smallest proportions of owner occupied and single family housing of the whole West Side. The latter's (tract 370) socio-economic and

[194] The tracts also differ in terms of their predominant land uses. The small population size of tract 361 with respect to the other census tracts can be explained by its predominant industrial and/or commercial land uses.

housing indicators figure far above the West Side-average[195]. The other two census tracts (371 and 372) lie closer around the West Side average, although they show some remarkable differences along certain variables: Whereas the median income is higher (and poverty level lower) in tract 372, the education levels of its population are below the West Side average. Precisely the opposite is true for tract 371. The St. Paul Housing Authority (PHA) considers Tracts 361 and 372 as high-poverty neighborhoods, as the percentage of its population living below poverty exceeds 15.6 percent, the poverty rate of the entire jurisdiction of St. Paul (table 6). Designating high poverty rates by comparison with city-averages is based on HUD-definitions fixed in the US Code of Federal Regulations (www.gpo.access.gov/cfr/index.html). The poverty rates of St. Paul census tracts can be seen in map 5.

If compared with the neighborhood environment of the average Hispanic in St. Paul (see last column in table 11, also table 6), the following features stand out: The West Side has higher proportions of recent immigrants, foreign-born residents and of those who speak another language than English at home, than the neighborhood of the average Hispanic in St. Paul. While West Side Hispanics have neighbors who fare better in terms of their incomes and housing-assets than those of the average Hispanic living in St. Paul, the inverse situation is true for educational achievement. This contradictory situation has already been observed in chapter 6.2.1, comparing characteristics of the total West Side and St. Paul population.

[195] They also figure above average compared to the neighborhood environment of the average white resident of St. Paul and similar to the metro area average (tables 6 and 9).

Map 5: Percent of population living below poverty in St. Paul census tracts, 1999

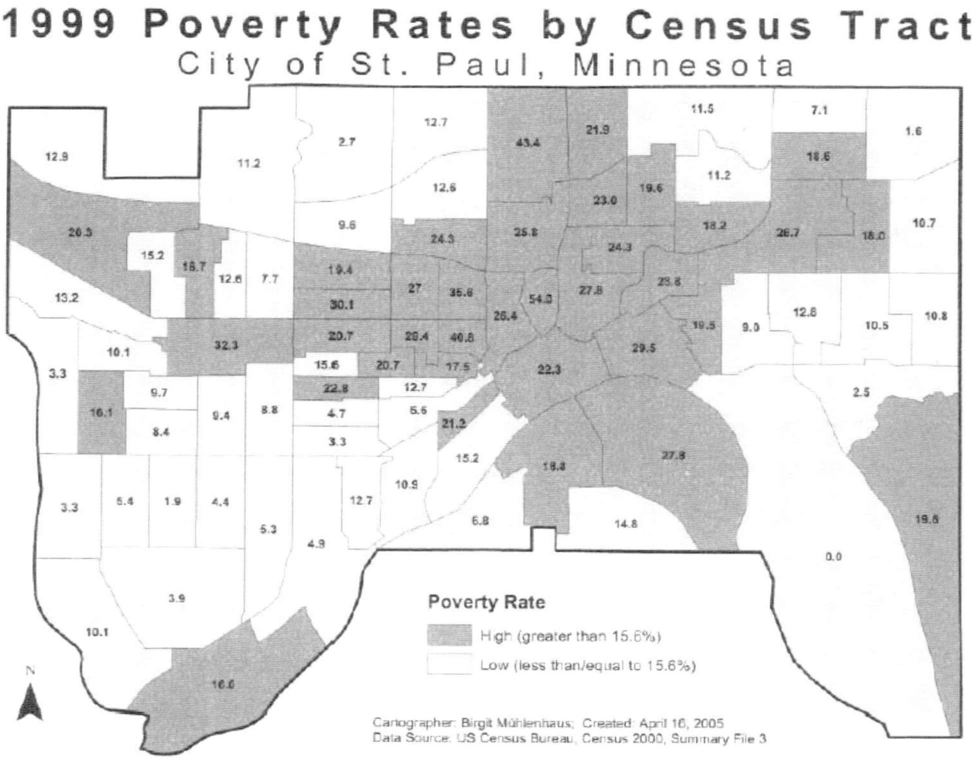

Source: St. Paul PHA

The predominant housing type on the West Side is single-family units, with 53% of households living in such homes. However in tract 361 or the "Flats", only 29% of the total housing stock is single-family units, the same proportion as housing structures with more than 50 units. In effect, most of the subsidized housing stock, usually large-unit structures are situated in tract 361[196]. The location of the public housing projects (Dunedin Hi Rise and -Terrace) and scattered site units owned by the Public Housing Authority of St. Paul can be seen in map 7 in chapter 9.1.3. The location of voucher-subsidized housing units of the St. Paul Public Housing Authority (PHA) is indicated in map 8 in the same chapter.

6.3 Mexicans and Latinos on the West Side

According to the Census 2000, the total Hispanic or Latino population on the West Side of St. Paul was 5,266 in that year representing 32.6% of the West Side's total population. This means a more than 50% increase of the Hispanic population in ten years time: In 1990, 3,390 Hispanics or Latinos were living on the West Side, corresponding to 22% of its population at that time.

Table 12 shows the growth of the Hispanic population on the West Side from 1970 to 2000, also compared to its proportions in the City of St. Paul and the Twin Cities Metro Area:

Table 12: Hispanic population in West Side, 1970 - 2000

	WEST SIDE			ST. PAUL	METRO AREA
Year	**Total population**	**Hispanic population**	**% of total population**	**% of total population**	**% of total population**
1970	17,047	2,106	12.4	2.0	0.8
1980	14,848	2,605	17.5	2.9	1.0
1990	15,312	3,390	22.1	4.2	1.5

[196] The multi-family building Dunedin Terrace has a total of 86 housing units, of which 12 are occupied by whites, 42 by African Americans, 2 by American Indians, 29 by Asians and one multi-race household. Nine households (may be white or black) or 10.5% of all households, are Hispanics. The Dunedin Hi-rise, exclusively inhabited by elder households, includes 136 housing units of which 86 are white, 43 African American, 2 American Indians and 5 Asians. 31 households or 22.8% of the households are Hispanics (PHA Monthly Management Report). Thus, in both public housing structures Hispanics are under-represented with respect to their share in the total West Side population, and even more so in tract 361.

2000	16,133	5,266	32.6	7.9	3.3

Source: Institute on Race on Race and Poverty, US Census (1970-1980). SF1 (P001H) for 1990, SF1 (P1H) for 2000.
*Enumeration by using the Spanish surname (see chapter 6.1).

Similar to the development already observed for the City and Metro Area, the Hispanic population on the West Side grew significantly in the 1990s, even though important increases can already be observed during the 1970s and 1980s. The figures also underline the quality of the West Side as a neighborhood particularly attractive to the Hispanic population, as compared to the City and Metro Area context. It has to be recognized though, that the Hispanic population on the West Side has grown only half as much as in the City of St. Paul and the Metro Area (view tables 3 and 4).

Thus, if growth rates instead of proportions of the Hispanic population are used as the variable of reference, the West Side cannot be projected to be the only significant Hispanic neighborhood in the City of St. Paul. While on the West Side the presence of Hispanics increased by 63% between 1990 and 2000, growth rates are much higher elsewhere, and notably in the neighborhoods or planning districts of the East Side of St. Paul (Greater East Side, Dayton's Bluff, Payne-Phalen and Sunray/Battle Creek/Highwood): The growth rates in these range from 95% in Sunray/Battle Creek/Highwood to 236% on the Greater East Side (www.st-paul.com, HACER 2002: 16). Table 13 illustrates this trend:

Table 13: Presence and growth of Hispanic population in West Side and East Side neighborhoods, 1990 - 2000

	WEST SIDE	**EAST SIDE**			
Year	**West Side (PD 3)**	**Sunray/BC/HW (PD 1)**	**Greater East Side (PD 2)**	**Dayton's Bluff (PD 4)**	**Payne-Phalen (PD 5)**
1990	3,240 (3,390*)	613	752	629	1,221
%	21.3 (21.2)	3.2	5.2	4.1	4.6
2000	5,266	1,197	2,529	1,890	3,325
%	32.6	5.9	9.5	10.7	10.5

	WEST SIDE	EAST SIDE			
Year	**West Side (PD 3)**	**Sunray/BC/HW (PD 1)**	**Greater East Side (PD 2)**	**Dayton's Bluff (PD 4)**	**Payne-Phalen (PD 5)**
% Growth 1990-2000	62.5 (57.9)	95.3	236.3	200.5	172.3

Source: http://www.st-paul.com.
*The Hispanic population figures differ from those in table 12, based on the (most reliable) 100-percent sample. Therefore. the latter ones, as well as resulting population proportions and growth figures are added in parenthesis.

Where do Hispanics who live on the West Side come from? Table 14 shows the most important national groups and the regional origin of the Hispanic population on the West Side in 1990 and 2000:

Table 14: National origins of Hispanics in West Side, 1990 and 2000

	Total Hispanic or Latino population	**Mexico**	**Puerto Rico**	**Cuba**	**Other Latinos**
1990	3,390	2,942	198	38	212
%	100.0	86.7	5.8	1.1	6.3
2000	5,266	4,311	221	54	680
%	100.00	81.9	5.1	1.3	12.9
Growth 1990-2000		46.5	11.6	42.1	220.8

Source: Census 1990, SF1 (P009) and 2000, SF1 (PCT11). Own compilation.

From table 14 two aspects stand out, echoing metro-, as well as nation-wide characteristics of Hispanic migration: Firstly, Mexicans constitute the big majority of Hispanic migrants on the West Side – this characteristic is even clearer than on the level of the Metro Area (view table 3). Secondly, "other Latinos" have increased their presence even more.

Since this research focuses on the Mexican population[197] of the West Side, in the following sub-chapters this country group will be looked at more in detail.

6.3.1 Residential locations

In the previous chapter (6.2.3) the distribution of the Hispanic population in the different census tracts of the West Side was shown. Table 15 illustrates the geographic distribution of the Mexican population on the West Side, compared to the one of the entire Hispanic population:

Table 15: Residential location of Mexican and Hispanic population on the West Side, 1990 and 2000

	West Side		**Tract 361**		**Tract 370**		**Tract 371**		**Tract 372**	
	1990	2000	1990	2000	1990	2000	1990	2000	1990	2000
Mexicans	2,942	4,311	520	626	236	359	901	1,245	1,285	2,081
%*	19.2	26.7	30.8	34.6	8.0	12.0	17.6	24.2	23.2	33.7
% Growth**		46.5		20.4		52.1		38.2		62.0
Hispanics	3,390	5,266	606	750	280	490	1,049	1,493	1,455	2,533
%*	22.1	32.6	35.9	41.5	9.4	16.4	20.5	29.0	26.2	41.0
% Growth**		55.3		23.8		75.0		42.3		74.1
Total	15,312	16,133	1,690	1,807	2,964	2,995	5,117	5,155	5,541	6,176
%	100	100	100	100	100	100	100	100	100	100

Source: Census 1990, SF1 (P009) and 2000, SF1 (PCT11). Own compilation.
* Percentage of the total population of the West Side or respective census tract.
* Percentage the population of the West Side or respective census tract has grown between 1990 and 2000.

With the big majority of Hispanics on the West Side being Mexicans, it was to be expected that the distribution of this national group is similar to the one of the total Hispanic population. Even so, the table shows interesting results. In all census tracts, the entire Hispanic population has grown more than Mexicans, suggesting an increasing presence of "other Latinos" apart from the traditionally strongest Hispanic groups (Mexicans, Puerto Ricans and

[197] If in the following I refer to the "Mexican population" or "Mexicans" of the West Side, foreign-born *and* US natives of Mexican descent are included.

Cubans) on the West Side. In relative terms, the census tract with the highest proportion of Mexican residents is 361 with 34.6% of its population being of Mexican origin in the year 2000. In absolute terms, most Mexicans live in census tract 372, which is also the tract in which the Mexicans have grown most between 1990 and 2000. Surprisingly, the tract with the second highest growth of the Mexican, and the highest of the Hispanic population, is tract 370 – the tract with the highest median incomes, education levels and housing ownership rates, as well as median values on the West Side (view table 12)[198].

6.3.2 *Demographic and socio-economic characteristics*

In what kind of households and families do Mexicans live on the West Side, with respect to other Hispanics and the total population of the neighborhood? Table 16 describes this looking at average household sizes, the presence of family households, as well as the one of families with children. The household and family situations of Mexicans in the different census tracts can be viewed in Annex 8[199].

Table 16: Household and family situation of Mexicans on West Side, in 2000

	Mexicans WS	**Hispanics WS**	**Total pop. WS**
Total pop.	4,311	5,266	16,133
Total hhs.	1,078	1,339	5,564
% / total Mex.	100.0	100.0	100.0
School-age population	1,126	1,397	3,687
%	26.1	26.5	22.9
Average hh size	3.70	3.67	2.91
1-person hhs.*	148	201	1,653
%	13.7	15.0	29.7
Family households**	874	1063	3,477

198 Again, it has to be taken into account that to begin with places with relatively few people are more likely to see relatively large changes, with the same absolute changes happening as in other places with more people.

199 The tables with the household and socio-economic situation in the different census tracts were annexed in order to allow for easier reading.

	Mexicans WS	Hispanics WS	Total pop. WS
%	81.1	79.4	62.5
Presence of children –18	548	617	2016
%	50.8	46.1	36.2

Source: Census 2000, for total population and Hispanics SF1 (P1, P1H, P12, P12H, P17, P17H, P18, P26, P26H). Presence of children for Hispanics in SF3 (P146H). For Mexicans SF2 (PCT1Mex, PCT3Mex, PCT8Mex, PCT9Mex). Own compilation.
* The percentages for the last three variables refer to universe of total households (hhs.), instead of population.
** Defined as households in which members are affiliated by birth, marriage or adoption.

Mexicans, as well as Hispanic households have bigger households and more children of school age in comparison to the whole neighborhood population. Not surprisingly thus, they also have less one-person- and more family households, as well as those with children. The demographic and family profile of the Mexican and Hispanic population on the West Side is similar. Interestingly however, the Mexican population alone, while including a slightly lower school-age population, shows smaller proportions of 1-person households and a higher proportion of family households and those with children. This may reflect a comparatively established situation of at least part of the Mexican population (the more longstanding one)[200], as opposed to 'other Latinos' with a higher incidence of recent and single arrivals.

Which are the present socio-economic characteristics of Mexicans on the West Side, with respect to the socio-economic and housing situation of Hispanics and the total population of the neighborhood? Table 17 provides an overview with respect to some selected socio-economic and housing variables. The information with respect to the different census tracts can be viewed in Annex 8.

[200] They are more established in the sense that a family could be founded or has joined the male or female immigrant pioneer who first came.

Table 17: Socio-economic and housing situation of Mexicans on the West Side, in 2000

	Mexicans WS	Hispanics WS	Total pop. WS
Total pop.	4,311	5,266	16,133
Total hhs.	1,078	1,339	5,564
% / total Mex.	100.0	100.0	100.0
SOCIO-ECONOMIC INDICATORS			
Median HH income 1999	38,257	39,576	36,392
Below poverty	862	1,012	2,563
%	22.2	19.2	16.0
to 4th grade*	134	156	469
%	7.48	6.9	4.0
College educated	128	239	1,858
%	7.2	9.4	19.4
HOUSING INDICATORS*			
Owner occupancy	536	645	3,261
%	49.7	48.5	58.2
Single family units	213	620	3,078
%	41.0	46.2	53.3
More than 30% income on rent	213	292	869
%	41.0	42.5	37.1
Median housing value	87,900	84,950	85,350

Source: Census 2000, for total population and Hispanics SF1 (P1), SF3 (P53, P87, P37, H30, H76, P152H, P159H, P148H, H12, H30, HCT30H, HCT39H, HCT42H). For Mexicans SF2 (PCT1), SF4 (PCT89, PCT142, PCT64, HCT2, HCT17, HCT59). Own compilation.

* For the educational attainment –related category "to 4th grade" the information about the Hispanic population is based in SF4 and does not include Hispanics of census tract 370. Universe of the two education variables is population 25 years and older.

** All housing indicators refer to universe of "occupied housing units", in the case of the renter-variable only to those occupied by renters.

Table 17 presents a somewhat complex picture that may partly be explained by a highly heterogenic Mexican and Hispanic population on the West Side:

Mexicans have a higher median income than the total population for the West Side, but less than Hispanics overall. The median housing value of Mexican home-owners from the West Side is likewise higher than the total population of the West Side and Hispanics. In contrast, a higher proportion of Mexicans earn an income below the poverty level as compared to the total and Hispanic population of the West Side. Less Mexicans than the total, but more than the Hispanic population, own their housing. Mexicans also pay a higher rent than they can afford[201] with respect to the total population, but not the overall Hispanic population of the West Side. With respect to their educational attainment, Mexicans are clearly below the West Side and Hispanics average.

How do Mexicans on the West Side fare compared to Mexicans in the entire City and in other neighborhoods of St. Paul? This comparison is important for a better understanding of the particularities of the Mexican population on the West Side and also as it puts into context the results of the qualitative study discussed in the following chapters.

Table 18 contrasts Mexicans on the West Side with Mexicans in the City of St. Paul and Mexicans in Payne-Phalen. The latter is one of the East Side neighborhoods with a high proportion of Mexican residents and high influx of Mexicans between 1990 and 2000[202].

---

[201] The US federal Department of Housing and Urban Development (HUD) defines a rental payment of more than 30% of a household's income as no more affordable (www.hud.gov, Community Planning and Development).

[202] I decided to contrast the West Side with Payne-Phalen as one of the other four East Side neighborhoods (see above) occurred for two reasons: First, after Dayton's Bluff it constitutes the East Side neighborhood with the highest proportion of Hispanic residents (10.5). Second, as opposed to Dayton's Bluff and the other East Side neighborhoods the borders of the census tracts of Payne-Phalen almost coincide with its neighborhood borders, which made up for a higher level of precision in the data used. Still, the sample data of SF4 only provided information on the Mexican population in three out of the eight census tracts of Payne-Phalen due to the small absolute numbers of residents of this group in the other five tracts. Thus, the information on the Mexican population for all variables, but the housing ownership one which was extracted out of SF2 (total population sample) is actually based on the three census tracts in Payne-Phalen with more than 100 Mexican residents.

Table 18: Demographic and socio-economic characteristics of Mexicans on West Side, City of St. Paul and East Side, in 2000

	West Side	St. Paul City	Payne-Phalen
Total Mexicans	4,311	18,147	2,542
% / total pop.	26.7	6.3	8.05
SOCIO-ECONOMIC INDICATORS			
Median HH income 1999	38,257	33,696	34,943
Below poverty	862	3,444	305
%	22.2	21.8	23.07
to 4th grade	134	552	65
%	7.48	7.51	12.3
College educated	128	681	38
%	7.2	9.27	7.2
HOUSING INDICATORS			
Owner occupancy	459	1,499	171
%	46.9	37.0	31.4
Single family units	442*	1,458	66
%	45.2	35.9	22.9
More than 30% income on rent	213	1,062	75
%	41.0	41.5	32.1
Median housing value **	87,900	85,300	82,800

Source: Census 2000, SF2 (PCT1Mex, HCT2Mex), SF4 (HCT17, PCT89, PCT142, PCT64, HCT2, HCT17, HCT59, HCT66) . Own compilation.

*For the West Side and Payne-Phalen: The "total Mexican population" and "owner occupancy" variables are the only ones in this table based on a total (Mexican) population sample, extracted from SF2. The other variables are extracted from sample data, which for the West Side include only census tracts 361, 371 and 372, and for Payne-Phalen the tracts 306.01, 310 and 316.

*The housing value for Payne-Phalen is relatively unreliable, as the SF4-variable HCT66 only provides values for the tracts 310 and 316.

Mexicans who live on the West Side seem to be better off socio-economically than Mexicans in the entire City of St. Paul and – more pronounced – in the neighborhood of Payne-Phalen. This is manifested by their higher median household income, more stable housing situation[203] and lower poverty rates. The status-gap however is much more salient with respect to the income- and wealth-related, than the educational variables: With respect to the college-educated members of this group, both Mexicans of the West Side and Payne-Phalen are situated even below the St. Paul-average. In contrast, clearly more Mexicans in Payne Phalen than on the West Side only, have no more than primary school education.

The relatively superior economic position of Mexicans on the West Side as compared to Mexicans in St. Paul and Payne-Phalen may be explained with a higher proportion of longstanding and thus more established Mexican households (also see next chapter). However, the low educational achievement of Mexicans on the West Side – already observed with respect to the entire Hispanic and West Side population - remains a salient feature. The higher proportion of Mexican renters on the West Side who pay a beyond-affordability level rent may be related to altogether higher housing costs on the West Side, both in the rental and in the ownership segment - an interpretation also supported by the lower median housing values of Mexican ownership housing in the rest of St. Paul and in Payne-Phalen.

6.3.3 *Immigrant situation and status*

The immigrant situation and status of the Mexicans on the West Side provide important information about the degree of consolidation – and thus, relative presence or absence of vulnerability – of this group. Therefore, it will be discussed in this chapter, and also be compared with the situation of Mexicans in the City of St. Paul as a whole (view Annex 8 for the corresponding figures for the West Side census tracts). Table 19 allows an appreciation on the immigrant situation of Mexicans on the West Side, based on the variables "recent immigrants" (year of entry after 1990), "foreign-born" and "non-citizenship":

---

[203] The housing situation of Mexicans on the West Side is considered more 'stable', due to their higher ownership rates and housing values – thus higher asset-ownership, as well as opportunities to increase these assets. The higher proportion of Mexicans living in single-family housing on the West Side than in Payne-Phalen or the whole of St. Paul is related to the higher ownership rates, as only few single-family homes are rental units.

Table 19: Immigrant situation and status of Mexicans on the West Side, in 2000

	Mexicans WS*	Hispanics WS	Total pop. WS
Total Mexicans	4,311	5,266	16,133
% / total pop.	26.7	32.6	100.0
Recent immigrants	995	1,304	1,300
%	23.1	24.8	8.1
Foreign born	1,432	1979	3182
%	36.3	37.1	19.4
Not a citizen	1168	1522	2240
%	29.6	28.5	13.6

Source: Census 2000. For total population and Hispanics SF1 (P1, P4, PCT11). For total population, Mexicans and Hispanics SF4 (PCT45, PCT43). Own compilation.

* The absolute numbers present an undercount, as they do not include the Mexican residents of tract 370. The percentages are therefore based on a limited universe and do not refer to the population number in the first row of the table.

Almost a third of Mexicans who live on the West Side are not citizens of the United States, indicating that an important number of them are in a situation of relative insecurity and/or vulnerability. Slightly more Mexicans are in this situation, as compared to the entire Hispanic population of the West Side. On the other hand, compared with the total Hispanic population on the West Side, a slightly lower proportion of Mexicans are foreign-born and recent immigrants. A reason, why relatively more Mexicans are non-citizens, *although* less of them are recent immigrants and foreign-born, might be that some of the pre-1990 immigrants have not yet become naturalized citizens – these are much more likely to be Mexican than to come from another Latin American country (view table 14).

How does the immigration situation and status of Mexicans on the West Side compare with the one of Mexicans in the City of St. Paul and the East Side neighborhood of Payne-Phalen?

Table 20: Immigrant situation and status of Mexicans on West Side, City of St. Paul and East Side, in 2000

	West Side	St. Paul City	Payne-Phalen
Total Mexicans	4,311	18,147	2,542
% / total pop.	26.7	6.3	8.05
Recent immigrants*	995	3893	538
%	25.2	21.5	38.6
Foreign-born	1,432	5766	613
%	36.3	35.8	46.4
Not a citizen	1168	4810	595
%	29.6	29.8	46.4

Source: Census 2000, SF1 (P1, P4, PCT11) and SF4 (PCT45, PCT43).
* The figures for the West Side and Payne-Phalen are only related to the total Mexican population of the census tracts for which data on the variable "year of entry" was available. This is why the total population number in the first row of the table does not correspond to the respective universes the percentages are based on.

Table 19 indicates that a higher proportion of Mexicans on the West Side are recent immigrants and foreign-born than in the entire City of St. Paul. Yet, fewer of them are recent immigrants, foreign-born and non-citizens than in the neighborhood of Phayne Phalen. Thus, the table indicates the double role of the West Side as, on the one hand, a neighborhood still attractive to many Mexican newcomers (table 14), and, on the other hand, one with a higher proportion of more longstanding US citizens of Mexican origin.

Combined with the figures in the socio-economic table in the previous chapter, table 18 confirms that other areas in the City of St. Paul, such as Payne-Phalen on St. Paul's East Side, have become more attractive - and probably also more affordable - to recent Mexican and Hispanic immigrants, i.e. those who arrived between 1990 and 2000 (table 12) than the West Side.

6.4 The West Side as a case

Before providing a summary of the present chapter, I want to link the empirical findings primarily based on neighborhood and city-statistics to the theoretical chapters of this document. Precisely, I want to reflect on the position of the West Side in an overall classification of (multi-) ethnic residential areas. This is important as it provides an additional indication about the transferability of the results of this research to other ethnic neighborhoods of the United States. Assumingly, this transferability is more likely to be given in neighborhoods with similar demographic and/or socio-economic characteristics.

Criticizing segregation studies for presenting the dominant racial urban structure as a dichotomy of majority and minority, or black and white, Johnston et al. (2003) propose an alternative classification of ethnic residential areas (also view White et al. 2005: 174). This classification captures the increasingly pluri-ethnic profiles of urban neighborhoods, while also taking into account opportunity disparities between the "host [non-Hispanic white] society which is the most powerful and has the greatest influence on the structuring of labor and housing markets, plus school catchment areas and the less powerful minority groups" (Johnston et al. 2003: 565)[204]. While Johnston et al. (2003) analyze the predominance of, and changes in types of ethnic residential areas on the census tract scale, I will apply this classification to the entire West Side neighborhood integrating four census tracts, without however testing the distribution of the respective neighborhood types on the City- and Metro Area-scale[205].

The classification scheme distinguishes between:

- Isolated host communities, in which the host or non-Hispanic white population forms 80% or more of the population. These are equivalent to what Marcuse (1997) terms as 'citadels' created by the dominant group to maintain or enhance its status (see chapter 2.3.3);
- Non-isolated host communities, in which the dominant group forms 50-80% of the population, thus living less isolated from other groups;

---

[204] The identification of the 'host society' with the non-Hispanic white population is problematic given the longstanding presence of e.g. the native or African American minorities in the US. This decision can nevertheless be justified in view of the ongoing socio-economic and power inequalities between the Anglo-white and other groups in the US. Furthermore, the authors themselves recognize that the categorization into four main ethnic groups constitutes an unsatisfactory simplification of multi-ethnicity, given the cultural heterogeneity within each of these groups (Johnston et al. 2003: 568).

[205] An application of the classification scheme to the entire City of St. Paul or Twin Cities' Metro Area would clearly go beyond the intentions of this document. Nevertheless I shall relate the West Side pattern to the one of the whole City or Metro Area.

- Assimilation-pluralism enclaves, with members of the host society living in a 30-50% minority, and two or more minority groups forming the remaining components;
- Mixed-minority enclaves, with several minority groups representing 70% or more of their population, with no one minority group being twice as populous as the size of the other minority groups;
- Polarized enclaves, in which one minority group is at least twice as large as all of the remaining minority populations, and accounts for 46 to 100% of the total population[206]; and
- Ghettos, in which one minority group forms 60% of the area's population and 30% of this group in the whole city lives in such areas. These correspond to what Marcuse (1997) terms as the 'classic ghetto' (see chapter 2.3.3).

Table 21 indicates that according to the presented classification scheme, between 1990 and 2000 the West Side evolved from a 'non-isolated host community' to an 'assimilation-pluralism enclave'[207]. This is the case as the non-Hispanic white or 'host' population constitutes less than 50% of the neighborhood's total population, the remaining part shared by several minority groups, in which the Hispanic population clearly prevails. At least three conclusions emanate from this: First, independent from the value statements implicit in the presented classification scheme, the West Side is far from representing a 'ghetto' neighborhood in which one numerically outweighing, in this case the Hispanic community, lived in 'isolation'. Second, the West Side has become more multi-cultural between the last censuses, with other minority groups, e.g. African Americans[208] experiencing a similar growth as

---

[206] The three types of 'enclaves' constitute a differentiation of what Marcuse (1997) considers as the benign type of segregation as a "voluntarily developed spatial concentration of a group for purposes of promoting the welfare of its members" (ibid: 228, see chapter 2.3.3). It has to be remembered that the value statement against the extreme forms of segregation (citadel and ghetto) by both authors (Marcuse and Johnston et al.) occurs against the background of power asymmetries running alongside racial and/or ethnic differences, i.e. host society and minorities.

[207] Although it presents characteristics of the 'polarized enclave' in that the Hispanic population is more than twice as large as all the remaining minority populations.

[208] It has to be noted here that many or even most of the growth of the African American population of the West Side can be attributed to immigrants from Africa, notably Somalis, rather than to an increase of native African American residents.

Hispanics. Finally, the ethnic and racial profile of the West Side neighborhood needs to be put into context with the ethnic and racial profile of the entire City or Metro Area.

Table 21: Racial composition of the West Side in 1990 and 2000*

	WEST SIDE	
	1990	2000
Total population	15,312	16,133
N-H white	10,009	7,868
%	65.4	48.8
N-H Black	479	961
%	3.1	6.0
Asian	1,175	1,269
%	7.7	7.9
Amer. Indian	395	236
%	2.6	1.5
Hispanic	3,390	5,266
%	22.1	32.6

Source: Census 1990 SF1 (P006, P009, P010). For 2000, SF1 (P1, P8). Own compilation.
*Table includes only population with "one race only". In the 2000 Census, 3% of the West Side population defined themselves as multi-racial.

Given that in the City of St. Paul the proportion of the 'host' or non-Hispanic white group has decreased from 80.4% in 1990 to 64.0% in 2000, the West Side is developing on par with the growing diversity of the City. The existence of Hispanic 'ghettos' or hyper-segregation, on the neighborhood-level or the scale of the entire City or Metro area, seems rather unlikely. This is not least due to the relatively small proportions of this minority-group city- or metro-wide, compared with other US metro areas, such as Chicago, New York or Los Angeles (table 5). Finally, complementing the presented classification scheme, it has to be remembered that the West Side shows a considerable income mix among its entire population and the Mexican-/Hispanic-community, thus disputing the notion of an economically depressed homogeneous 'ghetto' neighborhood.

6.5 Summary

In this chapter the 'local context' of this research was discussed, in terms of the City- and Metro area-environment and that of the West Side neighborhood. The historical presence of the Hispanic and/or Mexican population in the metro area, city and neighborhood was shown, as well as socio-economic and demographic characteristics, and the immigrant situation of both groups. Finally, the West Side was placed into a classification scheme of ethnic residential neighborhoods.

The Minneapolis-St. Paul Metro Area, as well as the City of St. Paul have historically experienced a relatively small migration of minorities of Third World countries. Even today, on the Metro Area scale 85 percent of the population is non-Hispanic white, and the same is true for 64 percent of the city population. These are high figures if compared to cities like Chicago and New York where the non-Hispanic white population constitutes 58 and 40 percent, respectively. This being said, the Metro Area and City have experienced important increases in their foreign-born population between 1990 and 2000, the majority of these due to the influx of Hispanic immigrants. Among Hispanics, Mexicans constitute by far the biggest country group and have doubled their presence in the city and Metro Area between 1990 and 2000. The historical and numerical dominance of Mexican immigrants to the Twin Cities notwithstanding, "new" Latinos from e.g. Ecuador, El Salvador and Peru have grown even more between 1990 and 2000.

The West Side of St. Paul can be considered a traditional immigrant neighborhood, with Mexicans forming its most continuous and longstanding migrant settlers. Although Mexican farm workers started to arrive in the neighborhood in the early 20th century, the West Side has witnessed an accelerated influx of Mexicans in the decade between 1990 and 2000 – parallel to similar developments in the city and Metro Area. Although other neighborhoods of St. Paul, notably on its "East Side", have experienced an even higher relative growth of Mexicans and Latinos between 1990 and 2000, the West Side continues to be the neighborhood in the City with the highest Hispanic and Mexican population – in 2000, 33 percent of its residents were Hispanics and 27 percent Mexican.

The West Side displays strong internal discrepancies in terms of the demographic and socio-economic characteristics of its population: While the "Flats" area (census tract 361) shows the highest concentrations of poor households and renters, as well as foreign-born residents, the Southwestern part of the "Bluffs" area (tract 370) is characterized by relatively high median incomes, housing values and ownership rates. In relative terms, most Mexicans live in the "Flats", however in absolute numbers their presence is strongest in two census tracts of the "Bluffs" (371 and 372). The socio-economic situation of Mexicans greatly varies in the different sub-areas of the West Side, too. 23 percent of Mexicans on the West Side are recent immigrants and 30 percent lacking full citizenship status. This suggests a situation of vulnerability and instability for this part of the Mexican population of the West Side, although in other neighborhoods of St. Paul, e.g. Payne-Phalen on the East Side, a much higher proportion of Mexicans is in this situation.

Placed in a classification of ethnic residential neighborhoods proposed by Johnston et al. (2003), some salient features of the West Side stand out: First, the ethnic diversity of the neighborhood, not least manifest in the ongoing presence of the non-Hispanic white ('host') population, and growth of the African American population. Dissimilar to the notion of a 'classic ghetto' (e.g. Marcuse 1997), the West Side presents a considerable income mix, both among its total and the Latino population. Second, the numeric predominance of the Hispanic population, although other minority populations grow at a similar pace. Third, while the West Side continues to be an unusually diverse neighborhood in the St. Paul City- and Twin Cities' Metro Area context, the ethnic change in the neighborhood between 1990 and 2000 is similar, but by no means extreme as compared to the one taking place on the city and metro scale.

7 Ethnic social networks and capital of the Mexican population on the West Side

In this chapter I examine the link between residential segregation of immigrants or 'ethnic' population groups and the development of social capital and social mobility in the context of my case study, the Mexican population on the West Side of St. Paul. The following questions will be specifically discussed in this chapter (see chapter 4)[209]:

1. What kind of social networks can be found among the Mexican population of the West Side and what can be said about their geography?
2. Do the social networks generate or hinder resources that impact on social mobility and other assets of 'value' for the individual immigrant, and if so, how?
3. How do the answers to these questions change with changing individual characteristics, e.g. gender, social class (income), first/second generation immigrants?
4. Does residential clustering in an ethnic neighborhood impact positively or negatively on the development of social networks and capital, and how?

The conceptual framework outlined in chapter 4 has determined the structure of the empirical analysis of this study. Therefore, the categories proposed by Bourdieu (size and volume of social capital; economic, cultural and symbolic capital) are used to assess the nature and extent of social capital generated among the Mexican population on the West Side. Also, Bourdieu's categories for the influence of the physical, on the social space (profits/deficits derived from the proximity to desirable agents and infrastructure, profits of position or rank) are applied to examine the 'site effects' of living on the West Side on its Mexican origin residents.

My principal information sources constitute the interviews conducted with Mexican or Mexican-American residents of the West Side, between November 2004 and May 2005. The interview guideline and a list of the inter-

[209] The research questions related to housing policies and planning are addressed in chapter 9. In that chapter, policy responses to ethnic segregation in other relevant sectors are discussed as well.

viewed residents and their socio-economic and household profiles can be viewed in Annex 2[210]. Expert interviews and complementary qualitative methods, e.g. observation, document review and neighborhood walks were further sources of information (see chapter 5).

The structure of this chapter follows the above research questions[211]: First, the social networks and relationships of Mexicans living in the West Side are discussed, followed by a reflection on their geography. Then, the impact of these ethnic networks on the development of mobility-relevant resources and assets (e.g. income, jobs) is assessed, both in terms of mobility advantages and disadvantages. Finally, the genuinely *spatial* effects of living in an ethnic neighborhood on the generation of social and other capital forms are discussed. The chapter closes with a summary of the foregoing discussions.

7.1 Ethnic social networks and relationships

As explained in chapter 6, the West Side has a long history of Hispanic and particularly Mexican presence in the neighborhood. The arrival of Mexicans on the West Side started in the early decades of the 20th century, continued with varying intensity in the course of the 20th century, and greatly increased in the 1990s. Several Mexican immigrant generations or cohorts cohabitate in the neighborhood. Immigration from other Latin American countries only became significant in the 1990s, although Hispanics from Puerto Rico and Cuba had already been coming to the neighborhood earlier (chapter 6.2).

Against this background, one assumption underlying my research questions requires immediate reframing: Due to the co-residence of several Mexican immigrant generations on the West Side, as well as of different cultural groups of Mexican or Hispanic origin, the existence of one ethno-based Mexican 'community' can all but be taken for granted. Rather, one needs to be aware of the existence of sub-groups within this Mexican population, with different socio-economic characteristics, cultural backgrounds and practices, as well as identities more or less related to their Mexican heritage. The statistical data in chapter 6 has already indicated a strong socio-economic heterogeneity of the Mexican population (view e.g. table 17). Up

---

[210] As pointed out in chapter 5, the true names of the interview partners have been replaced by pseudonyms.

[211] Also the interview guideline was organized according to these broad topics of interest (see chapter 4.4).

to what degree these sub-groups constitute micro-communities on their own is also assessed.

Thus, before elaborating on the types and degree of formality of the social relationships among the Mexican-origin population of the West Side, I describe the nature and elaborate on the reasons of the intra-ethnic differences in the neighborhood.

7.1.1 The heterogeneity of the Mexican population

Contrary to the outside perception[212] of the West Side as *the* Mexican 'community' in the Twin Cities' area, the study revealed considerable frictions inside this Mexican-origin population. The most salient rift runs between long-standing Mexican-American inhabitants, described as a formerly relatively homogeneous group[213], and recent Mexican immigrants to the West Side. Whereas a binary understanding of these two groups should be avoided, partly due to the importance of other categories of social differentiation (see below)[214], the conducted resident and expert interviews reveal that differences between these 'two' groups are strongly felt:

---

[212] I am including my own perception, prior to conducting the empirical study. 'Outside' is used here in geographic terms, i.e. in terms of not living in the neighborhood. It may be more appropriate to extend it towards the non-Mexican or non-Latino inhabitants of the West Side, i.e. to use inside-outside in ethno-cultural terms. However, a further discussion of this reaches beyond the purposes of this document.

[213] Many of the interviewed longstanding Mexican-American residents (nostalgically) mention that prior to the 1990s, the Mexican-American community on the West Side was small, relatively homogeneous in terms of their socio-economic conditions, and characterized by a high level of familiarity. The arrival of numerous Mexican and Hispanic newcomers in the 1990s changed this situation: "[Prior] to the big migration time (…) there was NOT a mass, but there was a lot of familiarity, not enough mass. Then you had mass, but no familiarity!" (Expert 7: 7). However, Expert 7 also maintains that the socio-economic and spatial mobility of some of its members was one factor that had already contributed to some socio-economic differentiation of this tightly-knit community.

[214] A binary definition of these groups is also rendered difficult due to the lack of a clear-cut dividing line, such as a particular moment in time separating 'longstanding' from 'recent' immigrants. For the purpose of this research, 'longstanding and 'Mexican-American' residents are defined as those who were born in the United States, as children of first- and more-generation immigrants. 'Recent-' and 'Mexican immigrants' are defined as those who have themselves migrated to the United States. One interviewee in the HACER-research (chapter 5.2.2) differentiates three West Side Mexican population groups based on the extent of their vulnerability: The first group is the long-term established families, the second immigrants without residence permit or citizenship and the third group the more established first genera-

"[You] also have this large, dramatic influx of immigrants that came into the area. And the interesting thing was that that created a lot of tension. Because even though they were both of Mexican origin, what you discovered, what I discovered, was we had HUGE cultural gaps, between these groups. I mean we had second, third, fourth generation Mexican-Americans, who've never been to Mexico, who didn't speak Spanish, maybe [not even] understood it, still eat some of their food, you know (...) FINALLY you tended to have Mexican-Americans here who started to move upwards socially. And then you got immigrants who would start at the lowest levels of economics. And you started seeing large numbers of (...) Mexicanos, which you know speaks also to a low-income, you know Spanish. So, in many ways the two groups couldn't be more different." (Expert 7: 6)

Whereas the longstanding Mexican-American residents of the West Side constitute a relatively established population group with US citizenship and employment, the recent Mexicans are characterized by unstable living conditions. Cultural differences between the more longstanding Mexican-American residents and the recent Mexican immigrants of the West Side are rooted in different degrees of permeation by the US-American culture[215], as well as different regions of origin, even among the Mexican newcomers[216]. Ronald, a third-generation male Mexican-American resident of the West Side puts it like this:

"We´ve got many more people [since new Hispanic immigrants arrived]. New people, uh, people that are bringing a Southwest uh uh attitude atmosphere to the community, you never would have seen a cowboy hat in our community and now there

tion immigrants, generally due to the several legalization initiatives in the last 20 years (see Box 3).

215 The practices and identities of the second- to fourth-generation Mexican-American with respect to their Mexican culture of 'origin' strongly differ from those of the recent Mexican immigrants. One example of this is the *Cinco de Mayo* celebration, organized on the West Side each year on the week-end of, or following May 5th (see chapter 6.2.1). Whereas from the perspective of the longstanding Mexican-Americans this festivity constitutes the peak manifestation of their Mexicanity, for the recent Mexicans the really important day is September 15th, Independence Day of Mexico: As the *Cinco de Mayo* is not much memorized in México, they "do not see the joke" (Esteban: 5) in this celebration. The women of the "Hispanic Women in Action" group (MHA), all relatively recent arrivals, also complain about the commercialization of Mexican culture in the context of the *Cinco de Mayo* celebration and of prices for food, drinks and games beyond their affordability.

216 According to the interviews carried out by HACER, a major part of the newcomers of the West Side come via California or Texas, i.e. chose the Twin Cities as secondary or tertiary migration destiny. This is also the case of five of the eight adult first-generation migrants of my interviews: Maribel, Elena, Rita, Linda and Manuel.

is you know hundreds and hundreds and thousands of them. (…) Uh, South-West as in Texas, and in Mexico, that sort of approach, you see cowboy hats for sale, cowboy boots for sale. That´s all new to us. There´s no cowboy in me, and I´ve lived here all my life (laughs)." (Ronald: 13)

While the 'objective' economic and cultural differences between longstanding and recent Mexicans or Mexican-Americans of the West Side dispute the dominant perception of 'the' Mexicans as one single group, the more important point is that these differences are strongly highlighted by the Mexicans of the West Side themselves. An important reason for this is that the outside homogenization of 'the' Mexican or Latino population represents a certain status-threat to the longstanding Mexican-Americans of the West Side:

"I think what happens, is that some of the folks who are second or third or fourth generation, you know, they're already pretty mainstream, you know. And I think, they don't wanna be lumped in once, in a sum and belong together with, you know, when you hear on the news, you know 'the Mexicans aren't making it in schools, they're dropping out of schools', or, 'it's the Mexicans doing', I mean, all the negativity, these folks want to make sure, they say, 'wait a minute, they're not talking about me, we're not like them', you know." (Expert 1: 5)

The perceived status gaps coupled with socio-cultural differences also appears in the reflections of this 21-year old male Mexican-American resident, when expressing his own ambiguity towards identifying with Mexican 'culture':

"It's because they [the recent arrivals] don't understand yet that this is a different country or a different state and that there are rules that need to be complied with, and that these rules are what keeps the community sane and together (…) Difficult to think about an example right now. But for instance, like leaving pork chops on the lawn, or run a business at the front of your house, selling tacos. To the American people it's just common sense stuff, but to them it's 'the only way to make a buck." (Arturo: 4f.)

The lack of communication and interaction between the longstanding Mexican-Americans with Mexican newcomers to the West Side is accentuated and magnified by their linguistic differences. Whereas most of the longstanding Mexican-Americans grew up without learning Spanish[217], this is the

[217] The reason for this usually stated by the interviewed residents is the intention of their parents to prevent them from being discriminated against by American mainstream society. Thus, rather than speaking to their children at home in their own language, parents would

language the Mexican newcomers are most acquainted with. The latter focus on the Spanish language however is not true for the mostly bilingual children of the newcomers who grow up in a US-mainstream institutional environment much more open and appreciative towards multi-lingual education and cultural diversity – a point elaborated more on further down.

The places of socialization of longstanding and recent West Side residents of Mexican origin differ considerably, partly due to socio-economic differences. Whereas longstanding Mexican-Americans can afford to get together in coffee shops or restaurants (Mexican or other) in- or outside the neighborhood on a regular basis, this is not the case for economically struggling recent immigrants[218]. However, common locations for socializing do exist[219]. For the young population in neighborhood these are schools or leisure centers, and for the adult population the different religious congregations, particularly the Mexican Catholic parish of Our Lady of Guadalupe (see chapter 6.2.1).

When asked about frequent locations for socializing in the neighborhood (see interview guideline, Annex 4), most of the interviewed Mexican or Mexican-American residents mention "Our Lady of Guadalupe". However, little interaction occurs at Church between long-term and recent Mexicans: On Sundays, the former participate in the English mass at 9 a.m., whereas the latter go to the Spanish masses at 11 a.m. and 1 p.m. According to the Church's priest, in spite of efforts by the Church to join the two groups e.g. by organizing bilingual meetings, they mostly socialize in different meetings

---

speak to their children in (an imperfect) English. This point will be discussed in more detail in chapter 7.2.3.

[218] Geographic mobility constitutes a particular challenge for recent female immigrants from Mexico, as most of them do not drive.

[219] According to Arturo, conflicts frequently arise at school between Mexican-American pupils and those who are children of recent Mexican immigrants. For instance, during his time as president of the Latino Club at High School, some pupils did not join the club as he did not speak Spanish. This points to the difficulty of positioning his identity in the midst of conflicting attributions by others: While his Mexican identity is rejected by (recent) Mexican schoolmates, the "High School tried to put me into the ESL classes, which is English as a Second Language" (Arturo: 4).

or events[220]. He considers the social rifts manifesting in the Church context as part of

"(…) the typical cycle when the immigrants come. Those who have been here for longer don't like the new immigrants, for a variety of reasons. The newcomers are hardworking families. The Mexican-Americans are hardworking families too, but settled in the United States way [back]. And it is a challenge for them to have to reach out to the newer immigrants." (Expert 14: 4)

Although the inter-personal relations between recent Mexican immigrants and longstanding Mexican-Americans are few, a more indirect link between the two groups exists. This is as most of the institutions on the West Side that serve the recent Mexican or Hispanic immigrants, e.g. Neighborhood House, have their origins in the migration history of the – today – longstanding Mexican-Americans or other immigrant groups of the time. Some longstanding Mexican-American residents of the West Side work or are otherwise involved in these organizations. The recent Mexican immigrants benefit of these institutions in a variety of ways, among these the opportunity for building and maintaining social relationships with co-ethnics. A categorization of the neighborhood organizations of the West Side is presented in the next sub-chapter.

In synthesis, two aspects need to be reiterated here: First, the idea of a unitary ethnic social network based on common ethnicity needs to be dismissed for the case of the West Side, in view of the large differences within its Mexican and Mexican-American population. Social interactions between these Mexican sub-groups are almost non-existent due to a variety of factual and constructed differences between them. The relationships inside the subgroups, albeit certainly dynamic, are characterized by mutual solidarity, particularly among some of the (mostly low-income) Mexican newcomers. Second, length of stay appears as the primary axis of difference among the Mexicans on the West Side. This is even more so as other categories of differentiation such as socio-economic status, citizenship status and cultural

[220] One example of the participation of the Mexican or Mexican-American groups in different events, apart from the Sunday masses, constituted the preparation of the Easter celebration which I witnessed on several occasions. On Good Friday, while the longstanding Mexican-Americans socialized in the "Lenten Enchilada dinner" in the parish hall, the recent Mexican immigrants dramatically staged the scene of the crucifixion of Jesus Christ on the square in front of the Church.

and regional background, are partly contingent on the moment of and the time passed since arrival.

7.1.2 Informal and formal social relationships

Taking into account the existence of Mexican sub-groups rather than of a unified community on the West Side, what kind of co-ethnic relationships can be found there, and what is their importance with respect to non-ethnic ones? I broadly categorize these networks according to their informal or formal character: Informal ethnic networks are those between family members, friends or more occasional acquaintances, formal ethnic networks are those that are entertained in the context of an organization or institution. While informal networks tend to be founded in emotional affinity and engagement, formal networks develop through commonly defined objectives and activities, usually in the context of an institution or organization (also see chapter 3)[221].

With respect to informal ethnic relationships, one commonality among the interviewed residents constitutes their attachment to the family. Both long-term Mexican-American and recent Mexican immigrants emphasize its importance, also as a contrast to the perceived little valuation of the family among the mainstream American population ("Because America is WELL known for not being very family oriented, you know", Elena: 10). On the one hand this is due to actively maintained relationships between family members e.g. in the context of family meetings, on the other hand also to an intrinsic value attributed to the family. Carmen, a 22-year old third generation female, when asked about the importance of her Mexican or Latino-, with respect to other-ethnicity contacts:

"I don't, I don't want to ever, put my family, second. So my family is always gonna come first, no matter what. And, because my family has, a Mexican background, they're always gonna be first, no matter what." (Carmen: 6)

---

221 There are other categorizations of social networks that cut across the informal-formal distinction. For instance, some authors distinguish between 'strong' and 'weak', or 'thick' and 'thin' social networks that may develop in the context of both informal and formal relationships (see chapter 3). Furthermore, formal and informal networks do not have to be considered as opposites as two persons may entertain both informal and formal social relationships (e. g. family members who are also members of a community group or parish).

The importance of the family[222] is also emphasized by the religious customs of the 'patronship', exercised in the context of baptisms, communions and confirmations. Through the nomination of friends as *comadres* or *compadres* of a child these friends do not only pay for the respective celebration, but ties between two different families are also strengthened and reiterated on a symbolic level, not least through their consecration by the Church. This custom is invariably exercised by long-term Mexican-Americans and recent Mexican immigrants and for the most part conducted among co-ethnics[223]:

> "Usually, if you choose comadres, this is because you get along well with them, you get along well with the children, you get along well with the family and so, usually, they are Hispanics. Mexicans." (Hermosa: 8)[224]

With respect to friendship relationships, among the recent Mexican immigrants these are predominantly co-ethnics. Among the interviewed female immigrants friendship encounters with other female Mexican immigrants are quite frequent, especially in the context of self-help or other immigrant-related service groups. This is particularly the case if the women are married, not in a full-time employment relationship and have small children – the latter constituting a reason for getting together with other mothers. In contrast, the male interviewees – and working mothers alike[225] - tend to point out time constraints for engaging in regular friendship contacts due to an intense work schedule.

---

[222] John, a 25-year old, third-generation Mexican-American is the only one painting a radically negative picture of his family: "I have brothers incarcerated, I have cousins murdered, from my family. My family, hum, is known as one of the worst families on, in this community. And that's why my name isn't, the best name to have, you know." (John: 3) The ambivalent role of the family with from the perspective of particularly young Mexicans will be elaborated on more in chapter 7.3.2.

[223] In the main text, quotations of interviews conducted in Spanish are presented in English, as I translated them. The Spanish originals are provided in the footnotes.

[224] "Usualmente, cuando agarras tú unas comadres, es porque te llevas bien con ella, te llevas bien con los niños, te llevas bien en la familia y entonces, usualmente, son Hispanas. Mexicanas." (Original wording)

[225] The leader of the women's self-support group "Hispanic Women in Action", Expert 4, confirms that the level of engagement of women with the group greatly depends on their employment hours and quantities.

Box 4: Elena and typical constraints on pursuit of formal or informal social contacts

At the time of the interview, Elena is 42 years old, mother of four children and divorced from her US-American ex-husband. She arrived in the Twin Cities in 1985, however prior to arriving in Minnesota stayed in Tijuana at the Mexican-US-American border for five years. In this city she had worked for an elderly woman with Altzheimer, an employment relationship she describes as extremely precarious: *"There I was like imprisoned, because my work was (...) 24 hours. (...) 24 hours seven days a week. No day off" (own translation). Doing this work, she earned a salary of 100 Dollars a week" (Elena: 2)*[226]. She came to Minnesota following the suggestion of a Mexican female acquaintance in Tijuana and who provided her first shelter in her and a friends' apartment in Downtown in St. Paul. However, the friendship soon broke apart.

Her first years in St. Paul, a city she loves, were marked by the vulnerability imposed by lack of citizenship and related instable work and personal relationships. After leaving her first shelter in Downtown, a Colombian friend of her former Mexican roommates took her to Guadalupe Church on the West Side. There a Mexican-American lady invited her to come live with her family on the West Side *("she said, 'I, I feel like that I can trust you'"*; Elena: 4), where she stayed for three years, at the same time working mornings and afternoons cleaning offices in Downtown St. Paul. In 1988, the lady told her to leave, out of fear that Elena's illegal residence status would have negative bearing on herself and her family: "*And she got very scared, and she asked me to go. (...) She asked me so I has to go and to quit my job. It was very devastating. I almost committed suicide"* (Elena: 6). In 1990, she managed to obtain her documents, which also provided the opportunity to commence her current, regular employment as housekeeper in a St. Paul public hospital. In the hospital she met her ex-husband, to whom she was married for approximately 10 years. After staying in a rental apartment in Downtown St. Paul in the first years, they purchased her present home on the West Side after having their first child.

Elena considers raising her children in decent conditions the central objective of her life. In spite of enjoying a relative degree of stability at the time of the interview (full citizenship, home ownership, stable employment), her life as a single-educating mother of four children, with little support from her husband and a moderate salary continues to be a struggle. It is against this background that apart from occasional get-togethers with her Mexican and Mexican-American neighbors (the former being something like a 'best friend') and telephone conversations with her sister (also living on the West Side) she finds it difficult to pursue or maintain regular social

---

226 "[Allí] yo estuve (ríe un poco) como que se puede decir que yo estuve en una cárcel, porque mi trabajo era de (...) 24 hours. (…) 24 hours seven days a week. No day off." (Original wording)

contacts. Asked about her spaces of socialization she states:
"I don't really do much, in that way (...), my mind is just like, go, uh, go to work, come back, and find what to do, maybe cook something what they [the children] can eat, and then pick up the kitchen and then go to bed." (Elena: 13).

Also Esteban, who came to the US three years prior to the interview, when asked about his regular social contacts states:

"Very difficult to give an answer. Yes, [we meet] with the family, my sisters in law, my brother, but not very often. From time to time, like every 8 days. But everybody has different work times, so sometimes it is hard to go see each other or find a time for a get together." (Esteban: 5)[227]

Among the long-term Mexican-American residents the social relationships or contacts vary greatly. Most of the interviewed long-term residents entertain friendship relationships with Mexican-American *and* Anglo-white persons[228], the latter often stemming from their professional occupations. Those with higher education skills and white-collar occupations (Harry as school principal, JAV as software engineer, Raul in marketing, Ronald in City Hall), tend to socialize more with non-Mexicans, as compared to their rather blue-collar co-ethnics (e.g. Engracia and Ramona as former fabric workers). However, for many of them their old-time Mexican friendships of the West Side, e.g. maintained in the context of religious customs such as the 'comadreship', continue to be important and transcend status-related differences. The latter aspect is expressed by Harry, school principal in a Minneapolis high school and a 54-old second generation immigrant to the West Side:

"I think that we all have that common bond, that we all knew where we came from and I could have some uh, uh, how can I put it some, uh, aura about me now that I'm better now that I'm more educated. I could, but, the reality is we all know where we came from and there is no, uh, pretense to it. So we all, we all feel pretty good about, and proud that we came from the West Side and feel good about whom we

227 "Muy difícil contestar a esto. Sí con la familia, las cuñadas, el hermano, [nos frequentamos], pero muy poco. De vez en cuando, cada ocho días. Pero todos tienen diferentes horarios de trabajo, así que es difícil encontrarse a veces, encontrar un momento para el convivio." (Original wording)

228 In contrast, very few of the interviewed Mexican or Mexican-American adult residents of the West Side state to regularly socialize with African American or Asian people. In the case of the younger interviewees (e.g. Carmen, Tamara, Marco) this is different, some of them being explicit about valuing racially diverse social settings.

are and what we did. So, our jobs or our education are kind of secondary, or even nothing, nothing to do." (Harry: 10)

With respect to formal relationships, among the Mexicans or Mexican-Americans interviewed for this research, more than half were involved in organizations, the majority of them as volunteers. Although not all of these organizations can be considered as 'ethnic', this strikes one as a rather high proportion and not representative of the actual organizational involvement of the Mexican population on the West Side. Rather, it may be the consequence of the interview recruitment that primarily drew on contacts through West Side organizations (see chapter 5).

Notwithstanding the interview bias mentioned, and assuming that the majority of Mexicans of the West Side are *not* involved in ethnic organizations, the interviews reveal certain patterns of organizational involvement: Most of the interviewed Mexicans who *do* participate in ethnic organizations (majority-membership by co-ethnics) are recent arrivals, female, mother of children and have low educational and skills levels. Typically, the involvement in such self-help organizations occurs in the form of voluntary work, as opposed to paid employment, and implies regularly scheduled interactions with co-ethnics, most of the latter also being females. The membership in ethnic neighborhood organizations tends to decrease with increasing length of stay in the United States, as well as with increasing income and/or educational levels.

Box 5: Linda, a 'typical' member of ethnic support groups

At the time of the interview, Linda, a female Mexican immigrant, is 28 years old, married and the mother of three children. She has arrived in Minnesota 5 years ago, following her husband who had come three years before her, himself following his father. Whereas her husband had directly migrated from Mexico to St. Paul, she came via Las Vegas, where she had spent six months with her brother and several uncles, her husband showing himself reluctant to be joined by her and their two eldest children. Her husband is employed as a house painter, in the same enterprise as this father and uncle. Apart from her primary occupation as housewife with child-rearing and house-keeping tasks, she works a few hours a week for Neighborhood House in the program "Plain Talk" (*Hablando Claro)* conducting sexual education for Hispanic parents, in Spanish.

She describes her time of arrival on the West Side as difficult, due to her inability to speak the English language and not knowing anybody. After a while she came to know about a women's group in her apartment building, targeted at Hispanic women

> for doing handcraft work, such as stitching. Through this group she learnt about a service organization called “West Side Family Center” who offered free child-care, and there, through acquaintances with other Hispanic women, heard about Neighborhood House and the group “Hispanic Women in Action” (*Mujeres Hispanas en Acción, MHA*) of which she was a member at the time of the interview. During the week she is involved in different support groups for Hispanic women: On Monday evenings a group facilitated by a psychologist in Minneapolis, on Wednesday evenings the “Hispanic Women in Action” group on the West Side and on Fridays a group against domestic violence offered by a Latino service group based on thc East Side of St. Paul.
>
> She describes that involvement in these organization accrues multiple benefits to her: The possibility of talking to somebody, of obtaining goods such as free winter jackets for her children, information about services and organizations, educational and/or work opportunities and finally the possibility to gain distance from her family and marriage environment.

The organizational landscape on the West Side is varied with respect to the nature and thematic focus of the neighborhood organizations. An overview of the organizations most frequently mentioned in the resident interviews is provided in Annex 7. Due to the numeric importance of the Mexicans and Latino population on the West Side, most of the organizations have developed some link with this group, although not all of them are explicitly targeted towards Mexicans or Latinos. Most of the organizations can be attributed to one of the following categories:

1. <u>Self-help or support organizations</u> facilitated by Mexican or Hispanic leaders and exclusively targeted at this ethnic or language population. The “Hispanic Women in Action” group, forming a subgroup of Neighborhood House, constitutes one example of such group.
2. <u>Social service institutions</u> of which the Mexican or Latino population may or may not form the predominant participants. Examples of this type are “Neighborhood House” (providing food delivery, parental and health education, youth promotion), “La Familia Guidance Center” (mental health services in Spanish) or “La Clínica” (medical services in Spanish). Organizations targeted towards the youth (e.g. sports and leisure groups, such as “Boys and Girls Club”) also form part of this category.

3. Community development corporations (CDCs) that provide business development- or housing-related services with an overall objective of West Side community development and/or upgrading. Examples of this organizational type constitute the "Riverview Economic Development Co-operation (REDA) or "Neighborhood Development Co-operation" (NEDA)[229].

The typical "clients"[230] of all these organizations constitute relatively recent Mexicans or Hispanic immigrants. Adapting to the needs of this clientele, the services of these organizations are relatively affordable as compared to the ones of American service providers e.g. hospitals, and completely or partly offered in the Spanish language[231].

The only institution on the West Side where the social networks of the recent Mexican immigrants and those of long-standing Mexican-Americans converge – and one forming a separate, fourth category of organization - is the Catholic Church, "Our Lady of Guadalupe". However, according to the priest of the parish the two groups rarely get involved with each other but rather co-exist side by side. Whereas for the older members of long-standing Mexican-Americans the Church constitutes THE site for active inter-ethnic networking, the recent Mexican or Hispanic families primarily participate in the Sunday masses or certain religious holidays[232]. However, they would not partake in the organization of Church events and festivals, not least due to linguistic and affordability discrepancies:

---

229 The West Side Citizens' Corporation (WSCO) also forms part of the West Side's CDCs however it maintains a rather remote link to the Hispanic population only.

230 Mexicans or Hispanics are not only clients of these organizations, but some of them work in them as employees – and tend to be rather longstanding Mexican-Americans. However, the proportion of Mexican/Hispanic employees is rather small and therefore not presented as the typical situation here.

231 If partly or totally offered in Spanish depends on whether the Hispanic population constitutes the only target group or one among others. Service providers such as "La Familia Guidance Center" and "La Clínica" cater specifically for the Mexican and Hispanic population. Others such as Neighborhood House or NeDA also provide their services to other immigrant groups or the native population in need.

232 According to the priest, the rosaries or "novenas" before Christmas are examples for such religious celebrations joined by the recent Mexican immigrants. In these cases, the longstanding Mexican-Americans would not partake, as it does not correspond to THEIR religious traditions. But for the most part, according to the priest, the support networks of the recent immigrants are outside of the Church.

"Because what the [old] families do is buy the food themselves, cook it and then sell it, and all the money comes to the Church. But a lot of them [the recent immigrants] do not have the money to do so, to buy all the food. So there is a lot of ways that they are excluded because of financial reasons and because of the language." (Expert 14: 3)

In synthesis, informal networks with co-ethnics are maintained by both recent Mexican immigrants and longstanding Mexican-Americans, albeit with different intensities and different functions[233], also depending on the individuals' gender and social status. Institutionalized or formal relationships with co-ethnics mostly occur between, and for, recent Mexican immigrants, the latter being most in need of the services offered by these networks, e.g. English language classes, training courses and food-shelves. The Church constitutes an exception, as both recent Mexicans and long-standing Mexican-Americans go there. Although the networks of the two groups do not, or only rarely converge in the context of Church activities or events, this organization fulfils a particular, and even sacred, function.

Both formal and informal networks shape social and spatial senses of belonging and foster ethnic residential segregation or clustering. They constitute 'pull-factors' for attracting recent arrivals to the neighborhood, as pointed out by Ronald:

"[In] Mexico or in in other Latino communities in the United States, further down South, specifically Texas, hum, the Church plays a great role in, in those communities, so when folks are new to this area (…), they often ask the question of of of whoever they meet, where do the Mexicans live. Most people still identify the West Side as the place **where the Mexicans live**, and the second question that person usually asks, that new arrival, is ′where is the **Guadalupe Church**′? (…) Guadalupe Church is a, is a the name itself is prevalent in many communities, around the country. So if you come out of Kansas, there is Guadalupe Church in Kansas, if you come out of Oklahoma, there is Guadalupe Church in Oklahoma, you come out of Texas, the Mexicans live around Guadalupe Church. Anyway you go, if there is a Guadalupe Church, the surrounding neighborhood will be Mexican. So, people are comfortable with that, identify that as a place where they get help, so when they get here, they will ask, ′Is there Guadalupe Church′?, because they know that that will be Mexican, and that will be Spanish speaking." (Ronald: 11, own emphasis)

---

[233] Whereas for the longstanding Mexican-Americans the ethnic networks mainly fulfill the function of bringing by social comfort, for the recent Mexican immigrants they are much more instrumental for getting by and ahead in the new society. This will be elaborated on in more detail in chapter 7.2.

The spatial dimensions of ethnic social networks will be elaborated on more in subsection 7.3 of this chapter.

With increasing length of stay and social status the relationships with co-ethnics are likely to become less important, compared to relationships developed in the context of e.g. educational- or work environments. In the present research this was particularly observed among the longstanding Mexican-Americans with a higher educational degree[234]. As Expert 9 from Neighborhood House states:

"Because so many people experience economic success or enough economic success to LEAVE a community and they do so, within a ethnic community." (Expert 9: 9)

Box 6: Ronald, an 'untypical' case of life-long engagement in neighborhood organizations

At the time of the interview, Ronald, a male second generation immigrant, is 55 years old, married and the father of four children. Born into a family with four siblings he was the first one born in St. Paul, in the 'old' community of the West Side "Flats", where his family settled in 1949, together with his grand-mother, aunts and uncle. His brothers and sisters had been born in the State of Kansas. Before settling in St. Paul, Minnesota, the extended family had passed by Chicago, in the quest of work.

Since his early childhood, Ronald was tightly involved in the organizational networks of the Mexican and the West Side community. During his youth Guadalupe Church, founded in the 1930s, formed "the contact point for (…) any kind of assistance program or any job opportunities" (Ronald: 2), and also for celebrations during school holidays. In terms of daily assistance, Neighborhood House constituted an important point of encounter, e.g. holding occasional food-shelves, as well as job referral programs for those in need. Additionally, during his childhood and adolescence, Neighborhood House would be the crystallizing point for any kind of youth recreation and organization activity: "I'd always been a part of Neighborhood House as a participant, as a kid, in the athletic programs, the social programs, the camping programs and everything" (Ronald: 4), mostly among other Mexican-American adolescents. Together with several other Mexican-American males he founded the "West Side Boosters Club" for the promotion of athletics in the neighborhood.

After serving the US Army in the Vietnam War, he obtained an employment in the Youth Department of Neighborhood House. His employment entry in several youth

[234] Among the interviewed residents of the West Side one had a Master's Degree (Harry), three other possessed college degrees (Juana, Monica, Raul) and one (Carmen) was attending college (see Annex 2).

promotion-programs at Neighborhood House on the West Side lead to work opportunities with the City of St. Paul government and administration, among others to run a civil service program for youth in low-income communities of St. Paul. At the time of the interview he had just been appointed "youth outreach coordinator" for a new city program, after having filled the position of "Director of the Citizen Service Office" of the city government in the previous three years.

Notwithstanding his professional advancement up to the level of the higher city administration, he continues being a West Side resident and strongly engaged with West Side organizations, mostly in advisory or governance positions: as a member of the Board of Directors of Neighborhood House, a trustee and member of the Men's Club at Guadalupe Church, a member of the West Side Boosters Club and an advisor for the West Side Citizens' Organization, WSCO.

7.1.3 The geography of social networks

Against the background of the academic discussions on transnational social networks (chapter 3.3), I researched the question of whether the social networks of Mexicans from the West Side are of a purely local nature (on the neighborhood or city level) or whether they transcend national borders, i.e. ranging towards the home country. Furthermore, if transnational social links (defined as the whole array of formal and informal practices linking individuals of two different nations; view Mahler 1998: 82) exist, it needs to be asked what the functions of these networks are.

Not surprisingly, on the West Side the geographic extension of ethnic social networks varies considerably among the longstanding Mexican-Americans and recent Mexican immigrants. In the case of the former, the ethnic social networks, whether formal or informal, are of predominantly local nature, except contacts with family members in the Twin Cities metro area, within the State of Minnesota or in other states of the US. None of the interviewed long-standing, i.e. second- and more generation, Mexican Americans stated that they were involved in transnational engagements, such as realizing phone calls or sending money or gifts to Mexico on a regular basis. Contacts with family or friends in Mexico or journeys to this country are rare among them. Some of the longstanding Mexican-Americans (Harry, Ronald, Theo, Carmen, John) ignore the regions of origin of their families. Others however describe the journeys to Mexico as an important aspect of their life due to the maintenance of family connections[235].

In contrast, for first-generation Mexican immigrants of the West Side, social contacts with the home country are frequent. The nature of these contacts greatly depends on the economic background and the citizenship status of the immigrants. For instance, journeys to Mexico are difficult in the case of an unresolved documentation situation, the latter being the case for most of the interviewed Mexicans who have been in the States for less than 15 years[236]. Exceptions hereto form temporary migrant experiences. Although examples of family members traveling back and forth between Mexico and the United States are occasionally mentioned, none of the interviewed Mexicans was in this situation him- or herself[237].

With journeys to Mexico being rather rare, almost all of the interviewed first-generation immigrants carry out regular, monthly phone-calls and send money to family elders in Mexico. Emilia, a 77-year old Mexican-American female who had arrived in Minnesota at the age of 19, regularly takes clothes to her home village in Mexico, for sale and for free. Three of the interviewed Mexicans (Maribel, Rita, Emilia) also have phone calls with family members who live in other cities or States in the US, as well as occasional visits, depending on their financial possibilities. However, in the case of most of the interviewed recent Mexican immigrants, members of their family (brothers and sisters, uncles, aunts or parents) are equally based in the Twin Cities – a consequence of the migration trajectory[238].

---

235 Francisco and Leon travel to Mexico and visit their extended families on a regular basis. Both of them have childhood memories of being in or traveling to Mexico, in the case of Francisco due to regular family journeys to his parents' home country, and in the case of Leon because of growing up in Mexico until the age of 6. In the case of most of the other interviewed Mexican-Americans the link to their home country is much more remote. For instance, Ronald states he travels to Mexico at times for holiday, and if so, to Cancoon, an international tourist destination.

236 This is an assumption, as except in the last three interviews carried out with recent Mexican immigrants, I did not directly ask about their citizenship status (see chapter 5.3.1).

237 For instance, for work purposes the brother of Linda travels back and forth between his hometown in México, where his family stays, and Las Vegas. The brother-in-law of Rita travels back and forth between Mexico, where his family stays, and Minneapolis.

238 Almost all of the recent Mexican immigrants state that they have either followed family 'pioneers' to the Twin Cities, or that they have been followed by family members.

Only the two most recent arrivals out of the recent interviewed immigrants on the West Side, Esteban and Mercedes, are saving money in the US for future housing or business investment in Mexico. However, the more typical case presented in the majority of the interviews with recent Mexican immigrants on the West Side, is the one of Linda. She has resolved to stay in the United States, thus rejecting plans to return to México prevailing in the first years after her arrival:

"So then we were like already thinking about; my husband was like, if I wanted us to buy a house, and I told him, well I think that, yes. Before I told him, no! As I told him, if we go back to Mexico, let's better buy a house in Mexico and that's it. But afterwards I said, well, we won't go back anymore, we're already here now (…). So, then we started with the necessary processes [for mortgage] and all that." (Linda: 8)[239]

In synthesis, among the recent Mexican immigrants of the West Side social relationships with family members and – to a much lesser degree – friends in Mexico are maintained through a variety of activities (journeys, phone calls, remittances, occasional gifts). This being said, these activities do not justify a notion of 'bifocality' or dual reference to the home and host country (Mahler 1998: 77ff.), except in the cases of Esteban and Mercedes who plan to go back to Mexico after saving a certain amount of money and gaining proficiency in English. Rather, the lives of the majority of these recent Mexican immigrants are much more locally focused, not least as a consequence of economic or legal restrictions[240]. This is reinforced by common decisions of new arrivals to move into a neighborhood where family members already live – thereby accentuating ethnic residential clustering. More or less regular phone calls or remittances to Mexico constitute the two most frequent manifestations of cross-national social interaction. These practices seem to be principally rooted in emotional ties with family members on the

239 "Entonces ya después, ya andábamos, este, mi esposo estaba que, que si quería que compráramos casa, y le dije, pues yo creo que. Antes le decía que no! Porque decía pues no, si nos vamos para México, mejor compramos la casa en México y ya. Pero después dije, no, dije, yo ni nos vamos a ir, ya estamos (...) Entonces ya, después empezamos ya, con los trámites, y todo eso." (Original wording)

240 A situation also observed by Mahler in the case of Salvadorian immigrants to Long Island (view Mahler 1998: 80).

one hand, and feelings of obligation, on the other[241]. Among the long-standing Mexican-Americans of the West Side cross-national social relationships with family or friends in Mexico are much more rare.

7.2 Social networks and the development of social capital

The research on the West Side showed numerous relationships between the social networks among co-ethnic and the development of *social capital.* In qualitative terms, the amount of social capital is defined as the volume of the economic, cultural or symbolic capital possessed by those to whom the person is connected – implying potential capital transfer effects on this person (Bourdieu 1986, chapter 3.1)[242]. Against this background, the empirical research focused on the question whether the social relationships among Mexican or Mexican-American co-ethnics on the West Side translate into mobility-benefits or -costs, and in which ways they do so.

Thus, in the following sub-chapters I discuss in what way the social networks among Mexicans on the West Side affect each of the constitutive factors of social capital: economic, cultural and symbolic capital. I also reflect on the relevance of other forms of capital, not included in Bourdieu's capital theory. Finally, I formulate an overall assessment of the amount of ethnic social capital on the West Side, also taking into account that this assessment might differ among individuals with different social characteristics.

7.2.1 Economic impacts

In what way do ethnic social networks influence the generation of income or wealth? The interviews with the Mexican and Mexican-American residents of the West Side suggest the following: First, the relevance of co-ethnic networks and acquaintances for economic advancement is highest among recent adult immigrants, generally with low skills levels. These co-ethnic networks and acquaintances mostly occur in the neighborhood context, hence their spatial dimension (see section 7.3). With increasing length of stay, i.e. in the

---

241 Until what degree such practices comply a status-reiterating function cannot be answered on the basis of the realized interviews, and much less from the perspective of the receiving end.

242 According to Bourdieu (1986), the amount of social capital depends on the size of formal or informal networks a person can mobilize, as well as on the capital weight inherent in these networks. I will focus on the latter aspect, as it constitutes the more decisive ones in Bourdieu's conceptualization and the difficulty of assessing the size of networks against an objective measure.

case of second- or more generation Mexican-American residents of the West Side, co-ethnic social networks are rather unlikely to be instrumental for economic advancement, especially in the case of Mexican-Americans with higher educational degrees.

For the recent adult Mexican immigrants their co-ethnic relationships bring about direct economic benefits, generally in the form of information about job opportunities. Almost all the interviewed recent Mexican immigrants on the West Side arrived in Minnesota following extended family members who had already been there for longer[243], who are usually of the *husband's* family. For instance Rita, 36, states:

"I came to Minnesota following my husband. This was in order to give him the opportunity to get together with his brothers, because in California he was alone, he did not have any family members staying there, it was only us [husband, wife and two children]. It was only myself who had family members staying there." (Rita: 1)[244]

Her husband Manuel, 43, describes a quite typical *male* job acquisition trajectory of recent Mexican arrivals on the West Side:

"Well, a brother of mine was here and so, he told if I wanted to come here, as there were opportunities and employment here. And so I came, and three days later I started working in a tomato packing enterprise. (…) Because my brother was working there." (Manuel: 1)[245]

In the case of recent Mexican immigrants, co-ethnic networks help with overcoming legal obstacles for finding employment. As the majority of Mexican immigrants who arrived in the 1990s lack full citizenship or even legal residence status, co-ethnic intermediaries assist – against remuneration - with the production of false documents. Possessing documents, albeit false, constitutes a minimum employment requirement by most businesses.

---

[243] Elena forms an exception here, arriving via the connection of a friend.

[244] "[Yo] me vine a Minnesota siguiendo a mi esposo. Porque, por darle este, por darle a mi esposo la oportunidad de compartir con sus hermanos, porque él en la California estaba sólo, no tenía familia, nada más nosotros. Nada más, pues nada más yo tenía familia." (Original wording)

[245] "Este, un hermano estaba aquí entonces a, me dijo no pues, si quieres venirte pues aquí [en Minnesota] hay oportunidades y trabajo. Y sí, me vine y, y a los tres días comencé a trabajar en una empacadora de tomates. (...) Porque mi hermano estaba, había trabajado antes allí." (Original wording)

Among recent female Mexican immigrants the employment experience greatly depends on their family situation, as well as on their level of adherence to traditional gender roles[246]. In most cases housekeeping and child-caring responsibilities lead to limited work opportunities. Thus, three of the interviewed female Mexican immigrants (Maribel, Linda, and Rita) are not employed or only work occasionally due to having small children. Mercedes works part-time in an ethnic grocery store on the West Side, an employment opportunity facilitated by her husband, who also works there. Hermosa, 39, at the time of conducting the interview did not work as, besides her household and family tasks, she was pursuing her studies to obtain a degree as a licensed nurse.

However, the employment trajectory of Hermosa seems quite typical in terms of the way female Mexican immigrants on the West Side obtain their employment, many times on a part-time basis. She got her first remunerated work in Minnesota in the cleaning service of a hotel after having participated in a preparatory class in the "Hispanic women in Action" group in Neighborhood House:

"In the context of Neighborhood House where I participated in the group, a lady came to the group and offered a class in hospitality. And this was about how to work in a hotel. So, when [after] I took this class with this lady, I went to a hotel. And then, well, they gave me the job in the hotel." (Hermosa: 6)[247]

The participation in formal ethnic networks such as the "Hispanic Women in Action" group tends to engender both direct and indirect benefits for employment acquisition for recent female immigrants. Direct benefits accrue if employment is accessed through reference by a co-ethnic friend or acquaintance. Benefits are more indirect if the participation in the group has helped

---

246 The adherence to traditional, i.e. patriarchal family life- and role models seems more likely in the case of less educated women, and arguably those of more rural areas of origin, such as Linda and Rita. For instance, Rita states that in spite of the difficulties to make ends meet economically, her husband does not allow her to work, due to the presence of children. On the contrary, in the families of Esteban and Mercedes, both of them from Mexico City and possessing a high school and technical school education, both husband and wife work. In the case of Esteban, also the child-caring responsibilities are distributed evenly between husband and wife.

247 "(En) el medio del Neighborhood House que yo asistía al grupo, una muchacha fue allá al grupo a dar clases como de hospitality. Y eso era cómo trabajar en un hotel. Entonces, cuando yo agarré este curso, con esta muchacha, fui buscar trabajo en un hotel. Y entonces, pues me dieron el trabajo en el hotel." (Original wording)

the women with something else that is useful for a later job search: e.g. on-the-job training like in the case of Hermosa for the cleaning job in the hotel, information about free English language courses, driving classes and employment agencies, or the promotion of 'soft' skills such as being able to speak in public or respond to employer expectancies in a job interview[248].

The interviews carried out with recent Mexican immigrants suggest that indirect employment-relevant benefits are more prevalent and probably even more important than direct ones. They are particularly important as they help to improve the job perspectives of the (mostly female) Mexican immigrants beyond their present situation, as well as improving their general living situation and capabilities. As the leader of the "Hispanic Women in Action" puts it:

"I see that the group, that the women are more, I mean that our mission is getting fulfilled. That the women feel more self-confident than when I first met them, because a lot of the women continue to be the same, and so, they speak English already, they already know better how to get around, and can already work in other things." (Expert 4: 1)[249]

The relevance of co-ethnic social networks for economic advancement, e.g. for obtaining employment, are not nearly as strong in the case of longstanding Mexican-American residents. Particularly in the case of the interviewed longstanding Mexican-Americans with a college- or university-degree (Monica, Juana, Raul, Harry, future: Carmen) co-ethnic networks play a near to zero-role with respect to facilitating employment or professional advancement – part of the reason being the relatively inferior educational levels of the population of Mexican origin from the West Side (chapter 6.3).

However, this does not mean that co-ethnic social networks do not bring by any economic benefit for these longstanding, relatively high-skilled Mexican-Americans from the West Side. For instance, Juana, a 39-year old software engineer and single-educating mother emphasizes the advantage of having her mother live in close proximity to her. This is because of the pos-

---

248 The skills development aspect will be further elaborated on in the subsequent chapter (7.2.2).

249 "(Veo) que el grupo, que las mujeres están más, o sea que la misión se está cumpliendo. Que las mujeres se sienten más este, más confidentes a cuando yo las conocí, porque muchas mujeres todavía siguen, son las mismas personas, y este, ya saben hablar Inglés, ya se pueden mover más, ya pueden este trabajar en otras cosas." (Original wording)

sibility to have her 11-year old daughter go there to after school – instead of to a paid child-care service.

In the case of two of the interviewed long-standing Mexican-American males, Ronald and Theo, their (formal) neighborhood contacts lead to employment connections and mobility outside the ethnic networks and community. For Ronald, 55, who was born on the West Side, the year-long work in the youth department of Neighborhood House has eventually resulted in his current high-responsibility occupation with the city government of St. Paul (see Box 6). Theo, in his 50s, also born on the West Side and son of a Mexican father and US-American mother, went from working in a West Side neighborhood recreation center to work in recreation centers in other neighborhoods in the city – considering this as a valuable opportunity for his "personal growth, to meet and experience other things, other than the West Side" (Theo: 8) and make new contacts. Apart from job mobility, he also experienced residential mobility to a higher-income suburb, having sold his first home on the West Side doubling the (absolute) value of its initial purchase price. However, he mentions that a lack of emphasis on education of the neighborhood High School and his consequent school drop-out constrained his tertiary education opportunities to begin with.

Thus, in the case of Ronald and Theo the mobility benefits engendered by ethnic neighborhood organizational networks ended up compensating to a certain degree for the educational disadvantages associated with growing up among co-ethnics and in an 'ethnic neighborhood'. This aspect will be further discussed in the subsequent section.

7.2.2 Educational impacts and symbolic values

The influence of ethnic social networks on the development of educational skills, or cultural capital, differs considerably among recent Mexican immigrants and their long-standing co-ethnics from the West Side. Whereas for recent immigrants – generally parting from low educational and skills levels - the formal and informal ethnic networks considerably help with skills acquisition, for second- and more generation Mexican-Americans this could not be observed. A second important difference, intersecting the first, arises if one compares the perspective of adults with that of children or youth of Mexican origin: Social contacts with co-ethnics tend to effectively promote employment-relevant skills and work perspectives for adults. In contrast, they are not unlikely to hold back the educational advancement of youth.

In the case of recent male Mexican immigrants the acquisition of skills is rarely explicitly mentioned. Most of the male immigrants or husbands of the interviewed women have acquired their current jobs via co-ethnic family contacts: Manuel in the construction sector, Esteban in a grocery store, Fermin in food processing and restaurant, the husband of Maribel as an assembly worker, the husbands of Hermosa and Mercedes in food processing and the husband of Linda in construction work. It can be assumed that after working for some time in these jobs, they have obtained some informal on-the-job-training instrumental for future job searches. Esteban, who is working in a Mexican grocery store on the West Side, mentions that the work in this store in the last two and a half years has helped him learn a lot, e.g. how to give food orders in English. It has also lead to employment mobility inside his present work as his former supervisor has sought him out as his successor[250].

Female (married) immigrants have obtained job- or skills development opportunities through socializing and spending their time in ethnic self-help groups. For instance, Hermosa, 39, accessed several vocational training workshops, job contacts and a community college scholarship through participation in the group "Hispanic Women in Action":

"Because there, everything happened. Because the woman who talked about the hotels [jobs] came there to make a presentation. From there she gathered a group for classes [in hotel services]. And normally, when they give classes in something, I always register. Because usually it helps me a lot. And learning a lot has helped me a lot. And it has opened doors for me." (Hermosa: 7)[251]

Forming part of more or less formal co-ethnic networks usually facilitates the information about free English language courses provided in some of the

---

[250] However, Esteban relates the employment situation in the ethnic grocery store as far from harmonious, due to the rivalries among Mexicans with different regions of origin, particularly between those coming from the capital and those from the provinces. His two former supervisors came from Guadalajara and, according to him, did everything to prevent him, coming from Mexico City, to succeed and to learn new things.

[251] "Porque allí todo lo. Porque la muchacha que habló de los hoteles llegó allí para dar una presentación. Con, este, juntó un grupo que quien quería tomar en las clases. Y pues, usualmente yo cuando van a dar clases de algo, yo siempre me apunto. Porque me sirve mucho. Y me ha ayudado mucho que, que aprenda mucho. Y me ha, me ha abierto puertas." (Original wording)

West Side institutions, like Neighborhood House[252]. Learning the English language is described as a challenge by most of the adult interviewees, but also as a necessity to get along and ahead in the new society[253]. Expert 8, member of a Hispanic research and advocacy organization and former resident of the West Side posits her aunt's social mobility as a consequence of language and other skills ultimately facilitated through her co-ethnic networks:

"And then she WALKED across the street to the Neighborhood House, where she took English classes. (…) She helps OTHER people in the English classes, and she's also given Mexican cooking classes for the Community Education Program. (…) Oh, and she also went to school, she went to school at St. Paul [Technical College], to be a cook. A Sous-Chef. So, she used to just cook at home, and she was always a good cook at home, but she went on to learn how to be a Sous-Chef, and worked in the St. Paul Athletic Club restaurant. And that's, Athletic Club, that's a private club! So, she was able to find some social mobility, in Minnea, in St. Paul, on the West Side, because she had family connections there, and those family connections had friends, right, so they set up (…) who came here with three little kids, so that she could go on and pursue her education and get a job, and her children could aspire to get an education. Now, her kids are all college educated. Her son's an engineer, her daughter's a financial [sic], her daughter makes more money than any of us." (Expert 8: 5)

However, the interviews with Mexican residents of the West Side suggest that ethnic social and family networks can have a detrimental effect on the school trajectories of children and youth. This may happen as adult family members, possessing few academic skills themselves, place a rather low value on education or are not acquainted with educational and child-welfare regulations in the United States[254]. It may also be due to time constraints experienced in the context of social and economic stress of many of the more recent immigrant families or due to institutional barriers occurring in the

---

252 This is even more the case for female immigrants, as the ability to attend English classes of the recent male immigrants is usually limited by their intensive work schedules. Thus, they tend to acquire some English skills through the contact with Anglo-American co-workers or clients, however depending on the intensity of this contact.

253 It can be assumed that the need to linguistically adapt to the host country, e.g. to obtain employment, is greater in an urban environment like the one of St. Paul and the Twin Cities with relatively small immigrant populations and enclaves as compared to urban areas with far larger immigrant groups, e.g. New York or Chicago.

254 Thus the importance, according to Experts 9 and 11, of sensitizing and involving parents in the education of their children.

context of segregation. The latter aspect is more extensively discussed in section 7.3.

The reasons for negative educational and overall social impacts of ethnic networks are gender-sensitive: Male youth are perceived to be at risk to get drawn in problematic peer-dynamics, e.g. gangs. This is effectively reflected in the case of John:

Box 7: John and negative educational impacts of ethnic social networks on male youth

At the time of the interview John is 25 years old and working as the teen coordinator in the Boys and Girls Club on the West Side. He grew up on the West Side as the son of a Mexican-Native American mother and Mexican father describing his 'ethnic' background as one rather hybridized through city life than determined by any one single ethnicity: "I am urban, I am more a city than ... I am a race and I am Hispanic and Native American, but I don't consider myself you know, all, completely that" (John: 1). His mother and father passed away in the course of his childhood and youth. According to John, both deaths were linked to alcohol and drug abuse.

John relates his youth as one strongly imprinted by a problematic and dysfunctional family and peer environment. His father came to the United States and from the very beginning was involved in drug dealing. His mother and father had been subjected to bad influences and child abuse during their youth and that was what he, his siblings (one of the same parents, two others of a different father and a different mother, respectively) and his cousins grew up with, too. When his mother passed away in 1988, he went to live with his aunt, also in the West Side: "[And], hum, her three suns and her old, uh, youngest, uh, her oldest daughter, and they were the ones, mainly, you know the drug abusers and drug addicts and everything at the time, and, they were, you know, sexual abusers to their, to their wives or their girlfriends, and I've seen that all, and I was raised by that (…)". Thus, he states having experienced all the negative sides of the West Side community, exemplified by his family and extended family peer environment. However, these influences were not all negative. Due to the help of his elder brother and to being involved with sports and the West Side's Boys and Girls Club he eventually "went to the other side, the good side, the positive side". Against the background of his own youth, he considers bringing about positive peer pressure and experiences to his own family and children and to youth of the neighborhood as his personal 'mission'.

John attended Roosevelt and Cherokee elementary schools and Humboldt high school on the West Side. As he did not finish high school in a regular manner he obtained an alternative high school degree (GED - General Equivalency Diploma) from an alternative learning center. Although he does not explicitly relate his family and peer environment to his school trajectory, the connection is implicit in the way he talks about the latter's implications on his life in general.

In contrast, the educational trajectory of young females seems to be threatened by the sometimes patriarchal view of their role in the households and as (future) mothers[255]. The case of Carmen reflects this:

Box 8: Carmen and negative educational impacts of ethnic social networks on female youth

At the time of the interview Carmen, daughter of a Mexican mother and Puerto Rican father, is 22 years old, a college student at the University of Minnesota and no longer living on the West Side. After growing up on the West Side until the age of 19, she moved away from there. Her present apartment is located between the St. Paul and Minneapolis University campuses. Apart from pursuing her studies at the University she works in a Mexican restaurant on the West Side and in a group home for handicapped persons in Eagan, a Twin Cities' suburb.

She directly ties the decision to move away from the West Side to the difficulty of 'balancing the bowl' between her college studies and family obligations: "Just because when I lived at home, and I was at school, there was a lot of, family issues, that I had to deal with, and there was a lot of family responsibility that I had to deal with. And I didn't, I really didn't want to do that. I wanted to focus on school" (Carmen: 7). As pursuing and concluding her college studies constitute high priorities for her, she did not concede to what she assumes to be her mother's desire: having her stay at home. She wishes to be able to make her brother leave the West Side, in order to distance himself from role models pernicious for his educational and general future: And I really really want him to go to college, and I really really want him to be successful, and I really want him to advance and like to do something with himself. Maybe move off from the West Side, if that is, ..., I don't want to say holding him back, but he's so caught up, in just not doing anything" (Carmen: 6). In a similar family scenario as in the case of John, she describes her father, her brother and her cousins as caught up in the life style of drugs and 'not working'.

In spite of her marking - also physical - distance to her family she takes pains in

---

[255] In a similar vein, Expert 7 recalls a case of a Mexican female student from Los Angeles whose father refused to attend her graduation ceremony: "Because her father, and I understand this, this is very common, her father didn't think that it was right for her to leave home. You know, a woman by herself, going away to college, very traditional in the community (...), and my understanding is that this is true of many other of her peers as well. And, fortunately she was strong headed enough [laughs] to go ahead with her desire and so she didn't try to step, go back and try to make peace with her father about it, so she didn't let him stop her, but I wonder how many other people did stop." (Expert 7: 5)

emphasizing the loyalty towards her family ("I don't want to ever, put my family, second", Carmen: 6), and the West Side: "I I really, I loved growing up there" (Carmen: 4). Living on the West Side and being among people 'like her' entails maximum comfort, however minimum chances for social and economic advancement. What appears as a loyalty conflict between the strong ties with the West Side and the opportunities out there also emerges when asked about plans for her future life. While stating that she would like to move away and seek out further opportunities, preferably in a warmer state than Minnesota, she also emphasizes that she would like to take her mother, brother and cousins with her, instead of doing this on her own.

However, the institutional environment may also be blind to cultural assets of immigrant populations – and thereby prevent them to unfold. The linguistic reality of the West Side constitutes a point in case. Almost all the adult Mexican-American interviewees were English speakers and most of them unable to speak Spanish[256]. This is at least true for the population growing up and going to school on the West Side until the 1990s. All of them point out the same reason for this situation, as explained here by Theo:

"I asked my Dad that once. I was in my late twenties. I said, Dad, how come we never learned Spanish at home? (…) He says, the reason we didn't teach Spanish is, because if you had, **if you wanted to get ahead**, you had to learn English. [Eva: Hmhmm]. So that was the priority. Cause, now I look back, if I could speak two languages, wouldn't that be intelligent?!" (Theo: 15, own emphasis)

The last two paragraphs suggest two important aspects: The first one is that also low-income or blue-collar parents want their children to succeed in society, although the idea of what this success entails may differ from that of, say, white-collar parents.

The second relates to the symbolic side of social or, for the present matter, cultural capital: The value attributed to certain capabilities, e.g. proficiency in a foreign language, is by no means constant, but rather contingent on a more or less favorable social and institutional environment. This environment, generally controlled by the most powerful members of a society, shapes people's (self-) esteem on the relevance of their knowledge, and materializes in institutional programs, e.g. educational curricula and strategies. The role of the educational institutions (e. g. schools and the school district) in shaping the educational achievement of Mexican youth on the West Side

[256] View field on Spanish language proficiency in interviewee matrix in Annex 2.

is directly related to spatial mobility-effects and will therefore be further elaborated on in chapter 7.3.

7.2.3 Social comfort

Up to now the instrumental benefits or costs of ethnic relationships or 'capital' were assessed, in terms of their contribution to economic or educational advancement of the respondents. However, the Mexican or Mexican-American interviewees from the West Side highlight an additional benefit: the notion of social comfort conveyed by socializing with and moving around co-ethnics, as well as the aspect of stability or empowerment.

Given the language barrier and the exposure to a foreign culture, it is not surprising that for recent Mexican immigrants being among nationals or co-ethnics is experienced as relief and comfort. Referring to her aunt again, Expert 8 emphasizes that much beyond the potential monetary value of ethnic social networks, they bring about a social connectedness that is instrumental in people's quality of life:

> "[There] is a measure of stability that she didn't have before. But I just think in terms of the quality of life. She used to go to the Neighborhood House all the time and she doesn't drive. You know a lot of the Mexican women of that age don't drive, they never learnt how to drive. And she could get everywhere she needed to, herself. She didn't have to rely on other people. She had a place to go to, where she had her own friends. And this is very important for people, as they get older." (Expert 8: 5)

Linda, a 28-year old Mexican female immigrant (see Box 5) emphasizes that the opportunity of socializing with female co-ethnics in the "Hispanic Women in Action" group has also contributed to moral support and her partial emancipation from patriarchal family structures:

> "It helped me to have connections with groups like, other groups of the community. And then also, to distract me like, of the stress of home and being locked-up there, and also I have got four children that almost drive me crazy [laughs]. (…) And so, if I go there [to the 'Hispanic Women in Action' Group] usually I take three of them with me and the little one stays with my husband at home. And this has also helped me in that my husband also takes up responsibilities with them [the kids]. I mean, to learn how to look after a child. And this is a way to make him know, and understand

me. That when he comes home, and all the children are around, I am also like. And now he understands." (Linda, 5)[257]

The notion of social comfort of being among co-ethnics is not limited to the recent Mexican immigrants, trying to preserve their own culture while at the same time trying to accommodate themselves with a new language and society. A considerable number of the longstanding and middle-class immigrants (Carmen, Dora, Leon, Ronald, Theo, Harry) emphasize the feeling of comfort associated with socializing with co-ethnics and in a neighborhood environment they have known for a long time. Some of them (Carmen, Dora, Leon, Ronald, Engracia) particularly highlight the comfort of being surrounded by what they identify with the Hispanic culture[258]. However, other long-standing Mexican-American interviewees (Francisco, Monica, Juana, Raul) do not highlight any particularities of their co-ethnic versus non-ethnic social relationships.

The Mexican-American interviewees who perceive socializing with co-ethnic social networks as comfortable do so due to a sense of shared experience and culture, and also as the co-ethnic social networks are perceived as a protection zone with respect to the outside- and potentially hostile world. As Carmen puts it, when explaining her perception of the West Side as a 'family community', as opposed to other Twin City neighborhoods:

"I really, I loved growing up there. I don't think I would have wanted to grow up anywhere else. Because it was such, I, I really felt comfortable and that side. Cause everybody was like me. Cause everybody, even though I didn't speak Spanish, eve-

---

257 "(....) a mi me ayudó como a tener como conexiones en, en grupos así de, otros grupos de la comunidad. O también este, como a distraerme que tal, como que se quita una el estrés que tiene de la casa y del encierro y y yo además que tengo cuatro niños, que casi me vuelven loco [ríe]. (...) Y entonces, si yo voy para allá, yo me llevo, casi por lo regular me llevo tres [al group de mujeres], y el más chiquito se queda con mi esposo aquí. Y eso también me ayudaba en eso, porque en eso que mi esposo también tiene, responsabilidad con ellos [los niños]. O sea, aprender a cuidar un niño, verdad. O sea es una forma para que sepa y, y, y me entienda a mí, verdad. O sea que yo también estoy, cuando llega, y están todos, entonces. Y ahora él entiende." (Original wording)

258 Some of the longstanding Mexican-Americans also express themselves positively about the fact that due to the great number of recent arrivals from Latin America, Hispanic traditions and holiday celebrations (such as Day of the Dead, Cinco de Mayo) are being reintroduced to the Mexican community of the West Side. On the other hand, cultural differences between the new arrivals and the long-standing Mexican-Americans are also highlighted.

ryone around me had dark skin and, we all, basically, came from the same place or knew each other's… circumstances. So [I] really liked that." (Carmen: 4)

Some of the longstanding Mexican-Americans explain the experience of social comfort when socializing with co-ethnics with their shared values. This, for instance, is expressed by Ronald, 55, when he mentions that he likes "being around people that look like me, that act like me and that come from a basic fundamental value system of what I come from" (Ronald: 11). Asked about these values, reference is made to a traditional West Side culture in which respect for others, dignity and pride were safeguarded and "mattered more than if you have had materialistic, tangible things" (Harry: 11). Self-reliance and service towards others are upheld as mentalities lived by – positive - parental role models, as well as at "Neighborhood House". This romantic historiography of life in the 'old' West Side community is particularly prominent among the older male Mexican-Americans community activists who witnessed the dislocation of the "Flats" neighborhood in their childhood (see chapter 6.2)[259].

As mentioned before, a shared identity among some of the longstanding Mexican-Americans also stems from growing up in a social group and neighborhood looked down upon by the majority population and the city government. Ronald, 55-year old and employee of the City of St. Paul emphasizes the importance of a Mexican-American peer group of six professionals for securing mutual support on a professional level dominated by the Anglo-white population:

"We talk about the work that we do and we trust in the fact that this other professional (…) have had a similar, or if not the same experience, and that, the values that are attached to the advice that we give one another is one, one, first and foremost probably culturally appropriate, and secondly, hum, professionally appropriate as well. Hum, in the City of St. Paul there is not a lot of Latinos that are working at the, at the level of government, in which this group works at. So hum, it´s important that we stay connected to one another and support one another hum, and share what we know, and what resources we have available with one another so that we can continue to be successful here." (Ronald: 11)

---

[259] These interviewees (Ronald, Harry, Theo) invariably mention the city's decision in 1957 to tear down the old West Side community on the "Flats" in order to build the flood wall and build the Riverfront Industrial Park. Similar ideas are expressed by long-term Mexican American West Siders in the HACER-interviews (chapter 5.2.2).

In synthesis, co-ethnic networks convey social comfort and what can be termed a sense of *well-being* to both recent Mexican immigrants and long-standing Mexican-Americans from the West Side, although the latter 'group' is not uniform in this regard. In the case of the older Mexican-American residents from the West Side, the shared experience of social exclusion or institutional discrimination (exemplified by the eradication of the old "Flats" community in the 1950s) seem to have strongly contributed to a sense of common or 'ethnic' identity[260]. None of the longstanding Mexican-Americans mention negative aspects of socializing with co-ethnics. However, for some of them it does not have much relevance beyond that of 'common' core family relationships. From the perspective of the recent immigrants (and some of the more longstanding Mexican-Americans) co-ethnic social contacts fulfill a double function: First, providing a feeling of personal belonging and preventing loneliness and isolation in a linguistically and culturally strange environment. Second, facilitating contacts to the social world outside the ethnic 'community'.

7.3 The 'neighborhood effect' on social capital and mobility

The focus of the previous sub-section was on the nature and volume of social capital generated among the Mexican population of the West Side. In this section I broaden the perspective[261] by asking, in what way living on the West Side favors or hinders the development of social capital and chances of social mobility.

---

[260] Skin color may play an important role in the degree of discrimination that is experienced. The fact that 22-year old Carmen, a college student, places the color of her skin at the first place of her self-description (see quote above), sustains this interpretation. At another point of the interview, she emphasizes the absence of comfort when socializing in a majority-white environment with her white co-workers: "Maybe just like, I don't know what we would talk about. Because, I don't know if they are interested in the same things I'm interested in. I don't know if if we have the same hobbies. (…) And they are like going to bars where there's a lot of , other white people, and I don', I would rather, my comfort zone is to go to a more, diverse setting." (Carmen: 6)

[261] The separation of social and physical effects realized here for analytical purposes is somewhat artificial. In principle I assume them to interact or even be mutually reinforcing (chapter 3.1.5). Therefore in the two previous sub-sections on ethnic social networks and social capital/mobility I do anticipate spatial aspects or implications for segregation at times.

7.3.1 Proximity to co-ethnics and ethnic infrastructure

For the interviewed residents of the West Side, the importance of the spatial proximity to co-ethnics and/or ethnic infrastructure greatly depends on their time in the US and, related to this, on their socio-economic location and English proficiency. Thus, the recent Mexican immigrants, particularly the – often less mobile - female ones, state that living in the West Side neighborhood is *instrumental* in accessing social contacts and services. In contrast, the longstanding immigrants rather emphasize the *emotional* value of the social comfort associated with being surrounded by co-ethnics and an 'ethnic' or culturally diverse atmosphere.

Typically, recent female immigrants greatly value the fact that most co-ethnics and ethnic infrastructure (service organizations, ethnic supermarkets, and social groups) are located within walking distance, as many of them do not drive. Living on the West Side helps them to overcome the linguistic barrier, due to services of local organizations offered in Spanish, as well as free English classes provided in the neighborhood. As Hermosa, 39 and mother of three children points out:

> "Well, I like that all the services are close by. Like the Hispanic shops, the banks where they speak Spanish, everything related to the language. Also because the schools are close by, even though my children are not there [on the West Side], but schools are nearby. The community resources are at hand as one says, they are just around the corner. And then, the area where I live it is quiet, not a lot of scandal. Everything. Everything is good." (Hermosa: 14)[262]

From the perspective of female Mexican immigrants who do not drive or are constrained in their mobility due to their household and child-care responsibilities[263], spatial proximity helps accessing social contacts and opportunities associated with these. Asked if living on the West Side is important in order to maintain the social contacts among Hispanic women in the "Hispanic

---

[262] "Pues me gusta que hay todos los servicios cerca. Como las tiendas Hispanas, los bancos que hablan español, todo está relacionado con el idioma. Este, también pues que hay las escuelas cercas, aunque yo a mis hijos no les tengo allí, pues hay las escuelas cercas, este. Los recursos de la comunidad están a la mano, como quien dice, cerca. Y este, pues el lado donde estoy yo, estamos tranquilo, no hay mucho escándalo. Todo. Está bien, todo." (Original wording)

[263] And associated male ideas on the female role in the family.

Women in Action" group, Hermosa, who has been on the West Side and in the United States for 13 years, responds:

"Well, it is not important to live on the West Side [talks in a slow, reflexive way], but, it is easier. Because, the group [Hispanic Women in Action] is there. It gets difficult if people from other areas come. Because sometimes they do not have transport, [so] they cannot come on a regular basis, or they do not drive, [so] they cannot come every week. So. On the one side it is important to be in the group as I have obtained many contacts, how they say, and a lot of knowledge. But on the other side, I think that maybe if I lived far from the West Side, maybe I would not have gone there. Because before I did not drive and all that. So." (Hermosa: 14)[264]

Thus, contrary to a more common view in the literature of ethnic clustering as an obstacle to contacts outside the ethnic community, the perception of the interviewed female Mexican immigrants rather suggests the opposite: A residential location nearby ethnic organizations and services, facilitates co-ethnic contacts, which tend to be useful for subsequent (job, educational) contacts in- or outside the West Side that may or may not be with co-ethnics[265]. Also, the proximity of the West Side to Downtown St. Paul is perceived as practical for accessing employment opportunities[266].

Recent male immigrants mention less the importance of being in close spatial proximity to co-ethnics for socializing purposes. Many of them state that they just do not have the time for socializing. However, especially for males

---

264 "Pues, no es importante vivir en el West Side [habla de una manera lenta, reflexiva], pero, es más fácil. Porque, el grupo [Mujeres Hispanas en Acción] está aquí. Lo difícil es si, gente de otra parte viene. Porque a veces no tienen transporte, no pueden venir seguido, o no manejan, no pueden venir cada ocho días. Entonces. Por una parte es importante estar en el grupo, que ya he tenido mucho contactos, como se dice, muchos conocimientos, pero por otra parte, yo creo que a lo mejor si viviera retirado del West Side, a lo mejor no hubiera podido ir. Pues porque antes no manejaba y eso. Entonces." (Original wording)

265 In the case of Hermosa the contacts at the "Hispanic Women in Action" Group assisted her with finding several low-skilled jobs outside the West Side (cleaning in a hotel, food-packing in a factory), as well as with accessing studies at the St. Paul Community College. With the latter she aims at obtaining a license to work as a nurse in the United States, by topping-up her Mexican degree in this profession.

266 Contrary to the 'spatial mismatch hypothesis' that emphasizes the divergence between low-income residential locations and entry-level job opportunities today in US metropolitan areas (for Twin Cities Orfield 1997: 58, for Atlanta Ihlanfeldt/Sjoquist 2000: 116, general Cutler et al. 2005: 204) no reference in this direction was made by the Mexican or Mexican-American interviewees. Rather the convenience of the West Side being located close to Downtown was highlighted, by interviewees of different occupational and/or skills levels.

(in many families the migrating 'pioneers') living with family members or friends on the West Side upon their arrival in the Twin Cities was instrumental for the fulfillment of a basic need: a first shelter.

From the perspective of the longstanding immigrants the spatial proximity to co-ethnics or 'ethnic' infrastructure looses its *instrumental* role for getting along in daily life, accessing shelter, jobs or other opportunities. The ties with ethnic institutions, i.e. networks such as self-help groups, tend to be much weaker, mostly because the longstanding Mexican-Americans do not need them.

Rather, for the longstanding immigrants the proximity to and partial use of ethnic infrastructure helps them to maintain their Mexican identity and a sense of place and belonging. The role of the Catholic Church of "Our Lady of Guadalupe" is particularly revelatory. It constitutes an important reference point for identity building and exemplifies the notion of social cohesion in a real (ethnic) 'community'. As Dora, 50, a female Mexican-American and community activist, points out:

"No matter how many communities they start and how many, how big they get, the West Side will ALWAYS be the original, you know, West, you know, Hispanic community. (...) Other areas are AREAS, they are not as community as we are. That's what I love too because here we have a Lady of Guadalupe Church, which people come from all over to go to Church here. Hum, they drive from EVERYWHERE (…) and that's like the most important thing about being in this community is the Church." (Dora: 1)

Many of the long-standing Mexican-Americans derive a strong sense of familiarity and comfort from the cultural diversity and the Hispanic atmosphere on the West Side[267]. Leon, 42, states:

---

[267] However, the diversity ideal expressed by some of the (mostly) longstanding Mexican-Americans does not necessarily correspond to the living reality in the neighborhood. As pointed out in chapter 7.1, the relationship between the recent and the long-standing Mexican-Americans is characterized by mutual, not least status-related animosities. Furthermore, tolerance and respect towards other minorities cannot be taken for granted. For instance, asked about other neighborhoods she would like to live in, Engracia states that she would not move to the 'Summit Area', another central city neighborhood, as there are "too many blacks" (Engracia: 10). A certain disdain towards the African American or black population is also not uncommon among the recent Mexican-American residents, e.g. when Esteban complains about black thieves in the West Side neighborhood.

"I like living in the West Side basically ′cause there is a lot of, a lot of ethnicity [difficult to pronounce]. Cause we are still with a lot of different cultures. And uh, mostly I would say because I grew up here, so I feel more comfortable and, and in comparison to Minneapolis, cause in Minneapolis now there is a big community, but it is really different. But here I still run into people I grew up with, you know." (Leon: 11)

Most of the long-standing Mexican-American interviewees highlight at some point their emotional connectedness to Mexican culture[268], and their appreciation of the very presence of this 'culture' on the West Side. Some of them also point out that due to the arrival of recent Mexican and Hispanic immigrants on the West Side Latino culture has become more visible[269]. Engracia, a female Mexican-American West Sider in her 60s, points to the fact that the arrival of many more Hispanic immigrants has allowed that a critical local client mass facilitated the establishment of ethnic stores:

"When I was growing up, we wouldn't have no Mexican stores to go buy products. My uncles who lived in Indiana, they would come once a year, visit us, they would bring us, all the Mexican products. Mexican chocolate, uh, *chicharrones*, the corn *tortillas*, hum, *chorizo*, *chicharron*, and I think, *jalapeños*. (…) So now we have more the influence of all the Hispanics being here, so we can have all the stores. And at that time there was nothing in Minneapolis; it was all in Saint Paul. And now there are all kind of stores and restaurants over there." (Engracia: 9f.)

While the emotional and comfort-conveying value constitutes the most frequently mentioned neighborhood effect of the West Side on the long-standing Mexican-American immigrants, it also plays an important role for the recent Mexican immigrants. Sometimes the positive experience of living in a cultural familiar environment is also mentioned in connection with the intention to forestall incidences of discrimination.

---

268 For instance, Dora, 50, states that "I′m SO MEXICAN! I'm SO involved in my culture, that I love the music, the food, the traditions, the ways, the customs, that that's why I never thought an Anglo person could every fit into my life" (Dora: 10). However, she also states that through Church she has started to get together with more 'white' persons than ever before.

269 This does not mean that the symbols and attributes of this Mexican or Hispanic culture lived by the recent immigrants and by the long-standing Mexican-Americans are identical. In an earlier point of this document reference has already been made on discrepant views on the *Cinco de Mayo* festival, or on the 'new' Southern US-culture brought in by the recent immigrants.

7.3.2 *Youth role models and education*

Most of the Mexican and Mexican-American interviewees consider living on the West Side as positive, for the diverse reasons mentioned above. However, the picture presented in the interviews is far from cloudless. Many of the interviewees mention that life on the West Side may imply the transmission of problematic peer role models to the youth, as well as bad educational outcomes. The first aspect is presented as a problem by many of the adult interviewees, particularly by mothers of young children. For instance, Hermosa, 39 and mother of three children, considers neighborhood gangs as the first (and only) aspect she does not like about living on the West Side:

"Well, I don't like that there are gangs. Because, they do a lot of harm to society. It's like, particularly if one has small children, one fears that one's own children get involved in the gangs. And as I have relatives who have adolescent children, and myself I have the adolescent, the 13 year old girl, so, therefore I do not like that they exist." (Hermosa: 14)[270]

Carmen, the 22-year old female college student, considers her family environment as a major constraint to pursuing her studies (view Box 8). While she herself has opted to move out of the West Side in order to be able to focus on her university education, she describes the family and West Side environment in the following way:

"Like, dropping out of high school, not working, because many of the men that he is seeing in his life are like that. They [now quickly talking] dropped out of school, my father dropped out of school, my brother, my father didn't have any more education, all of my uncles, well, one of my uncles on my father's side went to college." (Carmen: 6f.)

Also John, the 22-year old teen coordinator in a West Side youth organization (view Box 7), describes family dysfunction and peer violence as realities during his youth in the West Side neighborhood:

"I've been around murder, I've been around sexual abuses, drug abuse, drug sellers, everything that you see on the news that is negative, I've seen it. You know, I've seen it all. (…)" (John: 2)

---

270 "Pues, no me gusta que, haya pandillas. Porque, perjudican mucho la sociedad. Este, especialmente como uno tiene hijos chicos, eh, uno tiene temor que las pandillas involucren a los hijos de uno. Y como tengo familiares que tienen adolescentes, y como yo misma, que tengo la adolescente, la de 13 años, entonces, por ese lado, no me gusta, que haya eso." (Original wording)

While the family experience of John may be judged as particularly appalling and not representative of the one of all or most of the West Side youth, the recurrent mentioning of the gang problem, by both adults *and* youth[271], cannot be denied. The concern about gang activities and violence (with mostly youth involved) is partly supported by crime statistics. These indicate that between 1996 and 2000 violent crimes have increased in the neighborhood and figure higher as compared to St. Paul as a whole: by 880 per 100,000 people, compared to 851 to 100,000 in the entire city (HACER 2002: 45)[272]. Humboldt High School, the only regular public high school in the neighborhood, is believed to be strongly affected by gang activities. Tamara, 16-year old daughter of recent Mexican immigrants who has been living in the United States and Minnesota since the age of three, explains her deliberate decision against attending Humboldt High School:

"I don't like it because there is a lot of violence, I mean it is a bad school, I mean in terms of its students. The teachers are very good and all, but the students make it a bad school. You know I wanted to go to a school where I don't need to worry about anything else except my studies, and I knew that at Humboldt there would be whatever kind of problems and I would not be able to focus on my studies. And that is why I decided to better go to Highland [school in other St. Paul neighborhood]." (Tamara: 15)[273]

The concern about gangs or negative youth role models seems to cut across immigration cohorts and social status. However, the reaction to the problem differs considerably: While the more economically established West Siders (usually longstanding Mexican-Americans, rather than fresh arrivals) send

---

[271] The interviewees' opinions diverge as to whether gang-related violence increases or decreases in the neighborhood. For instance, while Tamara, 16, states that it seems to her as if gang activities have worsened, her brother Marco, 17, perceives that "they are bad, although not as bad any more as they used to be, due to more police presence in the neighborhood" (Marco: 5).

[272] However, the statistics also tell that property crime rates have decreased in the same period and compare quite favorably with those of the City of St. Paul: In 2000 they figured at 4,258 per 100,000 people compared to 6,439 (!) in St. Paul as a whole.

[273] "No me gusta porque es mucha, mucha violencia, yo pensaba que si, no, o son, es una escuela mala, o sea, los estudiantes. Los maestros son muy buenos y todo pero, los estudiantes hacen la escuela mala. Y o sea yo quería una escuela donde puedo no me tenía que preocupar por cualquier otra cosa no más que, mis estudios y yo sabía que si iba allí va a haber problemas con cualquier otra cosa y no, no poder concentrarme a mis estudios. Y por eso decidí yo mejor ir a Highland [escuela en otra área de la ciudad de St. Paul]." (Original wording)

their children to public and private schools outside the neighborhood or move out entirely, the more recent immigrants are more likely to have their children and youth attending the primary and secondary schools inside the neighborhood. The latter may be motivated by insufficient financial resources[274], a lack of information about alternative school options or may also be due to the convenience associated with children attending neighborhood schools – particularly for non-driving Mexican mothers. According to Expert 8, a former West Side resident, for some of her Mexican-American relatives the possibility of sending their children to schools outside the West Side constituted a key motivation *not* to leave the neighborhood[275]. Possible pernicious neighborhood effects on the educational outcomes of their children could thus be outweighed by the positive effects of strong social networks and affordable real estate prices on the West Side, with respect to middle or higher income suburban neighborhoods[276].

Apart from the problem of a negative peer influence in the neighborhood school environment, the interviews suggest that institutional deficits are responsible for bad educational outcomes. Theo, a 55-year old second-generation son of a Mexican father and a Caucasian-white mother of German heritage, states not having been appropriately prepared for higher, i.e. college education, at Humboldt School on the West Side. He considers this as the chief reason for dropping out after the first year at the university[277]:

"So, I wanna say this that, I know personally, I was not ready for college when I got out of High School. I don't, when I look back at my school, Humboldt High School on the West Side of St. Paul, the big emphasis for lots of us was sports. The empha-

---

[274] This is only correct in the case of the usually expensive private schools. In contrast, public primary and secondary education is free in the United States.

[275] The St. Paul school district introduced the so-called magnet-school model in the 1990s (Peebles 2004: 8, Schellenberg/Porter 2003: 3). This model conveys free choice to parents to send their children to public schools outside of their neighborhood. Expert 8 describes the problematic consequence of this in the following way: "You know there's an open school policy, so they argue to go somewhere else and as a consequence those who stay behind at Humboldt, are the ones whose parents don't know about or don't have the capacity to agitate for a better school system." (Expert 8: 2)

[276] This does not dispute an increasing scarcity in the lower price segments of the West Side's housing market (view Annex 9).

[277] He decided to discontinue his university education while waiting to get drafted for the Vietnam War. Describing his state of mind at the time: "I, I don't wanna be in school, I don't wanna be, do nothing, because the next month is the lottery [selection system for military service at the time], and I'm gonna be, I wanna do whatever I want, for one month." (Theo: 6)

sis on education was not there. As far as I'm concerned. My parents, uh, hardly ever went to a teacher's conference, the school never asked why, the school never inquired to me, [Theo], are you going on to School [university], after High School? And I don't wanna put all the blame, or blame, on the school." (Theo: 5)

He has sent his own children to private, catholic schools outside the neighborhood[278], under considerable financial sacrifices. He describes the preparation for higher education as starkly different to his own:

"But when I look at education today, my kids were getting ready for college, in eighth grade [approx. age of fourteen]. A big difference. And the emphasis to get ready for college, was in eighth grade. Seventh, eighth grade. And I look back now, there was never any emphasis for me going on to school EVER. You know. So. So uh. I guess I will put some blame in the school district." (Theo: 5)

The experience of Theo is replicated in the educational careers of other – older and young - Mexican-American interviewees who have attended Humboldt High School on the West Side. For instance, Ronald, 55, states having passed some college credits, however not finalized his studies. His son Arturo, 21, mentions that he went to the University of Minnesota after finishing high school, but stopped going, since he didn't know what he wanted to do there. John, 25, has left Humboldt School before attaining his high school degree, achieving a high school equivalent diploma afterwards (Box 7). Raul, 50, possesses a bachelor's degree in business management, but had attended a private high school in West St. Paul, an adjacent suburb to the West Side (see chapter 6)[279]. Carmen, 22, who now pursues her college education[280] and Harry, 55, who possesses a Masters Degree and works as a High School principal appear to be exceptions. This is underlined by Harry reflecting on the time he left Humboldt High School[281]:

---

278 Today, his daughter is pursuing her studies at the university while his son has already passed his.

279 Similar to Tamara, he describes the decision to pursue his high school education outside the West Side as a deliberate one. Asked what he does not like about the West Side: "I would say the school system. The school system was not desirable, that's why I decided to go to a private school. Cause I knew, if I went to the High School I was supposed to go there and finish. So I think uh, just the lack of good education." (Raul: 12)

280 After interrupting her college studies after the first year.

281 According to Harry, the small success rate of Mexican or Latino children at colleges or universities persists until today. According to him the colleges and universities up to the present, lack an effective retention strategy targeted at students of color. Hence the result of a relatively high student drop-out rate.

"[When] I graduated from High School, there were only about, six, I believe, Mexican, young men, who went on past High School and, of the six of us, I, Mexican that is, I'm not, I think I am the only one that, finished, school." (Harry: 8)

In the statements about the unsatisfactory educational outcome of West Side adolescents, blame is put on the educational entities (mostly Humboldt High School), and even more on the St. Paul school district. The Board of the district, which geographically almost corresponds to the St. Paul city jurisdiction, defines teaching approaches and personnel policies in the primary and secondary public schools in the City of St. Paul[282]. A number of the interviewed residents and experts accuse the school district of neglect towards the needs of an ethno-culturally diverse student and parental population. According to several interviewed experts (Experts 8, 9 and 11), the outreach to parents and their active involvement in school activities and policies form key conditions for pupils' educational success[283]. It also constitutes a condition for parents to be able to have their concerns addressed by the school board and district:

"And so, what you're seeing happen at that particular school [Humboldt High School], is neglect. It is neglect by the District. And, unless the parents in that community have the capacity to agitate the school board, you are not gonna see improvement in that school. Because, the district is so underfunded. And has, faces so many stresses that they don't respond to fire." (Expert 8: 2)

However, according to Harry, 54, aside from suffering from financial constraints the school district's political will to support the more vulnerable immigrant or other minority constituencies is also limited. According to him and other educational experts (Experts 8 and 11), support strategies required are for instance, bi-lingual and inter-cultural learning and teaching ap-

---

[282] Financially the school district depends partly on the allocation of federal resources for specific programs, but mainly on revenue from local property taxes. Due to their disproportionate numbers of low-income and renter households, the inner-city school districts tend to be subject to sever financial shortages, compared to their suburban counterparts (Polese 2000: 321ff.).

[283] The same experts also emphasize that this outreach and involvement tend to be more challenging in neighborhoods with high proportions of immigrant households, for a variety of reasons: Tight work schedules, family stress, lack of familiarity with the US school system and regulations, wrong outreach strategies, low emphasis on education. These problems as well as possible ways to overcome them will be taken up in chapter 9.

proaches, as well as additional funding, i.e. for personnel and learning facilities[284]. Recalling his years as principal of Humboldt High School:

"So we created a, uh, a rather assertive group of parents and community members, and uh, the Superintendent of the School Board became alert, said that, they were as assertive and aggressive as they were. And the interesting thing about that is that there are other areas of town, more affluent, and, and where Board members reside, that were as assertive and even at times more aggressive with THEIR needs, and it was never thought, uh in a negative light. But when the community from the West Side became aggressive and assertive, uh, that caused a problem for the Board and the Superintendent. Uh, a cynical person, which I can be at times, could relate that to institutional racism." (Harry: 3)

In synthesis, in the eyes of many of the interviewed residents, young and old, recent immigrants or longstanding Mexican-Americans, lower or higher status, living on the West Side may put youth and their educational outcomes at risk. Two reasons are pointed out for this: The first are problematic peer dynamics and cultures (e.g. gang violence) and in some cases problematic family role models. While male youth are believed to be more prone to succumb to these socially harmful role models, the careers of young females are sometimes hampered by patriarchal education models. The second are institutional deficits, notably on the part of West Side schools, particularly Humboldt High School, and the St. Paul school district. These institutional deficits do not only result in inadequate responses to the above challenges[285], but also in that potentials of a multi-cultural community environment go unrecognized or are even lost as long as they are not institutionally backed and acknowledged. For instance, Spanish language skill and thus proficiency has been lost by most of the second and third generation of Mexican-Americans on the West Side, due to a historically adverse social and institutional environment towards Spanish-speaking migrants (chapter 7.2.2). The language example also indicates that spatial proximity is not per-se a facilitator for the transfer of ethno-linguistic skills. In this sense, D.NH points to the importance of culturally familiar – positive –role models in the ethnic community. According to him, the latter, possess a higher degree of legitimacy among disadvantaged youth than mainstream (white) adults that did not confront the

---

[284] These needs as well as possible responses will be discussed in more detail in chapter 9.

[285] The question, whether these institutional deficits are (only) unable to adequately respond to the above challenges or are a reason that their existence cannot be answered at this stage.

race- and class-related mobility barriers during their childhood and youth. Possible alternative institutional arrangements and strategies will be discussed in chapter 9.

7.3.3 "Poor without knowing it"

Asked about what he liked about living on the West Side, Francisco, 42, stated that apart from having lots of friends it was

> " (...) **being poor and not knowing it** (laughs). Well, what I'm meaning is, just because it's like we have a lot of people that grew up like us, you know, and even though, we didn't have a lot of money, we really didn't mind, because a lot of people didn't have a lot of money on the West Side. You know. It's still kind of considered lower economic area, yeah, but, we didn't know that. You know, we grew up well, had a lot of friends, you know, we had places to go and play ball, you know there's a good, really good church there." (Francisco: 7, own emphasis)

Harry, 55, likewise recalls a sudden awareness about his family's poverty, when attending a University class. Reflecting like Francisco on the meaning of material wealth for well-being he puts:

> "I, I remember I didn't realize that I was poor, until my first year of College. And in my first Sociology class, the instructor uh, described the socioeconomic status that if you're, if you came from a family of this number of, uh, siblings, and, your Dad or your mother made this amount of money, you were considered, a, in poverty. And, I mean I wasn't even close, cause we had twelve kids and fourteen with my Mom and Dad, and so we were, by their standards, we were extremely poor. But, I'd, I'd never known, poverty in a sense of. My, my parents provided for us, we always had food, we always had clean clothes, and we had a healthy lifestyle. So." (Harry: 10)

Thus, Ronald, Francisco, Theo and Harry, all Mexican-American males between 40 and 50, describe their youth in the neighborhood in a similar way: They describe it as one in which certain elements of well-being (having friends, playing ball, going to Church, having enough to eat, being cleanly dressed, enjoying a healthy lifestyle) outweighed shortcomings in the economic field. Living in the ethnic neighborhood facilitated not to worry about these shortcomings, as everybody around was in a similar situation – and implicitly, similarly happy with the little they had:

> "The thing is interesting I look back, you know, we were all poor. So. But we didn't realize it. We didn't realize how poor we were." (Theo: 3)

Notwithstanding their predominantly positive memories attributed to this time, there is a problematic second side to this situation: Not to know about one's ′poverty′ as everybody around lives the same way, points to a potential and problematic isolation with respect to the outside world, i.e. the broader urban environment. Not being aware of the outer world's criteria of judgment nor of the means for changing this situation, may result in a situation of powerlessness and in a serious shortage of opportunities and choices. Not being aware of opportunities outside the neighborhood may impose considerable constraints on one's experiences and aspirations. Ronald, 55, recalls from his youth at Neighborhood House that

> " (…) growing up there [on the West Side] was virtually nowhere else to go. But our neighborhood. So, so, a lot of kids, I was fortunate enough that I had through Neighborhood House the opportunity to get outside the neighborhood, and to do some other things, but a lot of the kids that I grew up with didn't have that opportunity. And their, their, their worlds were very, very small." (Ronald: 12)

The problematic sides of the spatial isolation are however directly linked to, and arguably a consequence of the social and economic barriers imposed on the Mexican population on the lower West Side in the first half of the 20th century: Being considered second-class citizens, not being granted an equal quality education in public neighborhood schools, not being welcomed in majority-white private schools and in majority-white residential or business areas, being discriminated against in urban housing markets. Under the circumstances of a more or less explicit discrimination the spatial concentration of the Mexican population may become self-reinforcing in social terms.

Meanwhile, in the 1950s and –60s, the race- and class-related barriers even made them feel *inside* the West Side community. As Theo reflects on the motivations for his attending a primary school in Downtown St. Paul:

> "So, for first grade to fifth grade, I went to Assumption [school in Downtown St. Paul], which is actually a German Church. But interestingly enough, there were two Catholic grade schools on the West Side. St. Mathews, a German school, and St. Michael, an Irish School. And you know, I always wonder, why did we go across the river, across the bridge, to Downtown to Church? And I found out later, in my twenties, that back then, those parishes did not want Mexican kids at their schools. [Eva: Oh…]. St. Michaels wanted the Irish kids, and Irish is white. But as kids we didn't know that. I didn't know the politics back then. St. Matthews, was right on the West Side, so was St. Michaels by the way. And what did they want? They wanted the white kids, predominantly German kids, to go to that school." (Theo: 13)

At the turn of the 21st century, the institutional discrimination towards minority or immigrant groups in St. Paul and the US had decreased, not least against the background of a strict anti-discrimination legislation[286]. However, it is only against this historical background that certain status-relevant social and spatial practices can be understood. Ronald, 55, explains that socializing with his Mexican-American high-level city administration coworkers in Downtown St. Paul locations constitutes:

"(…) a conscious effort on our parts to, to show that Hispanic leaders, Hispanic City leaders, are, are visible in, in where other Anglo leaders and other City officials and people socialize. It's kind of a, a, Eva it's kind of a conscious effort to show that, that we can go where, wherever we want, whenever we want, and that we belong there too. So, hum, frankly it's, it's somewhat expensive to do that [laughs], but it's also something that we enjoy doing hum, hum, mostly because I think there was a time when, when we wouldn't have been welcomed. But now we are. That's kind of why we choose Downtown too." (Ronald: 8)

With de jure social and spatial mobility barriers having disappeared and the promotion of cultural diversity figuring high on US-policy agendas (e.g. in the educational field), this does not mean that the situation of low-income immigrant households or native minorities is effectively pursued on planning or policy levels. Neither does it grant an absence of informal discrimination. Planning and policy strategies for housing and community development will be discussed in more detail in chapter 9.

7.3.4 *The negative image of the West Side*

Many of the interviewed residents, particularly the longstanding Mexican-American West Siders, at some point of the interview mention the negative image of the West Side in the rest of the city. They perceive that inhabitants of the latter view the West Side as a low-income, 'Latino' neighborhood and one in which social deviant behaviors commonly associated with low-income minorities (crime, gangs, drugs etc.) abound. Asked what he dislikes about living on the West Side, Francisco, 42, states:

---

[286] The Civil Rights Laws were granted in 1964 and the Fair Housing Act in 1968 (see chapter 2.2). Whereas discrimination is outlawed for both public and private actors today, this does not mean that it does not exist anymore. For instance, HIS reports about discriminatory attitudes of teachers towards the few Hispanic children at her daughter's school, a majority-white public entity targeted at talented kids.

"You know the negative is I guess the perception, some people think that you know, where, maybe still to this day, they fear from the West Side, they still think that it's bad, that you're poor, that you're hanging out, that you might be part of a gang, or you know that you either have bad house or gang or a lot of trouble and things which are not totally true. So there is people out there, that are kind of like you know, they are prejudiced against people from the West Side." (Francisco: 8)

How does this negative perception of the West Side by the rest of the city manifest itself in the eyes of the interviewed residents? For the Mexican-American residents who have grown up with their siblings on the West Side 'Flats' (Theo, Harry, Ronald, Engracia), the removal of the residential neighborhood in 1958 symptomizes the historical disdain of the city towards the West Side community and its - predominantly Mexican - inhabitants:

" (…) the Port Authority, as it is still referred to, they, they told ALL the people, on the West Side Flats, that we have to move all of you, the flood is endangering your lives, and it's not healthy. So we're gonna buy you homes, whatever you have, and they gave them, whatever menial amount it was (…). And, and the governor says, we´re gonna take over this land or property for the betterment of the State or the people. Well in this, in this sense, they took over this land, and gave the people, menial amounts of money, to leave their homes. And so, what did they do? As soon as, as soon as the community was knocked down, they put up a HUGE flood wall. And what they did is, they put in, they put industry in there. For the tax base. And that's what they really wanted. They didn't care about the people." (Theo: 2)

Other, more contemporary, manifestations of the negative image of the West Side and other inner city neighborhoods include higher rates for car insurance, due to the perception that West Side car owners are more prone to car burglaries and other property infractions than those of e.g. suburban areas[287]. Several old West Siders describe the bewilderment of their upward mobile West Side friends about their decision to stay in, or move back into the West Side (Harry: 13, Expert 2: 1). According to Harry, politicians only display concern about the West Side community at the time of elections, however they do not come back afterwards. Furthermore, low upward dynamics in the

[287] The West Side forms part of the neighborhoods of the central city, for which insurance rates are higher than e.g. in suburban neighborhoods. In the context of the research on the West Side carried out by HACER, one interviewee states that her insurance rate went down after moving to West St. Paul, the suburb community immediately adjacent to the West Side.

real estate and housing prices on the West Side[288] reflect the perception of the West Side as a low-income neighborhood:

"(The) property values on the West Side have been undervalued for many, many years. Even though, it's close to Downtown St. Paul, it's close to all the major free-ways, you HAVE a main street, all these kinds of qualities that you would find in a, you know, livable community, it was underfunded, because of this reputation that it was a, 'ethnic', neighborhood. So, it wasn't really considered expensive real estate." (Expert 8: 3)

The negative perception of the West Side by people from outside the neighborhood contrasts with the predominantly positive perception of the neighborhood by its own residents. Values of the neighborhood, repeatedly pointed out by the interviewed Mexican and Mexican-American residents, include the inter-personal relations, the familiarity particularly among those who have lived in the neighborhood for a long time and a feeling of overall safety and security. Dora, 50, highlights that she always leaves her car and house doors unlocked, at least during the day. Harry states that his family has done likewise until recently. Monica, 32, mentions that she wants her kid to grow up in a real 'community' and close to her family. Juana, 39, as well as many other longstanding Mexican-American residents of the West Side, appreciates the possibility of walking in the neighborhood and chatting to acquaintances. Recent Mexicans *and* longstanding Mexican-Americans interviewed place a high importance on the Latino or culturally diverse environment of the West Side.

Many of the interviewed Mexican or Mexican-American residents contrast life in an inner-city community with life in the suburbs. The latter is perceived as impersonal or sometimes even socially hostile. Elena, a 42-year old first generation female immigrant puts it in a very visual manner:

"Uh, I don't feel like I belong in a suburb. Because first of all, the suburb, I don't think they will understand me. And I will be like, like a second-hand neighbor. And everybody would look at you like. They don't try to know you. People have a tendency not to know you. They judge you, with your appearance, and I don't think, you see lot of people hear things to get out of the West Side, they say, oh, let's go

---

[288] The housing prices of the West Side have nevertheless increased in the last years, not least in the context of the planned new development on the West Side Riverfront. In this sense the low purchase prices of houses on the West Side constitute a valuable equity to the Mexican or Hispanic households who already own a home there (Juana and Expert 2, Expert 5: 9).

live in the very rich, uh, neighborhood, because uh, the status living in there, and (…), they don't think, that their childrens or their families won't fit in there. Because, they won't understand you. So, for some people will work. And for some people don't work. So, I won't even THINK about that. Uh, about moving around here. Even if I had the money." (Elena: 17f.)

In a similar vein, Dora, a 50-year old Mexican American West Side leader, reflects about life in Woodbury, a growing suburb municipality located in the South of the Twin Cities metro area:

"Woodbury is a city in itself. It's got a hospital, it's got work-out gyms, it's got every store you can ever imagine, every restaurant ever imaginable, it's got beautiful homes, but, [lowers voice] I can never live in the suburbs! It's too, it's too, uh, nobody knows nobody! There's so many neighborhoods over there, that they don't even know their next door neighbor. They might wave or something, but they don't even know. There's no community." (Dora: 3)

In view of the discrepancies between the outside and inside perceptions of the West Side, two aspects may be outlined with respect to the former: First, by focusing on income (and arguably ethnicity) attributes, the *criteria* for judging the quality of life in the neighborhood are significantly narrowed. This echoes the elaborations on the notion of 'being poor' from the previous chapter. Second, by labeling the West Side as a 'poor' and 'Mexican' or 'Latino' neighborhood, an internal homogeneity is suggested that is at odds with both the economic and the ethno-cultural diversity of the neighborhood[289]. Ultimately the negative image of the West Side may be considered as a dominant society-based "outgrowth of perceptions about race and class" (Expert 8: 2, also see Harry: 12).

With respect to the inside view, the stigmatization of the West Side neighborhood by other city inhabitants seems to prompt two types of reac-

[289] The neighborhood statistics refute the notion of a homogeneous neighborhood, e.g. with respect to housing values, ownership rates, income levels and also race and ethnicity (see chapter 6). This is i.a. illustrated by the considerable differences of the different sub-areas or census tracts of the West Side, with respect to income levels and the presence of Hispanic or other minority households. The resident and expert interviews further indicate a significant heterogeneity of the West Side population, in terms of their socio-economic characteristics and socio-cultural practices. Furthermore, several interviewees highlight the culturally and socio-economically diversity, rather than homogenous character of the neighborhood.

tions[290]. These are contradictory only at first sight: The first, as mentioned above, decidedly contradicts the negative outside-image of the West Side, placing strong emphasis on the community connectedness and disputing rumors of high crime rates and other social ills presumably characterizing life in the West Side neighborhood:

"I walk the streets at any time in the day or night. You know, hey. People are getting bombed out and killed in the suburbs, more than in my neighborhood. What is the last time you heard of a murder over here? You know. Prominent neighborhoods. Rich homes. All these communities that claim to be the better neighborhoods. That's, that's what is on the news. You see murders in the West Side? We had our days, but [laughs], not in my time. Since I've lived here, we don't have no murders. Not that I have not heard of murders, named it, but, but I feel very safe." (Dora: 11)

Thus, the West Side is defended against an image felt to be unjust and unjustified. The presentation of the West Side as an almost perfect and harmonious 'community' nevertheless needs to be carefully considered[291], not least in view of the existing friction within the Mexican or Hispanic community.

The second reaction is that the negative image of the West Side held by the majority society is appropriated, albeit in different ways. This is particularly manifest in decisions regarding the purchase or location of housing property. For instance, Leon, 42, states that he would hesitate to invest in housing ownership on the West Side and would rather buy in the suburbs,

"'Cause here, even though our community is growing, it's always looked more as a low-income, and all that, that makes it different." (Leon: 12)

The fact that median housing values on the West Side are lower and increase less than those of the entire City of St. Paul corroborates Leon's perception

---

[290] The longstanding Mexican-Americans tend to more aggressively criticize the city's attitude towards the West Side and more vigorously highlight its positive sides than the recent Mexican immigrants. However, the latter also voice their appreciation of the West Side. The recent Mexican immigrants particularly stress the comfort associated with residing in a culturally closed community, as well as the instrumentality – and comfort - of having family members and organizations such as Neighborhood House and the "Hispanic Women in Action group close by.

[291] Needless to say that the defensive attitude of particularly the old West Siders with respect to their neighborhood, also needs to be taken into account in the interpretation of the interviews. This attitude might be particularly prevalent among those 'old' West Siders (Ronald, Harry, Francisco) who feel they need to justify their appreciation for the West Side vis-à-vis former neighborhood friends who decided to move out of the West Side.

(see table 10 in chapter 6)[292]. Although from an investment point of view low housing prices in a growth-promising neighborhood can even constitute a purchase incentive (an advantage experienced by two interviewees: Expert 2 and Juana), the investment into housing property on the West Side continues to be looked at as an insecure one. In contrast, the housing prices in some of the 'growing' suburban areas in the Southeastern Twin Cities Metro Area (Woodbury, Inver Grove Heights, Mendota Heights[293]) are believed to develop much more favorably, from the perspective of property owners.

Finally, a significant portion of upwardly mobile Mexican-American West Siders have moved out of the West Side, following the path of spatial assimilation proposed by mainstream American society: "(What) I see is that as people HAVE gotten more means, they DON'T stay within the community." (Expert 9: 8). While the interviewed Mexican-Americans who do no longer live on the West Side (Carmen, John, Theo, Harry) point out rather trivial reasons for their decisions (moving to neighborhood of partner, being closer to university, a fit housing opportunity), motivations of 'others' who have left the West Side are described as more linked to social status. As Expert 8 describes the attitude of her Mexican-American brother who has moved out of the West Side:

"I have a sibling who moved away to the suburbs. He has nothing good to say about the West Side. (…) All he sees is you know, projects [public housing]. Untended properties. And that's gonna influence his whole perception. Because now he lives near Lake Minnetonka [upmarket suburban municipality] and that's where he wants to be and. (…) And so, so it's just, he would make comments like, you can't get my mom out of the ghetto. Cause my ma wants to go to the West Side. And he says, yeah, you can't get my ma out of the ghetto. And that would be his perception. And I think, you know for him, he does crucify based just on the fact that you know, people don't take care of their lawns. And he says, oh, there is bunch of drug dealers

---

292 This is only compared to the central city average. However, price developments in some of the suburban areas may be much more favorable than those of the West Side. Furthermore, the interviews indicate that the physical qualities of the housing stock on the West Side (size of the site and house, quality of building material) is perceived as less convenient than those of (usually larger size, newer) housing structures in the suburbs.

293 These, together with West and South St. Paul, immediately adjacent to the West Side, are the suburbs most frequently mentioned by the interviewed longstanding Mexican Americans as, 1. possible places where they would move to when leaving the West Side, 2. areas where family members or Mexican American contacts have moved to.

there. How does he know? He doesn't live there, he hasn't lived there for 20 years!" (Expert 8: 2)

While the decision of many former Mexican-American West Siders to leave the neighborhood is directly or indirectly related to the West Side's negative image[294], there are also reasons relating to the actual use value of West Side homes. Several interviewees mentioned structural deficits of the West Side housing stock, or the small plot sizes (Linda, Hermosa, Monica, Leon, Fermin). These are physical characteristics related to the West Side's history as a working class neighborhood (chapter 6.2). Linda and her family moved to South St. Paul as houses on the West Side were not in a very good condition, plots too small and too costly for what they offered, compared to South St. Paul. Harry points out that when he started a family in the 1970s, the West Side housing was not attractive due to its bad quality and small plot sizes. Theo, after buying a nice Tudor-style house on the West Side and living there with his family for 17 years used the equity to buy another home in Mendota Heights on a much larger plot.

7.4 Summary

In this chapter, the ethnic social networks of the Mexican population of the West Side of St. Paul were discussed, as well as the role of these networks for the development of social capital and mobility. A further focus was placed on the question of how the neighborhood or physical environment by itself influences the opportunities for the development of social capital and mobility.

With respect to the social networks and relationships, the empirical research on the West Side has indicated the following: Contrary to the outside perception of a relatively homogeneous ethnic ′community′ the Mexican population of the West Side is highly differentiated – herein confirming information conveyed through the secondary analysis (statistics, HACER-research). These differences are of a socioeconomic and cultural nature, accentuated

294 The direct relationship is when people move out of the West Side in order to escape being associated with the negative neighborhood stigma. An indirect relationship would be if someone moved out due to better valuation rates of housing and real estate property elsewhere, as housing and real estate prices are at least partially influenced by neighborhood reputation. Even the deteriorated condition of some of the West Side housing, a direct effect of decade-long disinvestments in the neighborhood, is indirectly related to its negative image among better-situated housing market players.

through linguistic barriers and clear-cut in the perception of the longstanding Mexican-Americans, not least related to a fear of status loss. The differences are most accentuated between the longstanding Mexican-American residents and the first-generation Mexican immigrants, resulting in perceived and manifest divisions.

Thus, not surprisingly direct personal relationships between these two groups (the native and the foreign-born Mexicans) are rare. While for the more recent Mexican immigrants relationships with co-ethnics – family, friends, and acquaintances – constitute their main social contacts, among the long-standing Mexican-Americans social relationships are more diversified in ethno-racial terms. An important commonality among the recent Mexican immigrants and the more longstanding Mexican-Americans constitutes the value attributed to the family and the Church. Although both groups regularly attend Church masses and celebrations, they do it separately – also, but not only due to linguistic differences.

Contrary to the transnationalism-literature that stresses a 'bifocality' of immigrants (recent and longstanding ones) between their home and their host countries, the research on the West Side suggests that the life of even most of the recent immigrants is much more locally focused. With an increasing length of stay in the United States, the engagement with their home country seems to decrease. On the other hand, some of the recent immigrants refer to family members or acquaintances who travel back and forth between the US and Mexico. This finding disputes the notion of a one-directional and definitive migration as the predominant migratory pattern.

The interviews and other research methods have indicated that ethnic social networks fulfill a variety of needs for the population of Mexican origin. Again here, important differences can be stated between the experiences of the recent Mexican immigrants and those of the longstanding Mexican-Americans. For the recent Mexican immigrants, particularly females, groups such as the "Hispanic Women in Action" group or the services of Neighborhood House provide important economic and educational skills gaining opportunities: job references, training workshops, language courses, information about service and other institutions etc. For many of them, being able to socialize with co-ethnics provided a decisive step for further opportunities outside the ethnic networks – hence their 'bridging potential'. Also, in the case of the female immigrants the contact with co-ethnic females leads to an incipient liberation from patriarchal family structures. While the interviewed males socialize less in ethnic 'groups', contact with co-ethnic family members usually helped in finding their first jobs.

For the longstanding Mexican-Americans co-ethnic networks tend to be less important for their social mobility, especially in the case of those with higher educational degrees. However, family connections helped some of them (Dora, Leon, John, Arturo), with getting their first employment, in neighborhood institutions and businesses. An aspect emphasized by almost all of the interviewees is the social comfort associated with socializing with co-ethnics. In the case of recent immigrants the reasons for this are linguistic and cultural familiarity and the absence of discrimination, thus a sense of personal security. In the case of the more longstanding immigrants the reason for this is primarily seen in the trust instilled through a commonly shared history of dominant society-lead social exclusion and discrimination.

The 'neighborhood effect' on the development of social and other capitals appears to be ambivalent. The geographic proximity of co-ethnics is judged positive as it facilitates building and maintaining social relationships and related benefits, particularly for non-driving female immigrants. It facilitates the maintenance of a 'Mexican' or 'Hispanic' culture, be it through the possibility of buying Mexican food in the ethnic grocery stores or through assisting Latino celebrations taking place in the West Side neighborhood. The neighborhood environment is perceived to entail some risk for the young population, particularly for young males, due to the notorious prominence of gangs, not least in the West Side schools. While harmful peer role models are presented as one problem, institutional neglect towards the needs and potentials of a multi-cultural pupil and parent constituency is highlighted as a more fundamental one.

Finally, the interviews revealed a considerable discrepancy between the inside and the outside perception of the West Side. While the interviewed residents tend to highlight the positive sides of the neighborhood (i.a. good neighborhood relations and safety), the outside image of the neighborhood is dominated by common negative attributes to what is judged and reduced to be a low-income and Latino neighborhood. The negative outside image has problematic direct and indirect impacts on the Mexican immigrant and native-born population. Among these are historical disinvestments in the housing stock, low housing-asset building opportunities, upwardly mobile West Siders leaving the neighborhood and others.

8 Conceptual implications

The objective of this chapter is to point out the main conceptual implications of the study of the Mexican population on the West Side. The idea is to identify the most important patterns that determine variations in outcomes on the development of social capital and social mobility in the ethnic community, on the basis of the empirical study realized on the West Side. For the discussion of these patterns, additional conceptual approaches to the ones proposed by Bourdieu are used, as they show more explanatory power. The conceptualization in this chapter also provides the basis for the formulation of policy and planning recommendations in chapter 9 of this document.

The present chapter is thus divided into two content-related steps: In the first sub-section, specific *features* of social capital and 'site effects' in ethnic neighborhoods are pointed out. These features help to understand the potential strengths, but also the possible weaknesses of ethnic social capital. In the context of this study, the 'bridging' potential of 'bonding' ethnic networks has appeared as both an analytically and normatively important aspect. Also, the question is discussed of whether subjective 'well-being' as opposed to (rather objectively assessed) social mobility should form the basic criteria or reference point for the evaluation of social capital in ethnic neighborhoods.

In the second sub-section, the specific *conditions* for the achievement of social and other capital outcomes, as well as for the occurrence of certain positive or negative 'site-' or 'neighborhood effects', are pointed out. These are conditions on the individual, the neighborhood and on the macro-social level assuming that neither of them can be adequately understood without looking at the other issues. At the end of the chapter, its most important results are summarized.

8.1 Social capital and site effects in ethnic neighborhoods

According to Bourdieu, the amount of social capital a person is able to accumulate is determined by the size of informal and formal networks he or she can mobilize at a given moment and on the volume of economic, cultural and symbolic capital of the individuals a person is connected to – thus, on the convertibility of social into status-relevant resources (Bourdieu 1986). According to Bourdieu the physical or 'site effects' on a person's social and other capital, depends on profits or disadvantages derived from proximity to specific agents and material or social infrastructure, as well as on profits of position or rank.

So, what does the study on the West Side tell us about the social capital potential of ethnic networks and the site effects of ethnic neighborhoods? Tables 22 and 23 provide a summary of the identified benefits and costs associated with ethnic social networks, on the one hand, and living in an 'ethnic' neighborhood, on the other. Although these benefits and costs were assessed for the case of the West Side, their transferability to other ethnically segregated neighborhood environments is looked at further on in this chapter.

Table 22: Benefits and costs of ethnic social capital

	Social capital of ethnic social networks in terms of...			
	Economic benefits/costs	Cultural benefits/costs	Symbolic benefits/costs	Social benefits/costs; Well-being
Benefits	- Job opportunities - Free services from family members, e.g. child-care, English lessons and others - Scholarships for studying	- Skills training - English lessons - Driving lessons - Maintenance of own language and culture	- Valuing own culture - Value attributed to multi-linguistic and -cultural background by US society (present)	- Cultural familiarity - Absence of discrimination - Sense of social comfort - Women´s empowerment in patriarchal structures
Costs		- Parents as an obstacle to educational aspirations	- Little value to non-native language and culture by US society (past)	- Narrow environment for youth, lack of privacy

Table 23: Localization profits and deficits associated with living in an ethnic neighborhood

	Localization profits/deficits derived from ...	
	Proximity to valued agents and infrastructure	Position or rank; size of occupied space
Profits	- Walking distance to self-help groups and social services - Proximity to Downtown-jobs - Accessibility of same-language services and commercial infrastructure - Comfort associated with socially and culturally familiar environment - Concentration required to attain critical mass for specialized, ethnic services - Protection from outside judgment and discrimination	- Reputation of West Side among Hispanics as *the* Latino neighborhood of Twin Cities
Deficits	- Low-quality educational infrastructure - Contact with problematic peer role models, especially youth gangs - Unawareness of social and economic barriers reinforced through socio-spatial segregation (past)	- Negative image of neighborhood in the rest of the city - Self-perception as low-income neighborhood - Historical disinvestments in neighborhood - Low market values of housing and real estate property - Low use value of housing estates and old, dilapidated housing

The benefits and costs pointed out here cannot simply be compared or set off against each other. This is because some of them can be (subjectively or theory-guided) bestowed a stronger weight than others, and also since the occurrence of costs and benefits are contingent on particular conditions on the individual, neighborhood and macro-social or -institutional level. Also the respective weight of the costs and benefits will vary according to individual and supra-individual influences.

Before coming to the conditions for the social capital- and neighborhood-related outcomes, two issues related to the strengths and weaknesses of social capital will be addressed. The first challenges an aspect frequently stated in the literature, i.e. that ethnic social networks do not contribute to social mobility outside of the neighborhood or ethnic ′community′ context, although they may help getting along inside the community. Partly contradicting this statement, this study has revealed what can be termed a considerable bridging potential of ethnic social capital (Putnam 2000: 22, Putnam/Goss 2002: 9).

The second refers to the relationship between the 'instrumental' and the 'intrinsic' value of social capital. In other words, it reflects on whether 'social mobility' or rather 'well-being' should constitute the basic criteria of judgment of this value. This latter aspect also refers to the tension between a subjectivist versus an objectivist epistemology and constitutes a critical reflection of hitherto theories on ethnic social and spatial capital.

8.1.1 The 'bridging' potential of 'bonding' ethnic capital

In much of the literature on ethnic social networks and ethnic neighborhoods, the resources or capital potentially derived from these are assumed to be rather low. According to Bourdieu, poor households are likely to possess low social, economic, cultural and symbolic capital, and tend to be detrimentally positioned in the physical space, e.g. regarding their location of residence (Bourdieu 1999). De Souza Briggs assumes that while poor and minority neighborhoods and 'bonding' ethnic social networks may still assist people with 'getting along' on a daily basis they tend to bring about few opportunities for people to 'get ahead' (De Souza Briggs 1997, quoted in Goetz 2003: 217, quoted in Putnam 2000: 23). Other authors maintain that certain characteristics of social capital in ethnic neighborhoods may reinforce inside 'bonding', but prevent 'bridging' towards other cultural or socio-economic status groups (Uslaner/Conley 2003, Warr 2005: 304, Brisson 2005: 645, Colclough/Sitaraman 2005: 491, MacDonald et al. 2005, view chapter 3.4).

The research carried out on the West Side suggests that these assumptions only partially hold. They suggest an opposition between the respective categories (bonding and bridging, inside- and outside-orientation, getting along and ahead), which in view of the empirical findings does not exist[295]. Two factors can be pointed out to support this point:

[295] Most of these categories are discussed by Putnam/Goss in their overall reflection on the evolution of social capital theory (Putnam/Goss 2002: 10f.).

- The heterogeneity among the Mexican population of the West Side with respect to certain individual variables, e.g. immigrant cohort. This implies that ethnic social networks and the fact of living in an ethnic neighborhood fulfill entirely different purposes for different sub-groups within the Mexican population. It also implies that in some cases, e.g. in the relationship between recent Mexican immigrants and longstanding Mexican-Americans common ethnicity does not constitute a strong bonding criteria[296], at least not from the subjective view of individuals.
- The linkages between the apparently contrasting categories. For instance, most of the recent male immigrants from the West Side found their present employment – thus, economic mobility - through the help of family members or friends. Most of the recent Mexican female immigrants achieved their first, frequently casual, job opportunities through the participation in ethnic self-help groups in the West Side neighborhood. In some cases, these helped with accessing other opportunities *outside* the neighborhood. In the case of two of the longstanding male interviewees (Theo and Ronald) job entries in West Side neighborhood organizations provided stepping stones to higher level positions in other city areas or institutions.

Hence the 'bridging' potential of 'bonding' capital. Disposing of possibilities to get along may form an important contribution or even condition to get ahead. While much of the support offered in the ethnic neighborhood is indeed directed to a lower income and skills clientele, it is evident that most of the Mexican or Latino adult newcomers belong to this group and thus depend on these services. The same is true for employment achieved through co-ethnic family members and friends: While most of this employment may be entry-level, this is the one sought out by the - in their majority - low-skilled adult immigrants from Mexico and Latin America. An employment-housing mismatch as assumed in much of the literature as a typical disadvantage of central-city ethnic neighborhoods (e.g. Cutler/Glaeser 2006: 4) could not be identified on the West Side[297].

---

[296] A ´bonding´ element would be one based on perceived social commonalities, leading to joint practices and a notion of identity.

[297] The early settlement on the West Side in the first half of the 20th century occurred due to the low housing costs and the proximity of the meat packing plants and the railway that pro-

The ethnic neighborhood constitutes a favorable environment to service organizations directed at certain immigrant groups. This is as (e.g. linguistically) specialized services can be carried out more effectively and efficiently if they are located near to their clientele. This is especially the case with a low-income population that cannot afford to spend high transport costs and times to get to an organization or service provider, particularly if the latter results in opportunity costs for missed income-earning opportunities. It is against this background that Expert 9, leading employee of Neighborhood House, highlights the sociability and mobility obstacles recent immigrants may face in suburban, majority-white communities:

"And, it's a struggle for people of color in those other areas. Because, there aren't the support systems, there aren't the level, I mean, of, you know the connections that they have within the community. There aren't Neighborhood Houses. There isn't a 'home away from home' from them." (Expert 9: 9)[298]

In short, the results of this empirical study indicate that ethnic social networks and neighborhoods contain an important bridging potential towards contacts and opportunities outside the ethnic social or spatial community. However, the results also suggest that this potential does not materialize by itself. Rather, for it to unfold and have a broad impact, an active institutional support is required (view chapter 9)[299]. It is also against this background that the comfort associated with socializing with co-ethnics and living in the ethnic neighborhood needs to be carefully looked at. This is because part of this comfort can be explained by the discrimination expected in majority-white neighborhoods which should be addressed in the first place (see chap-

---

vided employment to many of the Mexican men. Although in the context of deindustrialization these work places do not exist any more, the proximity to Downtown-St. Paul – now predominantly service sector - employment is still mentioned as an advantage by some.

[298] He also mentions the problem Neighborhood House faces today to effectively cater to a more geographically dispersed Hispanic and Hmong clientele. This is "because of the gentrification of the West Side, partly due to Downtown, people we used to work with, would be working with, no longer live on the West Side" (Expert 9: 1), but most of them on St. Paul's East Side (view chapter 6.3). As a consequence, "it makes it hard for us, as people move to the East Side, we cannot always keep up with the cost of transportation to get people here." (Expert 9: 6)

[299] While this is true for the support needed by adult immigrants, this is even more imperative for the preparation of larger opportunities and capabilities for the young immigrant generation.

ter 7.3.4). The ambiguity of the comfort of co-ethnic, 'bonding' networking is expressed by Expert 7, a Latino Minnesota State politician:

"And so, I think that, if the thinking is that you can only get advantage by staying within your group, but the world really doesn't work that way. You know, one has to go out and attempt to make connections outside and comfortable areas, in order to pursue opportunities that otherwise may not be there, or even just to see opportunities you can't see, because you can only see them through your local lenses. So the disadvantage [of ethnic social networks] that, you know. In many ways the disadvantage is the same thing as the advantage. The advantage is that you are in a comfortable set of rules and understandings to which you can grow where there is more opportunities without feeling odd or feeling inadequate because of greater society's you know stereotyping of who you are and what your capacity is. " (Expert 7: 5f.)

8.1.2 *Instrumental versus intrinsic value of social capital*

The benefits and costs associated with ethnic social networks in the context of this study (view table 22) can be judged with respect to at least two basic criteria: The first represents the instrumental value of social networks, in the sense of their contribution to economic, cultural or symbolic benefits for the individual person. Here, the value or volume of social capital depends on the convertibility of social capital into monetary, educational or symbolic capital, thus on chances for social mobility. The second refers to what could be termed the intrinsic value of social capital. The focus here is on its significance for the attainment of individual *well-being*, rather than for social mobility.

While the contribution of social networks to social mobility can be measured by relatively objective criteria or indicators (e.g. increase in income and wealth, skills gains)[300], this is not the case of the measurement of well-being. On the contrary, according to Sen (2000, 2000a, 1999), the definition of individual well-being is strongly contingent on subjective and on (geographic and cultural) context-related criteria. This is the case as different individual situations, e.g. good or bad health, as well as local political and

---

300 The above should not suggest however that social mobility can be measured in an easy way. Whether certain economic or educational benefits (e.g. working in a tomato factory) should be considered as 'social mobility' is certainly a matter of discussion by itself. However, the relative nature of mobility or the opportunity for it should be taken into account, in the sense Elena puts it: "Opportunity for many people is to rise pretty high, but you have to consider from where you start." (Elena: 2) ([O]portunidad para mucha gente es subir bien alta, pero hay que ver de donde empieza uno." Original wording).

economic contexts, can lead to highly different appraisals of the use and utility of certain objective criteria, such as income- and skills-gains. The evaluation of social capital by subjective, rather than objective criteria may add some complication to the interpretation of research findings. However, subjective criteria need to be taken into account as they form the basis for individual and collective agency (Bourdieu 1990: 130).

What does the study of the Mexican population of the West Side indicate with respect to the relationship or weight of indicators of social mobility versus well-being? Although West Side residents were not directly asked about their criteria of well-being, the interview results provide some important indications on the matter. The first one is that people inside the 'ethnic' community and those outside of it use different definitions of personal poverty (as an antidote of well-being) (view chapter 7.3.3). This is reflected in some of the Mexican-American residents' comments on their childhood, during which they stated that they were "poor without knowing it". They did not consider themselves as "poor", as they had lots of friends and caring parents, lead a healthy life, had enough to eat and so on. It is also reflected in the words of Elena, a 42-year old first generation immigrant when she states:

> "Many people see me like poor, poor woman with four childrens. You know what? I probably I am, as, I would say a struggle, but sometimes, I don´t know my mind has not a break (…) Because I still think, you know what I think!, I think you will know that we are poor that you grow up, in the meantime, as long as you are full on the payroll (…) and have a clean place to live, you´re rich (laughs, Eva says: Sure). (…) Or they say, oh poor woman, doesn´t even have a car." (Elena: 12)

Many of the Mexican or Mexican-American residents stress the notion of social comfort and security associated with living on the West Side and socializing with co-ethnics. The comfort is a result of present or past experiences of mutual aid and solidarity, of cultural affinities, and also the absence of discrimination, contrary to what is expected in other neighborhoods or in the midst of a majority-white social context.

While much highlighted and appreciated by the people themselves, the 'intrinsic' value of ethnic social networks and neighborhood in conveying social comfort has historically gone unrecognized by the 'outside' society. This is pointed out by Expert 9 from Neighborhood House, referring to the city's decision in 1958 to tear down the houses on the - predominantly Mexican - West Side 'Flats' community:

"Because the old West Side was pretty, was a pretty, you know it was, 'those outside of here'. It was a ghetto, it was a slum. That's how people saw it, that's why it was wiped out. (…) People saw it as inadequate housing. But they didn't understand the social fabric that they were destroying doing that. And so, that had tremendous value, that social fabric. That was destroyed. Which is a pain that is still felt today on the West Side." (Expert 9: 8)

The value of ethnic social networks on their own right (providing a sense of belonging and community, a feeling of social comfort, stability and acceptance) can be better understood if one takes into account certain context-related conditions:

- The migration experience. Many of the first-generation adult immigrants perceive or remember it as one of personal uprooting and instability. Under these conditions, being able to communicate in one's own language and among individuals with a similar socio-cultural reference framework provides temporary relief and arguably strength to confront the challenges ahead.
- Past and present experiences of discrimination by the majority (Anglo-white) society. Particularly for the longstanding Mexican-Americans, the perception of racially motivated institutional ill-treatment (e.g. the eradication of the West Side 'Flats' community) and/or neglect, forms a strong identity-building factor. Likewise, the feeling of comfort expressed by some of the recent Mexican immigrants is also at least partly a result of experiences of discrimination in majority-white social and spatial contexts.

Thus on a normative level, the research on the West Side suggests that subjective criteria of well-being, among them the notion of social comfort and belonging, should be taken as seriously as tangible, material ones (a car, monthly income etc.). For the longstanding Mexican-Americans this inherent, emotional benefit of the ethnic neighborhood constitutes the decisive and for the recent Mexican immigrants a further crucial one. The important contribution of ethnic social networks and ethnic neighborhoods to conveying comfort and emotional security should be recognized.

The question still needs to be asked, to what degree the decision, for instance, to live in the ethnic neighborhood, is taken under conditions of free choice and deliberation. Based on Sen (2000, 2000a) I consider the latter to be a key ingredient of individual well-being and as conditions for people to realize their personal objectives of well-being.

The interviews with residents of the West Side suggest that the decision to move to the neighborhood has greatly been a matter of choice[301]. In most of the cases family members and, more seldom, friends already living in the neighborhood attracted the newcomers. In the first half of the 20th century, the proximity to the workplace (the meat-packing plants or railway in South St. Paul) constituted an additional motivation. Even though mentioned by few interviewees, it can be safely assumed that the decision to move to the West Side was also taken under affordability constraints – thus among a bundle of neighborhoods in St. Paul with affordable housing opportunities[302]. Incidences of direct discrimination in the housing market, e.g. racial steering by realtors, were mentioned by none of the interviewed Mexican or Mexican-Americans as a reason to live on the West Side.

Thus, Bourdieu's - instrumentalist - concept of social capital with material or symbolic status benefits or costs counting as its constitutive elements, needs to be complemented by the consideration of the intrinsic social or emotional dimension of social capital. Whereas this social dimension (manifested in the social comfort and belonging experienced in co-ethnic social relationships or the fact of living in an ethnic neighborhood) does not explain the incidence or absence of social mobility, it does explain the presence or absence of personal *well-being.* I assume the latter to be constitutive for residential mobility decisions. To what degree benefits in individual well-being are accompa-

---

301 This being said, it is important to point out the pitfalls of the concept of (residential) choice. As pointed out by Bourdieu, by virtue of the *habitus* individuals are much more likely to accommodate their tastes and practice-relevant decisions to the realm of the possible than to what they assume ,'is not for them' (1990a, 1987). Goetz (2003) points out that the residential choices of the poor are oriented by certain (economically based) choice constraints to begin with. These choice constraints lead to the dependence on certain amenities typically *not* provided in wealthy and/or suburban neighborhoods in the US, such as affordable rents or housing prices, public transport and certain services.

302 The neighborhood status and housing prices on the West Side have however changed. While at the time of the settlement of the first Mexicans in the 1920s the West Side might have been one of the city neighborhoods with lowest real estate and housing prices, this is no longer the case. For some very low-income Mexican or Hispanic immigrants the neighborhood is no longer affordable. This is also underlined by the decreasing availability of housing property in the lower price segments of the West Side housing market (view Annex 9).

nied by costs in individual choices or 'freedom' (Sen 2000, 2000a) needs to be assessed more in depth by future work.

8.2 Factors influencing social and neighborhood capital

The results of this research suggest that social capital or mobility outcomes in immigrant social networks cannot be judged uniformly, but vary according to certain factors or conditions. These factors are situated on various levels, i.e. of the individual, the neighborhood and also macro-social conditions. Their identification is important not only for the appreciation of the mobility – and well-being - relevance of ethnic networks and neighborhoods, but also for the formulation of policy recommendations and the development of policy.

8.2.1 Influences on the individual level

The sensitivity of social capital and - social and spatial - mobility outcomes to individual characteristics was mentioned several times during the presentation of interview results in chapter 7. The intention now is to point out the strongest influencing factors of the individual level and how they influence social capital and mobility. These factors are: immigrant generation, gender, social class and age.

In what follows I will point out *tendencies* rather than deliver exact measures or probabilities of social or spatial benefits versus costs. This is a matter of methodological coherence: The qualitative nature of most of the data generated in this study does not provide a basis for the quantification of results. By illustration of some tendencies in tabular form their communication will be facilitated. Thus, tables 22 and 23 are now complemented by individual demographic and socio-economic characteristics that contribute to social capital outcomes or neighborhood effects appearing as positive, negative or neutral.

The following two tables illustrate for whom social capital-related benefits (table 24) or costs (table 25) typically materialize:

Table 24: Individual factors influencing social capital benefits

	Benefits of ethnic network-related social capital in terms of…			
	Economic benefits/costs	Cultural benefits/costs	Symbolic benefits/costs	Social benefits-/costs; Well-being
	- Job opportunities - Free services, e.g. child-care, English lessons and others - Scholarships for studying	- Skills training - English lessons - Driving lessons - Maintenance of own culture	- Valuing own culture - Value attributed to multilinguistic and -cultural background by US society (present)	- Cultural familiarity - Absence of discrimination - Sense of social comfort - Empowerment in patriarchal structures
Individual criteria	***Benefits occurring among…***			
Immigrant generation	*First-generation immigrants*	*First-generation immigrants*	*All generations*	*All generations*
Gender	*Particularly fema-les*	*Particularly females*	*Both*	*Females*
Social class	*Low income and skills*	*Low income and skills*	*All social classes*	*All social classes*
Age	*Adults*	*Adults*	*Adults*	*Adults*

Table 25: Individual factors influencing social capital costs

	Costs of ethnic network-related social capital in terms of…			
		- Parents as an obstacle to educational aspirations	- Little value to non-native language and culture	- Narrow environment for youth
	Costs occurring among…			
Immigrant generation		*All generations*	*Both*	*All generations*
Gender		*Females*	*Both*	*Particularly fema-les*
Social class		*Lower income and skills*	*All classes*	
Age		*Youth*	*Adults and youth*	*Youth*

The tables show that in terms of their mobility relevance, ethnic social networks tend to benefit individuals with the following characteristics: first-generation, low income and –skilled, adult immigrants. Among the Mexican group on which this case study focused it can additionally be stated that female immigrants particularly derived social and other mobility-relevant 'capital' from their co-ethnic social networks. This must be considered against the background of the relatively subordinate status of females in predominantly male-dominated Mexican immigrant families[303].

The former does not mean that ethnic social networks impact negatively on social mobility prospects of the longstanding (more than first-generation) and higher class ethnic population. The case study with the Mexican population on the West Side suggests rather that ethnic social networks do *not* have a major influence on the mobility prospects of the more longstanding adult immigrants. This is particularly the case among Mexican-American adults with higher skills levels and occupational statuses for whom their institutionalized skills (e.g. university degrees) and/or work-related contacts form the major mobility-basis. Ethnic social networks tend to provide rather an emotional function, and to predominantly lie in the private, rather than the public or work sphere.

Young people, specifically young females, seem to be particularly exposed to mobility-related costs of ethnic social networks. The study indicates that family relationships (among 'traditional' Mexican families) can prevent young females from pursuing higher educational or professional careers[304]. Socio-economic struggles in some of the recent immigrant households might also distract parents' attention from their children's endeavors at school. The weight of the family-related, with respect to institutional barriers, as well as the importance of this phenomenon in general can however not be satisfactorily examined here and calls for further studies.

Independent of their mobility effect, ethnic social networks contribute to individual well-being. In the case study on the West Side this is a notion shared independently of social status, gender or immigrant cohort. However,

---

303 Hence the limited generalizability of this particular statement to other population groups. For these it would at least be necessary to re-check a possible assumption of disproportionate benefit of female ‚group' members.

304 In contrast, young males seem to be more prone to negative peer-group dynamics. These do not need to, but can be co-ethnic.

the emphasis placed on it by the longstanding Mexican-Americans can only be properly understood if historical experiences of social exclusion and institutional neglect against the Mexican ethnic and immigrant group are taken into account (see elaborations in previous chapters). These experiences had a strong identity-building effect; something less likely to occur among today's first generation Mexicans[305]. Among second- or more-generation youth ethnic identities are much more likely to get hybridized, particularly under conditions of increasingly multi-ethnic and cultural urban realities. As John, 25, points out:

"And that's the thing with like Hispanics, like, my friends, like my closed friends, we are all Hispanic, Mexican, Puerto Rican, but, we're not, like, bold, you know, the blood lines got thinner, as the races got into the city (…)." (John: 1)

The following two tables illustrate for whom spatial segregation-related benefits (table 24) or costs (table 25) typically materialize:

Table 26: Individual factors influencing positive site effects (profits)

	Spatial profits derived from …	
	Proximity to valued agents and infrastructure	Position or rank; size of occupied space
	- Walking distance to social groups and services - Proximity to Downtown-jobs - Accessibility of same-language services and commercial infrastructure - Comfort associated with socially and culturally familiar environment - Concentration required to attain critical mass for specialized, ethnic services - Protection from outside judgment and discrimination	- Riverfront development positively impacting on neighborhood image and housing market - Reputation as *the* Latino neighborhood in the City and Metro Area
Criteria	***Profits occurring among…***	
Immigrant generation	*Predominantly first generation immigrants, but also others*	*All generations, but particularly perceived longstanding MAs*

[305] Also today's Mexican immigrants report experiences of discrimination, although these are not as strong as the, partly institutionally sanctioned, ones in the past.

Gender	*Predominantly females*	*Males and females*
Social class	*Lower social classes*	*All social classes*
Age	*Adults*	*Adults*

Table 27: Individual factors influencing negative site effects (deficits)

	Spatial deficits derived from ...	
	Proximity to valued agents and infrastructure	Position or rank; size of occupied space
	- Low-quality educational infrastructure - Contact with problematic peer role models, especially gangs - Physical mobility hampered through violence - Unawareness of social and economic barriers reinforced through socio-spatial isolation (past)	- Negative image of neighborhood in rest of the city - Self-perception as low-income neighborhood - Historical disinvestments in neighborhood - Low market values of housing and real estate property - Low use value of housing estates and old, dilapidated housing
	Deficits occurring among...	
Immigrant generation	*All generations, but slightly more recent immigrants*	*All generations, but more perceived by longstanding Mexican-Americans*
Gender	*All genders, but slightly more male*	*All genders*
Social class	*All social classes, but probably more low class residents*	*All social classes*
Age	*Children and youth, indirectly parent-adults*	*Adults*

It is not surprising that first-generation adult immigrants of lower social status benefit most from the spatial proximity of co-ethnic households and/or ethnic services or commerce. There are several reasons for this: First, linguistic and often legal barriers limit their opportunities to socialize with US natives and access to jobs open to low-skilled natives. Second, they feel safer and more comfortable in a co-ethnic social and neighborhood environment, although most of them, particularly male immigrants, have co-workers belonging to other ethnic or racial groups. Third, recent immigrant arrivals tend to have a limited physical mobility, partly due to economic reasons (lack of income to possess a car, or pay public transport fees) and partly due to the gender-based household division of labor. Spatial benefits of proximity are accentuated as culturally or linguistically appropriate services (health, training, religious masses etc.) are usually located close to their clientele. In contrast, for more longstanding (beyond first generation immigrant) groups, the proximity of co-ethnic households and services is a matter of emotional comfort rather than need.

Children and (even more) adolescents are the ones experiencing negative site effects. This represents a serious matter indeed, as educational barriers experienced by them at present are most likely to result in mobility constraints in the future. The deficits result from the likelihood of being surrounded by harmful peer or adult role models in the neighborhood or family, as well as from educational entities ill-prepared to confront the challenges, but also use the potentials of a partly socio-economically burdened and non-native parent and student constituency. To the extent that parents of children anticipate and/or worry about social and educational risks their offspring is exposed to, they are an adult group also strongly affected by these locational disadvantages.

The study on the West Side indicates that living in an ethnic neighborhood provides rather limited profits of position or rank, independent of individual characteristics[306]. As long as the negative image is maintained by the dominant (middle class, Anglo-white) society, subjectively perceived locational advantages of the ethnic neighborhoods by immigrants or their descendants are unlikely to be capitalized upon, at least in a material sense. Tangible manifestations of this fact are housing disinvestments and little or slowly increasing housing values, as well as rapid residential turn-over implying that economically more successful households leave the neighborhood.

In synthesis, the analysis above helps to clarify at what points of the migration trajectory, for which age and gender groups and for which social classes ethnic networks and neighborhoods tend to encompass positive, or respectively negative effects. This represents an important innovation to previous studies on segregation in the USA, which either concentrate on the negative

---

[306] This being said, the image of the West Side is partly changing as a consequence of the processes of gentrification in parts of the neighborhood. Also, the diversity of the neighborhood with respect to income levels of its inhabitants, housing values and its housing stock (see chapter 6), may provide for more image-lifting options than in more homogenously low-income and/or minority neighborhoods.

aspects or remain vague about the conditions that lead to positive versus negative impacts.

The analysis suggests that the weight of the instrumental versus intrinsic dimension of social capital – social mobility versus well-being – changes with the length of stay of immigrants and their descendants in the country of destination: For immigrant newcomers the contact to co-ethnics and ethnic infrastructure tends to be of instrumental importance to get along and – related to this - ahead in the new society, although the aspect of socio-cultural comfort and familiarity is also essential. For second- and more generation descendants the comfort aspect associated with contact to co-ethnics and the ethnic neighborhood environment constitutes the dominant one. The neighborhood effect on the youth is more problematic, in big parts mediated and reinforced through the institutional deficits of neighborhood schools. Whereas living in an ethnic neighborhood comprises important or even essential *use* values from the perspective of an ethnic population, its exchange value is likely to be constrained by its negative low perception from the outside.

8.2.2 The neighborhood influence or the transferability of results

What aspects of the West Side neighborhood have a distinct influence on the results of this study about individual social capital and mobility outcomes? Answering this question is not only important in order to assess the transferability of the West Side case to that of other ethnic neighborhoods in the City of St. Paul or the United States. It is also helpful in order to come to a normative conclusion with respect to neighborhood features worth being encouraged or being discouraged in the policy and planning fields.

Three distinct characteristics of the West Side need to be highlighted that may differentiate it from the case of other 'ethnic' or high minority neighborhoods in St. Paul or ethnic neighborhoods in other cities in the United States[307]:

1. <u>The ethnic diversity of the neighborhood</u>: Although Mexican and Hispanic residents constitute the largest minority group in the neighborhood they coexist with a variety of other ethno-racial groups. Of the latter the non-Hispanic white population is the largest

[307] Two of these features have already been pointed out in chapter 6 when the West Side was discussed as a "case".

one and comprises almost 50% of the neighborhood inhabitants. At the same time the West Side constitutes one of the few majority-minority neighborhoods in St. Paul or the Twin Cities metro area.

2. The socio-economic diversity of its population: The variety of income groups, among the total *and* the Mexican and Hispanic population, is particularly evident if different sub-areas or census tracts of the neighborhood are compared. It is also reflected in the diverse housing stock of the West Side, although aggregate housing values in all the sub-areas of the West Side are lower than in the entire city of St. Paul. The planned development on the Riverfront on the northern edge of the neighborhood may add further income and wealth discrepancies to the neighborhood in the future.

3. The consolidated nature of ethnic infrastructure and networks: Institutions such as the Church of Our Lady of Guadalupe or the services of Neighborhood House geared towards the Hispanic population are tightly linked to the early Mexican migration of the first half of the 20th century. Although service institutions such as *La Familia* Guidance Center and *La Clínica* have been created or revitalized through the large influx of Mexican immigrants since the 1990s, they are founded on the basis of the social capital of longstanding Mexican-American residents.

The ethnic diversity of the neighborhood (with Hispanics, in the year 2000, forming 33% of the neighborhood population, Asians 8%, African Americans 6%, American Indians 2% and non-Hispanic whites 49%[308]) first of all points to the caution generally required when talking about 'ethnic' neighborhoods. In the political discourse, as well as in many scientific studies the 'ethnic' character of a neighborhood is identified pars pro toto with a particular national or ethno-cultural group – usually the majority-minority one, like the Mexicans or Hispanics on the West Side. In the meantime this ethnic group is likely to be heterogeneous in itself, as manifested in the differences between the various Mexican immigrant cohorts on the West Side -

---

[308] These are only some very general ethno-racial denominations. The designated ethnic or racial groups are internally heterogeneous, e.g. with respect to the different regional, national and cultural specificities included.

the latter constituting not the only, but the strongest differentiating factor[309]. Likewise, the existence of different ethno-racial groups (Hispanics, African Americans, Caucasian whites, etc.) and sub-groups within these indicates the existence of a multitude of ethnic networks and fractions. Both facts – intra- and inter-group differences – call for different approaches in policy and planning than in, say, culturally more homogeneous neighborhoods as this might be the case in some majority-African American neighborhoods.

In the City of St. Paul and the Twin Cities, for the major part of the 20th century the immigrants from Mexico and their descendants constituted a very small ethnic group (less than 2% until the 1970s, see chapter 6, table 6) in an almost complete white State- and City-environment. This constitutes a different situation to the one of Mexicans and Hispanics in high-immigrant destinations e.g. in the Southwestern USA. The small size and relatively homogeneous (mostly precarious) living conditions of the Mexican population during their early settlement decades may have lead to a strong internal cohesion on the one hand, while at the same time requiring interaction with other ethnic groups, at work or in the context of neighborhood institutions such as Neighborhood House. Thus, while the contemporaneous divisions within the Mexican population and the ethno-cultural diversity of the West Side may reflect a rather common picture of the social reality of immigrant neighborhoods, the long-lasting solidarity and the notion of 'community' among the 'old' Mexican-Americans of the West Side may be less likely to be found elsewhere[310].

The socio-economic diversity of the neighborhood – with median income levels in some sub-areas of the neighborhood figuring higher than in the St. Paul City average (table 9, Annex 8) - indicates that a variety of income groups are likely to interact with each other, e.g. in the context of school-,

---

309 The immigrant generation or cohort factor also lies partly at the root of other, e.g. the one of social class, measured by occupational status and educational skills. The first generation adults tend to have a lower occupational status, as well as skills level compared with the more longstanding, at least second generation Mexican-American adults.

310 This does not dispute the fact that within today's highly differentiated Mexican community of the West Side tight social networks of immigrant sub-groups exist as well. The "Hispanic Women in Action" group of Neighborhood House constitutes an example thereof. The point is rather that these ethnic sub-groups are small and likely to break apart latest in the context of the future socio-economic differentiation among their members' children and grand-children.

sports-, and other everyday activities of the youth. The diversity of the West Side's housing stock with respect to housing types and values means that living on the West Side entails higher neighborhood-internal mobility potentials than living in more homogeneously poor neighborhoods[311] - the predominantly negative image of the neighborhood in the rest of the city notwithstanding. This suggests that even Mexican households living in the 'poorer' sub-areas of the West Side in rental and/or public housing have the possibility of upward residential mobility inside the neighborhood, or that housing equity generated on the West Side may be subsequently invested in higher income neighborhoods elsewhere in the City or Metro Area. This was for instance seen in the example of Theo who has moved to a suburban neighborhood.

The fact that a number of ethnic service infrastructure and networks were created in the context of early 20th-century Mexican migration, or founded by longstanding Mexican-American leaders, may have increased their capacity to adequately respond to the needs of their Mexican/Hispanic constituency while, at the same time, offering links to non-ethnic contacts and institutions outside of the neighborhood (university etc.) – thus their ′bridging′ potential. Notwithstanding the frictions inside the Mexican community, the service networks developed by the 'old' Mexican immigrant families effectively assist today's immigrants in getting along and ahead in the new society. According to Expert 9 from Neighborhood House, the few longstanding Mexican-Americans who continue to be actively involved in the community[312] constitute the "anchors of the community" (Expert 9: 9) and positive role models and mentors for the immigrant youth.

In synthesis, the West Side neighborhood context may provide some positive components to the social networks and –mobility experience of its Mexican population that might not be found to the same degree in other ethnic neighborhoods. Incidences of self-help in informal, family- or vicinity-based networks are certainly also common in other 'ethnic' neighborhoods – and essential for the sense of well-being of immigrant newcomers. However the

---

311 The 'flip' side of this is that West Side housing has become no longer affordable for some of the lower income households.

312 The longstanding Mexican Americans are for instance involved in these neighborhood institutions as: director of La Familia Guidance Center, employee of Neighborhood House, members on the board of the same institution, all-time volunteer at the Church and so on.

chances for social mobility through the engagement in formal – more or less ethnic - social networks may be higher on the West Side than in other immigrant neighborhoods, even in the St. Paul or Twin Cities' context. A research carried out in other immigrant neighborhood types would however be instrumental in providing an empirically founded answer to this question.

8.2.3 The macro-social influence

In chapter 7 it was already indicated that the value attached to socializing with co-ethnics and living in an ethnic neighborhood also depends on external or macro-social factors. The extent to which social (and related economic, cultural) capital can be generated in ethnic neighborhoods greatly depends on how this neighborhood and its population are looked at from the outside.

In the case of the Mexican population in the West Side neighborhood, the external attitude towards ethnic social and place-communities has historically been characterized by depreciation towards social and cultural 'difference'. This depreciation manifests itself notably in the housing and educational, but also in other policy sectors:

- Housing: The perception of the West Side neighborhood and its housing stock is still permeated by negativity. According to one interviewed expert West Side homes and real estate have been "undervalued for many, many years (...) because of this reputation that it was a, 'ethnic', neighborhood" (Expert 8: 3). Indeed, housing values on the West Side are on average lower and increase less than those of the entire City of St. Paul. Accordingly, one of the interviewed residents considers buying a house on the West Side as not such a good deal, as "it's always looked more as a low-income" (Leon: 12) area. It can be assumed that vice versa, the negative image of the neighborhood has also played a role in limiting asset-building opportunities for West Side housing owners. It may also have contributed to a partly decayed housing stock in the neighborhood, as a consequence of decade-long disinvestment.

  The removal of the (in its majority) Mexican community from the West Side "Flats" in 1958, as well as similar urban renewal or slum clearing projects at the time, constitute institutionalized manifestations of the negative image of minority populations and their locations of residence likewise.

- Education: Many Mexican-Americans who grew up on the West Side in the mid 20th century, do not speak Spanish. This was as their parents made sure their children only spoke English at home, recognizing this language as a necessary condition to get ahead in US-society[313]. With the ability to speak several languages being valued and promoted in the US society and schools today, most Mexican immigrants now try to make sure their children retain their language of origin in addition to learning the English language – not least as an element of cultural pride. One may argue that linguistic retention constitutes an objective asset conveyed by socializing in co-ethnic social or vicinity context. However, the social utility of this asset (e.g. in peer encounters, recognition by teachers, employment searches etc.), as well as the value attributed to it strongly depends on the judgment of the overall society.

  Correspondingly, for many years teaching in West Side primary and secondary schools was carried out exclusively in English, in spite of the high presence of non-native students, many of them Mexicans. Only recently, have specific reading lessons for English-learners been introduced, Spanish-speaking staff been hired and extra-curricular activities developed that are targeted at a multi-cultural parent and student population[314]. Also, the City of St. Paul is now home to several Spanish-immersion or bilingual schools, partly in the West and East Side neighborhoods.

With respect to their general role in society, Mexicans and/or Hispanics are imagined as those who "aren't making it in schools, who're dropping out of school" (Expert 1: 5) or as illegal immigrants. The contribution of immigrants' labor to the US-economy tends to be disregarded, envied and/or reluctantly accepted, the latter in the sense that "[they] like them working, [but] they don't want to give them any benefits" (Expert 5: 5). All this is

---

313 Or inversely, the Spanish language as not being valued (e.g. by teachers, peers, prospective employers) and thus lacking instrumental utility.

314 This also shows that the external value judgments are by no means static, but subject to changes. These may only manifest in certain sectors (e.g. educational) and not in others. However it can be assumed that educational policies embracing multi-culturalism are somehow linked to a general more welcoming environment to cultural difference.

institutionally backed by a policy discourse that highlights the need for enforced repression on illegal immigrants on the one hand, while seeking out temporary solutions for ensuring the availability of cheap labor, on the other.

The case of the West Side indicates that the negative outside image towards the neighborhood and its population tends not only to be known, but partly appropriated by those subject to it (e.g., consideration of West Side as a "low income-area"). However, the case study also indicates that external and internal value judgments of the neighborhood do not always correspond. Particularly the longstanding Mexican-American residents of the West Side vigorously reject the negative outside image of the West Side, e.g. with respect to the perceived insecurity of the neighborhood (see chapter 7). Also, the external labeling of the West Side as 'the' Mexican or Hispanic neighborhood is rejected. Particularly the longstanding Mexican-American population emphasizes the socio-economic and cultural differences between themselves and the recent Mexican immigrant population, arguably for status-related reasons.

Another conflict is palpable in the mentioned evolution of the neighborhood image in the rest of the City. While most of the longstanding Mexican-Americans agree that there is a growing appreciation of the ethnic neighborhood history and culture among co-urbanites, the essentialising attitude behind this is looked at with suspicion. Like Carmen who describes her feelings when witnessing a 'tourist' group's visit to the West Side:

" (…) and there was all these white people walking around, they were like getting off the school bus and were like walking around and going in all the stores and they came in El Burrito [ethnic grocery store] and like buying stuff like they were tourists. Like if this were like a show or something like, I don't know, it was so weird to me, like they, yeah, like they have never been there before, and they were buying stuff like they were tourists, basically." (Carmen: 8)

In synthesis, perceptions and value judgments towards a certain social or ethnic population group and their residential location manifest in objectified and institutionalized forms, e.g. housing and real estate prices, school curricula, immigrant laws and so forth. The research indicates that those subject to the mostly negative outside image, ethnic minorities or residents of an 'ethnic' neighborhood, partly appropriate this image, e.g. by not wanting to buy housing property in the neighborhood or by moving out. Even if they do not appropriate, but reject it (defending the positive aspects of the neighborhood or implicitly criticizing the simplistic outside image) it tends to negatively affect their lives.

8.3 Summary

In this chapter some conceptual implications of this research were discussed and linked back to its theoretical framework. This conceptual discussion occurred alongside two different axes: The first were the concrete manifestations and outcomes of social capital in the ethnic neighborhood, as well as conceptually relevant factors that helped with their assessment: the 'bridging capacity' of 'bonding' social capital and the aspect of well-being. The second were the conditions on the individual, neighborhood and macro-social level that influenced these outcomes.

In section 8.1 the concrete manifestations of benefits and costs of ethnic social capital and 'site effects' in the West Side case were pointed out. It was highlighted that counting and setting-off benefits against costs is not possible as these manifest depending on individual characteristics, but also in factors beyond. Further the benefits or costs probably need to be attributed with different weighting (or valuing) qualifications and criteria. An important qualification constitutes the 'bridging' potential of social capital: Instead of merely assuming that acquiring a job or participating in training (e.g. through participation in a self-help group) constitutes a matter of fact incidence of social mobility, it is assumed that 'getting ahead' in society also requires the chance to 'bridge' beyond one's own group. The research on the West Side suggests that ethnic 'bonding' capital entails a considerable bridging potential, but that this needs to be actively promoted.

A second conceptually relevant issue forms the question whether social mobility or 'well-being' constitute the relevant criteria to assess the value of 'ethnic' social and neighborhood capital. In view of the emphasis placed in this research on the social comfort and security associated with socializing among co-ethnics and living in the ethnic neighborhood it is argued that subjective value judgments – basis of any individual agency – need to be taken into consideration to understand, for instance, their residential choices. This needs to be done in addition to the instrumentalist view of the value of ethnic social capital according to its economic, cultural and symbolic relevance. Taking into account the subjective value statements of the people reveals discrepancies in the understanding of individual well-being or – inversely – poverty. However, the comfort associated with living in the ethnic neighborhood on the West Side is also a consequence of past and present experiences of exclusion and discrimination.

In chapter 8.2 the specific conditions under which positive or negative social capital outcomes and neighborhood experiences occur are pointed out. On the individual level, immigrant cohort is the most decisive factor, at least in the case of the Mexican population of the West Side. While positive social capital and neighborhood benefits are particularly instrumental for first generation, relatively low-skilled adult immigrants, these benefits are not so clear among others. For today's longstanding Mexican-Americans of the West Side the aspect of social and emotional comfort brought by intra-ethnic socializing and living in the ethnic neighborhood is most important. The research has also revealed that the ethnic neighborhood effect may be harmful for the youth – at least under conditions of a non-supportive institutional framework. Given that the youth constitutes the human capital of the future this aspect is worrying indeed.

The multi-cultural character of the West Side, its socio-economic heterogeneity and the consolidated nature of its social (partly ethnic) networks may require some care in transferring the results of this study to other ethnic neighborhoods. However, I believe that the West Side shows a number of common or typical features of life in ethnic communities in US-cities, such as its ethnic diversity and the social and cultural differentiation within these. Finally, macro-social influences or external value statements are described as essential for the extent 'ethnic' social networks and life in ethnic neighborhood can be capitalized upon. The case of the West Side shows that the negative image of the neighborhood and the Mexican/Hispanic minority in the 'outside society' and corresponding institutional constraints may constitute important barriers for the well-being of an incipient and increasingly multi-cultural urban society.

9 Consequences for housing policies and planning

The objective of this chapter is to consider the implications of the findings of this research on the Mexican population on the West Side, for housing and other public policies. Thus, whereas the preceding chapters provided an analysis of the empirical data collected, this chapter contains normative conclusions of this analysis. Although strictly speaking these normative conclusions refer to the West Side case, the idea is that they also serve as a general indication on how to deal with residential segregation[315].

In this chapter the research questions 5 and 6, pointed out in chapter 4, are addressed:

- How can dominant housing policy and planning responses to residential segregation be assessed, or which are the more adequate ones?
- How can these be related to the challenges and (e.g. asset-creating) potentials of ethnic social networks?

The quest for enhancing residential choices, as opposed to focusing on ethnical and economic 'integration' in housing has gained momentum in the US in recent years. This is the case in the academic discussion on pros and cons of ethnically based residential segregation, but also among policy makers and practitioners confronted with political, economic and moral obstacles to desegregation (chapter 2.2). As the enhancement of choices can be considered an integral element for the achievement of personal well-being, it will be used as the point of departure for this chapter.

Thus, in the first sub-section I discuss the extent to which living on the West Side represents a matter of choice or of constraints from the perspective of its residents. This is done by looking at the factors that were pointed out as influential for residential decisions or patterns in chapter 2.1: income and social status, housing preferences and institutional practices. The respective importance of these factors for the Mexican population of the West Side is shown. In the second sub-section, residential segregation and deconcentration policies as the main current strategy to address segregation are assessed against the results of the study on the West Side. In the third sub-section, recommendations for promoting positive, but discouraging negative aspects

[315] Limitations of transferability however were already pointed out in chapter 8.2.2.

of residential segregation are provided. These recommendations are guided by the policy aim of enlargement of housing choice and capabilities, instead of 'forced' integration. Furthermore, they are based on the case study results on the contribution of residential segregation to individual mobility and well-being.

9.1 The 'choice' for residential segregation on the West Side

If the increase of housing choice is taken as a central criteria for orienting housing policies, certain limitations of the concept need to be taken into account. For instance, Bourdieu (1987) argues that people tend to accommodate with their limited choice (due to whatever reason) by presumably 'freely' choosing what they have within their small range of options (ibid: 589). In a similar vein Goetz (2003) points out that poor people's housing preferences tend to be oriented by certain needs[316] that constrain them to, rather than make them positively 'choose' certain neighborhoods and discard others. The affordability of the dwelling constitutes only one of these needs among others related to the housing environment. Therefore, any housing strategy (allowing or fighting housing desegregation) seriously focusing on housing 'choice', needs to take these into account.

The consequence of the latter is twofold: First that the concept of housing choice needs to be de-romanticized and complemented by the one of housing capabilities. The latter, defined as people's actual freedom to achieve residential and general well-being (view Sen 2000), also takes into account the possible constraints housing 'choices' are possibly rooted in[317]. On a normative level, it implies both the need to identify and to overcome these constraints. Second, methodologically, that apart from the subjective views of the people about their factual or would-be housing choice, the 'objective'

---

[316] These needs may be material or non-material, although Goetz only mentions the former (Goetz 2003: 10). Examples for material needs are: availability of public transport, of low-cost services and housing and proximity of employment. Examples of non-material needs are: existence of social networks, not feeling discriminated against, availability of culturally appropriate services. As the affordability of the dwelling constitutes only one factor among others related to the housing environment, any housing strategy (allowing or fighting against housing desegregation) seriously focusing on housing 'choice' needs to take these into account.

[317] These constraints could be, for instance, lack of political freedom of people, due to their fears of discrimination anticipated or experienced in majority-white residential areas. It could also be people's economic or cultural poverty.

scope of the latter needs to be assessed by looking at additional data sources. These may, for instance, be neighborhood historiography or statistics, as well as information on the housing market.

9.1.1 Income and social status

According to the conceptual model used in this thesis (chapter 4), the economic status of households constitutes an important aspect determining or limiting their housing choice. This is as in a housing market largely dominated by the private sector – which is the case in the United States – geographically differentiated housing and real estate prices determine the kind of environment people are able to live in. Thus, as a matter of fact, low income households (often minorities and recent immigrants) tend to cluster in neighborhoods with low housing and real estate values.

What can be said about the West Side in this regard? According to historical accounts, at the beginning of the 20th century at least the lower part of the West Side (the "Flats") attracted working-class and immigrant households due to its proximity to industrial work and cheap land prices (chapter 6). It can be assumed that at that time the West Side did not constitute the only, but one of the most affordable residential areas in the City of St. Paul. Several experts (Experts 2, 5 and 8) mention the disinvestments and relative undervaluing of the housing stock on the West Side in the course of the second half of the 20th century, hence a continuity of the low-price status of the area.

Today housing values on the West Side continue to be inferior to those of the entire City of St. Paul. Correspondingly, median incomes of West Side residents are lower than those of residents in the entire City of St. Paul (see table 10), although economic wealth levels vary considerably in different sub-areas of the neighborhood, also among the Mexican population (table 11 and Annex 8). Thus, for at least two reasons, the West Side can no longer be considered a 'low income neighborhood': First, since its housing values increase almost on a par with those of the City of St. Paul (see table 10 for the period 1990 and 2000). Second, since some of its sub-areas (census tracts 371 and 372) show aggregate income levels above City-average. Also, the Riverfront (former "Flats") area of the neighborhood is undergoing a process of redevelopment and upgrading, accompanied by the gentrification of adjacent neighborhood sub-sections[318].

As a result, purchasing home ownership[319] on the West Side starts to become unaffordable – or no longer cost-adequate, see chapter 7.3 - to recent and usually low-income immigrants, an issue mentioned by several of the interviewed Mexican residents and experts. This interpretation is corroborated by the relatively high incomes, housing ownership levels and median home values of the Mexicans on the West Side compared with those in St. Paul and the East Side neighborhood Payne-Phalen (see table 18). As Expert 2 of the community development cooperation REDA states:

"[In] general the profile of a standard Hispanic Latino family on the West Side, is going to be different than one that just arrived from let's say Mexico, that lives on the East Side or in Minneapolis. (…) They have been assimilated more if you will, they understand how things work, mainstream culture." (Expert 2: 3)

Nevertheless, the West Side neighborhood does include sub-areas with low-income and subsidized rental housing clusters, especially in the lower "Flats" area around the commercial corridor (see map 3, table 11). Census tracts 361 and 372 (see map 4) are labeled "high poverty" tracts by the St. Paul Public Housing Agency, as their poverty levels exceed the City average (table 10 and 11).

In synthesis, the fact that the West Side has historically offered more affordable housing than other neighborhoods in St. Paul or the Twin Cities' metro area, constituted a point of its attraction to immigrant, or more specifically low-income Mexican families. Since certain sub-areas (e.g. census tract 361) continue to show a concentration of affordable housing, the West Side is likely to attract low-income households, immigrants or not, for years to come. Although the affordability of housing assumedly constitutes a base

---

318 I understand gentrification as a process that implies the increase of housing property values and rents typically occurring in neighbourhoods formerly marked by disinvestment. As a consequence, an exchange of the hitherto lower-, by higher resident groups occurs (Beauregard 1986, Dangschat 1998, Smith 1986, Hamnett 1991).

319 A similar aspect is highlighted by Expert 2 with respect to the *commercial* property in the West Side neighborhood: "Property values have gone up. So, again, for a person immigrating here, whether it's from Latin America or anywhere else in the world, they may not choose the West Side for their first business. Just because it's more expensive. And, first because there aren't that many places to choose from. And second if there are, they're probably more expensive." (Expert 2: 4)

condition for people to settle in a neighborhood[320], none of the interviewed Mexican or Mexican-American residents mentioned it as a prime reason to move to the West Side[321].

9.1.2 Housing preferences

A further factor determining housing choice and urban residential patterns constitutes housing preferences of individuals and households. These preferences may refer to the dwelling as such, as well as to neighborhood environment, e.g. the availability of certain infrastructure and services, and characteristics of one's neighbors.

The question here is whether the 'choice' to live on the West Side constitutes a matter of positive preferences, e.g. resulting from the fact that the neighborhood better fulfills the needs of its Mexican residents than other city areas would do. Or, whether Mexicans choose or chose to move to the West Side in order to escape ill-treatment or being confronted with the more or less explicit prejudices of their fellow (majority-white) urban residents. If the latter were true, the existence of genuine alternatives could no longer be assumed, and this still without considering affordability constraints, (see Sen 2000: 52).

The resident and expert interviews of this research allow the most valuable insight into housing preferences of the Mexican population of the West Side.

According to the interviews it seems that moving to, and living on the West Side constitutes a matter of 'real' preferences, from the perspective of the Mexican population. When asked about their "life history on the West Side" (see interview guideline in Annex 4), the predominant motivation to move to the West Side constitutes to settle nearby fellow Mexicans, either family members or friends and acquaintances. As mentioned in the previous chapter, economic reasons are almost never referred to. If so, it is in the case of the software engineer Juana who highlights that she benefits from the com-

---

320 Having said this, it is still necessary to take into account the 'overpaying' rental households, who spend more than 30 percent of their income on housing. These form 41 percent of the West Side renters, as compared to 32 and 42 percent of renters in Payne-Phalen and St. Paul respectively (table 18).

321 Except for the Mexican-American Juana who emphasized that the good property investment on the West Side constituted one important reason for her to stay there. This was due to the relatively cheap housing on the West Side, compared with other neighborhoods she would have considered and been able to afford.

paratively low housing prices on the West Side. Or, it is in the case of Linda who complained about structural or maintenance deficits of the West Side housing stock and the latter's inordinately high cost that made her move to the first-tier suburb South St. Paul[322].

Following family members or friends constituted the most important reason to move to the West Side. The importance of this preference factor is emphasized by the fact that some of the interviewees state that in the case of leaving the West Side they would seek a neighborhood in which co-ethnics have settled before (view question 22 in interview guideline, Annex 4)[323]. However, as pointed out in chapter 8, the spatial or social benefits accrued by living on the West Side are judged differently by recent and longstanding Mexicans. This fact relates to the divergent housing needs and living situations of those pertaining to different immigrant groups.

Thus, for the (mostly low-income and low-skilled) recent or first-generation Mexican immigrants living on the West Side and in proximity to co-ethnics this represents a need for getting along and, related to this, ahead. This is as it facilitates the access to economic and educational opportunities and infrastructure. Beyond its instrumental aspect, living among co-ethnics corresponds to a more intrinsic need to live in a culturally and linguistically close environment. In a more negative sense, the latter is also related to the evasion of discriminatory attitudes by the majority society – an aspect pointed out by 26-year old Esteban, the most recent arrival of the interviewed Mexicans:

---

[322] The two experiences seem to conflict with each other: While Juana stated that she obtained more value for her money on the West Side (as a consequence of the undervaluing of the neighborhood's housing stock), Linda complained about the little value offered for overpriced housing structures on the West Side. Two possible explanations are highlighted for this contradiction: The first is the time lapse: Whereas Juana bought her house eight years prior to the interview, the experience of Linda was more recent, i.e. about one year prior to the conversation with her. During this time, the West Side housing market may have already considerably tightened. The other, in my view more pertinent explanation, is the co-existence of different price segments on the West Side. Whereas for the lower income levels the housing property prices may have strongly increased in view of a continuous demand, the situation may be different for the upper income levels among which the demand may (still) be more hesitant. Annex 9 supports this assumption.

[323] However, the majority of the interviewees do NOT want to move away from the West Side. In the case they do mention alternative neighborhoods, these are in their majority the ones in the Southeast-Metro Area, adjacent to the City of St. Paul and the West Side.

"Well, we would like to live in an area with not so much traffic and less noise, you know, (…) in the kind of areas where the Americans are. They are cleaner and quieter. For this reason we would like to live in this sort of territories [suburbs]. (…) But then we would not like to live there because the people there treat you as the 'bad Latino' or they look at you with a strange face, you know." (Esteban: 7)[324]

For most of the longstanding, multi-generational Mexican-Americans the preference to live on the West Side is rooted in a notion of personal comfort. It is however not motivated by distinct material needs[325], such as the use of ethnic infrastructure, or employment and/or training opportunities via social contacts. However, as extensively discussed in chapter 7.3, the social comfort noticed by many of the longstanding Mexican-Americans on the West Side seems to be strongly related to past, if not present experiences of discrimination.

In synthesis, practical advantages (in the case of recent immigrants) and social and emotional well-being (in the case of longstanding Mexican-Americans) lead to preference being an important aspect of choosing residence on the West Side. It has to be taken into account however that the 'comfort' aspect is related to the expected or experienced discrimination in majority-white areas – motivated by the memories of the 'old' Mexican-American West Siders or by contemporary, more subtle exposure to 'strange looks' (Esteban).

---

[324] "Pues, nos gustaría allí una área donde no haya mucho tránsito, no haya mucho ruido, pues (...) este tipo de áreas donde están casi los Americanos. Está más limpio, más tranquilo. Por ese lado nos gustaría vivir en ese tipo de territorios. (...) Por otro lado no por lo que (...) la gente como tratan uno de 'mal Latino', le hacen caras, ves." (Original wording)

[325] This does not mean that economic benefits do not play a role at all, but they do not constitute a priority. For instance, the decision of software engineer Juana to purchase a house in close proximity to her mother, who looks after her daughter for free, seems to be motivated by her willingness to maintain family ties rather than by financial shortages. A second example is youth promoter and single-educating mother Monica. She obtained a subsidized housing credit to buy and remodel a house on the West Side. Although it can be assumed that the subsidy constituted an important – material - condition for her being able to buy the house, it can be doubted that she would have pursued the opportunity if the house had been in another neighborhood.

Map 6: Location of public housing in St. Paul, year 2005

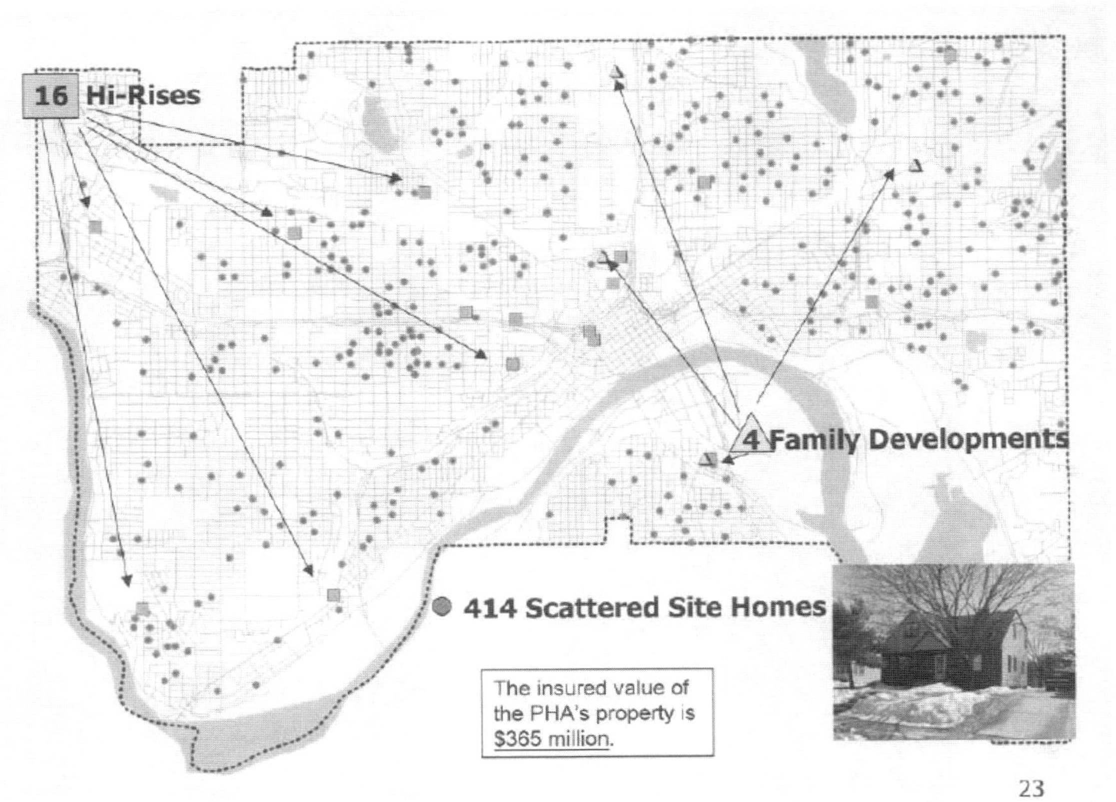

Source: St. Paul PHA

Map 7: Location of voucher units in St. Paul, year 2005

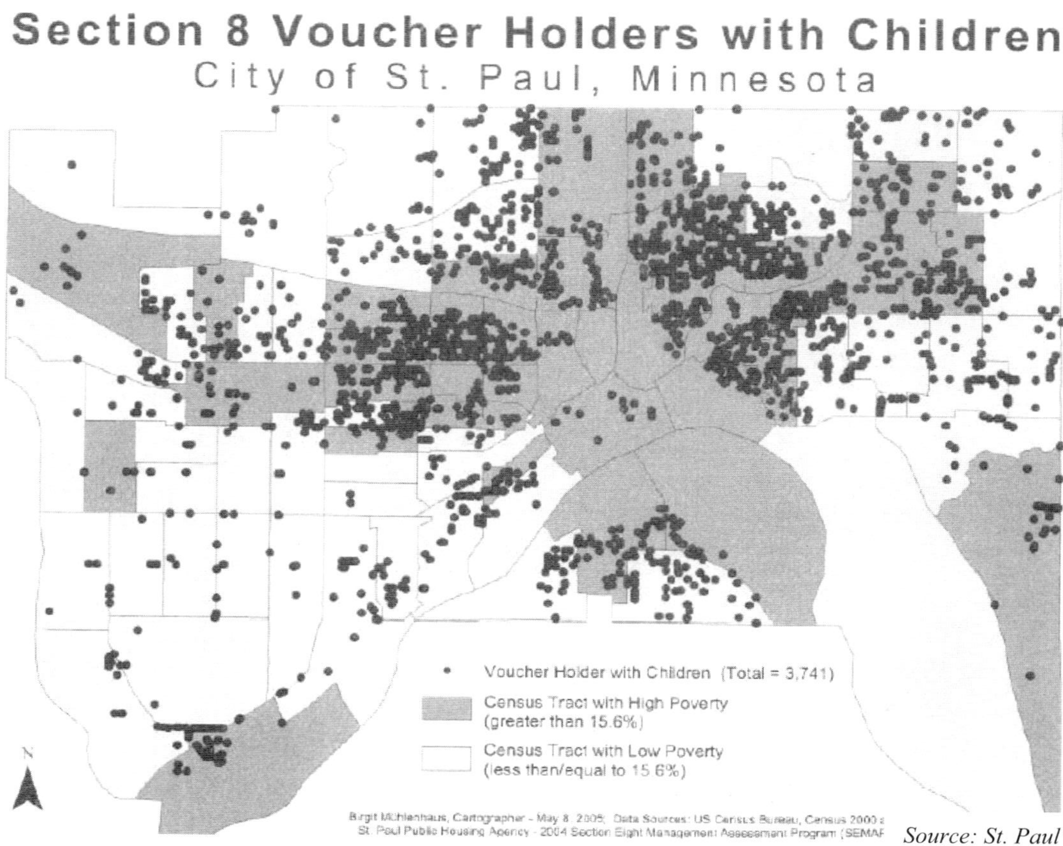

Source: St. Paul PHA

9.1.3 *Institutional practices*

The last factor that, according to the conceptual model this research is based on, determines residential choices and patterns are practices of public and private housing agents. These may be policy decisions, e.g. resulting in the concentrated placement of public housing projects or other subsidized housing in a certain neighborhood. In contrast, after the Fair Housing Act in 1968 housing policies explicitly pursued strategies to deconcentrate minority or low-income households (chapter 2.2). From the side of private housing agents (e.g. real estate agents, mortgage banks) unfair selling and lending practices, such as racial steering and blockbusting can contribute to maintain racial/ethnic and income segregation.

As already pointed out in chapter 6.2 the West Side shows an internal clustering of subsidized rental housing in its lower area corresponding to census tract 361 (map 4). Out of the four big public housing projects owned by the St. Paul Public Housing Agency, the smallest one, Dunedin Terrace, is located on the lower West Side (view map 6)[326]. One out of 16 Hi-Rises owned by the St. Paul PHA, Dunedin Hi-Rises with 136 units, is located just adjacent to the public housing (a so-called "Family Development") unit of the same name (map 6)[327.] In contrast, the scattered-site houses owned, and voucher units subsidized by the St. Paul PHA are located primarily in the central and south-eastern part of the West Side, corresponding to census tracts 372 and 371 (maps 6 and 7)[328]. The location of public housing and voucher units respectively can be seen in maps 6 and 7.

Box 10: Public housing in St. Paul

The number of US public housing programs is large. Their funding originates on several levels, i.e. federal, state, regional, county and city. Notwithstanding this variety, this section concentrates on the public housing stock owned and/or administered by the St. Paul Public Housing Agency (PHA), funded by the Federally De-

[326] The other "Family Developments" of the St. Paul PHA include 580 units (Mc Donough Homes), 314 units (Roosevelt Homes) and 298 units (Mt. Airy Homes). Their location in the City can be viewed in map 6.

[327] The Public Housing Agency disposes its Hi-Rises for older and disabled individuals or households only (interview Expert 10).

[328] This can be explained by the fact that the scattered-site and voucher units predominantly constitute single- or small multi-family units, which are less available in census tract 361 (see table 11).

partment for Housing and Urban Development (HUD). This focus can be justified for two reasons: First, for the prominent role of the agency in the provision and/or administration of affordable housing in the jurisdiction of St. Paul. Second, for its outreach to particularly low-income households: Compared with other public housing programs that target lower middle-class (rather than 'poor') households with 60% of a city's median income, the PHA-project- and tenant-based subsidies are directed at households with 20 to 30% of an area's median income (interview Experts 5 and 10). The Low-Income Housing Tax Credit Program (LIHTC) described in chapter 2.2 shows, nevertheless, a growing share in the subsidized housing provision in the US today, albeit targeted at 'higher low-income' households.

According to its Executive Director, the PHA-owned and –administered housing stock in St. Paul represents around 5% of the overall housing stock in the City, as compared to the public housing stock share in the entire US of approximately 2% (see chapter 2). However, according to estimates from the St. Paul PHA, only one out of five households of those who would qualify actually live in one of the subsidized PHA-units. Households stay on the PHA's waiting list from 3 to 5 years before getting housed, a typical or even low figure for the subsidized housing market in US-urban areas[329]. No new production of public housing units has occurred in St. Paul since 1986 and no vouchers have been added "since the late 1990s" (Expert 10: 2) – a situation corresponding to the one of national public housing (J.PHA Congress Testimony: 5).

The St. Paul Public Housing Agency owns around 4,300 project-based units, consisting of the four mentioned Family Developments (total of 1,673 units), 16 hi-rises (total of 2,476 units for seniors and disabled) and 430 single family, scattered-site units (PHA Management Report, March 2005: 16). In addition to its owned housing stock, it administers a further 4,000 privately-owned Section 8 voucher apartments, of which the owners agree to charge no more than an area-based Fair Market Rent (FMR). In a case the FMR-amount exceeds 30% of the household's income, the difference is covered by the PHA.

Whereas the public housing projects owned by the PHA are dispersed relatively evenly across the jurisdiction, the voucher units appear to be more concentrated[330] – a fact one of the interviewed experts of the St. Paul PHA perceives as somehow ironical: "And that probably belies some stereotypes, that the government concentrates poverty, and the private sector DISPERSES poverty. The map[s] will reveal

---

[329] According to a leading employee of the St. Paul PHA, in New York the time families stay on the respective PHA's waiting list is 17 years!

[330] They are concentrated around St. Paul's East Side (Payne-Phalen and Dayton's Bluff neighborhoods) and Summit-University area (Thomas Dale and Summit-University neighborhoods) – all of them considered low-income according to the HUD criteria (see map 5).

the reverse" (Expert 10: 1). The location of the project-based and voucher-units can be viewed in maps 6 and 7.

On the regional level, the Twin Cities' Metropolitan Council of Minneapolis/St. Paul acts as a provider of public housing in municipalities that lack an own PHAs (Goetz 2003: 96) and as a policy and planning agency. During the 1970s it reviewed applications of municipalities for federal infrastructure (e.g. highway) grants, depending of the municipalities' share in modest-income housing production. However, in the 1980s, the influence of the Met Council on municipalities' affordable housing production and the issue of fair-share housing began to disappear, in the light of federal budget cuts for affordable housing, changing priorities of the State's governor and changing demographics (Goetz 2003: 97ff.). The interviewed housing experts emphasize the "creativity" of certain, particularly first-tier suburban municipalities of the Twin Cities' region in the provision of affordable housing (e.g. combining diverse subsidy-sources). However, they also highlight the limited influence central city or regional agencies exercise on the affordable housing practices of suburban municipalities (interviews Experts 10 and 13).

On the State level, the Minnesota Housing Finance Agency (MHFA) offers below-market rate interest loans for first-time home buyers and for housing improvements, as well as home ownership education. Since its creation it has assisted more than 400,000 households in Minnesota with subsidized home loans (www.mhfa.state.mn.us).

Further affordable rental housing, subsidized in the context of the Low Income Housing Tax Credit Program (LIHTC), are also primarily located on the lower West Side or census tract 361[331]. In view of the concentration of low-income housing around the commercial corridor of the West Side several of the neighborhood housing experts state that "the neighborhood doesn't really want any more" (Expert 5: 7) of subsidized housing. Affordable housing units should be maintained and added in the wealthier sub-areas of the West Side: within "the higher buck housing" (Expert 5: 9). Since census tracts 361 and 371 are considered high-poverty areas (see map 5), the St.

331 Whereas the housing subsidies through the Public Housing Agencies are directed at households earning 30% of the median income of their jurisdiction, the Low Income Housing Tax Credit Program goes to households earning 60% of the median income, i.e. a higher income range (see chapter 2.2).

Paul PHA today has been requested to stop providing subsidies in these areas[332].

If compared to their overall presence in the neighborhood, proportions of Hispanic households living in subsidized units on the West Side are rather small. In the PHA-owned public housing projects on the West Side, 12% of the households living in the Dunedin Family Development and 23% of the older or disabled households residing in the Hi-Rise are Hispanic (PHA-Management Report, March 2005: 16). Only 2% of the households living in scattered-site units, and 3% living in voucher units in the entire City of St. Paul are Hispanic333. Of the 27 interviewed households none lived in PHA-subsidized housing. Two (Manuel, Rita) were living in the Bluff Park Units, a LIHTC-development and two others (Linda, Hermosa) had lived there prior to purchasing their present house.

However, it can be assumed that the relatively large availability of subsidized rental housing on the lower West Side has historically attracted immigrant households to the neighborhood. The Dunedin projects may have shown a larger presence of Mexican households in their first years. These former Mexican inhabitants may have now become home owners. The relatively small proportion of renter households among the Mexican population in census tract 361 (47% as compared to 62% of the total population, see Annex 9) confirms this assumption. In contrast, the public housing projects on the West Side predominantly house African-American and Asian households[334].

Notwithstanding the small percentage of Mexicans living in public housing units, the interviewed housing experts rather complain about the limited

---

[332] The Dunedin housing projects are located on the West Side since at the time of their construction (1959-1976, see Expert 10) no restriction related to the desegregation of public housing units was in place. In spite of the political discouragement of the concentration of low-income and non-white housing, high land prices and resistance of property owners (and sometimes local authorities as well) in wealthier communities have prevented an actual geographical expansion of subsidized housing (Experts 5, 10 and 12).

[333] The scattered-site and voucher-unit figures are not available on the neighborhood level. Although they may be slightly higher on the West Side than on the level of the entire City I expect them to show similar trends.

[334] In the Dunedin Family Developments African American and Asian households occupy 49 and 34 percent of the housing units respectively (PHA-Management Report, March 2005: 16).

availability of subsidized housing in the context of national policies and budget spending decisions:

"[We] know we are not serving all the people who would qualify from an income point of view. I think the statistics are, we serve about one out of five. So, for one family who would get in there, there would be four who need it and can't get in there. And, that's just an indictment I would make about the Federal Government that we just don't seem to have the will to provide adequate affordable housing." (Expert 10: 8)

In synthesis, the availability of subsidized housing on the lower West Side has contributed to the long-term settlement of Mexican and other immigrant households in the neighborhood. The placement of the Dunedin housing projects may have been a deliberate governmental decision following the removal of the 'old' Mexican Flats community and the erection of the flood wall in 1958. However, at least in the case of today's Mexican population on the West Side, it is hard to talk about institutionally steered ethnic concentration. Personal or household preference and the availability of cheap private housing seems to constitute a much stronger factor.

Getting back to the question of departure, to what degree is the residence of the Mexican population on the West Side the product of free choice? Out of the three factors discussed, housing preferences seem to be the most important factor influencing the residential location of Mexicans on the West Side. The interviews suggest that this preference is positively motivated by the desire to live near co-ethnics and make use of the (instrumental and emotional) benefits this nearness entails. However, the desire to evade anticipated or formerly experienced hostilities from the majority population also plays a role.

Furthermore, it is clear that especially for low-income recent immigrants the decision to live on the West Side arises from affordability and thus housing market constraints. Increasing the income of families or other relevant assets to better compete in the private housing market would thus be an important factor to increase their ability to choose to live in areas they are not yet able to consider[335]. These areas may be ethnic or non-ethnic.

---

335 One example of such asset is e.g. English proficiency – potentially of great assistance to negotiate with private home owners or rental and/or real estate agents.

However, even taking the affordability constraints as a given, it can be assumed that low-income Mexican families do have alternatives to living on the West Side. This is suggested by map 5 (chapter 6.2.3) showing poverty rates of St. Paul census tracts. It is also confirmed by the, albeit limited, availability of subsidized tenant- or project-based housing in other neighborhoods of St. Paul (see maps 6 and 7 with project-based and voucher housing locations).

9.2 Revisiting residential segregation and desegregation strategies

Based on the above thoughts on the factors leading to the decision of the Mexican population to live on the West Side, as well as the research results about the effects of this residential location, this section seeks to answer the following two questions:

- What is this research's eventual assessment on ethnically based residential segregation, and
- Based on the research, what conclusions can be drawn on the hitherto policy focus on ethnic/poverty desegregation?

9.2.1 Residential segregation revisited

The empirical study results in an assessment of residential segregation that, in view of the literature review in chapter 2.3, seems somehow trivial at first: Whether residential segregation is positive or negative depends. It depends on the macro-social framework, on the particular neighborhood- and city-context (e.g. degree of economic and/or ethno-racial fragmentation) and on individual characteristics and preferences.

The assumption is that these factors have both a significant impact on the freedom of choice involved in the decision to move to an 'ethnic' neighborhood, as well as on the effects of ethnic segregation, e.g. for the development of social capital, mobility and well-being – and whether these effects may be judged as positive or negative for individual outcomes. As the factors appear in a variety of combinations and may change over time, a categorical answer to whether residential segregation is 'good' or 'bad' seems more difficult.

With respect to the West Side, it was stated that ethnic clustering on the West Side appears predominantly a matter of preferences, rather than constraints. This is only true as long as individual affordability limits in the context of predominantly private urban housing market are regarded as secondary, as it can be assumed that the decision to move to the West Side occurred against affordability-related choice limits in the first place. It also needs to be reminded that anticipated discrimination does play a role in the 'choice' to move to an ethnic neighborhood, and that historically it played an even greater one.

Looking at the effects of living on the West Side for the building of individual social capital, and resulting mobility and well-being (chapters 7 and 8), both positive and negative aspects need to be mentioned. There is no doubt that for many Mexicans, living close to co-ethnics conveys important instrumental and social or emotional benefits. Whereas for recent, usually low-income and low-skilled immigrants the instrumental benefits (entry-access to employment and educational opportunities) play a greater role than for multi-generational Mexican Americans, social benefits are important for both. However, the research also showed that against the background of an adverse social and institutional environment (leading to negative stereotyping of the neighborhood and neglect), living in an ethnic neighborhood may have harmful effects. This is especially problematic in the educational field and for the youth.

Against this background, the importance of 'bridging' as a potential quality of ethnic neighborhoods, as well as criteria for orienting future housing and community development policies was highlighted. From the perspective of many recent Mexican immigrants, particularly females, socializing with co-ethnics on the West Side opened the doors to social and economic contacts beyond the ethnic social and geographic 'community'. This was especially the case due to the West Side's accumulated ethnic social and institutional capital since the settlement of the first Mexican laborers in the 1920s. However, West Side public schools seemed to rather hinder opportunities for future social mobility[336]. Also, the mainstream society's negative stereotyping in the past and present tended to craft social and inter-cultural barriers, rather than bridges.

In short, the case of the West Side has revealed both benefits and risks of ethnic neighborhoods. While the romantic view of a harmonious ethnic 'community' or group cohesion and consciousness needs to be rejected, mul-

---

[336] The West Side secondary school, Humboldt High School, was considered particularly notorious in this regard. In contrast, primary schools were hardly mentioned in connection with negative social effects.

tiple benefits in the economic, educational and social field can be related to ethnically based (sub-) group resources. The possible risks of ethnic clustering lie in a long-term social and economic isolation to which ethnically based spatial clustering may contribute. However, the research indicates that such isolation is neither inevitable, nor predominantly brought about by self-segregation as suggested by some authors (e.g. Uslaner/Conley 2003: 333). Rather the external social, political and institutional framework needs to be scrutinized.

9.2.2 Desegregation policy focus revisited

In chapter 2.2 of this document it was shown that previous policy and planning responses to residential segregation in the United States explicitly or implicitly sought to disperse minority and/or low-income households. These strategies were pursued in order to revert discriminatory housing policies and practices assumed to be the main causes of segregation (first generation desegregation programs). They were also pursued in view of the assumed pernicious effects of poverty concentration on the individual's and communities' social and economic opportunities (second generation desegregation programs). For several reasons, these strategies have shown limited success, both measured against their objective of desegregation and against the intended social and economic impacts. They have also been criticized from a normative perspective by authors seeking paths towards multicultural housing and urban policies (chapter 2.3 and 2.4).

The case of the Mexican community on the West Side largely confirms the critics of desegregation as a panacea against all kinds of social and economic problems. This is as on the West Side, living in proximity to Mexican or Mexican-American co-ethnics appears largely as a matter of individual or household's preference. It is also, as the positive effects of ethnic clustering on individuals, at least from their subjective points of view, are difficult to negate. However, the potential negative impact of the neighborhood on youth's educational and – as a result - employment career ought not to be overlooked, not least as a matter of future urban inclusion[337].

---

[337] The terms 'inclusion' is used here as an alternative to the more common one of 'integration'. This is, as in US policy language integration is directly linked to the normative goal of ethnic mixture in housing that can be criticized as ethno-centric by itself: It refers to the proportion of non-white minorities to white households disregarding the potential ethnic mix among these minorities. For instance, in the context of the Section 8 Management Assessment

Against this background, the interviewed housing experts consider the following as THE future housing policy challenge in the United States: Finding the right balance between granting people "the opportunity to live where they want to" (Expert 12: 7) and preventing opportunity constraints through the spatial concentration of social and economic disadvantage. This is to the degree that national and urban housing administrations entertain a philosophical debate as to what degree ethnic concentration should be allowed and to what extent it should be broken up, "forcefully if necessary" (Expert 13: 2). The latter debate is even more crucial with the Twin Cities' and other metropolitan communities becoming increasingly ethnically diverse.

Thus, from a housing policy perspective the results of this empirical study point to a number of dilemmas regarding ethnic desegregation:

- The choice versus integration dilemma: It constitutes a policy dilemma if people's choices are reduced in order to ultimately expand them[338]. On the level of their day-to-day operations, Public Housing Agencies are confronted with it if applicants for public housing refuse the housing unit offered to them. While from the 1980s onwards families had to accept the unit on the top of the list, in the meantime PHAs grant families a second choice, if they provide a 'good' reason for their refusal[339].

Program (SEMAP), census tracts are defined as racially concentrated if more than 20% of families are non-white minority households (interview Expert 13: 5).

338 This is a dilemma already faced by the integration maintenance approach described in chapter 2.2.

339 With 22% of answers, "Does not like the location" figures as the most frequent reason for the turndown of a unit (PHA Management Report, March 2005: 21). "Want 1 bedroom" and "Not ready to move" follow way behind with 11% and 10%. According to a policy analyst of the St. Paul PHA, Expert 13, colored households seem to be among the most frequent providing the first reason. Obviously, the category is quite broad and may also provide a pretext reason for white households who do not want to live in a minority area.

The placement of developer-driven pubic housing projects[340] constitutes another example. In principle, HUD does not allow the construction of such projects in minority- and low-income areas (such as census tracts 361 and 371 on the West Side). However, it now grants waivers for this prohibition if developers can prove that the units are marketed throughout an urban area (instead of only inside one ethnic community), or local councilors are able to show that they also make units available in 'non-concentrated' areas.

- Housing market dilemmas: In times of tight rental housing markets[341] the placement of affordable housing units in middle- or higher-income areas can prove extremely difficult. This limitation experienced in urban areas in the entire country (view chapter 2.2) was also highlighted for the jurisdiction of St. Paul and the entire Twin Cities' metro area. The above-mentioned waivers for project based voucher units are partly motivated by this practical obstacle, although waivers are not always granted, due to non-compliance with deconcentration regulations. The same dilemma applies to HUD's evaluation of PHA's ordinary Section 8 voucher program through the Section 8 Management Assessment Program (SEMAP)[342].
- Administrative problems: In the 1998 Public Housing Reform Act, the federal housing administration mandated the PHAs to foster the

340 These so-called project-based-assisted (PBA) units form part of the tenant-based voucher program. Under the so-called Supportive Housing Program, one PBA-model, private developers construct these units for particularly needy groups (chronic alcoholics, homeless etc.) and apply at the PHA for rental subsidies. Additionally, the developer can use the subsidy commitment of the Public Housing Authority as a guarantee with the bank or lenders, for the initial funding of the project. On the West Side, a local housing advocacy and research institution intended to build such a unit replacing a vacant unit on the West Side "Flats", the Commercial Club. In view of the resistance of the West Side community that was worried about the concentration of low-income housing in this area, adjacent to its commercial corridor, the project was eventually abandoned.

341 A common indicator to determine the tightness of the affordable housing market constitute the housing vacancy rates. A rate below 5% is considered very low. The rates are calculated for different price ranges. Usually, housing crisis tends to be most severe for the lower-end of the market (Goetz 2003: 110).

342 However, according to Expert 13, although the deconcentration indicators are annually assessed, their weight among 14 other indicators is limited and can be relatively easily compensated by a favorable operational record of a Public Housing Agency.

development of mixed-income public housing estates. This should be done by opening the latter to families with higher incomes – the 'working-', instead of the 'very poor' (view Goetz 2003: 58). While the effort to mix lowest-low income with highest-low income households results in considerable administrative burdens for PHA-staff[343], the degree to which families benefit from such strategy remains questionable. One of the interviewed housing experts highlighted that instead of calculating minority or income proportions in housing projects and neighborhoods, PHAs should rather concentrate on helping "ALL the families to increase their incomes, work with the community on job programs and education programs " (Expert 13: 4).

- Limitations of sectoral focus: As a matter of fact, HUD and public housing providers such as PHAs seek to enlarge housing choice and desegregation by way of housing strategies and instruments. However, as people's housing and neighborhood choices are influenced and constrained by a number of factors beyond housing (e.g. income-earning capacities, cultural and language skills, social needs) desegregation measures that focus on increasing housing affordability alone are not enough.
- Opposition of communities: The advantages and disadvantages of ethnically based spatial clustering as experienced on the West Side have been pointed out in former chapters and will not be repeated here. Resistance to desegregation by concerned residents, often ethnic communities, tends to be rooted in anticipated or already experienced disadvantages associated with life in majority-white neighborhoods[344]. Additionally, housing experts state that some ethnic communities view the desegregation policy goal as a result of paternalist, white-supremacist and assimilationist thinking:

[343] As a consequence, PHAs were required to report in detail the income distribution inside their public housing units, as compared to the city average. However, according to the St. Paul PHA housing analyst, HUD eventually took some pressure away from PHAs regarding this information, as it proved too complicated (Expert 13: 4).

[344] For instance, Goetz (2004) mentions considerable opposition to dispersal in the context of the Hollman vs. Cisneros consent decree from the side of the Southeast Asian community, as well as in other desegregation cases in the country (ibid: 283). View box below for further information on this case.

"Because WE're telling them that it's better that they are living nest door to rich people in Minnetonka [up-market municipality in western Twin Cities metro area] than with their family on the West Side. Because, this will make feel us better" (Expert 5: 9)

Lastly, the potential of housing estates and urban neighborhoods to bridge social gaps among individuals of different socio-economic and cultural background may be called into question. Or, turning the logic around, for socially and economically well-integrated Mexican-Americans from the West Side the location of residence is viewed as independent from their economic or educational whereabouts and mobility:

"[What] do you mean stay on the West Side? Cause you can make your home anywhere and pursue your job anywhere and achieve educational opportunities across the Twin Cities. Just because you live on the West Side, doesn't mean you're limited to that." (Expert 8: 6)

As one of the desegregation lawsuits considered most successful[345] in the country, the so-called Hollman-case in Minneapolis incorporates a wide spectrum of desegregation measures implemented by similar lawsuits in the country. At the same time, it illustrates the challenges typically experienced by desegregation policies.

Box 11: The Hollman vs. Cisneros[346] *case*

In 1992 attorneys of the local non-profit organization Legal Aid and the Minneapolis chapter of the National Association for the Advancement of Colored People (NAACP) filed a lawsuit against the Minneapolis Public Housing Authority (MPHA), the City of Minneapolis, HUD, and the Twin Cities Metropolitan Council (Goetz 2002: 1). The motivation for the lawsuit constituted alleged discrimination in the placement of public housing in Minneapolis (Goetz 2004: 284). Four out of five public housing projects with all together 770 units were located on the same site in

[345] It was considered successful as all elements of the proposed dispersal strategies have been implemented (Goetz 2004: 297). This also reflects the standpoint of at least two of the interviewed housing experts. For instance, Expert 10 from the St. Paul Public Housing Authority highlights that it is "one of the only lawsuits in the country that settled" (JHA: 8). Expert 12 from the HUD-office in Minneapolis believes that "other places in the country have not seen the success that we have seen here in Minneapolis" (Expert 12: 3).

[346] The lawsuit is named after Lucy Hollman, a first-hour community activist and the then-federal secretary of housing and urban development Henry Cisneros during the first Clinton administration (Goetz 2004: 283).

the traditional "North Side" African American neighborhood of the city and in a state of blight in terms of the physical conditions of the housing structures and units, as well as environmental conditions (Goetz 2002a: 5f., Goetz 2003: 15). The racial/ethnic and socio-economic neighborhood profile of the "North Side" starkly differed from the one of the average neighborhood in the metro area: In 1990, 5.8% of the population on the site was white, 45.7% black and 47.1% Asian, as compared to respectively 92.1%, 5.8% and 4.6% on the metro area level. 5.3% on the North Side were college graduates, 72.8% lived in poverty and 3.9% were homeowners, compared with respectively 27.1%, 8.1% and 68.7% in the metro area (Goetz 2004: 288).

According to the interviews with the housing experts, against today's legal housing standards it was obvious that the defendants would end up losing the lawsuit:

"[The] record was complete with statements from City Council members from the 1940s, and I read some of that. Who were on record saying, here is another opportunity to put federal housing, where should we put it? Let's put it in Near North Minneapolis, where the other negro housing is. And when that public record was found, of course they lost the case, because they HAD made deliberate decisions to concentrate it based on race." (Expert 10: 2)

With the consent decree being signed in 1995, the litigating parties agreed to a variety of remedies to deconcentrate the family public housing in Minneapolis. The following were the three pillars of the consent decree:

- Redevelopment of the "North Side". Aiming at creating an income mix in the area, the strategy included the demolition of the 770 housing units and the partly relocation of the families from the units.
- Issuance of 900 housing vouchers, for Hollman and other households. The housing vouchers were used in the context of a Special Mobility Program (SMP) and had to be used in 'non-concentrated' areas only. A city area was defined as 'minority concentrated' if it housed 20% more African American -, and 15% more poor households living in poverty compared to the regional average.
- A one-to-one replacement of the North Side units by scattered-site and project-based units: The aim was also that through the construction of single family units former public housing households would be moving to 'non-concentrated' areas within and outside the Minneapolis jurisdiction. How-

[347] However, the assessment of the actual impacts on the families, notably on school outcomes, may be premature at so short a time after moving.

ever, different than in the SMP-vouchers, this was not a requirement.

The strategy mix adopted in the context of the Hollman consent decree reflected a general characteristics of the deconcentration settlements of the 1990s in that "they were hybrids of two federal programs, HOPE VI and Moving to Opportunity" (Goetz 2004: 282) (chapter 2.2). Starting up as anti-discrimination lawsuits the majority of measures ended up focusing much more on the deconcentration of poverty aspect.

In the beginning of the 2000s, all the elements of the consent decree had been complied with and the 770 families re-housed – around 220 families in the original unit and the rest in other city or suburban neighborhoods (interview Expert 12: 4). Expert 12 from HUD in Minneapolis (still "[pinching himself], because sometimes I don't believe that we were actually able to do it", Expert 12: 4) considers the concerted effort of city and regional political and housing actors, as well as the eventual engagement of some suburban communities as central reasons of this success. Goetz (2004) points out that the affordable housing crisis witnessed by the Twin Cities' region from 1998 to 2002 contributed to a growing acceptance of subsidized housing some of the suburbs. This was as from an economic development of view it became necessary to marshal housing for suburban entry-level workers or simply people already living in these communities (Goetz 2003: 111, id. 2004: 294).

In spite of the mentioned success record, the 'deconcentration' process had to overcome considerable obstacles and showed unsatisfactory results, particularly if judged by the actual degree of spatial deconcentration achieved (Goetz 2004: 297). The obstacles lay in the difficultly to identify private landlords ready to co-operate in the voucher program, the resistance of a considerable number of suburban council members to accept and promote affordable housing in their jurisdiction, the opposition of particularly the Hmong immigrant community to be removed from the former "North Side" community and the very slow progress of relocation altogether.

The relocation of the former public housing residents, both in the voucher or replacement housing context, have in their majority occurred to areas close or adjacent to the city center: "Twenty percent of the families stayed within a 1-mile radius of the center of the original site, 39% relocated within a 2-mile radius, and 58% relocated within 3 miles" (Goetz 2004: 285). Only 13% of the families moved to the suburbs, the big majority of these to first-tier suburbs directly adjacent to the central city (ibid: 284). Although the socioeconomic characteristics of most of the communities former "Hollman" households moved to were significantly better than on the "North Side", they still tended to figure clearly below city- or metro-averages, and tended to worsen between 1990 and 2000 (ibid: 285). Families reported from their new neighborhoods an improved situation with respect to crime and drug problems, however no positive effects in terms of employment or school outcomes[347]. Particularly Southeast-Asian (Hmong) program participants complained about higher levels of social isolation in their new communities for themselves and their children, particularly if they were involuntarily relocated (Goetz 2002b: 20, Goetz 2003: 218).

The challenges experienced in the Hollman desegregation lawsuit parallel those witnessed by others in the United States (chapter 2.2). It is clear that the blight experienced in Minneapolis public housing might not be comparable to the situation of public housing residents in other extremely socio-economically fragmented urban areas. For instance, Chicago public housing families in the context of the Gautreaux case "got the hell out of" (Expert 13: 4) the inner-city Chicago area, when offered the vouchers. In contrast, in Minneapolis "public housing conditions and central-city neighborhood conditions have not inspired the residents to make a mad rush to the suburbs" (Goetz 2004: 298).

9.3 Policy and planning responses to segregation

What policy and planning related lessons can be drawn from the results of this research? In the previous chapters it was shown that residential dispersal as the focal policy response to residential segregation meets significant problems. These problems pertain to the limits of practicability of the dispersal approach, as well as to impact-related limitations on the desegregated households and individuals.

Yet, the case of the West Side and the St. Paul and Twin Cities urban context indicates that problems of the clustering of socially and economically disadvantaged groups should not be ignored either. These problems may be related to both causes and effects of segregation: e.g. economic or institutional barriers to increasing one's housing capabilities and choices, or social mobility constraints mediated through the spatial neighborhood context, e.g. in the form of a deficient educational infrastructure.

The results of this research suggest that broadening housing choices and capabilities of 'ethnic' or immigrant households, instead of residential dispersal, should constitute the overarching aim of US housing policies. With respect to the challenges and potentials of ethnic networks, the lessons-learnt and policy and planning recommendations spelled out here will be built on the following five principles:

- The role of 'ethnic' neighborhoods in conveying social comfort and positive social experience to their inhabitants needs to be recognized. This experience of comfort and sociability cannot invariably be replicated in other, e. g. majority-white neighborhood.

- Living in 'ethnic' neighborhoods and being involved in local ethnic networks can contribute to accessing opportunities outside of these – thus to social and physical mobility of immigrants. Hence the 'bridging' potential of 'bonding' social capital. Simply moving to wealthier neighborhoods may not convey the adequate kind of support to (at least recent) immigrants.
- However, the 'bonding' qualities and the 'bridging' potential of ethnic and neighborhood-related social capital need active institutional and policy support – as opposed to a 'laisser-faire' approach. Improving the outside image of an ethnic neighborhood constitutes an integral part of improving its 'bridging' potential.
- Although housing constitutes a crucial policy sector for advancing social and residential inclusion in US cities, it does not represent the only one. Specifically, measures to enhance individuals' educational and employment perspectives, as well as inter-cultural understanding need to be embraced in order to foster urban social inclusion.
- Housing and other, e.g. educational, policies should welcome instead of neutralize social and cultural multiplicity and 'difference' in their respective fields of influence. In this way a more affirmative attitude to an increasingly multi-cultural city reality would be created. However, they should also be responsive to group-sensitive negative consequences of segregation, e.g. of the youth.

9.3.1 Housing policy and planning recommendations

Strategies to enhance positive, and diminish negative aspects of residential segregation require action on several levels of intervention: On the level of agents in the neighborhood, in the respective cities and metro areas, as well as of actors on state and national levels. In order to effectively influence residential patterns, degrees and outcomes of segregation, they need to cover factors pertaining to both housing supply and demand.

Based on the results of the research, the following housing-related strategies can be recommended:

Provision of housing maintenance and rehabilitation loans to improve chances for housing-related asset building:

The underlying objective of this strategy is to enable individual households in an ethnic neighborhood to enhance their asset or wealth basis. Apart from enhancing their wealth basis, rising housing values may also lead to individual's increased choices and capabilities with respect to future housing mobility. Promoting housing or other capital investments in a hitherto disadvantaged area may also contribute to improving the image of a neighborhood and stop the chain of disinvestments many central city (minority or low-income) areas tend to be confronted with. In principle, this strategy can be fulfilled by neighborhood development corporations, as well as by finance organizations on the city, metro area or state level.

An example of such organization on the West Side constitutes the *Neighborhood Development Alliance (NeDA)*. This Community Development Corporation provides households with "very low-interest" (Elena) loans to repair or rehabilitate their housing units – provided these are 'old' housing units -, with financial support through the City of St. Paul. Additionally, they provide households with technical assistance for the rehabilitation work, in order to guarantee a long-lasting return on investment. ELW, a single-educating Mexican mother of four children, received a loan from NeDA in order to rehabilitate the basement of her detached dwelling.

Provision of group-specific social services in residential locations (e.g. public housing projects), as well as spatial pre-conditions for this:

The objective of this strategy is to increase the poverty-alleviating potential of public housing by providing complementary services needed by specific resident groups. For instance, immigrant households living in public housing projects may be in need of language-learning- or other start-up opportunities in the new society. As few housing estates are inhabited by one or two national groups only but tend to constitute multi-cultural residential spaces, problems of inter-cultural communication and relationships are also likely to exist. From the perspective of (ethnic) service providers, the spatial proximity of households residing in large housing estates constitutes an explicit advantage. While the social services are most likely to be provided by community organizations, the responsibility for the provision of communal space lies with the respective housing developer, e.g. public housing authorities.

In order to be able to provide such group-specific services, each of the so-called Family Developments (public housing projects) of the St. Paul Public Housing Agency (PHA) includes a community center. In these centers community agencies provide services for the residents "who MAY target individual immigrant populations" (Expert 10: 3) or several immigrant groups, depending on the resident constituency[348]. Examples of such services are free classes for English as a second language, employment promotion services for adults and youth, as well as meeting spaces for the teaching of handcraft or the organization of cultural events (view St. Paul PHA, Annual Report 2004). Similar services are provided in the communal space of the Bluff Park Homes on the West Side349.

Neighborhood upgrading linked with employment and business development opportunities

This strategy, similar to the one relating to the rehabilitation of dilapidated residential housing structures, pursues two related objectives: One is the improvement of individual or household socio-economic conditions by the enhancement of income-generating, i.e. employment or business start-up opportunities for its residents. The other is the 'upgrading' or revitalization of the neighborhood, in the sense that investments are carried out not only in its housing, but also in its commercial or services stock - not least as an image-lifting measure. While this entails a risk of gentrification[350], this risk does not dispute the importance to promote a dynamic housing and real estate market in potentially or actually disadvantaged neighborhoods. The (ethnic) population of the respective neighborhood should both have a stake

[348] The Public Housing Agency itself is not allowed to provide any services targeted to specific ethnic or racial groups, as they are not allowed to 'sort' residents with respect to their ethnic or racial group.

[349] The Bluff Park Homes estate was developed by NeDA, through the LIHTC Program (Neighborhood Development Alliance Report: 10).

[350] The West Side is a good example for the risk of gentrification entailed in capital investments in US central-city neighborhoods. Although in the time this study was carried out, in late 2004 and 2005, the Riverview Development was only in its planning stages, some concerns with respect to the possibly detrimental social impact of this development were voiced. The Hollmann redevelopment team in Minneapolis was confronted with similar fears "that the units that were going to be redeveloped, were going to be high-end luxury units" (Expert 12: 4), also in view of the close proximity to the Minneapolis CBD. It may be decisive in this context to which degree the (ethnic) population of a certain neighborhood has a stake in, and actually benefits from the redevelopments undertaken.

in, and benefit from the redevelopments undertaken. Revitalization activities are best executed by private agents (e.g. business owners), but usually require funding assistance from city governments or state institutions. Additional technical assistance may be provided by community development organizations.

The *Riverview Economic Development Association (REDA)* on the West Side was founded against the background that "in the early 80s this area, specifically the commercial corridor here on the West Side, was experiencing, was in the height of an economic downturn" (Expert 2: 2). During its 20 years of operation the organization has aimed at "promoting the positive aspects of St. Paul's West Side" (REDA, Annual Report 2003) by economic development, e.g. the provision of business start-up or extension loans, commercial revitalization and neighborhood marketing. Although the Association considers itself as representing the entire West Side population, in its marketing efforts it explicitly promotes its 'Latino image'. This is for instance by organizing the West Side Cinco de Mayo celebration or the branding of the West Side commercial corridor as "District del Sol". It assists business owners (e.g. owners of restaurants and grocery stores), many of them Hispanic, with their marketing towards their co-ethnics, but likewise to a non-ethnic client constituency outside the neighborhood, thus fulfilling an important 'bridging' function.

Linguistically specific home-ownership counseling

The objective behind this strategy is to entice individuals or families with a migration background to become home owners and thereby enhance their future housing choices and capabilities. This may be for instance through the building of financial wealth, as well through other benefits related to a secure home[351]. Individuals with a migration background tend to have more difficulties with obtaining information about home ownership regulations and models in their country of destination, not least as this information is not provided or available in their first language[352]. This is even more so if they

[351] These are, for instance, educational and health benefits. Educational benefits may accrue from enhanced opportunities for studying, e.g. for children and youth in an own study room. Health benefits may result from e.g. living in better isolated or less humid dwellings.

[352] Several of the interviewed first-generation Mexican residents of the West Side mentioned that it was important for them to deal with Spanish-speaking real estate agents when buying their first home.

do not have job- or loan-record considered credit-worthy. Such linguistically-specific home-ownership counseling is best executed by non-governmental agencies near to their client base. The latter does not dispute the need for them to be well-connected to city- or metro-wide housing providers and agents.

The *Neighborhood Development Alliance (NeDA)* on the West Side provides home-ownership counseling in Spanish and in English. Topics treated in the workshops or individual counseling include, for instance, teaching participants the steps how to buy a home, how to qualify for a mortgage, how much they can afford, how to work with a realtor and how to maintain a house (Neighborhood Development Alliance Report: 14). NEDA forms part of a metro-wide network of home-ownership counseling agencies, but is the only one staffed by bilingual and –cultural counselors and providing bilingual materials for Spanish-speaking persons – due to its spatial proximity to many Latino households. Thus indirectly, NEDA provides prospective home owners with the practical knowledge to buy houses where they choose to: "And it doesn't matter where they buy. And quite a few are buying in the suburbs. Cause they want what everybody else wants (laughs)." (Expert 5: 7).

<u>Development of more and diversified affordable housing models</u>

This policy recommendation is based on the notion of a shrinking governmental budget for affordable housing targeted to the lowest income groups[353], mentioned by all the interviewed housing experts (Experts 5, 10, 12, 13 and 15). The extent to which the demand for very affordable housing is not met by sufficient supply is expressed in the time households spend on the waiting lists of Public Housing Authorities in the big cities (see chapter 9.2), as well as in the proportion of households moving into PHA-public housing, as opposed to those who would qualify for it[354]. The proportion of Mexican residents on the West Side paying more than 30% of their income on housing (chapter 6, tables 17 and Annex 9) can be considered as an indicator of the need for more affordable housing for this particular group.

---

[353] According to the US public housing agencies these are households with an income up to 30% of the respective area's median income. It does not refer to programs catering to 'higher' low-income households (60% of median income), such as the LIHTC program of the US Income Revenue Service.

[354] According to Expert 10, in the city of St. Paul 20% of households who would qualify for public housing are actually moving in a PHA-unit (Expert 10: 8).

If the *US federal government* increased the budget for affordable public housing many households would, firstly, not be driven to overpaying for their respective housing units. An income-adequate expenditure for housing would also free their household budget for investments in other areas essential for individual and family well-being, such as health and education. This does not dispute the relevance or legitimacy of 'shallower' affordable housing programs, such as the Low Income Housing Tax Credit program (LIHTC). The principle to lure private housing developers into the production of affordable housing underlying the latter program seems valuable. However, this can only be considered a complementary strategy to the "big three" (Expert 15) PHA-led programs of project-based subsidies, Section 8 voucher units, and, as sub-category of the vouchers, project-based (PBA) voucher units[355].

Although the shrinking of the government budget for affordable housing is seen as a problem by all the interviewed experts, they also agree on the limitations of the traditional, large housing project-based model. Hence the necessity to develop affordable and other housing models, which are sensitive to the different economic, social and cultural needs of urban dwellers. In the words of the interviewed employee of the Federal Department of Housing and Urban Development, HUD, "it's really going to test our ability to understand who we're serving, understand that one size doesn't fit all" (Expert 12: 5). For instance, while the traditional single-family detached housing model accounts for the most Mexican households' desire of core family-centered housing ownership, it does not well respond to other needs and/or living conditions of this population group. These often lie in space limits in dense 'ethnic' center city neighborhood, as well as affordability constraints.

Preventing long-term low-income residential clustering

Whereas ethnically-based residential segregation does not appear to be a problem per se, the spatial concentration of very low-income and vulnerable households in one urban neighborhood or neighborhood sub-area does seem problematic: "[You] don't wanna build towers of concentration (...) you need a mix of opportunities" (Expert 5: 9). The objective of promoting a residential income mix in urban neighborhoods is thus, on the one hand, to

---

[355] Both the original Section 8 voucher program, as well as the project-based units implies the development and administration of units by private housing owners.

prevent the mid- or long-term erosion of their economic bases. This erosion is typically prompted by higher-income residents and businesses moving out, or refusing to invest in the neighborhood. On the other hand it is to prevent a social environment of generalized vulnerability. The latter also constitutes a more difficult environment for the operation of local schools and neighborhoods.

What follows out of this in terms of housing policy implications towards 'ethnic' neighborhoods, which tend to include an important number of low- or very low-income households? In view of the common intersection between minority and low-income status, what is the value of the ethnicity/race variable in assessing the quality of segregation in a certain neighborhood or area? What are the benchmarks for determining whether an area is below, or already beyond an acceptable level of income concentration? What is the appropriate geographic scale such considerations should be based upon?

Forced desegregation – be it with respect to income or race/ethnicity – cannot be recommended in view of the problems associated with it (chapter 9.2.2). A strategy oriented by enlarging people's housing *choices* and *capabilities* is therefore proposed in this document.

Examples for choice- and capability-enlarging strategies, apart from those already mentioned (city-wide home-ownership counseling, increasing affordable housing budget etc.) constitute metro area-wide information or referral systems about available affordable housing. These require an effective co-operation among city- and metro-wide housing agents (PHAs, private developers, funding institutions) and the maintenance by a specialized agency. The *Housing Link* in Minneapolis came out of the Hollman settlement (Box 10) and assists, via affordable housing data collection and analysis, renter households with getting information about available units and waiting lists openings, also outside of their city jurisdiction.

Efforts of *PHAs* to incite private property owners in middle-income neighborhoods to rent out to households with Section 8 vouchers, as well as to liaise with municipal councils outside of their jurisdiction for their own voucher's portability (chapter 2.2) constitute steps in the right direction. The federal housing administration, mediated through metropolitan area councils, should exercise pressure on recalcitrant suburban councils to set the (e.g.

zoning or institutional) conditions for affordable housing[356]. Anti-discrimination housing laws should be radically enforced by the federal government.

In view of the ongoing link between minority status and socio-economic disadvantage in contemporary US-America, a color-blind policy does not represent an adequate answer. Rather, affordable housing agents (PHAs, non-profit housing agents) should try to respond to group-specific housing- and non-housing needs, such as providing language- or other social services in their housing estates as this is done by the St. Paul PHA. In contrast, the presence of the white vs. non-white population in a neighborhood as criteria for racial 'integration' seems highly problematic. This is as the racial and ethnic diversity common in most 'ethnic' neighborhoods is not accounted for at all.

Merely income-related and quantitative indicators for the assessment of positive versus negative levels of income concentration should be complemented by: 1. Observations of additional income- and well-being related indicators (housing value, vacancy rates, and educational achievements) for each ethnic or racial group over time. This is in order to consider directions a neighborhood and its residents are moving towards. 2. Qualitative indicators, such as perceptions of residents as to the quality and safety of their housing, educational entities and neighborhood environment, and perceptions of developers and real estate agents about a certain area. A possible set of indicators for the assessment of residential segregation is proposed in chapter 9.3.3.

The case of the West Side, a relatively 'mixed' neighborhood concerning aggregate income levels, suggests that the neighborhood scale is too large to account for geographic concentrations of disadvantage. The different sub-areas of the neighborhood show fairly different social and economic profiles (chapter 6, table 11) and in the perception of the interviewed residents and experts, clear social designations[357]. Therefore, the Public Housing Authorities' use of the census tract level (including up to 4,000 residents) to observe socio-economic characteristics of urban areas seems adequate.

---

[356] The most effective way to exercise pressure seems to make federal infrastructure grants contingent on municipalities ('fair') shares of metro-wide affordable housing.

[357] Meaning that census tract 361 or the "Flats" area around the commercial corridor is known as the low-income area.

9.3.2 Policy and planning recommendations in other sectors

Expanding the 'bridging' capacity of households in ethnic neighborhoods and their genuine housing choices and capabilities requires a consideration of other opportunity-relevant sectors. For instance, employment and education constitute areas that determine individual social status, as well as housing and other mobility-relevant practices and choices (see chapter 3.2). In the context of the West Side, sector cross-cutting approaches, such as the promotion of culture-specific practices, as well as inter-cultural togetherness, have also turned out to be relevant.

Thus, based on the research, the following community development strategies can be recommended to increase individuals' housing choices and capacities:

Promoting local economic development and combining it with outside-oriented marketing

This strategy has two objectives. One is to provide individuals in ethnic communities with job and skills-enhancing opportunities in proximity to their residential location[358]. Also, residents coming from a common ethnocultural background provide a critical client mass to, e.g. owners of ethnic grocery stores or restaurants. The other objective is to enhance the economic basis of a neighborhood or, argued vice versa, to prevent an economic downturn of an area and overall neighborhood degradation. This strategy may be carried out by community- or city-based community organizations and usually requires a wide array of funding support from city or state levels.

The *Riverfront Economic Development Association (REDA)* constitutes an example of an organization promoting local economic development on the West Side. REDA supports their West Side member businesses in a variety of ways, e.g. by the rehabilitation of commercial housing stock or financial or training support for start-up businesses and business management (see previous chapter). Most of the REDA-members located on the neighborhood's commercial corridor are Hispanic. In spite of the 'natural' orientation of the Hispanic stores and restaurants towards their co-ethnic constituency,

[358] This is particularly relevant for non-driving women, a recurrent case among the recent Hispanic immigrant community.

Hispanic business owners “realize that the Gringos[359] are out there” (Expert 2a[360]: 3), i.e. market to other ethnic groups in- and outside the neighborhood. The “Hispanic Women in Action Group”, a group forming part of Neighborhood House, provides the female group members with contacts for jobs or training in hard and soft areas (accounting, financial management, leadership) relevant when looking for employment.

Strengthening educational capital of children and youth, with an affirmative attitude towards culture of origin

Children and youth of poor immigrant families tend to be confronted with distinct challenges both related to the process of cultural and linguistic change, as well as their parents’ pursuit for an economically and socially more stable life[361]. Schools badly adapted to the needs, but also the potentials of a multi-cultural student population constitute further detrimental conditions for the educational success of these children and youth[362]. Thus, on the one hand, the objective of the strategy of educational promotion of children and youth is to equip local primary and secondary schools with improved instruments to cater for their diverse student population. On the other, it is to provide children with the advantages of a local neighborhood school (opportunities for higher levels of parent involvement and community-school links, shorter school ways) while at the same time improving on educational quality and opportunity to pursue higher education in the future.

---

359 “*Gringo*” is a semi-pejorative expression used in Mexico and other Latin American countries to designate United States citizens. By some it is invariably applied to people from the global North.

360 Quotes from “Expert 2a” refer to the second interview conducted with this particular expert (Annex 3).

361 Almost all the interviewed recent Mexican immigrants, when asked about the reason for migrating to the United States, mentioned severe economic hardship or the impossibility of finding employment in their homelands, as the most important reason. An exception constituted the two young migrants from Mexico City, Esteban and Mercedes, who mentioned curiosity and interest to know something else as the most important motivation for their migration.

362 The institutional deficiencies mentioned by some of the residents, most of them Mexican-American, referred, for instance, to the use of outdated teaching methods, the lack of cooperation with neighborhood organizations and parents, and scant attention to the cultural diversity of students. Not least as a consequence of underfunding and –staffing West Side schools are reputed to give deficient preparation of children and youth for higher educational careers, e.g. in college or university.

Primary and secondary schools in the State of Minnesota have experienced a considerable ethnic and racial diversification in the last decades. The need to come up with strategies to lower traditional achievement gaps between colored and white students has become more urgent against these demographic changes (Peebles 2004: 5). Increasingly, strategies are recommended that draw on the – diverse - cultures of origin of the students and place an emphasis on an (inter-) cultural competent, as opposed to neutral educational environment (Peebles 2004: 9, Schellenberg/Porter 2003: 22)[363]. The latter includes promoting students' ability of inter-cultural interaction and understanding[364].

The *Roosevelt Elementary School (RES)* on the West Side provides an example for seeking out a wide array of educational strategies adapted to an ethnically diverse student population. Approximately 93 percent of the RES-students are students of color (Allen 2005: 2) and 92 percent of its students qualify for 'free and reduced lunch' (Expert 11: 3), the latter indicating high levels of economic need of the students' families. In spite of the difficult conditions the school is operating in (limited English proficiency of many students, struggling family backgrounds etc.) students' achievements have considerably improved in the past years according to the school-district wide testing scores. The interviewed expert from RPS highlights several strategies as essential for the schools' success story:

- Diverse staffing, in the sense that the ethnic background of students is reflected in the ethnic background of teaching or other professional staff. In this way, students are also confronted with positive role models from their own culture (Allen 2005: 2) and an intended maximum of parents is able to communicate with teachers in their own language.

---

363 The present emphasis on focusing resources on improving learning environments in majority-minority urban neighborhoods also comes as a response to the problems experienced with school desegregation programs, which e.g. involved busing initiatives. These problems are, for instance, the 'white' flight towards private schools, the limited options for desegregation inside the central city jurisdiction, long school ways for children and the costs involved in students' transportation (Peebles 2004: 4, Schellenberg/Porter 2003: 20, Expert 11: 1). .

364 Most 'ethnic' neighborhoods host students from more than two (e.g. white, Hispanic) ethnic or racial backgrounds. The West Side forms an example thereof, with important percentages of students and residents with an African-American and/or Asian background.

- Facilitation of parent-involvement. The importance of parent involvement lies in convincing parents of the importance of education and US public school regulations, particularly if they come from different cultural and low-skilled backgrounds. As parents might be adamant or insecure of such involvement, culturally adequate parent invitation strategies, e.g. barbecues announced in the Spanish language, need to be sought out.
- Supplementary education programs in children's or youth's native language: At RES, Spanish speaking students start with reading programs in their native language, in order to facilitate the subsequent transition into English-language reading (RES, 'Success for all brochure')[365]. By the end of the third grade all the students need to be proficient in English, in order to ensure that they are able to continue their school trajectory in an English-language learning environment.
- Co-operation with community organizations, in order to complement the school's efforts for students' educational improvement. Although the school employs a social worker, two counselors and an educator working on the involvement of Latino parents, it is in need of further support from the community. In this context, RES cooperates with the West Side's Neighborhood House in addressing attendance problems of Latino kids.

Promoting cultural specificity and intra- and inter-cultural togetherness

The objective of this strategy is to maintain the richness of a culturally diverse environment by valuing people's cultural heritage, and to improve the chances for a peace- and respectful co-existence of urban societies. A culturally affirmative environment is important as a matter of respect towards people's distinct identities, partly shaped through their cultural heritage[366]. In

[365] Children with other first languages than English and Spanish get extra-lessons by teachers instructed for teaching English Language Learners (ELL) (RES, 'Success for al' brochure).

[366] As pointed out in chapter 3.2, people's identities tend to be shaped by multiple dimensions or 'axes' of difference and not only ethnicity (Nagar/Leitner 1998: 227, Jacobs/Fincher 1998: 8, García Canclini 1995: 80ff.). However, in the case of recent immigrants ethnicity is likely to constitute an important basis on which to build common identities and practices. The same is true for population groups with a long history of racially or ethnicity-based discrimination. The object of discrimination (e.g. dark skin color) is likely to be transformed into the reference or 'rallying' point for common political struggle (Jacobs/Fincher 1998: 8).

more instrumental terms, culturally affirmative educational policies may contribute to increasing young learner's self-esteem as well as linguistic skills. Cultural specificity and diversity can be promoted in multiple fields and by a large spectrum of institutions, e.g. schools and community organizations.

On the West Side, the "Hispanic Women in Action" group (*Mujeres Hispanas en Acción*) has the mission of helping its female members to adapt to the new culture in Minnesota and the USA, while not losing their culture of origin (Expert 4: 1). The Mexican or Hispanic cultural roots of the female members are celebrated in a number of ways: By using the Spanish language in their group meetings, by celebrating Mexican and Latino holidays and traditions, by participating in Mexican or Hispanic community events, e.g. the *Cinco de Mayo* festival or Day of the Death and others. The group also creates networks with other Hispanic organizations or learning centers in the Twin Cities' region and has published the immigration experiences of some of its members in a bilingual book (Broshears 2002).

The promotion of inter-cultural or inter-group togetherness can be considered as equally important. Educational institutions play a particular important role in promoting inter-racial and –cultural understanding. Frictions may not only run along racial or ethnic, but also along other, e.g. socio-economic lines[367]. Therefore, educational, religious and other community organizations constitute important social and physical spaces for interaction across cultural and status-related boundaries.

Long-term immigrant communities, such as the West Side, also have the potential that long-term 'ethnic' leaders can enlarge their social networks and capital towards more recent immigrants to the neighborhood. In view of this potential, Neighborhood House connects recent immigrants with long-term resident leaders of the West Side, in the context of the "'New Americans' Minnesota Community Campaign" (Neighborhood House, Annual Report 2003: 10). The creation of the campaign is also due to the recognition that co-ethnic networks between different immigrant cohorts do not 'naturally' develop, largely due to status differences.

---

[367] In the case of the West Side, tensions between recent Mexican immigrants and long-standing Mexican-Americans are greatly related to socio-economic status discrepancies (view chapter 7.1.1).

Assisting suburban and rural communities with ethnic support structures

Two points need to be made here. The first concerns the nature of housing choice and capabilities: As many low-income households are in need of a housing *environment* with complementary support infrastructure (public transport, welfare services), building affordable housing in suburban, hitherto non-minority neighborhoods, may be a necessary, but not sufficient measure to enlarge housing 'choice'. Particularly low-income immigrant newcomers are in need of a housing environment with job, educational and other services in their language, or informal or formal co-ethnic networks that provide them with a sense of comfort and safety.

The second point is that apart from the reasons and level of choice involved[368], many low-income minority households end-up moving to suburban areas. These suburban areas tend to be badly equipped with (ethnic) support infrastructure or constitute an unwelcoming environment for non-native individuals and households. As pointed out by the interviewed expert from Neighborhood House:

"[It's] a struggle for people of color in those other [sub- or ex-urban] areas. Because, there aren't the support systems, there aren't the level, I mean, of, you know the connections that they have within the community. There aren't Neighborhood Houses. There isn't a 'home away from home' from them." (Expert 9: 9)

Thus the objective is to "try the experiment with density in that suburban environment" (Expert 9: 9) and thereby provide immigrant households with a more supportive and welcoming environment. It is also, on a second plan, to assist municipalities experiencing a recent immigrant influx with appropriate means and instruments to socially include the newcomers within their communities – e.g. by promoting inter-cultural learning and togetherness in community and educational entities. Non-governmental organizations experienced with social and community-based services to immigrant communities are best placed to do this work.

[368] These reasons may be related to the voluntary or involuntary dispersal of households through housing programs, but also to mobility decisions due to peri-urban or rural workplaces. The rural communities in the Southeast of Minnesota are a case in point. Mexican immigrants have historically been hired for – often seasonal - agricultural and industrial work there, and continue to be hired there. The suburbanization of commercial and service employment constitutes another reason for a rising housing demand in these areas (Orfield 1997: 57, Ihlanfeldt/Sjoquist 2000: 116, Bowen/Kimble 1997: 13f.).

As an example, one of the five strategic goals of Neighborhood House is to share their lessons-learnt with communities in peri-urban or rural Minnesota. This is in order to guide local governments and social services in these communities on "how best to integrate new immigrants and refugees into their communities" and "share the cultural competence (…) gained in over a century of serving multiple immigrant populations" (Neighborhood House, Annual Report 2003: 10). One strategy to do this is connecting immigrant newcomers with long-term, e.g. Mexican-American residents of the area, thereby tapping on the local ethnic social capital available. Other strategies consist of raising the capacities for civic engagement and advocacy of Latino leaders, fostering dialogues and partnerships, and increasing the awareness of the native population on the arrival of new immigrants, their contributions to social and economic development and on public policy on immigration (Neighborhood House, Annual Report 2003: 10).

9.3.3 Relevant indicators for the assessment of residential segregation

As a summary of my understanding on 'good' versus 'bad' aspects of residential segregation, a set of measurable indicators is presented here. On the one hand, these indicators concretize the findings of positive and negative sides of ethnic clustering derived from the research. On the other, they may serve as a practical tool for policy makers and practitioners in the housing and other policy and planning fields. In order to allow for case-specific flexibility, the indicators provide qualitative guidance rather than quantitative benchmarks for the assessment of segregation[369]. Further explanations to the indicators can be viewed in Annex 10.

Box 10: Neighborhood-related indicators for the assessment of ethnic residential segregation

1. <u>Income distribution</u>. Sub-indicators: Median income levels compared to city average; Income and poverty trends.
2. <u>Dynamic of housing market</u>. Sub-indicators: Trends in owner/renter housing, on a ten-year basis; Number of housing rehabilitation and other investment activities; Development of housing values with respect to the

[369] This is as numbers, e.g. of institutions addressing the needs of immigrants, are at least relative to the number of inhabitants of a certain neighborhood and need to be interpreted on a case-by-case basis. The list also does not provide weights in the sense of certain indicators to be more instrumental for positive segregation than others, nor propose specific measurement methods. This is something that needs to be addressed in future research endeavors.

housing value trends in entire city; Development of housing vacancies.

3. Intersection between income- and minority-status: Sub-indicators: Development of income levels per ethnic group; Development of poverty levels per ethnic group. Development of home ownership levels per ethnic group.
4. Existence of formal and informal ethnic institutions addressing the needs of recent immigrants. Sub-indicators: Number and activities of institutions or groups directed at certain ethnic population; Number of events/year organized by this group; Development of membership figures.
5. Availability of social spaces for inter-cultural encounters. Sub-indicators: Number and activities of institutions with intercultural constituency; Number of events/year organized by the groups; Development of membership figures.
6. Existence of 'bridging' activities: Sub-indicators: Number of free language courses offered; Number and kind of training courses; Number of business start-ups; Number of job-referrals towards in- and outside of the neighborhood; Number and kind of events including visitors from 'outside' the neighborhood.
7. Availability of youth spaces. Sub-indicators: Number of youth clubs; Number of sport clubs; Number and of activity of youth centers.
8. Performance levels and development of public schools. Sub-indicators: Performance of public schools compared with city average; Performance trends, on a yearly basis; Proportion of drop-outs compared with city average, and on yearly basis; Proportions of pupils that go and stay at college after secondary school, compared to city average.
9. Existence of gang activities in schools and neighborhood. Sub-indicators: Levels of youth violence, per type of violence, as compared to city average; Development of violence over time; Perception of youth and adults on gang activities.
10. Existence of 'no-go areas' and poverty pockets. Sub-indicators: Economically and socially disadvantaged sub-areas; Perception of insecurity of residents; Recurrent naming of 'bad' spots.

It needs to be added here that if in a specific neighborhood the kind of segregation present is judged as negative, the policy recommendations in chapter 9.2.3 and 9.2.4 provide for directions on how to improve the situation. Housing dispersal as a result of the identification of 'bad' residential segregation is not considered as an effective alternative.

9.4 Summary

In this chapter normative implications of the results of the research were discussed and recommendations for policy and planning responses to residential segregation in the housing and other sectors spelled out. The extent of housing choice and -capabilities involved in the decision of the interviewed Mexicans to move or stay on the West Side was used as a starting point to assess the conditions leading to segregation, in the present case study. Among three different influence factors assumed to be decisive for individual housing choice, preference seems to be the most relevant one in the case study. Recent Mexican immigrants derive objective and subjective advantages from settling closed to co-ethnics, and short- and long-term Mexicans associate living or socializing on the West Side with benefits in social comfort.

However, the prevalence of neighborhood preference should not defer from the existence of choice constraints. These may lie in affordability limits negatively affecting the availability of housing options to begin with. It is that more, socio-psychological mechanisms (or, in Bourdieu's terms, the *habitus*, see Bourdieu 1987: 285) may make individuals chose within the scope of the economically feasible, without feeling restricted in any sense[370]. Furthermore, anticipated or factual experiences of discrimination – authentic restrictions in the freedom to pursue their housing objectives! - may suggest that people prefer to opt in favor of a residential location with a high presence of co-ethnics or minorities.

Based on the results of the research with the Mexican population on the West Side, residential segregation and the quest for housing desegregation were revisited. The study results suggest that residential segregation may have both positive and negative influences on individuals, and whether the one or the other is true depends on individual characteristics, neighborhood conditions, and not least on the macro-social and –institutional context. Rather than providing a categorical assessment on segregation it is important to understand how these conditions are related to each other, and seek a complex, rather than simple set of answers, e.g. depending on group or co-

---

370 The empirical evidence for this phenomenon in the West Side case study is rather weak. Only Emilia, a 77-year old first generation Mexican lady mentioned with some sadness that she would like to live somewhere else, but "if it is not possible, it is not possible" (Emilia: 17, own translation) ["si no se puede, no se puede", original wording].

hort needs or particular neighborhood situations. Also, in the context of this research, housing desegregation has proved to be an unsatisfactory response to residential segregation, not only for reasons related to housing choice and needs of the concerned population groups, but also for political and practical obstacles.

Policy and practical responses were formulated aiming at encouraging the positive, while discouraging the negative aspects of residential segregation. Measures were proposed for the housing and other sectors crucial for individual and community capacity development (employment, education, intercultural togetherness). These measures drew on recognizing the comfort associated with socializing with co-ethnics, while encouraging that certain advantages of ethnic neighborhoods for enhancing individual mobility beyond the confines of the ethnic neighborhood are institutionally encouraged, as well. Finally, a set of relevant indicators for the assessment of the quality and type of segregation on the level of the individual neighborhood was proposed.

10 Conclusions

The research undertaken in the context of this dissertation has focused on the topic of residential segregation. The focus on this topic implied two particular and related challenges: The first was the large research tradition and – track of the topic of segregation in the United States, with a consequential need to familiarize and position myself in these discussions. The second challenge was to fill the research gaps rather intuitively perceived at first, by narrowing them down to precise research questions and placing them into a study approach and conceptual framework.

In order to provide my research questions and concerns with a link to the empirical reality, I studied them against the background of a particular case: The one of the Mexican population of the West Side of St. Paul neighborhood in the City of St. Paul in the United States. The empirical, as opposed to a merely theoretical approach to the topic, seemed justified due to the notion of not only content-related, but also methodological shortfalls in the hitherto discussions: the relative lack of qualitative studies on spatial ethnic clusters or 'communities' in US cities.

Thus, this research addressed relatively new aspects of residential segregation or clustering in conceptual and methodological terms:

- Conceptually, most research on minority segregation or clustering had focused on its *negative* aspects. This is largely due to the notion of a persisting discrimination and exclusion of the black American population, not only after the abolition of slavery, but also after the outlawing of any kind of racial discrimination through the enactment of the Civil Rights and Fair Housing Acts. It is also due to the notion of a surging – predominantly black - urban underclass in the context of economic restructuring from the 1980s onwards.

  Although built on legitimate theoretical and empirical claims, this discussion implicitly misses out (at least) two important aspects. One is the diversity of clustering experiences of minorities in United States cities, particularly in the context of an increasing immigration of non-white minorities from Latin America, Asia and Africa since the 1970s. The other is the assessment of minority community dynamics e.g. group-building (networking) and potential resources generated in this context.

Therefore, the present study has focused on an assessment of resources generated in immigrant communities particularly in the form of social capital and mobility. It has specifically analyzed how these resources are tackled by the spatial condition of clustering and has reflected on the possible implications of these findings for policies and planning.

- Methodologically, the majority of studies on residential segregation in the United States use a quantitative research setting and methods. This is a fact whether their center of interest lay on assessing motivations, i.e. causes for segregated living, or on evaluating changes in the quality of life of populations who had participated in residential mobility or desegregation programs. The genuine experiences of racial or ethnic individuals and groups have rarely been assessed in a qualitative manner.

  Contrasting this predominantly quantitative research tradition, the use of qualitative data collection and analysis methods lay at the heart of the present study. Thus, the perspective and experiences of residential segregation relating to the Mexican population could be assessed more fully than has been done in many previous studies.

Subsequent I want to redirect my attention to the focal research questions pointed out in chapter 4. For each of these, the most important features elaborated on in more detail in the former chapters, will be summarized briefly.

Review of research questions

What kind of social networks can be found among ethnic populations, in a segregated neighborhood? What are their most important characteristics?

In the conceptualization for the connection between social networks and the development of social capital and mobility (view chapter 4), formal and informal social networks were differentiated to begin with. In the analysis of the data generated in the interviews with residents and experts of the West Side, I therefore also distinguished between formal and informal ethnic networks. A relatively large proportion of the Mexican or Mexican-American interview partners in this research were involved in 'formal' ethnic neighborhood organizations. This allowed for an assessment of different types of organization and cycles of involvement, depending, for instance, on when they had actually arrived.

The research on the West Side suggests distinct patterns with respect to the kind of ethnic organizations and networks in ethnic neighborhoods. Formalized service institutions, that may or may not be managed by co-ethnics, are most likely to be used by recent immigrants who are most in need of the (language, information, and job or training referral) services they offer. In the case of the Mexican population the participation in formal ethnic networks is clearly gendered: most of them are female, married and mothers of small children. For many of the recent immigrants, however, employment and family work combined with legal insecurities may place serious constraints on their ability to network beyond their immediate family environment.

More longstanding co-ethnics are unlikely to participate in such formal networks, unless they are employed in them or involved in institutional management. The figure of the 'lifelong' ethnic community leader seems to form the exception, rather than the rule. Thus, in the context of a macro-social environment, in which a minority group or neighborhood is attributed with an inferior image, a common assumption of the literature on immigrant integration or assimilation becomes self-fulfilling: Many moving up the socio-economic ladder tend to distance themselves from their ethnic communities, both socially and spatially.

The research on the West Side suggests a further important point regarding ethnic grouping and organization. What is perceived as a 'group' or 'community' from the outside does not necessarily match the definitions inside the presumed group. In the present research class-based and socio-cultural friction between the recent and the long-standing Mexicans constituted a powerful example of such a mismatch between inside- and outside-attributions. Although the respective sub-groups had a common racial or 'ethnic' background, other variables proved more identity-relevant, particularly social status. This suggests that co-ethnic cohesion and common interest as a basis for, e.g. joint organization or political practice can all but be taken for granted.

Do the ethnic social networks generate or hinder resources that impact on social mobility and other assets of 'value' for the individual immigrant, and if so, how?

The results of this empirical study suggest that social networking with co-ethnics entails both benefits and costs for the individual person. According to the conceptual framework developed in this thesis, the benefits and costs can be differentiated according to the following dimensions: Economic, cultural/educational, symbolic and social. While the first three dimensions are derived from Bourdieu's concept of social capital, the latter is a dimension added on the basis of the results of this study.

The research on the West Side suggests that socializing with co-ethnics conveys mobility benefits and costs. Benefits include, for instance, information about job or training opportunities, referrals to service institutions, the possibility to celebrate the culture of origin and also the comfort entailed in feeling accepted – or, inversely, not rejected – by others. Costs include restricted opportunities in the educational field particularly experienced by children and youth. The constraints experienced by female youth lie in the co-ethnic social environment perceived as narrow and controlling, particularly due to their family and household responsibilities. Costs of co-ethnic networks for male youth lie in problematic adult or peer role models that restrict their educational and career aspirations and prospects.

With respect to mobility costs and benefits of co-ethnic socializing, three important issues need to be highlighted: The first is the 'bridging' potential of co-ethnic (bonding) social capital. This study has indicated that ethnic social networks have a considerable potential to facilitate (job, educational etc.) opportunities beyond them. The second is the 'intrinsic', as opposed to 'instrumental' value of social capital. The study results suggest that ethnic social networks convey an important social and emotional benefit to individuals, independent of their mobility-relevance. Hence the need to add a social, or emotional, dimension to Bourdieu's instrumentalist and objectivist categories. The third is that the (instrumental or intrinsic) benefits of ethnic social relations to the individual are strongly contingent on individual and supra-individual conditions. This point is addressed in the next question.

How do the answers to these questions change with changing individual characteristics, e.g. gender, social class (income), first/second generation immigrants?

Whether and to what extent individuals benefit from co-ethnic networks strongly depends on their individual situation and characteristics. The study on the West Side suggests that co-ethnic socializing entails important instrumental, or mobility, benefits for first generation, low-skilled immigrants, these are of minor, or even zero relevance to second- or more generation immigrant descendants. This is as recent immigrant arrivals tend to depend on (mostly, but not always legal) services offered by co-ethnic informal or formal networks: Referrals to welfare organizations, information about job opportunities, contact with free English lessons-providers and others. In contrast, in the context of the case study on the West Side, the longstanding English-speaking Mexican-Americans did not need these services.

Thus, the level of establishment in 'mainstream' American society greatly appeared as a function of the moment or cohort of arrival of people. This being said, the study did not look at mobility trajectories of Mexican-Americans who had grown up in non-ethnic social or spatial contexts. In any case, the benefits of co-ethnic networks for second- or more generation immigrant descendants lay chiefly in the social or emotional comfort conveyed by these networks, i.e. their intrinsic value. This value, defined not only as the presence of comfort, but also – negatively – as the absence of discrimination, is also valid for first-generation immigrants. Generally, however, the weight of the instrumental versus intrinsic dimension of social capital seems to decrease as immigrants and their descendants become settled in the country of destination.

However, it is not only individual, micro-level, characteristics that impact on the mobility relevance of ethnic social networks. Also macro-social influences do so. These manifest in the image of a group in society generally, including the legitimacy and value of its experiences and, e.g. linguistic, knowledge. In the case of the West Side, during most of the 20th century Mexican parents took pains not to speak Spanish with their children, considering English as a requirement to get ahead in US society – a consideration corroborated by the institutional, e.g. school, and social environment. Today proficiency in a foreign language is recognized as an asset, institutionally promoted and 'naturally' enjoyed by those growing up in a non-English family or peer context.

Does residential clustering in an ethnic neighborhood impact positively or negatively on the development of social capital and mobility, and if so how?

Analogous to the impact of co-ethnic relations on social capital and mobility, it is impossible to make a general assessment about the locational benefits or costs of living in an ethnic neighborhood. Rather, these depend on conditions of the individual and macro-social levels, as well as on the characteristics of the particular neighborhood or city environment. Proximity benefits of e.g. ethnic commercial and service infrastructure appear clearest for recent, low-skilled immigrants. This is due to their dependence on precisely this infrastructure, to their limited language or employment-related skills, and to their restricted mobility. For more longstanding immigrants, living or socializing in the 'ethnic' neighborhood is chiefly a matter of comfort, however not a practical need.

The tangible deficits of living in an ethnic neighborhood are most strongly experienced by children and youth. This is due to the perceived deficits of schools in the ethnic neighborhood, as well as to the proximity of potentially harmful peer and/or adult role models. However, the non-tangible deficits of living in an ethnic neighborhood, i.e. those of position or rank, concern all residents of this neighborhood. In the study on the West Side, these are again mostly motivated by the – more or less institutionalized - attitudes of the broader (macro-) social environment, and are best expressed by the term "neighborhood stigma". The stigma manifests in decade-long housing disinvestments and consequential low property value increases, institutional practices and socially upward mobile co-ethnics fleeing the neighborhood. The underlying motivation for the latter seems to lie in escaping the identification of the negative attributes of the neighborhood and its residents (low-income, low-skilled etc.) on oneself.

It is however important to mention that the mobility-, and also well-being impacts of living in an ethnic neighborhood also depend very much on the characteristics of the neighborhood and the broader urban environment. This aspect will be looked at in more detail below. But first I will look at the planning and policy implications of the above findings, as well as of those related to the success of previous answers to residential segregation.

What are adequate policy responses and how can previous policy responses be assessed?

In the present document, recommendations for policy and planning responses, particularly in the housing sector, are provided on the basis of two sets of information. The first is the experience with policy responses to residential segregation in the United States, mainly consisting of efforts to deconcentrate the poor and minorities, or, expressed in another way, to 'integrate' them in majority-white and wealthier neighborhoods. The second basis of the recommendations form the results related to the mobility- and well-being relevance of living in an 'ethnic' neighborhood and socializing with co-ethnics.

The desegregation policy focus is confronted with several serious dilemmas. First, up until now residential dispersal programs have lead to limited quantitative impact. This is due to frequent resistance of the receiving communities and of landowners, to tight housing markets, to limitations of the focus on the housing sector alone and ultimately also to the opposition of those to be dispersed – mostly immigrant or colored communities. Second, previous dispersal programs have lead to questionable qualitative impact, e.g. in terms of expected improvements in employment opportunities, or engagement in mobility-relevant social networks. The problem increases if people are dispersed against their will, assuming freedom of (housing) choice to be a central element of personal well-being.

Third, as the case study on the West Side has shown, living and socializing in an ethnically segregated neighborhood or cluster can provide opportunities for social and economic mobility outside of it – hence its bridging potential. It can also be of major significance for people's social and emotional well-being – hence its intrinsic value. Fourth, the study results have shown that different neighborhoods have diverging effects on individuals with different socio-economic and demographic characteristics. These effects can be both positive and negative. Five, they suggest that the outside perception and practices towards ethnic neighborhoods constitute powerful influencing factors on individual mobility opportunities and well-being.

The findings provide an important basis for the stating of policy and planning responses to segregation in the housing and other sectors. First, that desegregation does not serve as an appropriate policy objective to fight urban poverty and disadvantage. It should be substituted by the one of maximizing housing *choices* and *capabilities* to compete in the housing market and, ultimately, increase individual *well-being*. This entails the claim to fight persistent (policy- or market-related) obstacles to exercise freedom of housing choice, e.g. by strictly enforcing discrimination in the housing market, enhancing the budget for deeply affordable housing or opportunities for individual's and families' (economic, educational or housing-based) asset-building.

Second, the role of immigrant neighborhoods in conveying social comfort to their inhabitants needs to be recognized, and thus its significance of personal satisfaction and well-being. Third the role of ethnic social communities and neighborhoods in facilitating social- and physical mobility-relevant resources (contacts, hard and soft skills, employment opportunities) needs to be acknowledged. Thus, on a policy level, networks or organizations should be supported that convey this social and emotional support, e.g. to immigrant newcomers, and/or provide mobility-relevant services. Examples are housing estates with high proportions of immigrant residents where English language classes are given or opportunities for the celebration of cultural events provided. Low-interest housing maintenance or rehabilitation loans that serve to increase the asset base of property owners in the ethnic neighborhood constitute a further strategy to enhance the asset basis and mobility opportunities of individuals. Fourth, housing strategies need to be combined with measures in other sectors to effectively increase individual's social inclusion by enlarging their (housing) choices and capabilities.

Fifth, policy and planning responses should promote (cultural) diversity and be sensitive to the needs of specific groups. Children and youth constitute the groups most susceptible to possible detrimental effects of segregation. Particular efforts should therefore lie in improving the educational quality in immigrant communities, with an affirmative attitude towards their culture of origin. Such an affirmative attitude may consist of school staffing that – at least partly - reflects the ethnic origins of the respective student or parent constituency. It may also consist of (multi-) culturally blended efforts to involve parents in school matters.

The quest for the promotion of cultural diversity needs to be pursued on the symbolic level as well, e.g. by improving the majority society's image of immigrant communities and neighborhoods. This may be done through more multi-culturally oriented education, as well as by sensitization the (Anglo-white) majority community to the important role of immigrants for the social, cultural and, not least, economic wealth of the country.

Transferability of research results

The question of transferability of the results refers to the question if, and under what conditions these can be considered as *valid*. In order to answer this question, the specificities and the limitations of the studied case need to be recalled to mind, at least within the US context. In this document, particularities of the case study example were reflected on, with respect to the chosen population group (Mexicans), the selected neighborhood (West Side), as well as the urban environment (St. Paul, Twin Cities).

The selection of the *Mexican population* could be justified in view of the research questions and framework, as well as the characteristics of this particular immigrant group: In order to study experiences with ethnic residential clustering a population group had to be selected that was living in such clusters and numerously enough to be perceived as an ethnic community. Both conditions are fulfilled by the Mexican population in St. Paul. Migration experiences of Mexicans are likely to mirror those of other relatively low-skilled and poor arrivals from Third World countries, the status groups the research on residential segregation or social capital commonly is most concerned with. In contrast, results of this study are unlikely to reflect immigration or segregation experiences of white-collar, middle- or upper-class labor migrants to the United States. The influence of phenotypical and cultural affinity in explaining differential experiences with social and spatial segregation is also contested in the literature.

Box 12: The transferability of the results to the African-American community

In former chapters it was repeatedly pointed out that the US-literature on residential segregation has traditionally focused on the black/white antagonism and segregation, thereby neglecting the increasingly multi-ethnic urban reality of the country. But, do the results of this study suggest that the clustering experiences of a (partly low-income and -skilled) immigrant minority like the Mexicans fundamentally differ from those of a native minority group such as the African Americans?

It can be assumed that some of the crucial issues related to 'ethnic' social capital and mobility in the context of spatial clustering are valid as much for the African-American as for the Mexican community: This is, for instance, the social and emotional comfort associated with same-race or –ethnicity contacts and communities, and hence their inherent value for individual well-being. Also in the case of the African-American population, experiences of past and present discrimination by the majority-white society are likely to foster common identities, as well as social and political practices. Here also the decade-long stigma explains the pursuit of some to escape it through social and physical distance.

It can however be assumed that the problematic aspects of social and spatial segregation encountered on the West Side are more accentuated in majority-African American neighborhoods many of which are also economically disadvantaged. These are for instance family and peer relationships that hamper social mobility and deficient educational and social infrastructure. Co-ethnic or –racial networks may be much less instrumental for social mobility or 'bridging' beyond the community. This is also since the 'bridging' advantage constitutes a distinct experience of recent immigrant groups. In urban settings characterized by severe and racially marked polarization the 'flight' of upwardly mobile African American households from their neighborhoods of origin is likely to be much more accentuated than on the West Side.

However, the normative principles underlying the policy recommendations in this document are also relevant in the African-American community context: Instead of on residential dispersal or 'integration', the policy focus should lie on enhancing people's housing choices and capabilities. Respecting social or cultural 'difference' while fighting socio-economic injustice, e.g. in the form of housing market discrimination, may be even more imperative in the case of African Americans with a century-long record of exclusion and ill-treatment. Even more against this historical and symbolic background "it's viewed very cynical, that there is some federal government plans to deconcentrate poverty slash race" (Expert 10: 6).

The choice of the *West Side* as neighborhood case was equally justified in view of its characteristics. These are similar to those neighborhoods on which the segregation literature typically focuses. In the City of St. Paul and the Twin Cities metro area the West Side constitutes the neighborhood with the largest and most longstanding presence of Mexican immigrants. As Mexicans had already started settling on the West Side at the beginning of the 20th century, comparisons among different immigrant groups were possible. It has traditionally been perceived as an immigrant neighborhood of Mexican and other national or cultural groups.

The transferability of segregation or clustering experiences on the West Side to other types of 'ethnic' neighborhoods requires further discussion. In principle it can be assumed that neighborhood effects of the West Side are likely to correspond to those in *similar* kinds of neighborhoods. In chapter 6, the West Side was classified in a scheme that distinguishes types of ethnic residential areas, with respect to percentages of different population groups also based on assumptions about opportunity disparities between the majority-white population and minority groups.

According to the classification scheme, the West Side is described as an "assimilation-pluralism enclave", due to a relatively high presence of white residents as well as multiple racial or ethnic groups. This is, for instance, opposed to a "ghetto" type of neighborhood that is characterized by the clear numeric predominance of one particular minority group, e.g. African Americans. It is clear that the classification into different 'ethnic' neighborhood types does not form an objective in itself, but becomes filled with meaning when connected to information brought by the primary, qualitative data collected in this study.

It can be stated that the West Side neighborhood context provides some advantageous components to the social networks and –mobility experience of its Mexican population that might not be found, to the same extent, in other ethnic neighborhoods. These are, first, the absence of what could be termed a socio-spatial "isolation" of one particular group, in this case the Mexicans, on the neighborhood and city levels; second, the relative income mix in the neighborhood levels which implies, for instance, higher housing-related asset building or local business-development opportunities than in more economically 'depressed' neighborhoods; and third, relatively mature formal ethnic networks, e.g. the Church or "Neighborhood House", which may provide better start-up opportunities for recent arrivals than less consolidated and more informal networks in other immigrant neighborhoods.

The neighborhood context does not stand in a vacuum, but is connected to a larger urban context. Therefore, the question of the transferability of the results also needs to situate the City of St. Paul and the Minneapolis/St. Paul metro area with respect to other cities or metropolitan areas in the United States, e.g. with respect to their economic position and opportunities. I assume that higher-income urban areas provide better conditions for income-generation than economically depressed ones, although the occupational structure needs to be considered as well. This favorably tackles the economic mobility opportunities of lower skilled residents of an immigrant neighborhood.

The economic indicators for the City of St. Paul and the Twin Cities metro area (chapter 6) suggest that these are relatively well positioned compared to other urban areas in the United States. After all, its relative economic well-being constitutes one of the reasons why the urban region figures as one of the 'new' immigrant destinations in the country – a pull-factor repeatedly confirmed in the resident interviews. In spite of the important increase in its foreign-born population since 1990, the Twin Cities' urban region is still majority-white, compared to other urban regions in the United States.

In synthesis, the results of this case study with respect to experiences with ethnic residential segregation, its impact on social capital development and mobility, are likely to concur with those of

- Recent immigrant groups with similar class- or status-characteristics to those of the Mexican population. This can be assumed notwithstanding the considerable differences *within* the Mexican population, which have been accounted for by a maximum variation of selected Mexican or Mexican-American interview partners.
- Economically and culturally diversified 'ethnic' neighborhood contexts, with relatively consolidated ethnic services and networks and relatively extensive opportunities for intra-ethnic cultural exchange. The latter point may be particularly relevant for individual well-being, rather than for individual mobility.
- Economically well-positioned urban contexts with prevailing employment opportunities in the central cities, for higher *and* lower skills levels.

Finally, it needs to be pointed out that the statements on the influence of the neighborhood and city environment on the study results constitute assumptions only. A multiple case study-based investigation of the mobility relevance of ethnic segregation or clustering remains a task of future studies.

Future research topics and methodologies

In several chapters of this document I indicated possible points of departure for future studies. These are presented here in sum. While other authors may consider different priorities in the thematic field of social capital- and mobility-impacts of segregation, I am suggesting topics that seem relevant from the perspective of this particular research and methodological approach.

These are the following:

- *Extension of research to multiple case study scenario*: In the present document, the transferability of the results of this study on social capital and mobility experiences in other ethnic neighborhoods, could only be addressed in a hypothetical manner. An important contribution of future research endeavors would lie in expanding the neighborhood case study basis in order to ground some of the above assumptions empirically. Thereby the same or a similar methodological approach (focus on qualitative methods of research and analysis) should be adopted in other types of ethnic neighborhoods. The criteria for determining maximum variation should be oriented by the classification scheme by Johnston et al and those mentioned as relevant in the West Side context: Ethno-racial population mix, income and poverty levels and degrees of ethnic organization. A first logical step would consist of looking at other ethnic neighborhood types in the Twin Cities' urban context. Subsequently, the research should be extended to other urban regions in the United States and Europe with different population and economic characteristics.
- *Individual characteristics impacting on mobility decisions*: The question of who typically stays in the ethnic neighborhood, and who moves to non-ethnic settings could not be explored satisfactorily in the present study. The results of this case study suggest that upwards social mobility tends to precede spatial mobility. This is particularly the case if living in the 'ethnic' neighborhood is associated with stigma from the mainstream society. A study focused on this question would require a phased approach in which, first, in a quantitative sample, individual characteristics and trajectories of present and former residents of an ethnic neighborhood are compared, as well as mobility motivations of the latter group. In a subsequent step, a smaller sample of interview partners would be chosen in order to inquire into mobility motivations as well as residential experiences in ethnic versus non-ethnic environments.
- *Impacts of racial or ethnic clustering on children and youth*: The present study, in line with prior works on segregation, has indicated a potential risk of ethnic residential segregation or clustering on children and youth. The West Side case has further suggested that

ethnic clustering tends to impact differently on young women and young men. It has also shown that the institutional framework possesses an important influence on how potentials of a multi-ethnic community (e.g. linguistic and cultural wealth) are capitalized upon, and risks of a socially and economically burdened parent and student community mitigated. It would however be important to address the question of how spatial segregation impacts on children and youth in a more focused way. This could happen in the form of a longitudinal qualitative study following a sample of children and youth with maximal varying socio-economic backgrounds through their educational (and possibly occupational) trajectories. Additionally, these trajectories should be studied against the background of different educational approaches towards ethno-cultural diversity in a specific neighborhood setting, in order to assess their respective outcomes, advantages and limitations.

- *Transmission of neighborhood image on urban and neighborhood population*: In the context of the present study, the neighborhood image was pointed out as a factor forcefully influencing mobility prospects and living conditions in the ethnic neighborhood. The stigma laid upon the ethnic neighborhood by the 'rest of the city' is strongly perceived and partly appropriated by its inhabitants and fosters spatial mobility decisions of upwardly mobile co-ethnics. These mobility decisions are also a result of lower housing values or slow value increases with respect to those in other city or metro area neighborhoods.

  An open question remains, however, how the negative or positive image of a neighborhood, hence its symbolic value, is exactly transmitted? The respective influence of for instance media coverage, city policies or other opinion-forging channels, needs to be analyzed. Depending on the results of this analysis, appropriate policy and planning measures to improve the negative image of 'ethnic' neighborhoods need to be sought out, i.e. by targeting the most important image-producers. It can be assumed that both dispersal and in-place community upgrading strategies (moving people and moving resources) directed to the so-called 'problematic' or high poverty neighborhoods have a stigmatizing effect on their own. An image-tackling approach would be required then that reaches far beyond physical improvements on the neighborhood level, e.g. towards altering collective consciousness. But these are mere working hypothesis.

The question of appropriate policy and planning responses to ethnic residential segregation is far from exhausted. This is also due to the material and symbolic obstacles to urban social inclusion and the diversity of segregation experiences alongside specific individual and neighborhood conditions and social and policy contexts. In this document, I believe that some empirically grounded indications for future policy and planning practice, at different levels of intervention and in different sectors, have been provided. However, further research, e.g. with respect to strategies for housing and educational inclusion of immigrant children and youth in ethnic neighborhoods, constitutes a necessity for the construction of a socially just and multi-cultural urban togetherness.

Bibliography

Addison, Richard 1992: Grounded hermeneutic research. In: Miller, William L. / Crabtree, Benjamin F. (eds.) 1992a: Doing qualitative research. Sage publications. Newbury Park. London. New Delhi. P. 110 – 124.

Aguilera, M.B. 2005: "The impact of social capital on the earnings of Puerto Rican migrants." In: The sociological quarterly 46 (4) 2005. P. 569 – 592.

Alba, Richard / Nee, Victor 1997: „Rethinking assimilation theory for a new era of immigration." In: International Migration Review 31 (4) 1997. P. 826 - 874.

Allen, Rick 2005: "Promoting diverse leadership". In: education update 5 (47) 2005. P. 2 – 8.

Amin, Ash 2006: "The good city." In: Urban Studies 43 (5/6) 2006. P. 1009 – 1023.

Amin, Ash 2002: Ethnicity and the multicultural city. Living with diversity. Report for the Department of Transport, Local Government and the Regions and the ESRC Cities Initiative. January 2002.

Atteslander, Peter / Hamm, Bernd (eds.) 1974: Materialien zur Siedlungssoziologie. Kiepenheuer & Witsch: Köln.

Beauregard, R. A. 1986: The chaos and complexity of gentrification. In: Smith, Neil / Williams, Peter (eds.) 1986: Gentrification of the city. Boston. P. 35 – 54.

Bingham, Richard D. et al. 1997: Beyond edge cities. Garland Publishing: New York, London.

Blauw, Wim 1991: Conclusion. In: Huttmann, Elizabeth (ed.) et al. 1991: Housing segregation of minorities in Western Europe and the United States. Duke University Press. London. P. 391 - 402.

Boal, Frederick W. (ed.) 2000: Ethnicity and housing. Accommodating differences. Ashgate: Aldershot, Brookfield, Singapore, Sidney.

Bobo, Lawrence / Zubrinsky Charles 1996: "Attitudes on residential integration: Perceived status differences, mere in-group preferences or racial prejudice?" In: Social Forces 3 (74) 1996. P. 883 – 908.

Bohon, Stephanie A. 2005: "Occupational attainment of Latino immigrants in the United States." In: The Geographical Review 95 (2) 2005. P. 249 – 266.

Borrie, W. D. 1959: The cultural integration of immigrants. Unesco: Paris.

Bourdieu, Pierre 1999: Site effects. In: Bourdieu, Pierre 1999a: The weight of the world. Social suffering in contemporary society. Stanford University Press: Stanford. P. 123 – 129.

Bourdieu, Pierre 1999a: The weight of the world. Social suffering in contemporary society. Stanford University Press: Stanford.

Bourdieu, Pierre 1998: Practical reason. On the theory of action. Stanford University Press. Stanford.

Bourdieu, Pierre 1991: Language and symbolic power. Harvard University Press. Cambridge.

Bourdieu, Pierre 1990: In other words. Essays towards a reflexive sociology. Stanford University Press. Stanford.

Bourdieu, Pierre 1990a: The logic of practice. Stanford University Press. Stanford.

Bourdieu, Pierre 1987: Die feinen Unterschiede. Kritik der gesellschaftlichen Urteilskraft. Suhrkamp. Frankfurt.

Bourdieu, Pierre 1986: The forms of capital. In: Handbook of theory and research for the sociology of education. Greenwood Press. Westport.

Bourdieu, Pierre et al. 1991: Soziologie als Beruf. Wissenschaftstheoretische Voraussetzungen soziologischer Erkenntnis. Walter de Gruyter: Berlin, New York.

Bourdieu, Pierre / Wacquant, Loïc 1992: An invitation to reflexive sociology. The University of Chicago Press. Chicago.

Bowen, William M. / Kimble, Deborah 1997: Edge cities in context. In: Bingham, Richard D. et al. 1997: Beyond edge cities. Garland Publishing: New York, London. S. 3 – 21.

Bowes, Alison / Dar, Naira / Sim, Duncan 2000: Housing preferences and strategies: an exploration of Pakistani experiences in Glasgow. In: Boal, Frederick W. (ed.) 2000: Ethnicity and housing. Accommodating differences. Ashgate: Aldershot, Brookfield, USA, Singapore, Sydney. P. 170 – 178.

Boyte, Harry Chatten 1984: Community is possible: Repairing America's roots. Harper & Row: New York.

Breton, Raymond 1964: „Institutional completeness of ethnic communities and the personal relations of immigrants." In: The American Journal of Sociology 70 (2) 1964. P. 193 – 205.

Brisson, D.S. 2005: "Bonding social capital in low-income neighborhoods." In: Family relations 54 (5) 2005. P. 644 – 653.

Broshears, Trudy (comp. and ed.) 2002: Searching for a new horizon. Immigration journeys of Hispanic women. Buscando un nuevo horizonte. Jornadas de inmigración de mujeres Hispanas. Sexton: St. Paul.

Burgess, Simon et al. 2005: "Parallel lives? Ethnic segregation in schools and neighborhoods." In: Urban studies 42 (7) 2005. P. 1027 – 1056.

Burnley, Ian 1999: "Levels of immigrant residential concentration in Sydney and their relationship with disadvantage." In: Urban Studies 36 (8) 1999. P. 1295 – 1315.

Caesperlein, Gerold / Gliemann, Katrin 2003: Drehscheibe Borsigplatz. Ein Einwanderungsstadtteil im Spiegel der Lebensgeschichten alteingesessener Bewohner. Dortmunder Beiträge zur Raumplanung 114. Institut für Raumplanung der Universität Dortmund (IRPUD). Dortmund.

Calavita, Kitty 1995: Mexican immigration to the USA: The contradictions of border control. In: The Cambridge Survey of World Migration. Cambridge University Press: Cambridge.

Camarota, Steven A. / McArdle, Nora 2003: Where immigrants live. An examination of state residency of the foreign born by country of origin in 1990 and 2000. Backgrounder. Center for Immigration Studies.

Carpiano, R.M. 2006: "Toward a neighborhood resource-based theory of social capital for health: Can Bourdieu and sociology help?" In: Social science medicine 62 (1) 2006. P. 165 – 175.

Chandler, Mittie Olion 1992: Obstacles to housing integration program efforts. In: Galster, George C. / Hill, Edward W. (eds.) 1992: The metropolis in black and white: Place, power and polarization. Center for Urban Policy Research: New Brunswick. P. 286 – 305.

Clark, William A.V. / Blue, Sarah A. 2004: "Race, class and segregation patterns in U.S. immigrant gateway cities." In: Urban Affairs Review 39 (6) 2004. P. 667 – 688.

Clay, Philipp L. 1992: The (un)housed city: racial patterns of segregation, housing quality and affordability. In: Galster, George C. / Hill, Edward W. (ed.) 1992: The metropolis in black and white: Place, power and polarization. New Brunswick. P. 93 – 107.

Colclough, G. / Sitraraman, B. 2005: "Community and social capital: What is the difference?" In: Sociological inquiry 75 (4) 2005. P. 474 – 496.

Coleman, James S. 1991: Grundlagen der Sozialtheorie. Band 1: Handlungen und Handlungssysteme. R. Oldenbourg Verlag: München.

Cornwell, Terri Lynn / Murray, Sylvester 1992: Beyond black and white: Multicultural understanding and the sharing of power. In: Galster, George C. / Hill, Edward W. (eds.) 1992: The metropolis in black and white. Place, power and polarization. Center for Urban Policy Research: New Brunswick. 356 – 372.

Cutler, David et al. 2005: Ghettos and the transmission of ethnic capital. In: Loury, Glenn C. (ed.) 2005: Ethnicity, social mobility, and public policy. P. 204 – 221. Website Harvard University.

Cutler, David et al. 2006: When are ghettos bad? Lessons from immigrant segregation in the United States. In: Website Cornell University.

Dangschat, Jens 2005: "Local social capital for the 'social city'. Political geographies of social accommodation development with the example of Berlin-Moabit." Book review. In: Tijdschrift voor economische en sociale geografie 96 (3) 2005. P. 350 – 352.

Dangschat, Jens S. 1998: Segregation. In: Häußermann, Hartmut (ed.) 1998: Großstadt. Soziologische Stichworte. Leske + Budrich: Opladen. P. 207 – 220.

Dangschat, Jens S. / Friedrichs, Jürgen 1988: Gentrification in der inneren Stadt von Hamburg. Eine empirische Untersuchung des Wandels von drei Wohnvierteln. Hamburg.

Dawkins, Casey J. 2004: "Recent evidence on the continuing causes of black-white residential segregation." In: Journal of Urban Affairs 26(3) 2004. P. 379 – 400.

Denzin, Norman K. / Lincoln, Yvonna S. (eds.) 1994: Handbook of qualitative research. Sage publications. Thousand Oaks. London. New Delhi. P.

Denzin, Norman K. / Lincoln, Yvonna S. 1994a: Introduction. Entering the field of qualitative research. In: Handbook of qualitative research. Sage publications. Thousand Oaks. London. New Delhi. P. 1 – 17.

Denzin, Norman K. / Lincoln, Yvonna S. 1994b: Part III. Strategies of inquiry. In: Denzin, Norman K. / Lincoln, Yvonna S. (eds.) 1994: Handbook of qualitative research. Sage publications. Thousand Oaks. London. New Delhi. P. 199 – 208.

Denzin, Norman K. / Lincoln, Yvonna S. (eds.) 2003: Collecting and interpreting qualitative materials. Sage publications. Thousand Oaks. London. New Delhi. P. 259 – 309.

Dey, Ian 1999: Grounding grounded theory. Guidelines for qualitative inquiry. Academic Press. San Diego.

Dunn, Kevin 1998: "Rethinking ethnic concentration: The case of Cabramatta. Sydney." In: Urban Studies 35 (3) 1998. 503 – 527.

Eisenstadt, Michael G. / Kaltefleiter, Werner (eds.) 1975: Minorities in the metropolis. A German-American comparison. Eichholz Verlag: Bonn.

Fix, Michael E. / Capps, Randolph 2002: The dispersal of immigrants in the 1990s. November 26, 2002. Website Urban Institute.

Flick, Uwe 2003: Triangulation in der qualitativen Forschung. In: Flick, Uwe / Kardoff, Ernst von / Steinke, Ines (eds.) 2003: Qualitative Forschung. Ein Handbuch. Rowohlt Taschenbuch Verlag. Reinbek. P. 309 – 318.

Flick, Uwe / Kardoff, Ernst von / Steinke, Ines (eds.) 2003: Qualitative Forschung. Ein Handbuch. Rowohlt Taschenbuch Verlag. Reinbek.

Fong, Eric / Shibuya, Kumiko 2005: "Multiethnic cities in North America." In: Annual Review of Sociology (31) 2005. P. 285 – 304.

Fontana, Andrea / Frey, James H. 1994: Interviewing: The art of science. In: Denzin, Norman K. / Lincoln, Yvonna S. (eds.) 1994: Handbook of qualitative research. Sage publications. Thousand Oaks. London. New Delhi. P. 361 - 376.

Fortjuin, Joos D. et al. 1998: "International migration and ethnic segregation: Impacts on urban areas – introduction." In: Urban Studies 35 (3) 1998. P. 367 – 370.

Fossett, Mark / Warren, Warren 2005: "Overlooked implications of ethnic preferences for residential segregation in agent-based models." In: Urban Studies 42 (11) 2005. P. 1893 – 1917.

Frazier, John W. / Margai, Florence M. / Tettey-Fio, Eugene 2003: Race and place. Equity issues in urban America. Westview Press: Bolder.

Freeman, Lance 2000: "Minority housing segregation: A test of three perspectives." In: Journal of Urban Affairs 22 (1) 2000. P. 15 – 35.

Friedrichs, Jürgen 1981: Stadtanalyse. Soziale und räumliche Organisation der Gesellschaft. Opladen

Galster, George C. 1992: The case for racial integration. In: Galster, George C. / Hill, Edward W. (ed.) 1992: The metropolis in black and white: Place, power and polarization. New Brunswick. P. 270 – 285.

Galster, George C. / Hill, Edward W. (eds.) 1992: The metropolis in black and white: Place, power and polarization. Center for Urban Policy Research: New Brunswick.

Gans, Herbert J. 1997: „Toward a reconciliation of 'assimilation' and 'pluralism': the interplay of acculturation and ethnic retention." In: International Migration Review 31 (4) 1997. P. 875 – 892.

García Canclini, Nestor 1995: Consumidores y ciudadanos. Conflictos multiculturales de la globalización. Grijalbo: Mexico City.

Glaser, Barney G. 1992: Basics of grounded theory analysis. Sociology Press. Mill Valley.

Glazer, Nathan 1975: The integration of minorities from the point of view of social science. In: Eisenstadt, Michael G. / Kaltefleiter, Werner (eds.) 1975: Minorities in the metropolis. A German-American comparison. Eichholz Verlag: Bonn. P. 24-31.

Gilbertson, Greta 1995: "Women's labor and enclave employment: the case of Dominican and Colombian women in New York City." In: International Migration Review (29) 1995. P. 657 – 670.

Gilchrist, Valerie J. 1992: Key informant interviews. In: Miller, William L. / Crabtree, Benjamin F. (eds.) 1992: Doing qualitative research. Sage publications. Newbury Park. London. New Delhi. P. 70 – 89.

Glick-Schiller, Nina et al. (eds.) 1992: Toward a transnational perspective on migration: Race, class, ethnicity and nationalism reconsidered. Annals of New York Academy of Sciences, 645. New York: New York Academy of Sciences.

Glick-Schiller, Nina et al. 1992a: Transnationalism: A new analytic framework for understanding migration. In: Glick-Schiller, Nina et al. (eds.) 1992: Toward a transnational perspective on migration: Race, class, ethnicity and nationalism reconsidered. Annals of New York Academy of Sciences, 645. New York: New York Academy of Sciences. P. 1 – 24.

Godehart, Susanna 2007: The transformation of townships in South Africa. The case of KwaMashu. SPRING Research Series (SRS) 49. SPRING publications: Dortmund.

Goering, John / Coulibably, Modibo 1991: Public housing segregation in the United States. In: Huttmann, Elizabeth (ed.) et al. 1991: Housing segregation of minorities in Western Europe and the United States: Duke University Press. London. P. 305 – 334.

Goetz, Edward 2004: "Desegregation lawsuits and public housing dispersal. The case of Hollmann v. Cisneros in Minneapolis." In: Journal of the American Planning Association 70 (3) 2004. 282 – 299.

Goetz, Edward 2003: Clearing the way. Deconcentrating the poor in urban America. The Urban Institute Press. Washington.

Goetz, Edward 2002: Hollmann vs. Cisneros. Report Nr. 1.

Goetz, Edward 2002a: Hollmann vs. Cisneros. Report No. 6.

Göschel, Albrecht 2001: „Integration und Stadt". In: Deutsche Zeitschrift fuer Kommunalwissenschaften (1) 2001. P. 5 - 11.

Goldberg, Barry 1992: Historical reflections on transnationalism, race, and the American immigrant saga. In: Glick-Schiller, Nina et al. (eds.) 1992: Toward a transnational perspective on migration: Race, class, ethnicity and nationalism reconsidered. Annals of New York Academy of Sciences, 645. New York: New York Academy of Sciences. P. 201 – 215.

Goldring, Luin 1998: The power of status in transnational social fields. In: Smith, Michael Peter / Guarnizo, Luis Eduardo 1998: Transnationalism from below. Transaction Publishers. New Brunswick. P. 165 - 195.

Gordon, Milton M. 1964: Assimilation in American life. The role of race, religion and national origins. Oxford University Press: New York.

Guarnizo, Luis Eduardo / Smith, Michael Peter 1998: The locations of transnationalism. In: Smith, Michael Peter / Guarnizo, Luis Eduardo 1998: Transnationalism from below. Transaction Publishers. New Brunswick. P. 3 – 34.

HACER (Hispanic Advocacy and Community Empowerment through Research) 2002: Los Latinos en el West Side de St. Paul. Latinos on the West Side of St. Paul. HACER.

Hamnett, Chris 1991: The blind man and the elephant. The explanation of gentrification. In: van Weesep, Jan / Musterd, Sako (eds.) 1991: Urban housing for the better-off: Gentrification in Europe. P. 30 – 51.

Häußermann, Hartmut (ed.) 1998: Großstadt. Soziologische Stichworte. Leske + Budrich: Opladen.

Häussermann, Hartmut / Siebel, Walter 2001: „Integration und Segregation – Ueberlegungen zu einer alten Debatte." In: Deutsche Zeitschrift fuer Kommunalwissenschaften (1) 2001. P. 68 – 77.

Hanlon, Bernadette et al. 2006: "The new metropolitan reality in the US: Rethinking the traditional model." In: Urban Studies 43 (12) 2006. P. 2129 – 2143.

Hanhörster, Heike / Mölder, Margit 2000: Konflikt- und Integrationsräume im Wohnbereich. In: Heitmeyer / Anhut (eds.) 2000. P. 347 – 400.

Helper, Rose 1991: Introduction to American policies and programs. In: Huttmann, Elizabeth (ed.) et al. 1991: Housing segregation of minorities in Western Europe and the United States. Duke University Press: London. P. 303 - 304.

Heitmeyer, Wilhelm / Anhut, Reimund (eds.) 2000: Bedrohte Stadtgesellschaft. Soziale Desintegrationsprozesse und ethnisch-kulturelle Konfliktkonstellationen. Juventa: München, Weinheim.

Hermanns, Harry 2003: Interviewen als Tätigkeit. In: Flick, Uwe / Kardoff, Ernst von / Steinke, Ines (eds.) 2003: Qualitative Forschung. Ein Handbuch. Rowohlt Taschenbuch Verlag. Reinbek. S. 360 – 368.

Hopf, Christel 2003: Qualitative Interviews – ein Überblick. In: Flick, Uwe / Kardoff, Ernst von / Steinke, Ines (eds.) 2003: Qualitative Forschung. Ein Handbuch. Rowohlt Taschenbuch Verlag. Reinbek. S. 349 - 360.

Hubermann, A. Michael / Miles, Matthew B. 1994: Data management and analysis methods. In: Denzin, Norman K. / Lincoln, Yvonna S. (eds.) 1994: Handbook of qualitative research. Sage publications. Thousand Oaks. London. New Delhi. P. 428 - 443.

Huttmann, Elizabeth (ed.) et al. 1991: Housing segregation of minorities in Western Europe and the United States. Duke University Press. London.

Huttmann, Elizabeth D. / Jonnes, Terry 1991: American suburbs: Desegregation and resegregation. In: Huttmann, Elizabeth (ed.) et al. 1991: Housing segregation of minorities in Western Europe and the United States. Duke University Press: London. P. 335 – 366.

Iceland, John 2004: "Beyond black and white. Metropolitan residential segregation in multiethnic America." In: Social science research (33) 2004. P. 248 – 271.

Ihlanfeldt, Keith R. / Scafidi, Benjamin P. 2004: "The neighborhood contact hypothesis: Evidence from the multicity study of urban inequality." In: Urban Studies 39 (4) 2004. P. 619 – 641.

Ihlanfeldt, Keith R. / Sjoquist, David L. 2000: The geographic mismatch between jobs and housing. In: Sjoquist, David L. (ed.) 2000: The Atlanta paradox. Russell Sage Foundation: New York.

Jacobs, Jane / Fincher, Ruth (eds.) 1998: Cities of difference. Guilford Press: New York.

Jargowsky, Paul A. 1997: Poverty and place. Ghettos, barrios and the american city. New York.

Johnston, Barry A. 1991: Housing segregation in the urban black population of the Midwest. In: Huttmann, Elizabeth (ed.) et al. 1991: Housing segregation of minorities in Western Europe and the United States. Duke University Press: London. P. 243 – 271.

Johnston, Ron et al. 2003: "And did the walls come tumbling down? Ethnic residential segregation in four US metropolitan areas 1980 – 2000." In: Urban Geography 24 (7) 2003. P. 560 – 581.

Jones, Delmos 1992: Which migrants? Temporary or permanent? In: Glick-Schiller, Nina et al. (eds.) 1992: Toward a transnational perspective on migration: Race, class, ethnicity and nationalism reconsidered. Annals of New York Academy of Sciences, 645. New York: New York Academy of Sciences. P. 215 - 218.

Kaplan, David H. / Woodhouse, Kathleen 2004: "Research in ethnic segregation I: Causal factors." In: Urban Geography 25 (6) 2004. P. 579 – 585.

Kardoff, Ernst von 2003: Qualitative Evaluationsforschung. In: Flick, Uwe / Kardoff, Ernst von / Steinke, Ines (eds.) 2003: Qualitative Forschung. Ein Handbuch. Rowohlt Taschenbuch Verlag. Reinbek. P. 238 - 250.

Kato, Yuki 2006: "Planning and social diversity: Residential segregation in American new towns." In: Urban Studies 43 (12) 2006. P. 2285 – 2299.

Kelle, Udo / Erzberger, Christian 2003: Quantitative und qualitative Methoden: kein Gegensatz. In: Flick, Uwe / Kardoff, Ernst von / Steinke, Ines (eds.) 2003: Qualitative Forschung. Ein Handbuch. Rowohlt Taschenbuch Verlag. Reinbek. S. 299 - 309.

Kao, Grace 2004: "Social capital and its relevance to minority and immigrant populations." In: Sociology of Education (77) 2004. P. 172 – 183.

Kraus, Neil 2004: "Local policymaking and concentrated poverty: the case of Buffalo, New York." In: Cities 21 (6) 2004. P. 481 – 490.

Krysan, Maria / Farley, Reynold 2002: "The residential preferences of blacks. Do they explain residential segregation?" In: Social Forces 3 (80) 2002. P. 937 – 980.

Kuzel, A.J. 1992: Sampling in qualitative inquiry. In: Miller, William L. / Crabtree, Benjamin F. (eds.) 1992: Doing qualitative research. Sage publications. P. 33 – 46.

Lamnek, Siegfried 1989: Qualitative Sozialforschung. Methoden und Techniken. Band 2. Psychologie Verlags Union: München.

Lauria-Perricelli, Antonio 1992: Towards a transnational perspective on migration: Closing remarks. In: Glick-Schiller, Nina et al. (eds.) 1992: Toward a transnational perspective on migration: Race, class, ethnicity and nationalism reconsidered. Annals of New York Academy of Sciences, 645. New York: New York Academy of Sciences. P. 251 – 258.

Le Monde 2006, April 21: "Les Latinos aux Etats-Unis. Sûrs de leur force."

Lewis Mumford Center (LMC) 2001: Ethnic diversity grows, neighborhood integration lags behind. December 18, 2001. Website LMC.

Lichtenberger, Elisabeth 1986: Stadtgeographie. Teubner Studienbücher: Stuttgart.

Logan, John R. 2003: America's newcomers. June 18, 2003. Website LMC.

Logan, John R. 2002: Hispanic populations and their residential patterns in the metropolis. May 8, 2002. Website LMC.

Logan, John R. 2002a: Separate and unequal: The neighbourhood gap for blacks and Hispanics in metropolitan America. October 13, 2002. Website LMC

Logan, John R. 2002b:. The suburban advantage. New census data show unyielding city-suburb economic gap, and surprising shifts in some places. June 24, 2002. Website LMC.

Logan, John R. 2001: The new Latinos: Who they are, where they are. September 10, 2001. Website LMC.

Logan et al. 2001: From many shores: Asians in Census 2000. Ocober 6, 2001. Website LMC.

Loury, Glenn C. (ed.) 2005: Ethnicity, social mobility, and public policy. Cambridge.

Li, Wei 1998: "Anatomy of a new ethnic settlement: The chinese ethnoburb in Los Angeles." In: Urban Studies 13 (36) 1998. P. 479 – 501.

MacDonald et al. 2005: "Growing up in poor neighborhoods: The significance of class and place in the extended transitions of 'socially excluded' young adults." In: Sociology 39 (5) 2005. P. 873 – 891.

Mahler, Sarah 1998: Theoretical and empirical contributions toward a research agenda for transnationalism. In: Smith, Michael Peter / Guarnizo, Luis Eduardo 1998: Transnationalism from below. Transaction Publishers. New Brunswick. P. 64 – 100.

Mahler, Sarah 1995: American Dreaming. Immigrant life on the margins. Princeton University Press. Princeton.

Marcuse, Peter 1997: "The enclave, the citadel and the ghetto: what has changed in the post-fordist city." In: Urban Affairs Review 2 (33) 1997. P. 228 – 264.

Marcuse, Peter 1993: "What's so new about divided cities?" In: International Journal of Urban and Regional Affairs 17 (3) 1993. P. 355 – 365.

Massey, Douglas / Denton, Nancy 1993: American Apartheid: Segregation and the making of the underclass. Cambridge.

MacDonald et al. 2005: "Growing up in poor neighborhoods: The significance of class and place in the extended transitions of 'socially excluded' young adults." In: Sociology 39 (5) 2005. P. 873 – 891.

McClure, Jane 1992: "A story of change, pride, perseverance. The Mexican-Americans and their roots in St. Paul's past." In: Ramsey County History 27 (3) 1992. P. 4 – 12.

McKenzie, Roderick D. 1974: Konzepte der Sozialökologie. In: Atteslander, Peter / Hamm, Bernd (eds.) 1974: Materialien zur Siedlungssoziologie. Kiepenheuer & Witsch: Köln. P. 101 – 112.

Meinefeld, Werner 2003: Hypothesen und Vorwissen in der qualitativen Sozialforschung. In: Flick, Uwe / Kardoff, Ernst von / Steinke, Ines (eds.) 2003: Qualitative Forschung. Ein Handbuch. Rowohlt Taschenbuch Verlag. Reinbek. P. 265 - 275.

Merkens, Hans 2003: Auswahlverfahren, Sampling, Fallkonstruktion. In: Flick, Uwe / Kardoff, Ernst von / Steinke, Ines (eds.) 2003: Qualitative Forschung. Ein Handbuch. Rowohlt Taschenbuch Verlag. Reinbek. P. 286 - 299.

Middleton, Alan et al. 2005: "Social capital and neighborhoods that work." In: Urban Studies 42 (10) 2005. September 2005. P. 1711 – 1738.

Miller, William T. / Crabtree, Benjamin F. (eds.) 1992: Doing qualitative research. Volume 3: For primary care. Sage publications. Newbury Park. London. Delhi.

Miller, William L. / Crabtree, Benjamin F. 1992: Primary care research: A multimethod typology and qualitative road map. In: Miller, William T. / Crabtree, Benjamin F. (eds.) 1992a: Doing qualitative research. Volume 3: For primary care. Sage publications. Newbury Park. London. Delhi. P. 3 – 28.

Miller, William L. / Crabtree, Benjamin F. 1992a: A template approach to text analysis: Developing and using codebooks. In: Miller, William T. / Crabtree, Benjamin F. (eds.) 1992: Doing qualitative research. Volume 3: For primary care. Sage publications. Newbury Park. London. Delhi. P. 93 - 109.

Nagar, Richard / Leitner, Helga 1998: Contesting social relations in communal places. Identity politics among Asian communities in Dar Es Salaam. In: Jacobs, Jane / Fincher, Ruth (eds.) 1998: Cities of difference. Guilford Press: New York.

Nee, Victor et al. 1994: "Job transitions in an immigrant metropolis: ethnic boundaries and the mixed economy." In: American Sociological Review (59) 1994. P. 849 – 872.

Neubert et al. 2000: Armutsmindernde Wirkungen des Ressourcenmanagementprojekts PATECORE in Burkina Faso. Deutsches Institut für Entwicklungspolitik (DIE). Berichte und Gutachten. Berlin.

New York Times 2001, June 29: "The World: Adjoining; Rethinking segregation beyond black and white."

O'Connor, Alice et al. (eds.) 2001: Urban inequality. Evidence from four cities. New York.

Orfield, Myron 1997: Metropolitics. A regional agenda for community and stability. Brookings Institution Press: Washington.

Park, Robert E. 1974: Die Stadt als räumliche Struktur und als sittliche Ordnung. In: Atteslander, Peter / Hamm, Bernd (eds.) 1974: Materialien zur Siedlungssoziologie. Kiepenheuer & Witsch: Köln. P. 90 – 100.

Patterson, Orlando 1997: The ordeal of integration. Washington.

Peebles, Thandiwe 2004: Comprehensive desegregation/integration plan and budget. Submitted December 15, 2004. Unpublished document.

Pelemann, Katleen 2002: "The impact of residential segregation on participation in associations: the case of Moroccan women in Belgium." In: Urban Studies April 39 (4) 2002. P. 727 – 748.

Pessar, Patricia 1998: The role of gender, households, and social networks in the migration process: A review and appraisal. In: Kasinitz, Philipp / Farley, Reynold (ed.s) 1999:

The handbook of international immigration: the American experience. Sage Foundation. New York. Pp. 53 – 70.

Petersen, William 1958: "A general typology of migration". In: American Sociological Review (23) 1958. P. 256 – 266.

Polese, Mario: Learning from each other: Policy choices and the social sustainability of cities. In: Polese, Mario / Stren, Richard (eds.) 2000a: The social sustainability of cities. Diversity and the management of change. University of Toronto Press. Toronto. P. 308 – 334.

Polese, Mario / Stren, Richard (eds.) 2000a: The social sustainability of cities. Diversity and the management of change. University of Toronto Press: Toronto.

Popkin, Susan J. 2002: The Hope VI Program – What about the residents? Policy brief. Published December 2002. Website Urban Institute.

Portes, Alejandro 1998: "Social capital. Its origins and applications in modern sociology." In: Annual Review of Sociology (24) 1998. P. 1 – 24.

Portes, Alejandro 1997: „Immigration theory for a new century: some problems and opportunities." In: International Migration Review 31 (4) 1997. P. 799 – 825.

Portes, Alejandro 1987: "What's an ethnic enclave? The case for conceptual clarity." In: American Sociological Review (52) 1987.

Portes, Alejandro / Jensen, Leif 1987: "What's an ethnic enclave? The case for conceptual clarity." In: American Sociological Review (52) 1987. P. 768 – 771.

Price, C.A. 1959: Immigration and group settlement. In: Borrie, W. D. 1959: The cultural integration of immigrants. Unesco: Paris. P. 267 – 287.

Priemus, Hugo 2000: Colorful districts: west European cities moving towards multi-ethnicity. In: Boal, Frederick W. (ed.) 2000: Ethnicity and housing. Accommodating differences. Ashgate: Aldershot, Brookfield, USA, Singapore, Sydney. P. 225 - 232.

Putnam, Robert 2000: Bowling alone: The collapse and revival of American community. Simon & Schuster. New York.

Putnam, Robert / Goss, Kristin A. 2002: Introduction. In: Putnam, Robert (ed.) 2002: Democracies in flux: the evolution of social capital in contemporary society. Oxford University Press. Oxford.

Quillian, Lincoln 2002: "Why is black-white residential segregation so persistent? Evidence on three theories from migration data." In: Social Science research 2 (31) 2002. P. 197 – 229.

Ream, Robert K. 2005: "Toward understanding how social capital mediates the impact of mobility on Mexican American achievement." In: Social Forces 84 (1) 2005. P. 201 – 224.

Robinson, David 2005: "The search for community cohesion: Key themes and dominant concepts of the public policy agenda." In: Urban Studies 42 (8) 2005. P. 1411 – 1427.

Rouse, Roger 1992: Making sense of settlement: Class transformation, cultural struggle and transnationalism among Mexican migrants in the United States. In: Glick-Schiller, Nina et al. (eds.) 1992: Toward a transnational perspective on migration: Race, class, ethnicity and nationalism reconsidered. Annals of New York Academy of Sciences, 645. New York: New York Academy of Sciences. P. 25 – 52.

Ryan, Gery W. / Bernard, Russel H. 2003: Data management and analysis methods. In: Denzin, Norman K. / Lincoln, Yvonna S. (eds.) 2003: Collecting and interpreting qualitative materials. Sage publications. Thousand Oaks. London. New Delhi. P. 259 – 309.

Saltman, Julie 1991: U.S. neighborhood stabilization efforts. In: Huttmann, Elizabeth (ed.) et al. 1991: Housing segregation of minorities in Western Europe and the United States. Duke University Press: London. P. 374 - 390.

Sandercock, Leonie 2003: Cosmopolis II. Mongrel cities in the 21st Century. Continuum. London, New York.

Sandercock, Leonie 1998: Towards cosmopolis. Planning for multicultural cities. Wiley. New York.

Sanders, Jimy M. et al. 1994: "Job transitions in an immigrant metropolis: Ethnic boundaries and the mixed economy." In: American Sociological Review (59) 1987. P. 849 – 872.

Sanders, Jimy M. / Nee, Victor 1987: "Limits of ethnic solidarity in the enclave economy." In: American Sociological Review (52) 1987. P. 745 – 773.

Schellenberg, Stephen J. / Porter, Cindy 2003: School choice in established magnet school systems: Voluntary desegregation after thirty-five years. A paper presented as part of the symposium "Are school choice and charter schools resegregating public schooling?" at the Annual Meeting of the American Educational Research Association. Chicago, Illinois, April 24, 2003. Unpublished document.

Schnur, Olaf 2005: "Exploring social capital as an urban neighborhood resource: Empirical findings and strategic conclusions of a case study in Berlin-Moabit." In: Tijdschrift voor economische en sociale geografie 96 (5) 2005. P. 488 – 505.

Schuck, Peter 2003: Diversity in America. Harvard University Press. Cambridge.

Sen, Amartya 2000: Inequality reexamined. Cambridge, Massachusetts: Harvard University Press.

Sen, Amartya 2000a: Development as freedom. New York: Anchor Books.

Sen, Amartya 1999: "Democracy as a universal value". In: Journal of Democracy 10 (3) 1999. P. 3 – 17.

Siisiäinen, Martti 2000: Two concepts of social capital: Bourdieu vs. Putnam. Paper presented at ISTR Fourth International Conference "The Third Sector: For what and for whom?" Dublin, Ireland.

Simpson, Ludi 2005: "On the measurement and meaning of residential segregation: A reply to Johnston, Poulsen and Forrest." In: Urban Studies 42 (7) 2005. P. 1229 – 1230.

Sjoquist, David L. (ed.) 2000: The Atlanta paradox. Russell Sage Foundation: New York.

Smit, Dan / Purchase, Juana 2006: A review of the international experience with inclusionary housing programmes: Implications for South Africa. Johannesburg. Unpublished document.

Smith, Michael Peter / Guarnizo, Luis Eduardo (eds.) 1998: Transnationalism from below. Volume 6, Comparative urban and community research. Transaction publishers. New Brunswick.

Smith, Neil 1986: Gentrification, the frontier, and the restructuring of urban space. In: Smith, Neil / Williams, Peter (eds.) 1986a: Gentrification of the city. Boston. P. 15 – 34.

Smith, Neil / Williams, Peter (eds.) 1986a: Gentrification of the city. Boston.

Squires et al. 2002: Experiencing residential segregation. "A contemporary study of Washington, D.C." In: Urban Affairs Review 38 (2) 2002. P. 155 – 183.

Strauss, Anselm / Corbin, Juliet 1994: Grounded theory methodology. An overview. In: Denzin, Norman K. / Lincoln, Yvonna S. (eds.) 1994: Handbook of qualitative research. Sage publications. Thousand Oaks. London. New Delhi. P. 273 – 285.

Strauss, Anselm / Corbin, Juliet 1990: Basics of qualitative research. Sage publications. Newbury Park. London. New Delhi.

Thomas, William I. / Znaniecki, Florian 1996: The Polish peasant in Europe and America. University of Illinois Press: Urbana and Chicago.

Tomlins, Richard 2000: Addressing the housing needs of minority ethnic communities: towards a pluralistic ethnic housing policy. In: Boal, Frederick W. (ed.) 2000: Ethnicity and housing. Accommodating differences. Ashgate: Aldershot, Brookfield, Singapore, Sidney. P. 163 – 169.

Uslaner, Eric M. / Conley, Richard S. 2003: "Civic engagement and particularized trust. The ties that bind people to their ethnic communities." In: American Politics Research 4 (31) 2003. P. 331 – 360.

Vigdor, Jacob L. 2003: "Residential segregation and preference misalignment." In: Journal of Urban Economics (54) 2003. P. 587 – 609.

UNDP (United Nations Development Program) 1992: Human Development Report.

van Weesep, Jan / Musterd, Sako (eds.) 1991: Urban housing for the better-off: Gentrification in Europe.

Wacquant, Loïc 1999: America as social dystopia. The politics of urban disintegration, or the French uses of the "American model". In: Bourdieu, Pierre 1999a: The weight of the world. Social suffering in contemporary society. Stanford University Press: Stanford. P. 130 – 139.

Waldinger, Roger (ed.) 2001a: Strangers at the gates. New immigrants in urban America. University of California Press: Berkeley, Los Angeles, London.

Waldinger, Roger / Der Martirosian, Claudia 2001: The immigrant niche. Pervasive, persistent, diverse. In: Waldinger, Roger (ed.) 2001a: Strangers at the gates. New immigrants in urban America. University of California Press: Berkeley, Los Angeles, London. P. 228 – 271.

Warr, D.J. 2005: "Social networks in a 'discredited' neighborhood." In: Journal of sociology 41 (3) 2005. P. 285 – 308.

Werbner, Pnina 2001: "Metaphors of spatiality and networks in the plural city: a critique of the ethnic enclave economy debate." In: Sociology 3 (35) 2001. P. 671 – 693.

White, M.J. et al. 2005: "Mapping social distance - Ethnic residential segregation in a multi-ethnic metro." In: Sociological methods research 34 (2) 2005. P. 173 – 203.

Wilson, Franklin D. / Hammer, Roger B. 2001: Ethnic residential segregation and its consequences. In: O'Connor, Alice et al. (eds.) 2001: Urban inequality. Evidence from four cities. New York. P. 272 – 303.

Wilson, William J. 1990: The truly disadvantaged. The inner city, the underclass and public policy. The University of Chicago Press: Chicago.

Wind, John de / Kasinitz, Philipp 1997: "Everything old is new again? Processes and theories of immigrant incorporation." In: International Migration Review 31 (4) 1997. P. 1096 – 1011.

Wolff, Stephan 2003: Wege ins Feld und ihre Varianten. In: Flick, Uwe / Kardoff, Ernst von / Steinke, Ines (eds.) 2003: Qualitative Forschung. Ein Handbuch. Rowohlt Taschenbuch Verlag. Reinbek. S. 334 - 349.

Wolfreys, Jim 2000: "In perspective: Pierre Bourdieu." In: International Socialism Journal (87) 2000.

Wortham, Anne 2002: „America and Immigration. Are we a melting pot?" In: Current January (436) 2002. P. 8 – 15.

Wuthnow, Robert: The United States: Bridging the privileged and the marginalized? In: Putnam, Robert (ed.) 2002: Democracies in flux. Social capital in Western societies. Oxford University Press. Oxford, New York. P. 59 - 102.

Young, Iris M. 2000: Inclusion and democracy. Oxford University Press: New York.

Young, Iris M. 1990: Justice and the politics of difference. Princeton University Press: Princeton, New Jersey.

Zhou, Min 2001: Progress, decline, stagnation? The new second generation comes of age. In: Waldinger, Roger (ed.) 2001a: Strangers at the gates. New immigrants in urban America. University of California Press: Berkeley, Los Angeles, London. P. 272 – 307.

Zhou, Min / Kim, S.S. 2006: "Community forces, social capital, and educational achievement: The case of supplementary education in the Chinese and Korean immigrant communities." In: Harvard educational review 76 (1) 2006. S. 1 – 29.

Zubrinsky Charles, Camille 2003: "The dynamics of racial residential segregation." In: Annual Review of Sociology (29) 2003. P. 167 – 207.

Zubrinski Charles, Camille 2001: Processes of racial residential segregation. In: O'Connor, Alice et al. (eds.) 2001: Urban inequality. Evidence from four cities. New York. P. 217 – 271.

Policy documents

Testimony of St. Paul PHA-director to House of Representatives, May 2005.

St. Paul PHA deconcentration analysis, January 2004.

Websites

factfinder.census.gov: American Fact Finder. Census figures of the 1990 and 2000 Census and general information on the American Census.

www.brookings.edu: Brooking Institution.

www.brookings.edu/es/urban/livingcities/MinneapolisStPaul.htm: "Living Cities" Report, Minneapolis-St. Paul in Focus.

www.census.gov: United States Census Bureau.

www.ciser.cornell.edu: Cornell University, Cornell Institute for Social and Economic Research. Article Cutler et al. 2006.

www.economics.harvard.edu: Harvard University, Department of Economics. Article Cutler et al. 2005.

www.gpoaccess.gov/cfr/index.html: Code of Federal Regulations.

www.hud.gov: US Federal Department for Housing and Urban Development.

www.huduser.org/publications/hsgfin/phase1.html: Information on pair-testing methods.

www.metrocouncil.org: Twin Cities Metropolitan Council.

www.migrationinformation.org: Migration Information Source.

minneapolis.about.com: About Cities and Towns. Minneapolis / St. Paul.

mumford.albany.edu: Lewis Mumford Center for Comparative Urban and Regional Research.

mumford.albany.edu/census/data: Lewis Mumford Center, America's Community Survey.

mumford.albany.edu/census/report.html: Several reports (indicated in bibliography).

www.mhfa.state.mn.us: Minnesota Housing Finance Agency.

www.novoco.com/low_income_housing/facts_figures/research_center.pdf: Jackson, Pamela J. 2007: The Low-Income Housing Tax Credit: A framework for evaluation. CRS Report for Congress. March 7, 2007.

www.rchs.com: Ramsey County Historical Society.

www.st-paul.gov: City of St. Paul, USA.

www.stpaulpha.org: St. Paul Public Housing Agency.

www.universallivingwage.org: Information on calculation of minimum living wage in United States.

www.urban.org: Urban Institute, Washington. Several articles.

usa.ipums.org/usa/index.html: Integrated Public Use Microdata Series.

www.wsco.org: West Side Citizens Organization.

www.wilder.org: Wilder Research Center.

www.geomyideal.com: Several photos of houses and buildings on West Side.

Brochures from visited institutions and others

A cultural guide to Saint Paul's West Side: Murals, sculptures, gardens, markets, restaurants, bakeries.

Kids Discover Aztecs. Soldiers of a feather flock together.

NeDA, Neighborhood Development Alliance Report: Ten Years Building homes, partnerships and a great neighborhood.

Neighborhood House, Annual Report 2003.

PHA Monthly Management Report: Management Report of the Public Housing Authority of St. Paul, March 2005.

REDA, Riverview Economic Development Association, Annual Report 2003: Twenty years of community partnerships.

RES, Roosevelt Elementary School, 'Success for all' brochure.

St. Paul Public Housing Agency: Annual Report 2004.

West Side Neighborhood Learning Community brochure.

Annexes

Annex 1: Variables accessed in American Fact Finder

Census year	Summary File	Variable label	Variable name
1990	**1**	P001	Persons
		P001H	Persons (Hispanic)
		P006	Race
		P009	Hispanic origin
		P010	Hispanic origin by race
		H003	Tenure
	3	P031	Language spoken at home
		P036	Year of entry
		P042	Place of birth
		P057	Educational attainment
		P080A	Median household income in 1989
		P117	Poverty status in 1989 by age
		H061	Value
		H061A	Median Value
2000	**1**	P1	Total population
		P1H	Total population (Hispanic or Latino)
		P3	Race
		P4	Hispanic or Latino, and Not Hispanic or Latino by Race for the population 18 years and older
		P7	Race (Total population)
		P8	Hispanic or Latino by Race (Total population)
		P12	Sex by age (Total population)
		P12H	Sex by age Hispanic or Latino
		P17	Average Household Size
		P17H	Average Household Size (Hispanic or Latino Householder)
		P18	Household size, household type and presence of own children
		P18H	Household size, household type and presence of own children (Hispanic or Latino householder)
		P21	Household type by age of householder
		P26	Household type by household size
		P26H	Household type by household size (Hispanic or Latino

Annex One

Census year	Summary File	Variable label	Variable name
			householder)
		PCT11	Hispanic or Latino by specific origin
		H4	Tenure
	2	PCT1Mex	Total population (Mexican)
		PCT3Mex	Sex by age (Mexican)
		PCT8Mex	Average household size (Mexican)
		PCT9Mex	Household size, household type, and presence of own children (Mexican)
		HCT2Mex	Tenure (Mexican)
	3	P19	Age by language spoken at home by ability to speak English for the population 5 yrs. and older
		P22	Year of entry for the foreign-born population
		P23	Year of entry by citizenship status for the foreign-born population
		P37	Sex by educational attainment for the population 25 yrs. and older
		P53	Median household income in 1999 (Dollars)
		P57	Aggregate household income in 1999 (Dollars)
		P87	Poverty status in 1999 by age
		P146H	Households by age of householder by number and presence of own children (Hispanic or Latino)
		P148H	Sex by educational attainment for population 25 yrs. and older (Hispanic or Latino)
		P152H	Median household income in 1999 (Hispanic or Latino)
		P159H	Poverty status in 1999 by age (Hispanic)
		PCT11	Language spoken at home by ability to speak English for the population 5 yrs. and older
		PCT 20	Place of birth by year of entry by citizenship status for the foreign-born population
		H7	Tenure
		H12	Tenure (Hispanic or Latino householder)
		H30	Units in structure
		H74	Housing value for (Dollars) for specified owner-occupied housing units
		H76	Median value (Dollars) for specified owner-occupied housing units

Annex One

Census year	Summary File	Variable label	Variable name
		HCT30H	Units in structure (Hispanic householder)
		HCT39H	Gross rent as a percentage of household income in 1999 (Hispanic householder)
		HCT42H	Median value (Dollars) (Hispanic householder)
	4	PCT43	Sex by place of birth by citizenship status (for Mexicans)
		PCT45	Sex by year of entry for the foreign-born population (for Mexicans)
		PCT64	Sex by educational attainment for the population 25 yrs. and older (for Mexicans and Hispanics)
		PCT89	Median household income in 1999 (Dollars) (for Mexicans)
		PCT142	Poverty status in 1999 by sex by age (for Mexicans)
		HCT2	Tenure (for Mexicans)
		HCT17	Tenure by units in structure (for Mexicans)
		HCT59	Gross rent as a percentage of household income in 1999 (for Mexicans)
		HCT66	Median value (Dollars) for specified owner-occupied housing units (for Mexicans)

Annex 2: List of resident interviews on the West Side

NO.	Informants* (interview date)	Gender	Age	Family situation	Social class (education, current employment)	Duration in WS (US)	Members in organizations	Interview language
1	Carmen (30.11.04)	Female	22	Not married, no children	Full-time college student; work in restaurant and in NGO	Born in WS, third generation	No	English
2	Francisco (30.11.04)	Male	46	Not married, no children	High School (?); Rec. Center Director	Born in WS, second generation	No	English
3	Maribel (7.1.05)	Female	47	Married, four children	Sixth grade; Child care	16 years (29 years)	Yes (Hisp. Women´s organization)	Spanish
4	Monica (10.11.05)	Female	32	Not married, one child	College degree; Programme Director at NGO	29 years	Yes (Owners Association, neighborh. NGOs)	English
5	Juana (8.11.05)	Female	39	Not married, two children	College degree; Softwear Engineer	Born in WS, second generation	Not very, slightly through daughter	English
6	Elena (18.11.05)	Female	42	Divorced, four children	Fourth grade; Hospital janitor	19 years (24 years)	No	Spanish & English
7	Dora (20.1.05)	Female	50	Married, four children	BS; Registered nurse	23 years (born in Kansas, USA), second generation	Yes (Very active in Church)	English
8	Leon (25.1.05)	Male	42	Not married, no children	High School; Hair dresser / cosmetologist	Born in WS, second generation	No	English
9	Ronald (27.1.05)	Male	55	Married, four children	High School, some college credits; Coordinator St. Paul Parks and Rec. Dept.	Born in WS, second generation	Yes (sev. Neighborh. Organizations)	English
10	John (2.2.05)	Male	25	Not married, four	Alt. High School; Teen Director at	Born in WS, third	Employed in	English

NO.	Informants* (interview date)	Gender	Age	Family situation	Social class (education, current employment)	Duration in WS (US)	Members in organizations	Interview language
				children	NGO	generation	neighborh. NGO	
11	Hermosa (7.2.05)	Female	39	Married, three children	High School, some college; Registered Nurse (in Mexico)	13 years (13 years)	Yes (Hisp. Women´s organization)	Spanish
12	Linda (14.2.05)	Female	28	Married, three children	8th grade; at home, some community work	5 years (5.5 years)	Yes (Hisp. Women's organization)	Spanish
13	Engracia (22.2.05)	Female	"60s"	Married, one son	GED, retired, formerly assembler in factory	Born on the WS, second generation	No, but some volunteering in Church	English
14	Emilia (24.2.05)	Female	77	Widow, 9 children	Two years at school, formerly office cleaner	50 years (born in Arizona, with 5 years to Mexico, then directly to MN)	No, but some volunteering in Church	Spanish
15	Raul (28.2.05)	Male	50	Married, four children (out of 2 marriages)	BA, currently unemployed; marketing	Born on the WS; third generation	Yes (Hisp. Veterans Group), but not much	English
16	Rita (10.3.05)	Female	36	Married, four children	Sixth grade (?), currently at home with children	7 years, came via California	Yes (MHA, CLUES group)	Spanish
17	Theo (3.3.05)	Male	50s	Married, three children	Some college; Rec Center Director	Born on the WS; second generation (father Mexican, mother Caucasian white)	?	English
18	Harry (8.3.05)	Male	54	Divorced, three children	Masters Degree, High School Principal	Born on the WS, now lives in Mendota Heights; second generation	Yes (NH, Boosters, Church)	English

NO.	Informants* (interview date)	Gender	Age	Family situation	Social class (education, current employment)	Duration in WS (US)	Members in organizations	Interview language
19	Manuel (14.3.05)	Male	43	Married, four children	Sixth grade, roofing	7 years (17 years, in Los Angeles)	No, but in St. Paul Church before	Spanish
20	Ramona (15.3.05)	Female	66	Single, 1 daughter	GED, filer at bank	Born on the WS, second generation	No, but some volunteering at Church	English
21	Tamara (18.3.05)	Female	16	Single	High School	13 years	Yes (Neighborhood House, WS Safe Neighborhood Council, WSCO)	Spanish
22	Arturo (30.3.05)	Male	21	Single	Recreation, High School degree, some college	All his life, fourth generation	Employed in Neighborhood Center	English
23	Tonia (29.3.05)	Female	42	Married, four kids	Lower, High School, work in post office	14 years	No, formerly participation in women support group	Spanish
24	Esteban (5.4.05)	Male	26	Living with partner, but not married	Lower, High School, work in grocery store	3 years	No	Spanish
25	Mercedes (11.4.05)	Female	27	Married, two kids	Lower middle, technical college, work in grocery store	3 years	No	Spanish
26	Fermin (13.4.05)	Male	44	Married, four kids	Lower, 9th grade, cook, work in soft drink company	24 years (before 4 years in Chicago)	No	Spanish
27	Marco (9.5.05)	Male	17	Single	In High School	13 years	Yes (NH, as work)	English

* The true names of the informants have been replaced by pseudonyms.

Annex 3: List of expert interviews and institutions

No.	Informants (interview date)	Name of institution	Type of institution	Level of intervention	Target group	Work sector(s)	Mexican or Latino members and/or employees?	Mexican or Latino leadership?
1	Expert 1 (23.11.04)	Neighborhood House (NH)	NGO	West Side Neighborhood and City	Immigrants (focus on Latinos)	- family support - health education - youth promotion - community building	Yes (few)	No
2	Expert 2 (18.1.05, 11.5.05)	Riverview Economic Development Association (REDA)	Community Development Corporation (CDC)	West Side Neighborhood	Hispanic business owners	- business training - business start-up and rehab loans - neighborhood promotion	Yes (many)	No
3	Expert 3 (24.1.05)	West Side Citizens' Organization (WSCO)	Community Development Corporation	Neighborhood, City	West Side residents	- building and construction codes - environment - youth promotion - representation of WS in City of St. Paul (as Ward Council)	Yes (few)	No
4	Expert 4 (31.3.05)	Hispanic Women in Action	Self-help group (part of NH)	WS Neighborhood (predominantly)	Hispanic women	- cultural retention - skills development and empowerment	Yes (exclusively)	Yes

No.	Informants (interview date)	Name of institution	Type of institution	Level of intervention	Target group	Work sector(s)	Mexican or Latino members and/or employees?	Mexican or Latino leadership?
						- social support		
5	Expert 5 (4.5.05)	Neighborhood Development Association (NEDA)	Community Development Corporation (CDC)	WS Neighborhood	West Side residents	- housing development - housing rehab and loans - housing ownership information	Yes (some)	No
6	Expert 6 (10.5.05)	City of St. Paul Planning and Economic Development Department	Public	City	Residents of City of St. Paul, planning community	- housing and economic development	No	N.A.
7	Expert 7 (10.5.05	Minnesota House of Representatives	Government	State of Minnesota	Minnesota population	- policy making	N.A.	N.A.
8	Expert 8 (13.5.05	Hispanic Advocacy and Community Empowerment through Research (HACER)	Research organization	State of Minnesota	Hispanic and Latino population	- research, advocacy	Yes	Yes
9	Expert 9 (29.5.05)	Neighborhood House	NGO	East Twin Cities Metro Area	Immigrants (focus on Latinos)	- family support - health education - youth promotion - community building	Yes (some)	No
10	Expert 10	St. Paul Public Housing Author-	Public	City of St. Paul	Low-income population of St.	- administration of public housing	N.A.	N.A.

No.	Informants (interview date)	Name of institution	Type of institution	Level of intervention	Target group	Work sector(s)	Mexican or Latino members and/or employees?	Mexican or Latino leadership?
	(1.6.05)	ity			Paul	stock		
11	Expert 11 (2.6.05)	Roosevelt Primary School	Public	West Side neighborhood (predominantly)	Primary school children (1st through 3rd grade)	- primary education	Yes	Yes
12	Expert 12 (7.6.05)	Federal Housing and Urban Development Department (HUD)	Public	Federal	Twin Cities' Metro Area	- housing policy making and enforcement	N.A.	N.A.
13	Expert 13 (14.6.05)	St. Paul Public Housing Authority	Public	City of St. Paul	Low-income population of St. Paul	- administration of public housing	N.A.	N.A.
14	Expert 14 (5.7.05)	Our Lady of Guadalupe	Church	Parish	Members of congregation, West Side community	- religious and social services	Yes (many)	No
15	Expert 15 (13.7.05)	Housing Link	NGO	Twin Cities Metro Area	Housing providers and low-income population	- rental housing research and information	N.A.	N.A.

Annex 4: Interview guideline for resident interviews

INTRODUCTION

Thank you very much for being available for this interview! My name is Eva Dick, I am from Germany and I am doing this research with the University of Minnesota and the University of Dortmund in Germany, for my PhD studies in urban planning. I am doing the research about the living situation of the Mexican population in the West Side of St. Paul, and therefore conducting a lot of interviews with Mexicans and Mexican-Americans living in the West Side, or working in organizations on the West Side. I am very interested in hearing about how experiences of the Mexicans and Mexican-Americans on the West Side have changed over time. Therefore I talk to persons of different ages and of different duration of stay here in the neighborhood, but also in the US.

I have prepared an interview guideline with questions I would like to ask you. However, please feel free to bring in other issues you find important about the West Side and your experiences there. Feel free to take the time you need in answering the questions. The interview usually takes about 1 hour, but certainly that differs a little in each interview.

I want to ask you for permission to use a recorder, as I cannot take notes fast enough to remember all that was said in the interview. However, our conversation is confidential, nobody else will be allowed to listen to the tapes and the information you give me will not be used in connection with your name.

LIFE HISTORY IN THE WEST SIDE

1. Do you remember **how it was when** you (or your family) **moved to the West Side**? (*if moved to the West Side, continue with question no. 2; if always lived in the West Side, jump to question no. 4)*
2. **Where** did you (or your family) move **from**? (*Probe: Did you know somebody already living in the West Side when you moved here?*)
3. **Why** did you (or your family) move to the West Side?
4. **When** did your family come to the **US** and to the Twin Cities? (*Probe: cities the family lived before; different family members staying in different places in the US)*
5. **What other family** members live in the West Side?

GETTING ALONG AND AHEAD

(*If person moved to West Side, is a 'recent' immigrant, continue with question 6; if person has been living in West Side all of her/his life, jump to question 7)*

6. Who helped you to **get started** in the West Side when you moved here? Or: Did you have somebody to get started? (*Probe: everyday infrastructure, job, housing, child-care etc.)*
7. Who helped you to **find housing**? (*Probe: information about ads, location of ads, recommendation or knowledge of somebody who left his/her apartment etc.)*

8. How did you find your **current job**? *(Probe: is the job in the West Side, does it have to do with contacts in the West Side; former job, process of job search, persons and agents who helped; maybe ask about them)*

9. Whom do you turn to **if you need help**, e. g. borrow something; or help with job, place to stay, family problem, talk about problems? *(Probe: Mexican or non-Mexican, different 'types' of help, can you provide an example?)*

10. Whom do you **celebrate** with? (*Probe: occasions of celebration, e. g. religious ceremonies and events, importance of church and religion, sports, Mexican or non-Mexican context)*

SOCIAL NETWORKS AND SPACES

11. **Whom** do you socialize with on a regular basis? (*Probe: Mexican or non-Mexicans, number of Mexicans vs. non-Mexicans, type of social contacts, activities, contacts living in- or outside the West Side, Mexicans moving out of the WS?)*

12. **Where** do your Mexican / Mexican-American contacts live? (*Probe: live in West side, number of Mex. friends living in the West Side, as compared to number of Mex. friends living outside the West Side; are friends from the West Side or not, moved away from West Side)*

13. **Where** do you spend time (more casual: hang out) with your friends or family? *(Probe: places to hang out with Mexican vs. non-Mexican friends and family, in the West Side or not, specific places, e.g. church, park, where do you go to church)*

14. **How** do your Mexican / Mexican-American contacts **differ** from your non-Mexican contacts? (*Probe: importance of Mexican / Mex.-American vs. non-Mexican social contacts, type of activities, social and physical places to socialize, deliberate 'choice' of non-Mexican contacts, for x reason?)*

15. Do you keep in touch with **family and friends in your home country / town**? How do you keep in touch? (*Probe: where is it, how often, how intense, what kind of contact, e. g. regular visit, sending mail, gifts, money etc.)*

16. Are you a member of a **neighborhood organization** or association? If yes, what do you do in this organization and which are the organization's main activities and objectives? (*Probe: are you a member of an immigrant organization? Do you go to Church?)*

17. Do you **volunteer** in the neighborhood? In what way exactly?

PROS AND CONS OF WEST SIDE

18. What do you **like about** living in the West Side? (*Probe: are there particular places you feel strongly attached to, e. g. church; is it important to live in the West Side to maintain social contacts you value, for your well-being)*

19. What do you **dislike about** living in the West Side? (*Probe if mentioned: perception of rest of the city of the West Side, personal experiences with 'negative' social status of West Side, what would you like to change?)*

20. What **other neighborhood** would be as good or better as the West Side? (*Probe: What exactly would be different in other neighborhood, what impact would other neighborhood have on Mexican(-American) social contacts?)*

21. **Has the West Side changed** in the last (5) years (*or, if people moved there more recently: "since you have moved here"*? In what way?

FUTURE PLANS

22. Do you expect to be living in the West Side **5 – 10 years from now**? (*Probe: Where else? Other place in Twin Cities, MN, US, home country?)*

ADDITIONAL DEMOGRAPHIC AND SOCIOECONOMIC INFORMATION

Time of living in Twin Cities, and in the US:

Cities in the US before moving to Minneapolis:

Housing tenure:

Highest education level:

Your profession (previous jobs):

Number of wage earners in family:

Other income sources:

Your gender:

Your age:

Marital status:

Presence and number of children:

Thank you very much! These are all the questions I have. Is there anything else about your life or experiences in the West Side you would like to add?

Annex 4: Guia de preguntas para entrevistas en el West Side

INTDRODUCCION

Muchísimas gracias por ser dispuesto/a de darme esta entrevista! Mi nombre es Eva Dick, soy Alemana y estoy haciendo una investigación con la Universidad de Minnesota y la Universidad de Dortmundo en Alemania, para mis estudios doctorales en planificación urbana. Estoy haciendo la investigación sobre las condiciones de vida de la populación Mexicana en el West Side, y por eso intento hacer muchas entrevistas con Mexicanos o Mexicanas (Mexicano-Americano/as) que viven o/y trabajan en el West Side. Estoy muy interesada en cómo las experiencias de los Mexicanos y Mexicano-Americanos han ido cambiando a lo largo de los años, ya que los Mexicanos ya han venido desde hace muchos años al West Side. Por esto trato hablar con personas que han venido al West Side, pero tambien a EEUU, en diferentes momentos y con personas de edades diferentes.

He preparado una guía de entrevista con preguntas que me gustaría ponerle. Sin embargo, si hay otros temas que le parecen importantes en cuanto a sus experiencias aquí, le pido que les mencione, aunque no pregunte directamente sobre esto. También me parece muy importante que tome todo su tiempo en responder a las preguntas. La entrevista normalmente dura más o menos una hora, sin embargo esto puede variar un poco en cada conversación.

Me gustaría pedirle su permiso para usar una grabadora, ya que no puedo tomar notas lo suficientemente rápido para retomar todo lo que hablamos. Sin embargo, nuestra conversación es confidencial, y ninguna persona adicional podrá escuchar lo que hablamos. Le garantizo que la información de usted no voy a usarla en conexión con su nombre.

HISTORIA DE VIDA EN EL WEST SIDE

23. **¿Cuánto tiempo** lleva usted en el West Side? O más abiertamente: Usted recuerda cómo fue cuando llegó al West Side? (*si vino al WS, continuar con pregunta no. 2; si siempre ha vivido en el WS, continar con pregunta no. 4)*
24. **¿Desde dónde** usted se mudó? (*Verificar: Usted conoció a alguién quién ya vivía en el WS cuando usted llegó?)*
25. **¿Porqué** mudó usted al West Side?
26. **¿Cuándo** su familia llegó a los EEUU y las Ciudades Gemelas? (*Verficar: ciudades en las cuales la familia vivió antes; diversos miembros de la familia viviendo en diferentes sitios en los EEUU)*
27. **¿Cuáles otros miembros de su familia** viven en el West Side?

ORIENTARSE EN LA VIDA COTIDIANA Y AVANCAR EN LA SOCIEDAD

(Si la persona mudó al West Side o es unA imigrante reciente, continuar con pregunta no. 6; si la persona ha vivido toda su vida en el West Side, saltar a la pregunta no. 7)

28. ¿Quién le ayudó a orientarse en el West Side cuando usted llegó? O: Usted ha tenido a alguién para ayudar a orientarla acá? (*Verificar: infraestructura cotidiana, trabajo, casa, cría de niños etc.)*

29. ¿Cómo encontró su **casa** actual? (*Preguntar más: información sobre anuncios, locación de los anuncios, recomendación de alguién quién quitó su casa etc.)*

30. ¿Cómo encontró su **trabajo actual**? *(Verificar: ¿el trabajo se encuentra en el West Side?, ¿tiene algo que ver con contactos socials en el West Side?; ¿cuál fue el trabajo anterior, cuál fue el proceso de búsqueda de trabajo, cuáles fueron personas o agentes que ayudaron?, quizás preguntar también sobre las experiencias de estas personas)*

31. ¿A quién se dirige **si necesita ayuda**, por ejemplo pretar algo, ayudar con la búsqueda de un trabajo, encontrar una casa, un problema de familia, hablar sobre un problema? *(Probe: Mexican or non-Mexican, different 'types' of help, can you provide an example?)*

32. ¿Con quién usted **celebra**? (*Verificar: ocasiones, frecuencia e importancia de celebración, por ejemplo ceremonias o eventos religiosos, de deporte; si tienen que ver con el contexto Mexicano o no)*

REDES Y ESPACIOS SOCIALES

33. **¿Con quién** socializa regularmente? (*Verificar: Mexicanos o non-Mexicanos, número de Mexicanos comp.. con non-mexicanos, tipo de contactos y actividades sociales, contactos Mexicanos que viven en, o fuera del WS, Mexicanos que se fueron del WS)*

34. **¿Dónde** viven sus contactos Mexicanos o Mexicano-Americanos (no olvidar)?

35. **¿Dónde** pasa su tiempo libre con sus amigos y amigas Chicanos o su familia? *(Verificar: sitios para pasar el tiempo con contactos Mexicanos y non-Mexicanos y familia, en el West Side o no, sitios específicos, por ejemplo iglesia, parque; ¿dónde va a la Iglesia?)*

36. **¿En qué sentido** usted piensa que sus contactos Mexicanos o Chicanos serían diferentes de sus contactos no-Mexicanos? (*Verificar: relativa importancia de los unos y de los otros, tipo de actividades, espacios sociales y físicos para socializar; ¿selección de contactos no-Mexicanos a propósito, por una razón x?)*

37. ¿Usted queda en contacto con su familia y/o amigo/as en **su ciudad o país de orígen**? Cómo queda en contacto? (*Verificar: dónde queda la ciudad de origen; frecuencia e intensidad de contacto; tipo de contacto, por ejemplo visita regular o periódica, enviar correo, regalos, dinero etc.)*

38. ¿Usted es miembro de una **organización barrial** (del West Side)? En el caso que sí, ¿qué es lo que hacen en esta organización y cuáles son sus actividades y objetivos más importantes? (*Verificar: ¿usted es miembro de una organización étnica? ¿Usted va a la Iglesia?)*

39. ¿Usted realiza un **trabajo voluntar** en el barrio (West Side)? En el caso que sí, ¿el cuál?

VENTAJAS Y DESVENTAJAS DEL WEST SIDE

40. ¿Qué **le gusta** del hecho de vivir en el West Side? (*Verificar: ¿hay sitios muy importantes para usted, por ejemplo una iglesia?; ¿es importante vivir en el West Side para mantener los contactos sociales que son importantes para usted?*

41. ¿Qué es lo que **no le gusta** del hecho de vivir en el West Side? (*Verificar en el caso de que se mencione: percepción del resto de la ciudad del West Side; experiencias personas con el estatus 'negativo' del West Side en el contexto urbano general; ¿qué le gustaría cambiar?*

42. ¿**Cuál otro barrio** estaría para usted igual de bien o todavía major que el West Side? (*Verificar: ¿Qué exactamente sería diferente en otro barrio?; ¿cuál sería el impacto de vivir en otro barrio sobre sus contactos Mexicano/as o Chicano/as?)*

43. ¿Diría usted que el **West Side cambió** en los últimos (5) años (*o, si persona mudó más recientemente: desde que usted ha llegado*)? ¿De qué manera?

PLANES FUTUROS

44. Usted piensa vivir en el West Side de acá en **5 – 10 años**? (*Verificar: ¿Dónde? ¿Otro sitio en las Ciudades Gemelas, en MN, EEUU, país de orígen?)*

INFORMACIÓN DEMOGRÁFICA Y SOCIOECONÓMICA ADICIONAL

Tiempo de vivir en Ciudades Gemelas y EEUU:

Ciudades en EEUU antes de venir a Ciudades Gemelas / St. Paul:

Propiedad o alquiler de vivienda:

Nivel más alto de educación:

Profesión (trabajos anteriores):

Número de asalariados en la familia:

Otras fuentes de ingreso:

Su género:

Su edad:

Estado civil:

Presencia y número de niños:

Muchísimas gracias! Estas son todas las preguntas que yo tengo. Hay algo sobre su vida o sus experiencias en el West Side que le gustaría añadir?

Annex 5: Guideline for expert interviews (standard)

INTRODUCTION

- *Present myself, institutional context of my research*
- *Inform about subject of my research: social relations between Mexican residents in the West Side; why the West Side? History as THE neighborhood in the Twin Cities that has attracted large proportion of immigrants; long history of Mexican community; larger picture or interest: how do social relations and networks between people of the same national or ethnic origin develop over time in a neighborhood; what influence does the fact of living in the same neighborhood have on these social networks and also on the living conditions of the immigrants; policy and planning initiatives responding to potentials and needs of 'ethnic' neighborhoods; background dispersal politics of neighborhoods with large concentration of minorities.*
- *Talking to Mexican American residents of, and to persons working in organizations on the West Side or impacting on community development of the West Side*
- *Interview will take about one hour*
- *Permission to record the interview?*

Questions for expert interviews

1. Can you tell me about the **work** you are (your organization is) doing **on the West Side**? (*Probe: job title and role, if applies: history of the organization, focal field or sector, major 'issues' of Mexican population)*
2. What kind of **work** are you doing with the **Mexican or Latino population**? *(Probe: focus or not on Mexican or Latino population, specific activities)*
3. Which would you describe as the **most important needs of the Mexican or Latino population**, in your field of work? (*Probe: needs of Mexican or Latino, with respect to needs of rest of the community, heterogeneity of Mexican or Latino population)*
4. How does your **organization** (or yourself) **addresses the needs** of the Mexican or Latino residents of the West Side? (*Probe: communication and decision-making procedures, representation of Mexicans or Latinos in organization, culturally specific services, examples)*
5. **Apart from your own field of work**, which are the **biggest problems** for the Mexican or Latino, but also the entire West Side community? (*probe: link or intersection of person's work field with other community development fields; probe if applies: intersection of housing with other development fields, such as education and employment)*
6. What can **community development agents** and **policy makers and planners** do to address the situation of the Mexican / Latino or other immigrants on the West Side? (*probe if applies: how to enhance social, economic and cultural capital of immigrants, while promoting expressions of cultural specificity, how to promote positive, while discouraging negative aspects of*

ethnic clustering, link between housing and other key development areas, interaction between ethnic community and State)

7. What is your assessment on the **advantages and disadvantages of the spatial concentration** of ethnic households, versus their dispersal? (*probe: assessment of, or example for the situation of the Mexican residents of the West Side, advantages ethnic households may have in majority-white, suburban areas)*

8. What is your assessment of the **costs and benefits of ethnic social networks**? (*Probe: situation of Mexican social networks on the West Side, social networks for getting along vs. getting ahead, spatial proximity affecting social mobility*)

9. Is there **anything else** I should now about the Mexican community on the West Side?

Thank you very much for this interview!

Annex Five

Expert interview (Expert 4)

1. Can you tell me about the **history of your organization** or group? (*Probe: when it started, reasons to start it, how it developed over time etc.)*
2. When did you start working for your organization?
3. Which are the main **activities and objectives** of your organization? (*Probe: how activities and objectives developed over time, challenges for organization to adapt to changes in the neighborhood, role and main activities of the person in the organization)*
4. How does MHA **meet the needs of the Mexican American** residents of the West Side? (*Probe: special focus or not on Mexican population, specific situation – or not – of Mexican population etc.)*
5. How has the West Side **changed** in the last years (since you remember) and how does your organization deal with these changes?
6. Which are **advantages** of the West Side for its Mexican American or Latino residents (*probe: specificity of WS, with respect to other communities, e. g. suburbs, type of advantages)*?
7. Which are **disadvantages** of the West Side for its Mexican American or Latino residents? (*Probe: type of disadvantages, specificity of WS, with respect to other communities)*
8. Which are the biggest **challenges** of the West Side, from the perspective of the Mexican American and Latino, but also the entire community? (*follow-up if mentioned: diversity and integration; Mexican and other Latino and immigrant communities; specificity of West Side with respect to other neighborhoods in the Twin Cities, challenges for community development)*
9. What can **policy makers**, **planners** and **community development agents** do to improve the situation of the Mexican-American, Latino and other immigrants on the West Side? (*follow-up on planning and policy issues, if mentioned)*
10. Is there **anything else** you think I should know about the Mexican community in the West Side?

Thank you very much for this interview!

Annex Five

Entrevista de expertos (Expert 4)

1. Puede contarme sobre la historia de su organización o grupo? (*Verifica: cuando comenzó, porqué comenzó, comó se desarrolló en el curso del tiempo)*
2. Cuando empezó usted a trabajaar para su organización?
3. Cuáles son las actividades y los objetivos principales de su organización? (*Verifica: cómo se desarrollaron las actividades y los objetivos a lo largo del tiempo, retos para adaptar a cambios en el barrio, papel y actividades principales de la persona en la organización)*
4. Cómo asista su organización a la población Mexicana-Americana del West Side? (*Verifica: focus o no sobre populación Mejicana, situación específica – o no – de populación Mejicana, razon de focalizar)*
5. Cómo ha cambiado el WS en los últimos anos (desde que usted se acuerda) y cómo ha reaccionado su organización a eso?
6. Cuáles son las ventajas del West Side para sus residentes Mexicanos o Latinos (*verificar: diferencia del WS, en comparación con otras comunidades, p. ej. Suburbs, tipo de ventaja)*?
7. Cuáles son las desventajas del WS para sus residentes Mexicanos o Latinos? (*Verifica: tipo de desventaja, diferencia del WS, en comparación con otras comunidades)*
8. Cuáles son los retos más grandes del West Side, de la perspectiva de la comunidad Mexicana o Latina, pero también de la comunidad entera? (*verifica su mencionado: diversidad e integración, cosas particulares del WS en comparación a otros barrios en Ciudades Gemelas, retos para desarrollo de la comunidad)*
9. Qué pueden hacer políticos, planificadores o agentes de desarrollo de comunidades para mejorar la situación de los Mexicanos, Hispanos u otros imigrantes del WS? (*verificar: seguir con aspectos de política y planificación)*
10. Hay otra cosa usted quiere que sepa sobre la comunidad Mexicana en el WS?

Muchas gracias para esta entrevista!

Annex Five

Expert interview (Expert 10)

1. Can you tell me about the main housing programs of the St. Paul Housing Authority?
2. Do you have special (housing related) services directed at immigrants, e. g. the Mexican population?
3. From your experience with the Public Housing Authority in St. Paul, which are the main locations, as well as types of housing of Latino residents? (*Probe: aspect of housing choices and preferences; specific preferences of Mexican or Latino residents, with respect to Hmong or other immigrants; importance of social networks, cultural aspects etc.*)
4. What can housing agents and housing policy makers do to improve the general living situation (opportunities etc.) of immigrant families? Can you name an example? (*Probe: Which are the biggest problems immigrant families face; ways of influencing housing location by public housing entities or agents; appropriate strategies or incentives to prevent 'concentration of poverty')*
5. Which are the advantages and disadvantages of the spatial concentration of ethnic or immigrant households? Can you name examples? (*Probe: situation of Mexican or Latino immigrants, West Side as a housing location; impact of different housing types and locations, e. g. scattered site or more concentrated housing units, single or multi-family units, tenant- vs. project based, on well-being or opportunities of families*)
6. What is your assessment on the North Side redevelopment in Minneapolis (Hollmann case)? (*Probe: Impact of relocation programs on families, moving to suburbs or other city areas*)
7. Which are, from the St. Paul PHA's and your own experiences, the lessons-learnt for appropriate housing strategies for immigrant (and low-income) households? (*Probe: key players to influence and to be involved in strategies)*
8. Is there anything else you would like me to know about the St. Paul PHA's perspective on housing for immigrant families?
9. Do you have any recommendations on who I should also talk to, as housing expert? (E. g. somebody from HUD)

Thank you very much for this interview!

Annex Five

Expert interview (Expert 11)

1. Can you tell me about **how it came that you started to work** at Roosevelt Elementary School, the **history** of Roosevelt Elementary and some **special features**? (*Probe: reasons for special features*)

2. Do you have special (housing related) services directed at immigrant, e. g. Mexican school kids? (*Probe: when these activities started and why*)

3. Which would you describe as the **most important problems of Mexican or Latino students** on the WS, in your field of work? (*Probe: needs or problems of Latino kids as compared to kids from other immigrant groups, are problems related to location of WS or specific to the WS?,* ***problems of schools on the WS****)*

4. How does Roosevelt Elementary School **addresses these needs**? (*Probe: other education stake-holders in the community; relationship with parents, community organizations or other educational institutions of WS; what is done and what could/should be done more; Roosevelt vs. other schools on the WS*)

5. What are in your assessment the biggest problems of the WS Schools? (*probe: specificity of WS location or 'immigrant' neighborhoods, share some of the interviewees' opinion on* ***'bad' schools'*** *on the WS; different challenges of elementary and high schools?)*

6. What can **community development agents** and **policy makers and planners** do to address the problems of the Mexican / Latino or other immigrant students on the West Side, in the field of education? (*Probe, if mentioned: advantages and disadvantages of magnet schools vs. neighborhood schools, connection of educational with other sectors, e. g. housing; assessment on housing dispersal for the sake of a better education or 'better schools' for children; how to level educational standards of students, citywide, without compromising respect for cultural specificity;* ***role of School District****, view residents' comments*)

7. Which are the **advantages and disadvantages of the spatial concentration** of ethnic or immigrant households? Can you name examples, specifically from the field of education? (*Probe: positive or negative assessment on impact of residential segregation on educational and related opportunities; educational 'issues' on WS; how can negative aspects be addressed, how do they address them in Roosevelt School*)

8. Which are, from your own experiences, the **lessons-learnt** for appropriate educational strategies targeted at immigrant (and low-income) students or families? (*Probe: key players to influence and to be involved in strategies)*

9. Is there **anything else** you would like me to know about the Roosevelt Elementary School and the West Side's educational situation?

Thank you very much for this interview!

Annex Five

Expert interview (Expert 12)

1. Can you tell me about your work at HUD (focal activity, work fields)?

2. How would you describe HUD's position towards the issue of residential segregation or racial/ethnic and income concentration? (*Probe: development of HUD's position over time, present situation, differences between income and racial/ethnic segregation)*

3. Which are the main policy instruments HUD uses – today - to deal with or influence the spatial concentration of low-income or ethnic households? (*Probe, if mentioned: focus on tenant-based, as opposed to project-based public housing, Section 8 and related programs, e. g. Moving to Opportunity, Hope IV, moving counseling etc., performance rating of PHAs*)

4. Does HUD differentiate normatively and in terms of programs between low-income vs. racially/ethnically based segregation? (*Probe: specificity of spatial concentration of immigrant households?)*

5. How would you assess the success of approaches or policies of HUD against deconcentration? (*Probe: have they worked operationally, did they have the desired impact or outcome on the target population, e. g. in terms of betterment of opportunities, what did not work)*

6. Could you please name an example? *(e. g. Hollmann lawsuit in Minneapolis or others)*

7. Do you think there is a discrepancy between minority housing choices or preferences and HUD policy or program goals? (*Probe: refer to importance of social networks for first generation immigrants, based on my interviews; on what Expert 10 said about opposition of especially African American communities against deconcentration etc.; how can these discrepancies be deal with?)*

8. What would you say are the lessons-learnt for HUD on dealing with residential segregation? (*Probe: how to prevent the bad aspects of it while encouraging the positive aspects; is it a hopeless dilemma and ambiguity for housing policies or are there ways to walk the fine line?, key players to be involved in approaches)*

9. Which are the advantages and disadvantages of the spatial concentration of ethnic or IMMIGRANT households? Can you name examples? (*Probe: specificity of residential segregation of immigrants with respect to other populations; policy implications of this*)

10. Is there anything else you would like me to know about HUD's perspective and policies on residential segregation, specifically towards immigrant residents? (*other housing policy programs, e. g. the lack of affordable housing supply with respect to the demand)*

Thank you very much for this interview!

Annex Five

Expert interview (Expert 13)

1. Which are the actions the St. Paul Public Housing Authority takes to encourage the participation in the Section 8 Voucher Program of owners located outside areas of poverty or minority concentration? Do you also try to engage jurisdictions outside the City of St. Paul? Which kind of INCENTIVES would you use to engage them?

2. Which are the delineated areas of poverty or minority concentration used by the St. Paul PHA? Do you have maps available showing these areas? What do these maps suggest in terms of the overlay of low-income and racial concentration? How do the West Side census tracts fare in these maps?

3. How is "minority concentration" (referred to in the "expanding opportunities" indicator) defined, in terms of proportions of racial or ethnic minorities?

4. What does HUD do to enforce its deconcentration goals with the PHAs? Have you already tried to obtain a "waiver" from HUD, in order to be able to build housing units in concentrated areas? How does this program exactly work?

5. How do you assess the success of promoting the Voucher Program in non- concentrated areas, also in terms of preferences of the minority households?

6. Which PHAs have to submit data on the "deconcentration bonus" indicator (I did not fully understand the CFR-explanations)? Is the St. Paul Housing Authority requested to deliver this information?

7. Do I understand it right, that the "deconcentration bonus" indicator only refers to low-poverty, but not low-minority areas? Why is that so?

General policy questions:

8. How do you assess, from the point of view of minority or immigrant families (and their housing choices or preferences) the success of deconcentration efforts in public housing - also the Section 8 Voucher Program?

9. Is there, or should there be a way in the public housing sector to deal with specific housing or services needs of immigrant residents? Or with housing preferences?

10. From your perspective, which are the most important lessons-learnt on racial and low-income housing deconcentration?

Thank you very much for this interview!

Expert interview (Expert 14)

1. Can you tell me how you came to Guadalupe Church? (*Former jobs, if also with Hispanic community, since when at Guadalupe Church)*
2. Which are the special features of Guadalupe Church and community, with respect to other parishes you have known? (*specificity due to Mexican-American community)*
3. What are the activities / situations the Mexican / Latino community gets involved in? *(masses, events, different groups of the Hispanic community involved in different things)*
4. How do you assess the relationship between the 'old' and the 'new' Mexican or Latino families at the Church? Could you give me an example? *(tensions, indifference, solidarity?, perspectives)*
5. Has the relationship between 'old' and 'new' Mexican/Latino families changed in the last years? *(Also from what you've heard of predecessors)*
6. What are the advantages and disadvantages of the spatial concentration of ethnic or IMMIGRANT households? *(example: West Side)*
7. Which are the advantages and disadvantages of ethnic social networks? *(how do they manifest themselves at Guadalupe Church)*
8. How do you assess the future role of the Mexican/Hispanic community in the Our Lady of Guadalupe parish? *(only new immigrants?)*
9. Is there anything else you would like me to know about the Mexican/Hispanic community in Our Lady of Guadalupe Church?

Thank you very much for this interview!

Expert interview (Expert 15)

1. Can you tell me about Housing Link's history and key work areas?
2. How would you describe Housing Link's position towards the issue of racial/ethnic and income-based concentration? (*Link to Hollmann case, implicit or explicit position, e. g. per statutes; performance checks with respect to deconcentration; if yes, by whom and how*)
3. Which are the main instruments Housing Link uses to promote Metro-wide housing opportunities of low-income and minority households? (*Explicit focus on minority concentration at all?*)
4. How would you assess the success of Housing Link's approaches to promote metro-wide access to affordable housing opportunities? (*actual distribution of households affected by Housing Link's activities in Metro-area; impact of spatial dispersion on the targeted households, e. g. in terms of betterment of opportunities, examples)*
5. Has Housing Link experienced obstacles to realize its mission to promote access to affordable housing Metro-wide? (*kind of obstacles, reasons, by whom and on which levels, examples*)
6. What is your assessment on the advantages and disadvantages of the spatial concentration of minority or IMMIGRANT households?
7. What is your assessment on the Hollmann case, in terms of the process itself and its impact on the (former) low-income and/or minority residents of the Near North Side?
8. What should housing agents (service agencies, housing authority, policy makers) do in the future to improve housing choices and other opportunities of low-income and minority households?
9. Is there anything else you would like me to know about the Housing Link's experiences and perspectives on minority/low-income concentration and housing choices?

Thank you very much for this interview!

Annex 6: Participation in neighborhood events during research

Date	Organization	Event*	Locality	Objective	Hispanic presence
7.2.05	WSCO	Riverfront Development on the West Side	Humboldt School	Information about proposal of developer group	Minimal (approx. 1%)
18.2.05	Guadalupe Church	Lenten Enchiladas	Guadalupe Church	Social event, fund raising	Big majority
9.3.05	Hispanic Women in Action	"Hablando Claro" (Straight Talk)	Rio Vista Neighborhood Center	Sexual health education for women	100%
30.3.05	Hispanic Women in Action	Immigration law information	Rio Vista Neighborhood Center	Information about legal novelties in immigration law	All
12.4.05	Guadalupe Church	Lenten Enchiladas	Guadalupe Church	Social event, fund raising	Big majority
25.4.05	Guadalupe Church	Lenten Enchiladas Representation of crucifixion of Christ	Guadalupe Church	Social event, fund raising Religious ritual	Big majority All
13.4.05	Hispanic Women in Action	"Hablando Claro" (Straight Talk)	Rio Vista Neighborhood Center	Sexual health education for women; parents talking about sexuality to kids	100%
3.5.05	TOR (interviewed resident)	5th of May Lunch	Hall at Riverfront	Celebration of Mexican-American event	Big majority
7.5.05	Several	*Cinco de Mayo* celebration	West Side commercial strip	Mexican and Latino culture celebration	Many
25.5.05	WSCO	Riverfront Development on the West Side	Humboldt School	Discussion of Riverfront development proposal	Minimal (1%)

Date	Organization	Event*	Locality	Objective	Hispanic presence
				by WS community	
2.7.05	Guadalupe Church	Church service	Church	Religious	All

* The regular meetings of the Mujeres Hispánicas en Acción group, from December 2004 onwards, are not mentioned here. However, specific training sessions held in this group are.

Annex 7: West Side neighborhood organizations

Name of institution	Type of institution	Target group	Activities	Mexican or Latino members and/or employees?	Mexican or Latino leadership?
Baker Center	Social service institution	Children and youth from the neighborhood	- Leisure activities	Unknown	Unknown
Boys and Girls Club	Social service institution	Children and youth from the neighborhood	- Sports and athletic	Yes (partly)	Unknown
Hablando Claro (Straight Talk)	Self-help group	Hispanic parents and youth	- Sexual and HIV/AIDS education	Yes (exclusively)	Yes
Hispanic Women in Action	Self-help group (part of NH)	Hispanic women	- cultural retention - skills development and empowerment - social support	Yes (exclusively)	Yes
La Clínica	Social service institution	Hispanics residents of West Side and other St. Paul neighborhoods	- medical services	Yes (partly)	Unknown
La Familia Guidance Center	Social services institution	Hispanic residents of West Side and other St. Paul neighborhoods	- mental health therapy and prevention services	Yes (exclusively)	Yes
Neighborhood Development Association (NEDA)	Community Development Corporation (CDC)	West Side prospective and present home-owners	- housing development - housing rehab and loans - housing ownership information	Yes (some)	No
Neighborhood House (NH)	Social services institution	Immigrants population on West Side and East Metro Area	- family support - health education	Yes (few)	No

Name of institution	Type of institution	Target group	Activities	Mexican or Latino members and/or employees?	Mexican or Latino leadership?
			- youth promotion - community building		
Our Lady of Guadelupe	Church	Members of congregation, West Side community	- religious and social services	Yes (many)	No
Riverview Economic Development Association (REDA)	Community Development Corporation (CDC)	Hispanic business owners in "District del Sol" (central comercial corridor on West Side)	- business training - business start-up and rehab loans - neighborhood promotion	Yes (many)	No
West Side Boosters	Sports association	Youth of West Side	- athletics	Yes	Unknown
West Side Citizens' Organization (WSCO)	Community Development Corporation	West Side residents	- building and land use - environment - education and youth promotion - representation of WS in City of St. Paul (as Ward Council)	Yes (few)	No

Annex 8: Mexicans in West Side census tracts

Household and family situation of Mexicans on West Side census tracts, in 2000

	Mexicans WS	Tract 361	Tract 370*	Tract 371	Tract 372	Hispanics West Side	Total pop. West Side
Total pop.	4,311	626	359	1,245	2,081	5,266	16,133
Total hhs.	1,078	168	88	300	522		
% / total Mex.	100.0	14.5	8.3	28.9	48.3	100.0	100.0
School-age population	1,126	157	88	367	514	1,397	3,687
%	26.1	25.1	24.5	29.5	24.7	26.5	22.9
Average hh size	3.70	3.49	3.56	3.91	3.84	3.67	2.91
1-person hhs.*	148	37	9	41	61	201	1,653
%	13.7	22.0	10.2	13.7	11.7	15.0	29.7
Family households**	874	122	71	248	433	1063	3,477
%	81.1	72.6	80.7	82.7	83.0	79.4	62.5
Presence of children –18	548	70	41	164	273	653	2016
%	50.8	41.7	46.6	54.7	52.3	47.4	36.2

Source: Census 2000, for total population and Hispanics SF1 (P1, P1H, P12, P12H, P17, P17H, P18, P26, P26H). Presence of children for Hispanics in SF3 (P146H). For Mexicans SF2 (PCT1Mex, PCT3Mex, PCT8Mex, PCT9Mex). Own compilation.
** The percentages for the last three variables refer to total households (hhs.), not population as universe.*
*** Defined as households in which members are affiliated by birth, marriage or adoption.*

Socio-economic and housing situation of Mexicans in West Side census tracts, in 2000

	Mexi-cans WS	Tract 361	Tract 370*	Tract 371	Tract 372	Hispa-nics WS	Total pop. WS
Total Mexicans	4,311	626	359	1,245	2,081	5,266	16,133
% / total Mex.	100.0	14.5	8.3	28.9	48.3	100.0	100.0
SOCIO-ECONOMIC INDICATORS							
Median HH income	38,257	32,500	N/a	45,127	37,143	39,576	36,392

Annex Eight

	Mexicans WS	Tract 361	Tract 370*	Tract 371	Tract 372	Hispanics WS	Total pop. WS
1999							
Below poverty	862	81	N/a	308	473	1,012	2,563
%	22.2	12.2	N/a	25.9	23.3	19.2	16.0
to 4th grade	134	62	N/a	18	54	156	469
%	7.48	20.8	N/a	3.5	5.5	6.9	4.0
College educated	128	0	N/a	56	72	239	1,858
%	7.2	0.0	17.7	10.9	7.4	9.4	19.4
HOUSING INDICATORS							
Owner occupancy	536	89	54	150	243	645	3,257
%	49.7	53.0	61.4	50.0	46.6	48.5	58.2
Single family units	442	70	n/a	136	230	620	3,078
%	45.2	37.3	80.2	48.2	41.8	46.2	53.3
More than 30% income on rent	213	34	n/a	73	106	292	869
%	41.0	47.9	n/a	50.7	34.8	42.5	37.1
Median housing value	87,900	85,500	76,400	91,400	86,800	84,950	85,350

Source: Census 2000, for total population and Hispanics SF1 (P1), SF2, SF3 (P19, P22, P52, P87, H7, H30, H76, P152H, P159H, P148H, H12, HCT30H, HCT39H, HCT42H). For Mexicans SF2 (PCT1), SF4 (PCT89, PCT142, PCT64, HCT2, HCT17, HCT59). Own compilation.

** As a consequence of the small number of Mexican households in census tract 370, information with respect to this national group is retained. Therefore, only housing tenure figures are available for the Mexican population in SF2.*

Immigrant situation and status of Mexicans in West Side census tracts, in 2000

	Mexicans WS**	Tract 361	Tract 370*	Tract 371	Tract 372	Hispanics WS	Total pop. WS
Total Mexicans	4,311	626	359	1,245	2,081	5,266	16,133
% / total pop.	100.0	34.6	12.0	24.2	34.2	32.6	100.0
Recent immigrants	995	98	34	307	590	1,304	1,300
%	23.1	15.7	N/a	24.7	28.4	24.8	8.1
Foreign born	1,432	170	N/a	449	813	1979	3182
%	36.3	25.5	32.0	37.3	39.3	37.1	19.4
Not a citizen	1168	126	26	377	665	1522	2240

Annex Eight

	Mexicans WS**	Tract 361	Tract 370*	Tract 371	Tract 372	Hispanics WS	Total pop. WS
%	29.6	18.9	5.1	31.3	32.1	28.5	13.6

Source: Census 2000. For total population and Hispanics SF1 (P1, P4, PCT11). For total population, Mexicans and Hispanics SF4 (PCT45, PCT43). Own compilation.

** The figures for census tract 370 refer to the Hispanic population as a whole, due to the small number of Mexicans in this tract. For the variable "recent immigrants" there has been no information available, not even for the whole Hispanic population, very likely also for reasons of confidentiality.*

*** The absolute numbers present an undercount, as they do not include the Mexican residents of tract 370. The percentages have to be considered an approximate, rather than precise value.*

Annex 9: Housing values on the West Side 1990 – 2000

1990

Housing values in $	Numbers	Percentages
Below 20,000	46	1,73
20,000-39,999	166	6,26
40,000-59,999	1075	40,52
60,000-99,999	1366	51,49
100,000-124,999	18	0,68
125,000-149,999	19	0,72
150,000-174,999	12	0,45
175,000-199,999	10	0,38
Above 200,000	0	0,00

Source: Census 1990, SF 3 (H61). Own compilation.

2000

Housing values	Numbers	Percentages
Below 20,000	6	0,21
20,000-39,999	78	2,71
40,000-59,999	202	7,02
60,000-79,999	876	30,46
80,000-99,999	889	30,91
100,000-124,999	415	14,43
125,000-149,999	227	7,89
150,000-174,999	71	2,47
175,000-199,999	58	2,02
Above 200,000	54	1,88

Source: Census 2000, SF 3 (H74). Own compilation.

Annex 10: Neighborhood-related indicators for the assessment of residential segregation

Indicators	Sub-indicators	Explanations/comments
1. Income distribution	1.1 Median income levels compared to city average	
	1.2 Income and poverty development	*To be measured by comparison of census data on ten-year basis.*
2. Dynamic of housing market	2.1 Trends of owner/renter housing	*Increase in ownership housing can be considered positive due to increase in asset building. Similarly, an increase in renter households may indicate de-creasing neighborhood investment. However, has to be treated carefully.*
	2.2 Number of housing rehabilitation and other investment activities	*This can also indicate a gentrification trend inclu-ding the displacement of more vulnerable groups.*
	2.3 Housing value development	*To be measured by comparison of census data on ten-year basis.*
	2.4 Housing vacancy development	*Same*
3. Intersection between poverty- and minority-status	3.1 Development of income-levels per racial/ ethnic group	*Same*
	3.2 Development of poverty level per racial/ ethnic group	*Same*
	3.3 Development of home-ownership levels per racial/ethnic group	*Same.*
	3.4 Development of distribution of population groups.	*To be measured by comparison of census data on ten-year basis.* *Important for putting into context income-related data. For instance, with many new immigrants settling in a neighborhood it is not surprising that income-, poverty- and rental levels start going up.*
4. Existence of formal and informal ethnic insti-	4.1 Number of institutions or groups directed at	*NGOs, CDCs or CBOs in the community, however*

Indicators	Sub-indicators	Explanations/comments
tutions	certain ethnic population	*not public services, e.g. schools.*
	4.2 Number of events/year organized by this institution or group	
	4.3 Development of membership figures	*Figures need to be seen in relation with e.g. immigration numbers and resident numbers.*
5. Availability of social spaces for inter-cultural encounters	5.1 Number and activities of institutions with intercultural participation	*NGOs, CDCs or CBOs in the community, however not public services, e.g. schools.*
	5.2 Number of events/year organized by this institution or group	
	5.3 Development of membership figures	*Figures need to be seen in relation with e.g. immigration numbers and resident numbers.*
6. Existence of 'bridging' activities	6.1 Number of free (English)language courses offered	*Number of activities need to be seen in relation to resident numbers.*
	6.2 Number and kind of training courses	*Same*
	6.3 Number of business start-ups	*Same*
	6.4 Number of job-referrals in- or outside of the neighborhood	*Same*
	6.5 Number of events including visitors from out side the neighborhood	*This does not mean that pure 'ethnic' events are not valuable. However, these are also seen as an opportunity for increasing intercultural exchange and understanding.*
7. Availability of youth spaces	7.1 Number of youth clubs	*Number of activities need to be seen in relation to resident or youth numbers.*
	7.2 Number of sport clubs	*Same*
	7.3 Number and activities of youth centers	*Same*
8. Performance levels and activities of public schools	8.1 Performance of neighborhood public schools compared with city average	*To be looked at with school district data, on a yearly basis.*

Indicators	**Sub-indicators**	**Explanations/comments**
	8.2 School performance trends.	*On a yearly basis.*
	8.3 Proportion of drop-outs, compared with city average.	*To be looked at with school district data, on a yearly basis.*
	8.4 Proportion of pupils that go and stay in college after secondary school, over time.	*Individual school data, on a yearly basis.*
9. Existence of gang activities in schools and neighborhood	9.1 Levels of youth violence, per type of violen ce, as compared to city average	
	9.2 Development of violence over time	*To be measured on a yearly basis.*
	9.3 Perception of youth and adults on gang acti vities	*To be inquired on the basis of interviews*
10. Existence of 'no-go areas' and pockets of poverty	10.1 Existence of economically disadvantaged sub-areas	*To be determined on the basis of census data.*
	10.2 Perception of insecurity of residents	*To be inquired on the basis of interviews*
	10.3 Recurrent identification of same 'bad' neighborhood spots	*To be inquired on the basis of interviews*

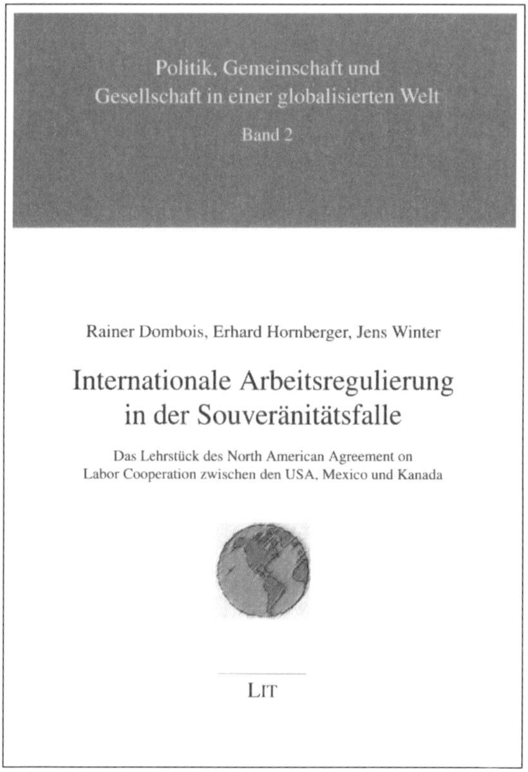

Rainer Dombois; Erhard Hornberger; Jens Winter

Internationale Arbeitsregulierung in der Souveränitätsfalle

Das Lehrstück des North American Agreement on Labor Cooperation zwischen den USA, Mexiko und Kanada

Die Globalisierung hat auch die Debatte über die Möglichkeiten und Perspektiven internationaler Arbeitsregulierung, insbesondere die Durchsetzung internationaler Sozialstandards neu entfacht. Im vorliegenden Buch werden die vielfältigen Aushandlungsprozesse und die Wirkungsweise des 1993 zwischen den USA, Mexiko und Kanada als NAFTA-Nebenabkommen ausgehandelten North American Agreement on Labor Cooperation untersucht. Das internationale Arbeitsregime wird als Lehrstück für die Probleme und Dilemmata internationaler Arbeitsregulierung im Spannungsfeld zwischen internationalen Beziehungen und nationalen Arbeitsbeziehungen und Souveränitätsansprüchen analysiert.

Bd. 2, 2004, 328 S., 29,90 €, br., ISBN 3-8258-7694-2

LIT Verlag Berlin – Hamburg – London – Münster – Wien – Zürich

Fresnostr. 2 48159 Münster

Tel.: 0251 / 620 32 22 – Fax: 0251 / 922 60 99

e-Mail: vertrieb@lit-verlag.de – http://www.lit-verlag.de

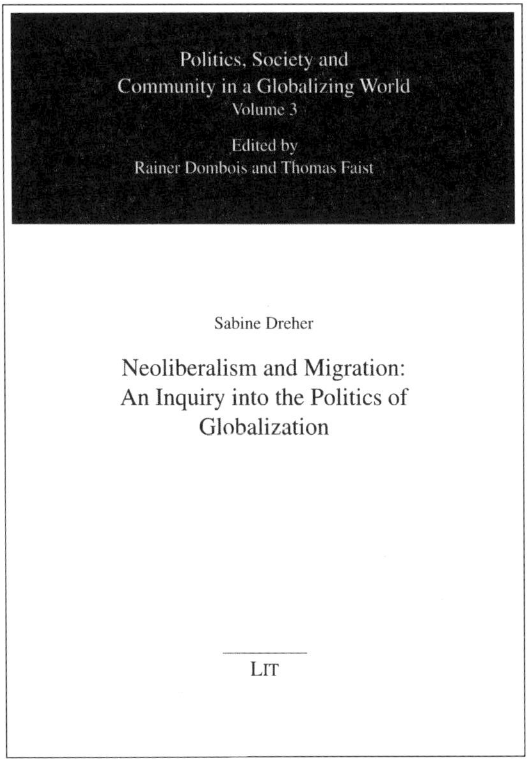
Politics, Society and
Community in a Globalizing World
Volume 3

Edited by
Rainer Dombois and Thomas Faist

Sabine Dreher

Neoliberalism and Migration:
An Inquiry into the Politics of
Globalization

LIT

Sabine Dreher
Neoliberalism and Migration: An Inquiry into the Politics of Globalization
This series is dedicated to theoretical contributions and systematic empirical studies of political, economic and cultural formations which cross the borders and boundaries of states. The focus is on the main areas of public policy: security, human rights, legitimacy of political systems, welfare, and developments in the Global South. This third volume looks at the role of neoliberalism in the institutionalization of differential rules for capital and migration flows in the global economy.
Bd. 3, 2007, 288 S., 25,90 €, br., ISBN 978-3-8258-8187-0

LIT Verlag Berlin – Hamburg – London – Münster – Wien – Zürich
Fresnostr. 2 48159 Münster
Tel.: 0251 / 620 32 22 – Fax: 0251 / 922 60 99
e-Mail: vertrieb@lit-verlag.de – http://www.lit-verlag.de

Politik, Gemeinschaft und Gesellschaft in einer globalisierten Welt

Band 4

herausgegeben von Rainer Dombois und Thomas Faist

Kathrin Ruhl, Jan Schneider, Jutta Träger, Claudia Wiesner (Hg.)

Demokratisches Regieren und politische Kultur

Post-staatlich, post-parlamentarisch, post-patriarchal?

LIT

Kathrin Ruhl; Jan Schneider; Jutta Träger; Claudia Wiesner (Hg.)
Demokratisches Regieren und politische Kultur
Post-staatlich, post-parlamentarisch, post-patriarchal?
Demokratisches Regieren und politische Kultur tragen zunehmend post-patriarchale, post-parlamentarische und poststaatliche Züge. Obwohl diese Diagnose auf den ersten Blick eindeutig erscheint, führt sie sogleich zu weiteren Fragen: Haben sich patriarchale Strukturen tatsächlich überlebt oder nur eine andere Gestalt angenommen? Wovon genau ist die Rede, wenn Folgen der Globalisierungtthematisiert werden? Was bedeutet „Europa" – in Bezug auf den Begriffsinhalt wie auch für Theorie und Praxis von Demokratie? Handelt es sich bei governance-Prozessen wirklich um neue Handlungsmuster und Prozeduren der politischen Willensbildung und Entscheidung? Mehr denn je ist die Politikwissenschaft derzeit gefordert, mit sich rasant vollziehenden Wandlungsprozessen in diesen Bereichen Schritt zu halten, sie zu orten, zu beschreiben, einzuordnen und zu deuten. Der vorliegende Band beleuchtet die Problemfelder anhand von Einzelbeispielen und lässt Handlungs- und Systemlogiken nachvollziehbar werden, die längst – und teilweise kaum hinterfragt – zu einem Bestandteil politischer Kultur geworden sind.

Bd. 4, 2006, 312 S., 19,90 €, br., ISBN 3-8258-9396-0

LIT Verlag Berlin – Hamburg – London – Münster – Wien – Zürich
Fresnostr. 2 48159 Münster
Tel.: 0251 / 620 32 22 – Fax: 0251 / 922 60 99
e-Mail: vertrieb@lit-verlag.de – http://www.lit-verlag.de

Ulrich Raiser

Erfolgreiche Migranten im deutschen Bildungssystem – es gibt sie doch

Lebensläufe von Bildungsaufsteigern türkischer und griechischer Herkunft

Aus dem Blick der gegenwärtigen Bildungsdebatte geraten die Kinder aus Einwandererfamilien, die in Schule und Studium erfolgreich sind. Ihr Erfolg basiert, so die These dieses Buches, auf dem vitalen Glauben der Familien an einen sozialen Aufstieg in der Aufnahmegesellschaft – ein migrationsspezifisches Kapital, das den Motor für eine erfolgreiche Schulkarriere bildet. Auf der Grundlage 24 lebensgeschichtlicher Interviews entsteht somit eine Typologie bildungserfolgreicher Migranten deren Erfolgsgeheimnis in der familiären Deutung der Migrationserfahrung liegt.

Bd. 6, 2007, 200 S., 19,90 €, br., ISBN 978-3-8258-0659-0

LIT Verlag Berlin – Hamburg – London – Münster – Wien – Zürich

Fresnostr. 2 48159 Münster

Tel.: 0251 / 620 32 22 – Fax: 0251 / 922 60 99

e-Mail: vertrieb@lit-verlag.de – http://www.lit-verlag.de